Style in Theory

CONTENTS

ACKNOWLEDGMENTS

The list is one of the most styleless forms around—readers of Umberto Eco's *The Infinity of Lists* might, conceivably, disagree—but we are content to resort to it here in acknowledging the invaluable help of those who in one way or another have contributed to the various events and discussions that have driven our work on the place of style in theory for the last three years: Catherine Belsey, Arthur Bradley, Stella Borg-Barthet, Saviour Catania, Simon Critchley, Tony Fisher, Maria Frendo, Arleen Ionescu, Josef Lauri, Francesco Marroni, Joseph Muscat, Peter Vassallo.

In Bloomsbury, Haaris Naqvi has been unfailingly available and helpful. We have benefitted hugely from his advice and expertise in every stage of the collection's preparation, as we have also from that of Srikanth Srinivasan, James Tupper, and Ally Jane Grossan, whom we thank for their patience and care during the work on the proofs and on the rest of the production process.

We have had long and rich exchanges with all the contributors in this volume on style, theory, literature, philosophy, and the spaces in between. Their commitment to the project has been unstinting, and we are grateful for their enthusiasm, support, and patience, not to mention their style in practice.

Special thanks go to Mario Aquilina and Janice Sant, for the graciousness and care lavished in their additional help with the editing, and for their amazing good humor. Thanks, too, to Vanessa Psaila, for her help with various aspects of the manuscript.

Lucienne Bugeja, Liz Groves, and Maria Muscat helped with various practicalities in our meetings on style in theory over the last three years.

To Anne-Marie, Antoinette, Benjamin, Helena, Joe—thanks for putting up with it.

–Ivan Callus, James Corby, and Gloria Lauri-Lucente

Introduction

Style in theory: Between literature and philosophy

How should an Introduction to a volume on "style in theory" be framed? Inevitably, its frame, its framing, cannot serve containment. The essays it prefaces will neither capture style, which is famously indefinable and elusive, nor settle theory into any comfort zone, whether between literature and philosophy or elsewhere. The matter is not helped by theory being a discourse and a discipline about which the jury is out, busy debating whether theory is—some would say "was"—a distinct discourse or discipline in the first place. It is uncertain whether the credibility lies with those bystanders testifying that theory is dead or, instead, with those witnesses affirming that it is still very much alive, though perhaps leading a different existence. Not, then, an auspicious start. Let us make it worse, by contending that literary theory has never tended to bother much with style anyway.

It is possible to twist and turn, and to nuance and disclaim—which would itself be very much in the style of theory, this tactic being one of the mannerisms, or stylized gestures, of theory that we recognize and which are, manifestly, already taking over this Introduction—but it looks like the contention can stand. Style, as the very aspect of expression which theory might be presumed to be well primed to investigate—especially since one cannot expect other disciplines to do that work—is that which theory has not, in fact, really investigated. Uninterested, broadly speaking, in any props provided by the protocols of stylistics or the algorithms of stylometers, theory ranks style lower in its priorities than aesthetics, politics, or ethics (to mention vaster concerns), or issues like those raised by "code," the "matheme," "the question of the animal," or, simply, "life," to mention more specific *topoi* that have recently attracted significant attention (see, for instance, Hayles 2006; Badiou 2007,[1] Derrida 2008, Thacker 2010). Any doubts that theory is incurious when it comes to "the question of style" (Nancy 2008, 18) are dispelled when one seeks to recall a major work on style written by the figures routinely referenced in commentaries on theory: Saussure, Propp, Bakhtin, Benjamin, Jakobson, Barthes, Althusser, Gadamer, Bataille, Foucault, Adorno, Lacan, Genette, de Man, Blanchot, Deleuze, Guattari, Lyotard, Derrida, Said, Kristeva, Jameson, Eagleton, Irigaray, Spivak, Baudrillard, Agamben, Bhabha, Cixous, Butler, Greenblatt, Žižek, Stiegler, Nancy, Badiou, and any other who might be added to this list (off catalogues like those provided, for instance, by Leitch et al., 2010). The effort of memory may be significant, but we think we are right in anticipating that the results of the recall will not be insuppressible. Indeed, the impression arises that it is not entirely certain that a concern with the elements of writing does not sit incongruously with *some* of those named.

To be sure, there is the occasional study that counters that impression. Foucault's *Death and the Labyrinth: The Work of Raymond Roussel* (1987), or Derrida's *Spurs: Nietzsche's Styles* (1979) come to mind. Both go beyond the kind of closely analytical commentary that leaves "the question of style" largely incidental (arguably, this occurs even in texts like Deleuze's *Proust and Signs* [1973] or Barthes's *S/Z* [1975]). It is, of course, easy to protest that many of the figures in that list have, ironically, produced individual texts or discrete bodies of work that bear analysis precisely on the basis of the distinctiveness or singularities of the style(s) that emerge(s) there. It can also be countered, as is seen below, that theory is as much about styles of thought as about styles of expression. But we think that our contention is viable. For though the counterresponses anticipated here may motivate the slightly more thoughtful but still defiant first sentence of our second paragraph, it remains hard not to conclude that style is what is ex-centric in theory.

[1]Interestingly, however, Badiou has characterized his affiliation to mathematics in terms of *style*, favoring the "grand style," as opposed to the "little style" (2004).

Is that terrible? Well, yes, up to a point. If literary theorists are not to talk about style, then who is? After all, it is quite odd for a discourse to downplay one of its natural objects of study. Indeed, an assumption that drives this book is that the differences that exist between literary criticism and literary theory—and, intuitively, there are quite a few, though we do not have the space here to explore either the contention or those differences—do not include an inattention to rhetoricity. For it is easy to prove, of course, that theory is compelled by rhetoric. An attention to rhetoric, however—whether theory turns to it generally (Derrida 1982) or extendedly yet specifically, through considering or itself deploying devices like paragram (Kristeva 1969), allegory (de Man 1982), the punceptual (Ulmer 1988), and the diverse examples that Genette studies in relation to the "mimological" (1995) or, broadly, "figures" (see Genette 1966, 1969, 1972), all of which are open to becoming conceptualized and conceptualizing—is surely not quite the same as an attention to style. So does that attention arise more insistently in literary criticism—for instance in what Leo Spitzer, as a pioneer in stylistics, exemplified, if we can even agree that he is more a critic than a theorist—to confirm that style is indeed ex-centric in theory? To put it hyperbolically: is theory *definable* by its relative indifference to style?

It would be ironic, of course, if that were so, as there is much within theory that speaks insistently on the importance of attention to "the remainder," or *reste*, which is "not amenable to reason or any form of calculation" (Miller 2009, 78). Hence, if style, in its own candidacy for consideration as a remainder, is ex-centric to theory, what emerges there is the intractability of the relation between theory and style and how vexatious style is to theory. Theory could on this account be presumed to garner interest in style in the wake of all the auditing of all the rhetorical resourcefulness of a text. Once stylistics is done, one could say, then theory might stir itself toward style. And yet we might possibly need to say "yes": theory is definable by its indifference to style, at least if the subtext of the title of Jonathan Culler's important collection of essays, *The Literary in Theory* (2007), is anything to go by. For the charge that theory is not even very interested in literature, let alone style, is of course an idea that has long had currency (see, for instance, Steiner 1989), though Culler confirms that "[t]he *eclipse* of literature in theory is a very *recent* phenomenon" (Culler 2007,

5; emphasis added). Our own subtitle to this collection of essays, *Between Literature and Philosophy*, further suggests that theory's conflicted nature over its disciplinary (dis)affiliations must find itself reflected in where it stands on style, both in terms of its own shaping and in view of its ambivalence over its readiest gravitations. Style *might* bear an established relation to the literary—there is a "but" developing in this paragraph, to be marked below—and the genealogies of that relation are, indeed, traced in various essays in this book, even as they acknowledge that Barthes's *Writing Degree Zero* (1984) was striking in its time precisely because it overturned assumptions on the necessity of that relation and suggested that the literary can also be styleless. Indeed: the literary, clearly, is not reducible to style, which is itself irreducible, for style is a remainder which eludes critical protocols, while being necessarily constitutive of other discourses too. Culler's judicious observations are more vital still. "What we call *theory* for short," he says, "is manifestly not theory of literature, despite the fact that *theory* has served as the nickname for 'literary and cultural theory'" (Culler 2007, 4). If that is so—and here is the "but" emerging irrepressibly—then the question of *literary* style, and possibly even style *tout court*, cannot be expected to be prominent in theory. If we are to speak of style in theory, therefore, it seems that literature cannot be expected to be central to that debate. Style has already slipped beyond literature's framing to lie between it and something else. Yet it is interesting to observe, as that is absorbed, that it otherwise seems inescapable that criticism *must* continue to privilege *literary* style, this being enduringly presumed to be the instantiation of style that will most completely exercise analysis, at least where writing is concerned. Whereupon it is intriguing that if "the resistance to theory" is/was relatable to "the resistance to the use of language about language" and to "the universal theory of the impossibility of theory" (de Man 1986, 19–20)—so that the resistance to theory is also a resistance to the attention to style—then the language (or style) in question is again not cast, there, as inevitably literature's. All the rest, then, is *not* literature—or not about literary style, at any rate, even or *especially* in theory's attention to what remains when all else has been accounted for.

As texts like *Allegories of Reading*, *Blindness and Insight*, or *Aesthetic Ideology* show, de Man tended to read philosophy when he was not reading literature (Pascal, Hegel, Kant, Rousseau, Schiller,

Nietzsche, Heidegger). That can be said of many included in the long list of theorists above, a good number of whom are in fact more classifiable as philosophers than anything else. It is one of the reasons, in fact, why philosophy is accorded such a prominent role in the essays in this volume. But just to make things more uncertain and our subtitle potentially dissatisfying, theory finds itself situated between and across various discourses, not just literature and philosophy. Linguistics, theology, psychoanalysis, cultural studies—to mention a few—could all figure there. In an earlier book, Culler had made that point. "Writings from outside the field of literary studies," he wrote, "have been taken up by people in literary studies because their analyses of language, or mind, or history, or culture, offer new and persuasive accounts of textual and cultural matters. . . . The genre of 'theory' includes works of anthropology, art history, film studies, gender studies, linguistics, philosophy, political theory, psychoanalysis, science studies, social and intellectual history, and sociology" (1997, 3–4). In that respect, the apparent downplaying in our subtitle of linguistics and popular culture when considering the question of style in theory seems particularly poorly judged. Culler himself has always been at pains to show the importance of both. *Structuralist Poetics* (1975) put in the foreground the importance of linguistics to the rise of (structuralist) theory. The natural progression, it could be presumed, is to go with cognitive stylistics or with cultural studies, about which more below. Significantly, *The Literary in Theory* has an important essay on "Doing Cultural Studies" (240–53). Why, then, have we converged on literature and philosophy in considering style in theory, when theory is "an unbounded group of writings about everything under the sun" (Culler 1997, 3)? Might it have been better to approach "style in theory" in terms of what style could hypothetically and more diversely be? And where, to draw a further obvious objection, is politics in all this? What are the politics of theory's style(s)?

More fundamentally still, has theory thought about its own style(s)? Has it been autotelic, self-referential, metatheoretical in that respect—or has it disregarded its own challenge to itself, the challenge of its own style(s)? Let us proceed carefully, on the basis of five broad points that in our view need to be addressed in reaction to those questions.

(1) *Style in Theory and Literary Studies*. We shall keep to literature and literary studies for just a while longer in the first of our

five points. Style's relative neglect in literary theory, we might want to say, is both understandable and regrettable. It is understandable because critique, we notice, has always edged away from narrowing foci on the signature rhetoric and writing of the author, text, or corpus that is inferred thereby. A life in letters has rarely been enough—even to a reclusive scholar like Petrarch who, like Cicero and Quintilian before him, extended his gaze to law, government, politics, diplomacy, religion and much else besides. It can hardly be surprising that critique itself strays beyond close scrutiny of the textures of expression and of the fabrics of reception and appreciation they weave to work also (rather than instead) with broader cloth. A *De re publica* is always liable to emerge from the same pen that produced a *De oratore*. Scholars of writing have, indeed, always worked to retain affiliation to the traditions of criticism while shaping them away from any presumption that style, tone, or rhetoric ought to be naturally privileged. Style, then, was never quite an overriding concern in literary criticism. Theory is not flouting any trends there.

If, however, this is regrettable, it is to the extent that inattention to style may have grown disproportionate. A strong expression of that suspicion can be found in the work of the late Frank Kermode, whose work has the rare ability to resonate powerfully with literary critics of different persuasions. Kermode, it is well to recall, was not averse to the ways of theory. As Michael Payne noted in an interview with him, Kermode had "cautious investments in literary theory," and "his book *Shakespeare's Language* . . . suggests that theory and poetry have more in common than we often admit" (Kermode 2003, 53 and 55). As it happens, however, *Shakespeare's Language* reacts to a situation where "Every other aspect of Shakespeare is studied almost to death, but the fact that he was a poet has somehow dropped out of consideration" (2000, vii). Kermode writes to counter "modern critics, who on the whole seem to have little time for [Shakespeare's] language; they tend to talk past it in technicalities or down to it in arcanely expressed platitudes" (vii). The scarcely veiled target is theory and its habitual modes and styles—of thought, as much as of expression. Kermode's fear is that "in the end you can't get rid of Shakespeare without abolishing the very notion of literature" (viii). Self-evidently wishing to safeguard both, he runs very closely together concerns with—and loyalties to—language, Shakespeare, and the value of literary culture, and regrets that "Shakespeare's words" are "only rarely invoked" in contemporary critical approaches (viii). He does so in a book—*Shakespeare's Language*—which, he tells Payne, was "an attempt at writing for both academics and the general reader" (2003, 61): an endeavor one would not think to impute to theory. Kermode demonstrates evident wistfulness over "the aesthetic [being] out of fashion" (2003, 57). Value, then, and "the concept of organic unity" remain a concern to Kermode, who reiterates that "we've suffered a bit from the condemnation of the aesthetic as an ideology" (52), a point renewed by Catherine Belsey recently when she expresses the regret, this time of someone more avowedly "theoretical," that pleasure in literary criticism is not accorded greater space (2011, passim). The effects of that on the attitude to style in theory are discernible in the not insignificant fact that the terms *stylish*, *stylishness*, or *stylishly* occur very rarely in these pages. Clearly, it was not enough that as editors we consider them to be terms of approbation and that we are partial to what they designate. The theoretical unconscious, evidently, is a powerful thing, and in more than one sense its operations makes it difficult to have the *measure* of style, in theory or elsewhere.

At stake is an issue that Kermode cannily flags up without specifying style in theory directly. It concerns a certain kind of deadening stylization in theory, which then makes it timely to conduct an "autopsy" of literary criticism:

> There's a nice little book, by a man called Mark Bauerlein, in which he gives a list of certain expressions which recur in modern theoretical discussion; he simply asks what they mean, and whether the people who are using them have any idea what they mean, or whether there isn't a kind of bandwagon of jargon terms which people help themselves to (apologies for the mixed metaphor) and coast along simply by using this language. (66–7; see Bauerlein 1997)

This reflects the perception that "style in theory" is an almost oxymoronic phrase. It is one thing to speak about the "construction"—a word, incidentally, that Kermode (2003, 67) mentions as one of the "expressions" queried by Bauerlein—of style in theory, and quite another to look for style and stylishness in theory. That is particularly so if theory comes across, instead, as a discourse that exemplifies a line in *Rosencrantz and Guildenstern are Dead*. Theory, some would aver, is "tied down to a language which makes up in obscurity what it lacks in style" (Stoppard 1967, 77).

Style, however, *is* present in all manner of ways in theory and in literary studies, as the essays in this volume attest. In any case, it is hardly consistent to bemoan the perceived diminution of value in literary studies, and then not move to acknowledge what there is of value in theory when it comes to considering style. These essays, this framing introduction will assert, do that. And they do so in a manner that pays attention to theory being "between literature and philosophy," in ways considered below.

(2) *Style in Theory and Philosophy. Can* theory be stylish, or at least style-aware, is what we are asking, and what might there be of value in that? And how can theory afford style at all, when it is so invested in philosophy? The difficulty is the perceived incompatibility in the style of thought of the two discourses. Again, let us proceed slowly. In an almost too well-known response to a question of Derek Attridge, Derrida once said that "[s]till now, and more desperately than ever, I dream of a writing that would be neither philosophy nor literature, nor even contaminated by one or the other, while still keeping—I have no desire to abandon this—the memory of literature and philosophy" (1992, 73). This "dream" is a particularly influential poststructuralist attribute within theory, it must be said. Its effects are not necessarily discoverable in the other constituencies of theory, like (to give another list) formalist approaches, structuralism, New Historicism, feminism, queer theory, Marxism and post-Marxism, ecocriticism, reception-oriented approaches, postcolonialism, or posthumanism. But since it is poststructuralism that bears arguably the closest affiliation to philosophy, it is there that we might need to trace the issues that arise concerning theory when it finds itself between literature and philosophy. The *between* suggested in Derrida's dream weighs heavily on theory and on this volume's project as well, and not only because of our subtitle. The thrust toward liminality, hybridity, inbetweenness, and their valorization is among the readiest—one might say "stylized"—reflexes of theory. It complements performative and quasi- or crypto-literary writing in some of the texts of theory, which some will find inventive and others, admittedly, tiresome. In that sense, "style in theory," yes—or literary style, in theory.

The difficulty, however, is that given current vicissitudes in the academy, theory is "out of style" and perhaps, too, out of *that* style more particularly. "High theory," for which one might read this version of poststructuralism and its "dense mixing of styles" (Kamuf 1985, 11), is certainly precarious. That, too, is something the bystanders say. But in a more fundamental *manner*—one less subject to changing fashions—style will always have been *out of style*. Style, in this sense, marks a faultline in the history of Western thought and culture that can be traced back to Plato and beyond. That faultline—and it is precisely one of *style*—is, putatively, between philosophy and poetry, or literature. On one side is philosophy's relative disregard for style in its overriding pursuit of truth, and on the other is poetry's—literature's—all-consuming interest in style, even—perhaps especially—at the expense of truth. This is, of course, too conveniently styled a story to rise above the level of caricature. But over the years, and as a result of what theory inclines to—in its dreams—that story has been sufficiently pervasive and compelling to give shape to "theory" as the discourse that emerged *out of the faultline of style, between literature and philosophy*. According to that account, theory is a miscegenated, polymorphous discourse that actively resists the aporias of style, refusing to recognize the traditional division of intellectual labor of philosophy and literature. *Style* would therefore be nothing less than the exorbitant *atopos* or *non-lieu* of *theory*.

Theory, then, has always been simultaneously *in* and *out of* style, and, like style—this, at least is the story it has most commonly told itself—it exists in sharpest relief as the *between* of literature and philosophy. But what of style—in theory—today? And what of theory—out of style—today? If the preceding account of theory and style as the interstices of philosophy and literature is at best a thumbnail sketch, how much more suspiciously should it be considered in the context of the humanities' supposedly post-theoretical present? These issues are responded to below. Before we go there, however, let us note that in an essay that takes, as its title, "All the Rest is Literature," Jean-Luc Nancy comments that "[t]he misfortune of a dreadful style in writing has befallen more than one philosopher—perhaps all of them" (Nancy 2008, 17). Philosophy is *the* discourse without style, as "the philosopher writes badly, and sometimes he or she does nothing but scribble," in a different reflex that is "not an accident, but rather an infirmity that is cosubstantial with and congenital to the exercise of philosophy" (17). Philosophy, indeed, is convinced that "*truth* demands a laborious science without style" (Nancy 2008, 61; emphasis in original): what in an essay called "Philosophical Style" (1997), Nancy refers to as "the ideal of an absence of style . . . an infinitely sober prose that ultimately effaces itself in presentation" (1997, 20). Yet this is itself a stylistic judgment and it is precisely what leads to an inbetweenness between philosophy and literature, to an oscillation between the two discourses. The dynamic is inescapable:

> [O]ne must already possess in advance the aesthetic and literary categories that enable one to assess a style, or a lack or absence of it. In other words, one has to be in possession of *literature*. Literature can, in effect, either well subordinate philosophy to itself as a genre and bring to bear on it the only kind of judgment that does not arise from philosophical decision, or it can altogether exclude philosophy from its domain, from style. But in order to make use of this notion of literature, and in order to delineate either of these partitions [*partages*], one needs philosophy. (Nancy 2008, 17–18, emphasis in original)

Theory is the discourse with the most developed attention to these oscillations, and in this sense "theory" names the response to the "need" felt at—and *as*—"the end of philosophy" for "another style" (1997, 19). Perhaps it is only in theory's attentiveness to the radicality of that demand—which in effect (though in more than mere *effects*) and precisely out of (and *as*) fidelity to "the question of style" (19) calls for an absolute indifference to any "ideal or model of 'style'" (21)—that the between of literature and philosophy can, in "renewed tension . . . turning style against style" (21), resist the temptations of complacency. And this is why any review of style in theory *must* be as much about philosophy as about literature, as the essays in this volume collectively are, for they understand that the question of style is as philosophical as it is literary. But that does, rather, raise the question of what stylistics, then, must do.

(3) *Style in Theory and Stylistics. Qu'est-ce que le style?*, a collection of essays positioned in the French tradition of *stylistique*, includes the suggestion by Robert Martin that style has a "statut

préthéorique" (Martin 1994, 13). Style, whether approached in its larger meaning or in the narrower sense of *literary* style, corresponds to a pretheoretical "intuition" (13) that escapes the moment one attempts to contain it. This is a simple enough point, but it rings true and it is important. It is not encountered as pregnantly in the critical, philosophical, or theoretical writings on style as one might think. Even in Martin, it is something of a stray remark. More crucially here, it is an admission from within stylistics that style will forever remain irreducible to its protocols: elusive and indefinable, as was acknowledged at the start of this Introduction. Its consequence, Martin argues, is that the passage from the pretheoretical to the theoretical can only proceed as a function of established conceptions in language and in the fundamentals of aesthetics (13). It is the equivalent, within stylistics, of the idea expressed by Nancy that one "has to be in possession of *literature*" to attend to style, the question of which will always have been posed within philosophy—this putatively styleless discourse—already. Style, therefore, is pretheoretical, but it perhaps can only be noticed as such in post-theory. Style, we conclude, is between and after the non-moment and the moment of theory: always there, before theory; never quite there, never quite in theory, for it is always beyond it.

This, however, is not the style of stylistics. Style has different disciplinary identities, different linguistic identities, even different national identities. It is always in passage, in movement, in translation. In this volume we have tried to be diligent in marking those trajectories and cross-identities, and in translating religiously wherever needed but keeping the original visible. One identity we have not rendered, however, is the style of cognitive stylistics, which, we think, has drifted past Martin's "intuition" even while it proposes "the notion that meaning is embodied, and that mind and body are continuous; the notion that categorisation is a feature of prototype effects, so that categories are provisional, situationally dependent and socio-culturally grounded in embodiment too; and the notion that language and its manifestations in reading and interpretation is a natural, evolved and universal trait in humans, continuous with other perceptual and tactile experience of the environment" (Stockwell 2007). This is not quite the style in theory, or the style of theory—and yet, why should it be? Cognitive stylistics brings the idea of "mind style" (see Fowler 1977) to intersections with the (pre-)(con)textual in interesting enough ways, especially in the midst of "the cognitive turn" (Toolan and Weber, 2005). If theory is such a miscellany, as Culler said, can it not also embrace this, especially since the emphasis on context there brings style back to the political? Definitely—but, in this book, we have kept to one style of approach, in expectation of synthesizing work in other contexts.

(4) *Style in Theory and Politics*. On that question of style and the political, or the polemical, we shall not say much, confident that the first essay in this collection has some rather compelling things to say about it and that a number of the essays here are aware that "style maps a will onto a world" (see van Eck, McAllister and van de Vall 1995, 19). The study of style may, admittedly, be overwritten by a political unconscious (see Jameson 2002). It would be quite a witless response to style, however, to think that a preoccupation with it is, tendentially, apolitical, when so much about style is about suasion, about the shaping of expression that, whether deliberately or otherwise, is canny about ethos, pathos, logos, and the beguilements that lie between rhetoric and effect. And, furthermore, it would be to ignore Rancière's Schillerian suggestion that it is precisely style's elusiveness, its self-sufficient "unavailability" (2009, 34) or "indifference" (e.g. 2009, 28–40; 2011, 138), that announces the "radical separation of the sensorium of art" (2009, 40) and preserves a considerable metapolitical potency. Style, then, in theory and beyond, *is* political. And, to that extent, an attention to style in theory must be timely. It responds to the times.

(5) *Style in Theory and Contemporary Culture*. We have seen above how style in theory may need to wonder whether theory is out of style. What is certain is that the style in theory as this might be "constructed" in deconstructive hegemonies has been complemented (rather than supplemented) by positions that superadd themselves to theory's constituencies. In the process, they move the debate on, but it is doubtful if they quite change style in theory. Rancière's *Mute Speech*, for instance, retains the "alembicated style" of theory (Rockhill 2011, 25), and it is not only because of that that it is recognizable as a *theoretical* performance, for it positions itself, once more, "between literature and philosophy." At the same time, it is evidently perturbed, though it would perhaps be good for it to be more so. "The age of literature," Rancière writes, "is not only the age of war between forms of writing" (114); quite in the style of theory, however, he remains in *writing*,

and goes on to develop his thoughts about "mute-loquacious" (114) speech—rather, for instance, than in what has been called "technesis" (Hansen 2000) or its analogues or, since one can also follow Stiegler and thereby be more recognizably in the style of theory, "technics" (Stiegler 1998; 2009; 2010). A "failure to form the instrument necessary for literature" (Rancière 2011, 114), we rather think, is not in the style of theory—and yet it is precisely the style of theory, when theory is caught in between literature and philosophy, to disremember its transmediatic milieu. We mention this here because style is as "an absolute manner of seeing things" (to quote Rancière quoting Flaubert, before he insists that "'Absolute' means not bound, freed" [116]). If, truly, "Style is not a manner of sentences because it is primarily a manner of conception" (118), primed to "pierce the Idea" (114, 119), then style in theory, if it is to approximate the absolute must free itself from itself, from *style in theory* to the extent that this is knowable, practised, *intuitive*. The larger problems with style in theory, therefore, occur when style in theory is not surprising, not unsettling, not *not* itself.

You might well ask, therefore—are you holding a surprising book?

*

You will not have been surprised, in the question above and in this sentence as well, that the theoretical rediscovers the mode of direct address to the reader, unconventional though that is. A book about, or of, theory will always contrive something surprising, though we hope there are more substantial surprises in the following pages. But if you answer in the affirmative, we must hope that the word *surprising* is used less than disingenuously in your response.

We do not want to say much about the book itself. That too is not surprising. The essays speak for themselves, we feel, and we certainly do not wish to rehearse the convention in introductions of this type whereby each essay is summarized and its claims on scholarship's posterity advertised. Like others within theory, we have noticed that we have an aversion to the institution of the abstract—that way, eventually and by an *extensio ad absurdum*, lie the tyranny and twittering of the 140-character message. Theory has a different gearing, a different measure, a different *style*. It has, indeed, been instructive to discover just how recalcitrant the theoretical is to the conventions of the institution of the style guide. Theory's value is in that, too: it will *not* be *styled*. Not amenably, anyway.

We shall not, however, say nothing at all about the essays in this collection. A few points, then. The essays here are not the productions of a collective. They are not a project. They are as eclectic as theory itself, even if they eschew the mode of style in theory that could have gone further in relation to (3) and (5) above. But then style in theory is never absolute enough. Even when it is unbound—"in between"—it is never entirely disaffiliated from itself, and even in the process of self-renewal through self-revisioning of its style(s), it continues to tend toward literature and philosophy a little more than toward everything else that makes up its miscellaneity. And, like us, the authors of these essays felt that the first duty in this volume was to consider theory in a return upon itself and its styles, tones, modes, and modalities, as well as the approaches, readings, forgettings, and rememberings that might be summoned thence.

In the eclecticism there are patterns, as one might expect. These are reflected in the sequence of the essays. They move from a concern with the histories, genealogies, cultural memory, and developing repertoires of style in theory (Mazzotta, Lauri-Lucente, Sillars); to theoretical readings of style in philosophy, literature, and culture (Anton, Burnham, Müller, Rabaté, Corby, Hughes); to explorations of style in avowedly theoretical writing which are not loath to resource the affordances of print and textual play and/or ratify the implications, formal and conceptual, of style's ludic-cum-conceptual potentialities in lieu of literature and philosophy (Garnier, Milesi, Aquilina, Sant); to, finally, consideration of style in theory in life and in death (Herbrechter, Callus).

In the course of all that, it emerges that style was never, after all, ex-centric to theory. The value of style, of theory, of style in theory, becomes appreciably evident in those essays, and it is that value which this introduction has sought to frame.

Ivan Callus
James Corby
Gloria Lauri-Lucente

References

Badiou, Alain. 2004. "Mathematics and Philosophy: The Grand Style and the Little Style." In *Theoretical Writings*, edited and translated by Ray Brassier and Alberto Toscano, 3–20. London: Continuum.

—. 2007. *Being and Event*. Translated by Oliver Feltham. London: Continuum.

Barthes, Roland. 1975. *S/Z*. Translated by Richard Miller. London: Jonathan Cape, 1975.

—. 1984. *Writing Degree Zero & Elements of Semiology*. Translated by Annette Lavers and Colin Smith. London: Jonathan Cape.

Bauerlein, Mark. 1997. *Literary Criticism: An Autopsy*. Pennsylvania, PA: University of Pennsylvania Press.

Belsey, Catherine. 2011. *A Future for Criticism*. Oxford: Wiley-Blackwell.

Culler, Jonathan. 1975. *Structuralist Poetics: Structuralism, Linguistics, and the Study of Literature*. London: Routledge & Kegan Paul.

—. 1997. *Literary Theory: A Very Short Introduction*. Oxford: Oxford University Press.

—. 2007. *The Literary in Theory*. Stanford: Stanford University Press.

Deleuze, Gilles. 1973. *Proust and Signs*. Translated by Richard Howard. London: Allen Lane.

De Man, Paul. 1982. *Allegories of Reading: Figural Language in Rousseau, Nietzsche, Rilke, and Proust*. New Haven, CT: Yale University Press.

—. 1983. *Blindness and Insight: Essays in the Rhetoric of Contemporary Criticism*. 2nd edn. London: Routledge.

—. 1986. "The Resistance to Theory." In *The Resistance to Theory*, 3–20. Minneapolis: University of Minnesota Press.

—. 1996. *Aesthetic Ideology*. Minneapolis: University of Minnesota Press.

Derrida, Jacques. 1979. *Spurs: Nietzsche's Styles*. Translated by Barbara Harlow. Chicago: University of Chicago Press.

—. 1982. "White Mythology: Metaphor in the Text of Philosophy." In *Margins of Philosophy*, translated by Alan Bass, 207–72. Brighton: Harvester Press.

—. 1992. "'This Strange Institution Called Literature': An Interview with Jacques Derrida." Interview by Derek Attridge. London: Routledge.

—. 2008. *The Animal that Therefore I Am*. Edited by Marie-Louise Mallet. Translated by David Wills. New York: Fordham University Press.

Foucault, Michel. 1987. *Death and the Labyrinth: The World of Raymond Roussel*. Translated by Charles Ruas. London: Athlone Press.

Fowler, Roger. 1977. *Linguistics and the Novel*. London: Methuen.

Genette, Gérard. 1966. *Figures I*. Paris: Seuil.

—. 1969. *Figures II*. Paris: Seuil.
—. 1972. *Figures III*. Paris: Seuil.
—. 1995. *Mimologics*. Translated by Thaïs E. Morgan. Lincoln: University of Nebraska Press.
Hansen, Mark. 2000. *Embodying Technesis: Technology Beyond Writing*. Ann Arbor: University of Michigan Press.
Hayles, N. Katherine. 2006. "Traumas of Code." *Critical Inquiry* 33: 136–57.
Kamuf, Peggy. 1985. "Translator's Note." In *The Ear of the Other: Otobiography, Transference, Translation*, by Jacques Derrida, edited by Christie V. MacDonald. Translated by Peggy Kamuf, xi–xii. New York: Schocken.
Kermode, Frank. 2000. *Shakespeare's Language*. London: Allen Lane.
—. 2003. "Value after Theory: Frank Kermode." Interview by Michael Payne. In *life.after.theory*, edited by Michael Payne and John Schad, 52–77. London: Continuum.
Kristeva, Julia. 1969. *Séméiôtikè: Recherches pour une sémanalyse*. Paris: Seuil.
Leitch, Vincent B., William E. Cain, Laurie A. Finke, Barbara E. Johnson, John McGowan, T. Denean Sharpley-Whiting, and Jeffrey J. Williams, eds. 2010. *The Norton Anthology of Theory and Criticism*. 2nd edn. New York: W. W. Norton & Co.
Martin, Robert. 1994. "Préliminaire." In *Qu'est-ce que le style*? Edited by Georges Molinié and Pierre Cahné, 9–13. Paris: Presses Universtaires de France.
Miller, J. Hillis. 2009. *For Derrida*. New York: Fordham University Press.
Nancy, Jean-Luc. 1997. *The Sense of the World*. Translated by Jeffrey S. Librett. Minneapolis: University of Minnesota Press.
—. 2008. *The Discourse of the Syncope: Logodaedalus*. Translated by Saul Anton. Stanford: Stanford University Press.
Payne, Michael and John Schad, eds. 2003. *life.after.theory*. London: Continuum.
Rancière, Jacques. 2009. *Aesthetics and Its Discontents*. Translated by Steven Corcoran. Cambridge: Polity.
—. 2011. *Mute Speech*. Translated by James Swenson. New York: Columbia University Press.
Rockhill, Gabriel. 2011. "Introduction: Through the Looking Glass—The Subversion of the Modernist Doxa." In *Mute Speech*, by Jacques Ranciere, 1–28. New York: Columbia University Press.
Spitzer, Leo. 1928. *Stilstudien*. 2 vols. Munich: Mynchen Hueber.
Steinmetz, Rudy. 1994. *Les styles de Derrida*. Brussels: De Boeck-Wesmael.

Stiegler, Bernard. 1998. *Technics and Time, 1: The Fault of Epimetheus*. Translated by Richard Beardsworth and George Collins. Stanford: Stanford University Press.

—. 2009. *Technics and Time, 2: Disorientation*. Translated by Stephen Barker. Stanford: Stanford University Press.

—. 2010. *Technics and Time, 3: Cinematic Time and the Question of Malaise*. Translated by Stephen Barker. Stanford: Stanford University Press.

Stockwell, Peter. 2007. "Cognitive Poetics and Literary Theory." *JLT* 1(1): 135–52.

Stoppard, Tom. 1967. *Rosencrantz and Guildenstern Are Dead*. New York: Grove Press.

Thacker, Eugene. 2010. *After Life*. Chicago: University of Chicago Press.

Toolan, Michael and Jean Jacques Weber. 2005. "Introduction to the Cognitive Turn: Papers in Cognitive Literary Studies." *European Journal of English Studies* 9(2): 107–15.

Ulmer, Gregory B. 1988. "The Puncept in Grammatology." In *On Puns: The Foundation of Letters*, edited by Jonathan Culler, 164–89. Oxford: Blackwell.

van Eck, Caroline, James McAllister, and Renée van de Vall. 1995. *The Question of Style in Philosophy and the Arts*. Cambridge: Cambridge University Press.

1

Style as polemics

Giuseppe Mazzotta

We usually speak of the "spirit" of a place or of a historical period, say, the Baroque period with its contorted lines and its hyperboles, or of the Old Delhi bungalows and bazaars vibrant with noises, with baskets of peanuts and piles of ginger, and we know what we mean by it: the essence of that place or the *genius loci*. We even speak directly of a "French style," or "Greek style," to mean, respectively, the spectacle of country-houses, chateaux, ateliers, the Louvre, Provincial furniture, or the rugged landscape of whitewashed villages perched on rocky hills and the silhouette of the Parthenon. This sort of style evokes for us the look of things, the taste and unique quality of a whole culture, and calling it the "spirit" of a place or its style is a way of pulling together impressions drawn from architecture, sounds, ways of life, and values.

When we leave behind issues pertinent to travelogues and turn to an appraisal of style in related literary and philosophical theories, we are confronted with polemics, even when we turn our sentences into interrogatives. It is as if style, from the Latin *stilus* or *stylus*, meaning stake or a pointed weapon, never lost its etymological resonance. Derrida, for one, encapsulates the common concerns with the stylistics of our times by seeking to explore "la question du style" in an epochal modern thinker such as Nietzsche (Derrida 1979; see also Kofman 1984). Style, in this context, does not just designate the unique, distinct voice of Nietzsche. For Derrida, rather, his reflection is a strategy, a way of putting into question the very possibility of a fixed sense as well as the likely desire to impart a unidirectional intention to a text's meaning. We witness the triumph, in many ways a liberating experience, of the style of suspicion. The reason for the questioning is to be found in the groundlessness of our knowledge and our beliefs. In this sense, Nietzsche marks a new departure in the style of traditional philosophical speculations on account of his aesthetic philosophy, his way of abandoning traditional metaphysics and seeking to systematically yoke together literature and philosophy. As is widely known, he found this mode of representation in part thanks to his friend Burckhardt's studies on the Renaissance, but mostly in the aesthetic vision of the world expressed by the ancient Greeks.

There can hardly be any doubt that Nietzsche's aesthetic insight inaugurates philosophy's modern, radical turn, at odds with the metaphysical, rational abstractions of nineteenth-century German thought, for instance in Kant and Hegel. It is this aesthetic insight that triggers his project of reorientation of the intellectual, moral, and political tradition of Western thought. One needs to pinpoint the essential trait of his aesthetic vision. Over his world hovers a theory of art, which shows him, as *The Birth of Tragedy* argues, that we are trapped in a double bind, the foundation of which are two mythical categories of representation. On the one hand, we grapple with the vast display of illusions and appearances, namely, Apollo's dream-world that is steadily evoked as the expression of surface values and as a meditative style. On the other, we witness the exposure of the "horror of existence," the chaos of tragic contradictions and the depths or "abyss" of the will that is dramatized by the wild ecstasy of Dionysus and is expressed in a joyous, adventurous language of passion. This aesthetic vision leads Nietzsche to propose, among other things, as one can read at the opening of *Human, All Too Human*, the announcement of a new Enlightenment for the modern age. The emblem of the new epoch is a new style, a style to which Nietzsche refers as one of "historical philosophizing," one which we call perspectival thinking. Or, in other words, "Everything, however, has come to be; there are no eternal facts: just as there are no absolute truths. From now on therefore, *historical philosophizing* will be necessary, and along with it the virtue of modesty" (Nietzsche 1997, 17).[1]

The question of style turns up, in the wake of Nietzsche, in most modern philosophical speculations (as well as in Derrida's

---

[1]All italics in quotations are those of the author quoted unless otherwise indicated.

own deconstructive project). Style is again a question for so-called les enfants de Nietzsche (to use the title of Sarah Kofman's study of the *Ecce Homo*), and they include Deleuze, Bataille, Blanchot, Klossowski, Derrida, and Kofman herself, etc. (see Kofman 1993). Within this philosophical ambit, style is not reducible merely to a question of techniques, craft, or to the power to wrap one's thoughts in a sort of gauze of artificiality and eloquence. To the contrary, these representatives of the "French Nietzsche" (a critical strain that focuses on Nietzsche's semiotics) grasp style as a mode of thought that reflects on the meta-literary aspects of narratives, that reaches out toward enigmatic utterances (under the influence of Heidegger), and plays with etymologies, puns, and bold webs of metaphorical resonances in order to eschew the temptation of metaphysics.

We could call it an extraterritorial, cosmopolitan style of thought, which apparently shuns history but which comes through as a form of suspicion toward what are perceived as superannuated, grand philosophies of culture. And yet, for all its abstractions, this newfangled stylistic mode of philosophizing coincides with a perception of the phenomenal, material, and physical realities of experience. We are all too familiar with some avant-garde, postmodern versions of philosophical style: Lyotard's skeptical views of grand meta-narratives, Ansell-Pearson's neo-baroque fascination with simulacra and artifices, or Roland Barthes's view of style as a "metaphor" (Barthes 1970, 12).[2] The past, so they argue, can only be retrieved from a detached, ironic perspective. To grasp how much they all owe to Nietzsche's inimitable and yet, paradoxically, exemplary style we should briefly look at the precise genealogy of Nietzsche's own adventurous understanding of style: the traditions of pre-Socratic aphorisms and, more generally, the framework of the Sophists.

The term, from *sophizo*, refers to those teachers of ancient Greece (Protagoras, Gorgias of Lentini, who held that nothing exists, Cratylus, etc.) condemned by Socrates and Xenophon for their redefinition of wisdom or *Sophia*, and for teaching not the truth but the appearances of the truth as well as the strategies of rhetorical arguments to pursue them. Like latter-day lawyers, atomists, and

---

[2]For some thoughtful comments on postmodern projects such as Lyotard's, cf. Ansell-Pearson 1997, especially 3ff.

Heracliteans, but unlike Socrates, the sophists treated knowledge skeptically as a thing that could be sold for a price, and, thereby, they severed it from any idea of a metaphysical *truth*. Plato hated their conjunction of wisdom and the marketplace, a sort of relation that cast religion, ethics, law, and politics to a matter of viewpoints to be decided by the power of one's rhetoric. In our time, the sophists are viewed with increased sympathy. Their thinking that nothing exists, and that if anything did exist we could know nothing about it, comes through as an act of liberation from the shackles of metaphysical, abstract generalities.

There is no doubt that when Nietzsche asks in *Truth and Falsity in an Ultramoral Sense*, "What therefore is truth?," he answers in the specific sophistical mode of the *sophistai* (those who possess wisdom). He grasps and endorses the power principle that underlies their ancient revival of eloquence. So, "What therefore is truth? A mobile army of metaphors, metonymies, anthropomorphisms: in short a sum of human relations which became poetically and rhetorically intensified, metamorphosed, adorned, and after a long usage seems to a nation fixed, canonic, and binding: truths are illusions of which one has forgotten that they *are* illusions; worn-out metaphors which have become powerless to affect the senses; coins which have their obverse effaced and now are no longer of account as coins but merely as metals" (Nietzsche 1965, 508).

Nietzsche's reflection goes on to acknowledge his puzzlement about the origin of the human impulse to truth. The brunt of the passage, which restates one of Vico's aphorisms in his *New Science*, gravitates nonetheless within a temporal horizon. The metamorphosis of an originary metaphorical figure into a subsequent *proper* or literal noun takes place within the flow of time. The sense of the contingency and shiftiness of figurative language cannot but trigger a deep distrust against any idealism, against all illusions of eternity or omnipresence, and the belief in nature's infallible laws. The reader, moreover, cannot but be struck by the metaphor of a "mobile army" of metaphors: the metaphor for the play of metaphors implies a war-like, polemical understanding of language. It can destroy or protect from destruction, and, as if it were a praxis, it can modify the material ambiance of the world.

The idea of figurative language as a polemical weapon and a form of power pervades Nietzsche's thought. His polemics turn against Socrates, and it is equally well known that in his *Philosophy in the*

Tragic Age of the Greeks, as he focuses on the *style* of the philosophers, he arranges his argument around the idea of an opposition between two styles, the metaphorical style (which designates the richness of life and its affirmation), and the needy, ascetic style of the rationalist philosophers. Within this radically dualistic pattern, Nietzsche places Heraclitus against Aristotle, an opposition which repeats the original duality between Dionysius and Apollo, Euripides versus Aeschylus—and they all reenact the struggle between sublime imaginative, aesthetic beauty versus dry scientific constructions of reality. These sharply drastic, reductive dualities are certainly questioned by Nietzsche as he shows the tenuousness of conceptual boundaries. Nonetheless, he distances himself from Aristotle, who is accused of the intellectual crime of rejection of Heraclitus. Aristotle is acknowledged as "the greatest man of the concept"; at the same time, on the basis of his strict adherence to the authority of the *logos* and the "concept," he attacked Heraclitus' devaluation of the "principle of non-contradiction." (I take these considerations from Kofman 1993, 18–22.)

The style of interpretive violence Nietzsche adopts, and he may well do so ultimately to argue for the desirability of an imaginative and intellectual openness over and against the rigidity of closed systems, is certainly designed to arouse the consciousness of the sources of violence in the contradictory assertions and values occurring in history. In effect, however, the "philosophy of the future" he advances can be defined as a way of thinking that opens up to an unpredictable future and leaves behind the narrow scaffolding of dogmatic constructions. Yet, his thinking still presupposes a belief in the existence of objective categories, such as the Dionysian impulse and the Apollonian dream. What determines the superiority of the Dionysian category over the Apollonian one is a question of the will to power. From this standpoint, Nietzsche's idea of a style, as necessarily polemical, as necessarily the locus for the staging of clashing viewpoints, is far from being radical or new. Actually, it is rooted in ancient Hellenistic grounds and echoes not just the sophists but a whole tradition of philosophical theories of style that stretches from Aristotle well into the early modern period.

Nietzsche's polemic with Aristotle, conducted in the name of the energy and affirmation of multiplicity, comes to a focus on one specific issue. He does not attack Aristotle's theory of style. Rather, in his radical skepticism toward dialectics and all abstractions, he finds that Aristotle brackets the exploration of the complexity of human personality and suppresses the mythical origins of Western culture. If Nietzsche means by this charge that Aristotle did not regard *poetics* or what can be called the aesthetic faculty as the source of all knowledge (though, like Plato, he casts Homer as the very voice of Greek wisdom), he is right in pointing out the rational thrust of the Greek philosopher. Aristotle writes in the unabashed conviction that the *logos* of Greece, defined by him as the power of speech and reasoning, is the home of all understanding.

Accordingly, both his *Poetics* and his *Rhetoric* devote an extraordinary attention to what one can call an *ethics* of style, to the persuasion that style always entails a revaluation of values (Aristotle 1982, 1954). Aristotle views both texts as therapeutic of the disorder within language and the values it embodies. In the *Poetics* the judgment over the proper style of literary language and of the theater carries ethical and political implications. In the *Rhetoric*, his thoughts range from the classification of metaphors to questions about the foundation of good style "in the correctness of language" (III, 5, 1407a). At the same time, forensic and political oratory (with subtly ironic remarks about Gorgias), their rhythm, and their order of moral contents are treated with extraordinary detail. What particularly the philosopher puts at the forefront of his reflections is the notion of rhetoric as a system of assertions and refutations, as a game of opponents who plead in court and refute each other (III, 17, 1418b). Like rhetoric, which poses as a remedy to all differences, style embodies a system of order and, at the same time, it barely conceals the fact of oppositions and differences (the barbarisms) within the social reality.

In the *Poetics* (chapters 19–22) language (along with character, plot, thought, melody, and spectacle) is viewed as a constituent part of tragedy. The qualities of style—*lexis*—are listed: the virtue of clarity is primary. But the text quickly moves to an analysis of "an impressive style" (chapter 22, 1458), that which surpasses the ordinary and includes "foreign words, metaphors, expanded words, and whatever departs from normal usage" (1458a). The foreign words, a sort of an incomprehensible riddle, produce barbarisms, which threaten the clarity of the ordinary Greek language. Confronted with this stylistic crisis, Aristotle recommends ". . . a blend . . . of these ingredients, since the unfamiliar element (the foreign word, the metaphor, the ornamental word, and the other types mentioned) will save the diction from being commonplace and drab, while the colloquial element will ensure clarity" (22, 1458b). The confluence of two idioms, the assimilation of the "foreign" elements to the natural ones to form an ordered style, no doubt, reflect Aristotle's ethical theory of the "median" between virtues and vices (*Nicomachean Ethics*, II, chapters 5–9). The ethical model for style subordinates rhetoric to ethics as if they were part of the same practical and political science.

Aristotle never formulates a critique of the foreign or the "stranger" (a figure that steadily recurs in ancient philosophical texts), but he is not alone in reflecting on ways in which style and language can cope with the intrusion of what is alien to Greek self-consciousness. Let me turn briefly to the famous speech of Pericles, the leading statesman in fifth-century Athens, as it is reported by Thucydides in the *Peloponnesian War* (II, 35ff.; the speech is available in Kagan and Viggiano, 205–10). The speech, as is known, was part of the funeral ceremonies held, by ancient custom, to remember and honor the soldiers who had first fallen in battle. Because of his eminence and widely acknowledged wisdom, Pericles was chosen to deliver their eulogy. Rather than directly eulogizing the valor and sacrifice of the soldiers, Pericles chose to deliver the panegyric of the city of Athens, of the liberal democracy it created and the values it promoted. These values, so he argues, are worth dying for.

In this classic of political oratory (the genre that Aristotle places at the heart of his *Rhetoric*), Pericles' speech unfolds by joining together rhetoric, politics, and ethics, that is, by recalling the bare facts of Athenian culture: "I shall begin," he is recorded to say, "with our ancestors; . . . Our constitution does not copy the laws of neighboring states; we are rather pattern to others than imitators ourselves. Its administration favors the many instead of the few; this is why it is called a democracy. If we look at the laws, they afford equal justice to all in their private differences; if to social standing, advancement in public life falls to reputation for capacity; . . . The freedom which we enjoy in our government extends also to our ordinary life. . . . But all this ease in our private relations does not make us lawless as citizens . . ." (II, 36, 1–372).

The Athenians' historic achievements (democracy, freedom, laws) were made possible by their common, unquestionable commitment to the principles of human reason and of a rational philosophy bent on understanding man's place in the city and, concomitantly, the place of the city in a man's life. What freed the Athenians—and here lies the basis for the singularity of their culture, their privilege to establish their city as a model for others to imitate and become, thus, "the school of Hellas" (II, 41, 1)—was their abiding exercise of reason, which was viewed as coextensive with the vast scope of the *logos*.

It is widely believed that Thucydides was present at the commemoration of the dead soldiers, that he heard Pericles' eulogy and transcribed it *verbatim* in his history-writing. His presence allowed him to cast himself as an eye and ear "witness," and it provided him a rhetorical mode that lends an aura of authenticity to his historical narrative. In adopting this narrative strategy, moreover, Thucydides could lay the foundation for our grasping the essentials of style as a powerful polemical weapon. The real purpose of Athens' violent enemies, so in effect Pericles and Thucydides together argued, was the destruction not just of the city but of reason itself. To the city's enemies, Pericles opposed a communal style marked by the "we" and the "our" in his speech to stress that both speaker and audience shared the values of common memory, aspirations, thoughts and, in one word, of the *logos*.

The theatricality of the public ceremony, which hinged on Pericles' live performance, transcends the historian's effort to capture the "living" voice of Pericles. In reality, it gave Thucydides' text its concrete, irreducible quality. It was, actually, a decisive rhetorical strategy because it created the conditions for Thucydides' rescuing his political ideas of a constitutive of democracy, or of what he liked his audience to think democracy was, from the pitfall of indulging in the repertory of commonplace formulas and abstract ratiocinations. The fiction of the "living" voice, with its scale of sounds, pauses, cadences, rhythm, as well as the gestures of the body etc., turned his account into a concrete, truly memorable experience. Thanks to this piece of oratory, the *logos* could only be identified as a question of language and as a matter of style. It is possible to say that a peculiar fusion of language and style occurs. Style always presupposes language. In effect, it can be said that the ancient logos, inherited from the ancestors, revives and even has its origins in Pericles' style, just as Pericles' style could only have existed within the matrix of the Greek *logos*. Finally, the singularity and cadence of the "living voice"—so did Thucydides obliquely intimate—could transfigure into life the death of the soldiers they were commemorating. They could bring them back to the historic and at the same time symbolic life of the undying city.

These classical traditions of style were not lost in the development of Roman culture and its early modern ramifications. I will briefly refer to Petrarch (1304–74), who systematically took up, absorbed, and acknowledged his dependence on the classical traditions and refined their energies. The wonderful essay by Gloria Lauri-Lucente included in this collection sheds light on the many facets of Petrarch's sense of style.

I would like to focus on a genre Petrarch deployed while living in Avignon, a genre known as the *invective*, which was common currency for someone like Demosthenes (e.g. the *Philippics*) and Cicero, and it extended among Italian humanists of the following century, such as Valla and Poggio Bracciolini, to name only a few.

Traditionally, an invective stages a high-pitched public verbal confrontation in the tribunal or theater of public opinion between two contenders. Akin to a war of words or *logomachia*, an invective is marked by harsh, even bombastic charges and countercharges ranging from incompetence to immorality, and even calumnies about character, and is shaped by the belief that words are invested with the quasi-magical power to destroy lies and create reality anew.

Petrarch's *Invective against a Physician*, written in 1355, does all of this and more as it targets a physician, whose name Petrarch never gives, and who was notable for his engagement as the physician entrusted to look after the health of Pope Clement VI in the years of the Black Plague till his death in 1352. Petrarch's invective dramatizes a fierce struggle, the juxtaposition of two radically polarized worldviews, that of the physician, who is cast as a sort of Aristotelian philosopher of nature, and that of Petrarch, the Augustinian humanist/rhetorician. No mediation is possible between them. Petrarch heaps hyperbolic contempt on his opponent, the court-physician who is treated as an enemy, an illiterate, a self-appointed priest of science, and an impostor who is after money and does the work of death. To this vision, Petrarch opposes his conviction in the primacy of the therapy of the soul, the value of moral philosophy, and his belief in the world-shaping power of poetry. The struggle between these two styles of living is not merely an academic exercise. The invective, on the contrary, is really addressed to the Pope. From this point of view, Petrarch warns the Pope of the intellectual and moral dangers inherent in the alliance he has enacted between theology and science and urges him to espouse a modern theology of interiority Petrarch himself represents.

Undoubtedly, from Nietzsche to Aristotle, Thucydides, and Petrarch, the question of style is always an ideology and a strategy of power. Every author I have here examined questions values of science, nation, religion, and ethics. At the same time they all signal the need for a new turn in thinking, to master, dispose, and judge newly emergent values. They establish a new theory of culture and civilization, but, on closer inspection, the turn appears as no more than a repetitive, persistent and unchanging response to existing cultural circumstances. This is to say that the questions of style cannot be reduced to a conceit or a mere technique of formal ornamentation. Quite to the contrary, a writer's style unfailingly traces the filigree of genuine struggles going on in political life and its finite circumstances. And in the case of Nietzsche we are invited to take seriously his sense of the multiplicity of styles as the fitting reflection of the modern condition. Not for nothing, I suspect, he chose to end his *Human, All Too Human* with a meditation known by "The Wanderer," which I transcribe as my conclusion:

> Anyone who has come even part of the way to the freedom of reason cannot feel himself to be anything other than a wanderer upon the earth though not a traveler *toward* some final goal: for that does not exist. (1997, 302)

This sort of prose evokes the style, the spiritual perspective of a St Paul, of Dante, the poet of exile or of the desert, or even of a Kierkegaard. Their self-conscious displacement and marginality to the various institutionalizations of culture (political, literary, ethical, etc.) allow them to challenge its myths and, thereby, explore new frontiers of thought.

2

Petrarch and the birth of style in the *Collatio laureationis* and the *Familiares*

Gloria Lauri-Lucente

Throughout his statements in his Latin prose in a direct manner, and in his poetry in the vernacular in an indirect manner, Petrarch conceives of style as an act of supreme self-referentiality and self-definition through which the distinctive voice of the individual poet is established. Style is the *labor limae* for which Petrarch is so famous, a phrase that begins with Horace, becomes one of the pivotal components underlying the rhetorical strategies of Petrarch's entire literary corpus, and ultimately, through Petrarch himself, is codified as it enters into contemporary Italian to indicate linguistic refinement. Perhaps the best avenue to the poet's self-glorifying treatment of style in the *Familiares* (Petrarch 1997a; 1997b; 1975b; 1985), the epistolary corpus in Latin on which the following paper will be concentrating, is the *Collatio laureationis*, or the *Coronation Oration* (Petrarch 1975a; 1955), which Petrarch delivered when he was crowned poet laureate in the Senatorial Palace on the Capitoline Hill in Rome on Easter Sunday in 1341.

In the *Oration*, notions of style are intertwined with the discussion of *aemulatio* of prior tradition and prior poets, as the old is transformed into the new through poetic agon in a type of violent competition and displacement between battlefield foes that Harold Bloom himself probably could not have depicted more convincingly. Any stylistically effective metamorphosis of prior examples takes place within the realm of rivalry and competition, since emulation of prior models suggests approbation and, along with approbation, envy and malice (Pigman 1980, 18). Beyond affirming through tropes of martial conquest the importance of the thematic of poetic triumph and poetic fame, as well as the concomitant achievement of immortality through success and notoriety, Petrarch's overarching concern in the *Coronation Oration* is with variation and metamorphosis: metamorphosis of the prior tradition, of images and characters as described within the prose and the poems of Petrarch, but, most pointedly—and here Petrarch differs from most of his contemporaries in terms of the rise of the individual subject in the late Medieval and early Renaissance period—with the metamorphosis of Petrarch's speaker himself.[1] What this means is that metamorphosis is no longer only the *object* of poetic discourse but also a function of the *subject* of lyric poetry itself which then becomes the very "matter" of Petrarch's story, a matter that is at once lyrical and narrative and that concerns the individuality of the speaking voice over time as it is transformed through *labor limae* to create the subject in all its ever-changing varieties. This is why the self-referential "vario stile" or "varied style" in the opening sonnet of Petrarch's *Canzoniere* signals the deep meaning of what Petrarch and the Petrarchan tradition are all about—from the past to the present and aiming, however egocentric it might sound, toward the Petrarchan future.[2]

At the very heart of the *Coronation Oration* is the knowledge that there will be a Petrarchan tradition and that this Petrarchan tradition will follow Petrarch himself: a tradition inaugurated by him, which looks not only backward but also forward, a tradition born out of the new and bringing with it many followers, a

---

[1]On the characteristic trait of self-referentiality and subjectivity which sets Petrarch apart from his contemporaries, see Giuseppe Mazzotta (1993, 2–3), who writes that "with his insistence on subjective individualism and his steady concentration on the innermost landscape of the mind, Petrarch is said to generate an epoch-making transition to modernity."

[2]On the modernization of tradition through this backward and forward movement, see Marco Santagata (1993, 33), who writes that in his Latin works, Petrarch is a "restauratore," ("restorer") whose intent is "to renew by looking backwards" ("rinnovare guardando all'indietro").

tradition through which the concept of the triumphant "poetic" self is created. Petrarch writes:

> sicut quosdam pudet per aliorum isse vestigia, sic alii multoque plures sunt qui, sine aliquo certo duce, iter arduum aggredi reformidant. . . . Audacter itaque fortassis, sed non, ut michi videor, maligno proposito, ceteris cessantibus, me in tam laborioso et michi quidem periculoso calle ducem prebere non expavi, multis posthac, ut arbitror, secuturos. (Petrarch 1975a, 1268)

> (while there are some who think it shameful to follow in the footsteps of others, there are far more who fear to essay a hard road unless they have a sure guide. . . . Boldly, therefore, perhaps, but—to the best of my belief—with no unworthy intention, since others are holding back I am venturing to offer myself as guide for this toilsome and dangerous path; and I trust that there may be many followers.) (Petrarch 1955, 306)

In this trope of the path, Petrarch puts himself at the head of a new tradition, and insists on the vitality and originality of this new poetic self which never borrows heedlessly or imitates unthinkingly, but rather recasts classical images, themes, and poetic developments into another mold and into a new style. In fact, the very essence of Petrarch's humanist style is to be sought in "that mode through which the individual consciousness seeks to distinguish itself, to affirm its incomparable originality" (Jameson 1974, 334) through "an invention in *form*" rather than "a discovery of new *content*" (306), as Fredric Jameson would put it.[3] It is this very insistence on style as being the outward manifestation of a unique act of poetic self-creation which has the potential of inaugurating a new tradition that has earned the *Oration* Ernest Hatch Wilkins's famous appellation as the very "first manifesto of the Renaissance," whose distinctive "mingling of elements old and new" universalizes the singularity of the artist's signature and establishes its superiority over that of its predecessors (Petrarch 1955, 300).

Petrarch's relationship with tradition that repeats itself and also changes itself over time through the process of individual and collective metamorphosis leads us into consideration of his meditations

---

[3]All italics in quotations are those of the author quoted unless otherwise indicated.

on his imitative strategies in another set of expository writings, the *Familiares*, a collection of 24 books of letters written between 1325 and 1366 and addressed to both fictitious and real interlocutors. *Imitatio*, for Petrarch, means the imitation and transformation of prior examples into something new and "better" ("melius")—as regards competition, "the better" is the key element here since the successful introspective mastery of the past will coincide with the act of transcending prior tradition and positing a new authorial voice through the meticulous analysis of such metaphors whose undeniable suggestiveness governed the discussion of imitation in classical times (Petrarch 1997a, 1.8.44 / 1975b, 1.8.46). In this regard, alongside the image of the path through which the dominant self proclaims its triumph in the *Oration* over prior tradition, the two principal metaphors running throughout Petrarch's Latin letters on imitation are the metaphor of the bees, as we shall soon see, and that of filial resemblance which, interestingly enough, turns out to be remarkably similar to Wittgenstein's notion of family resemblance (see, for example, Wittgenstein 2001, 27–8). These three metaphors are primarily images of motion, generation, productivity, and time, which is to say, they are all images of projection and desire. Within this deep, vast network of imagery, along with the concern for metamorphosis, is another underlying thematic interest, that of concealment, which is essentially a question not *only* of stylistic technique but rather one of *both* stylistic technique and substance. This is true because style is the substance of a great deal of Petrarch's poetry. It is through style that the old is transformed into the new—and here the pun on style, *stilus*, or pen, is central; it is also through style that the truth of both the world and poetic tradition infused with that world is most forcefully expressed.

To take up once again the image of the path first, we should turn to a letter addressed to Cicero, *Familiares* 24.4. Whereas Cicero is acknowledged as Petrarch's master in the less arduous ways of prose, the supreme guide in the more tortuous and restricted paths of poetry is Virgil: "Accessit et alter poetice vie dux; ita enim necessitas poscebat, ut esset et quem solutis et quem frenatis gressibus preeuntem sequeremur" (Petrarch 1997b, 24.4.228) (In the realm of poetry we followed another master since necessarily we had to follow one supreme guide in the unencumbered ways of prose and another in the more restricted paths of poetry) (Petrarch 1985, 24.4.319).

This notion of following a guide in the sense of imitation along a path—a path which for Petrarch will establish a new tradition in which he supersedes the guide and becomes the leader himself for all who follow him—is a recurring notion which he picks up from Seneca. In Epistle LXXXIV, "On Gathering Ideas," Seneca writes:

> Confragosa in fastigium dignitatis via est; at si conscendere hunc verticem libet, cui se fortuna summisit, omnia quidem sub te, quae pro excelsissimis habentur, aspicies, sed tamen venies ad summa per planum.
>
> (It is a rough road that leads to the heights of greatness; but if you desire to scale this peak, which lies far above the range of Fortune, you will indeed look down from above upon all that men regard as most lofty, but none the less you can proceed to the top over level ground.) (Seneca 1991, 284)

Taking his cue from Seneca, Petrarch goes on to explain this game of oneupmanship in the establishment of a new tradition in terms of poetic creation which begins in competition and ends in something new and triumphant—a competition which delights not in sameness but in imitation, not in blindness, ineptitude, or servile resemblance but in the superiority of the imitator's genius, not in following slavishly a guide but in parting ways with such a guide if necessary in order to venture into the inaccessible and the unknown.

Petrarch, the solitary hero in search of unexplored paths, enacts a radically new sense of the omnipresent past that he inherits through his self-reflexive literary intelligence which makes him keenly aware of the temporal distance separating his culture from that of his forebears. It is because of this heightened awareness toward the past that a new sensibility finds prototypical expression in Petrarch, without which the poet would have remained a prisoner of his precursors. In a passage infused with a notable moral quality, Petrarch writes:

> Sum quem priorum semitam, sed non semper aliena vestigia sequi iuvet; sum qui aliorum scriptis non furtim sed precario uti velim in tempore, sed dum liceat, meis malim. (Petrarch 1997b, 22.2.108)

> (I am one who intends to follow our forebears' path but not always others' tracks; I am one who wishes upon occasion to make use of others' writings, not secretly but with their leave, and whenever possible I prefer my own.) (Petrarch 1985, 22.2.214)

Only by embarking on a new path, even though following a guide to a certain extent, can the poet transform the old into the new, thereby providing the basis for the metamorphosis of prior tradition through his leadership, as the new guide supplants the old, and is spurred on by a type of ambition that equals and even surpasses that of Ulysses when he ventures beyond the pillars of Hercules.

> usque ad hoc tempus vita pene omnis in peregrinatione transacta est. Ulixeos errores erroribus meis confer: profecto, si nominis et rerum claritas una foret, nec diutius erravit ille nec latius. (Petrarch 1997a, 1.1.7)

> (I have spent all my life, to this moment, in almost constant travel. Compare my wanderings with those of Ulysses: if the reputation of our achievements were the same, he indeed traveled neither more nor farther than I.) (Petrarch 1975b, 1.1.7–8)

The analogy which Petrarch draws between his own peregrinations and those of the ambiguous and enigmatic figure of Ulysses is key to our understanding of his self-referential comments on style. In his insightful analysis on what motivates Petrarch to cast himself as Ulysses, Giuseppe Mazzotta concentrates on both the "stubbornly enigmatic, elusive character" of this "multifarious, polytropic hero" whose restlessness refuses "to be fixed in time or space," and also on his ability to fully exploit "the simulations and dissimulations" of style which must be guarded jealously and made known only to himself (Mazzotta 2009, 315–16). Mazzotta writes:

> As Dante's representation in *Inferno* 26 shows, Ulysses speaks covertly, forever hidden in the tongues of fire, and yet his language attains sublime heights of rhetoric; he is the bearer of a secret knowledge (the secret of self-knowledge) but remains unknown to others, and, in the Homeric version, he keeps his identity concealed even from his wife Penelope. (315)

The notion of concealment and secrecy lies at the very heart of the second of our three sets of images in terms of imitation, that of the bees, which, like that of the path, comes to Petrarch via Virgil and Seneca.[4] In a letter to Tommaso da Messina on inventiveness and talent, Petrarch comments on Seneca's formulation as regards bees and originality: "Cuius summa est: apes in inventionibus imitandas, que flores, non quales acceperint, referunt, sed ceras ac mella mirifica quadam permixtione conficiunt" (Petrarch 1997a, 1.8.39) (His loftiest advice about invention is to imitate the bees which through an astonishing process produce wax and honey from the flowers they leave behind) (Petrarch 1975b, 1.8.41).

This example of the bees is a central point in Petrarch's conceptualization of the way poetry should work, as new poetry takes the best from the old and creates something different and entirely new, something lovely and, as we have seen, something *better* than what the tradition has had before. Rather than simply reproducing what others have left behind them, poetic production involves recreation and new creation at one and the same time. It is precisely the notion of being better that makes the notion of imitation one of transformation and rebeginning in true Renaissance fashion, while providing the conceptualization for metamorphosis not just of certain poems or of certain elements of the poetic tradition but of the entire tradition in Petrarch's name, to be followed by those who come after him. The rebirth and creation of a new poetic sensibility thus takes on the form of a genuine and enlightened triumph over prior tradition which is ultimately metamorphosed into the Petrarchan tradition through style. Such a process of assimilation of one's sources requires an ability to select, to

---

[4] "nos quoque has apes debemus imitari et quaecumque ex diversa lectione congessimus, separare, melius enim distincta servantur, deinde adhibita ingenii nostri cura et facultate in unum saporem varia illa libamenta confundere, ut etiam si apparuerit, unde sumptum sit, aliud tamen esse quam unde sumptum est, appareat." ("We also, I say, ought to copy these bees, and sift whatever we have gathered from a varied course of reading, for such things are better preserved if they are kept separate; then, by applying the supervising care with which our nature has endowed us,—in other words, our natural gifts,—we should so blend those several flavours into one delicious compound that, even though it betrays its origin, yet it nevertheless is clearly a different thing from whence it came") (Seneca [1991, Epistle LXXXIV, 278–9]).

conceal ("absconde")[5] and to inscribe within one's memory the exempla that have been read and meditated upon, as the following passage demonstrates:

> Hec visa sunt de apium imitatione que dicerem, quarum exemplo, ex cuntis que occurrent, electiora in alveario cordis *absconde* eaque summa diligentia parce tenaciterque conserva, nequid excidat, si fieri potest. Neve diutius apud te qualia decerpseris maneant, cave: nulla quidem esset apibus gloria, nisi in aliud et in *melius* inventa converterent. Tibi quoque, siqua legendi meditandique studio reppereris, in favum stilo redigenda suadeo. (Petrarch 1997a, 1.8.44, emphasis mine)
>
> (From their example, select and *conceal* the better ones in the beehive of your heart and hold on to them with the greatest diligence and preserve them steadfastly, lest anything should possibly perish. And be careful not to let any of those things that you have plucked remain with you too long, for the bees would enjoy no glory if they did not transform those things they found into something else which was *better*. You also, if you find anything of value in your desire for reading and meditating, I urge you to convert into honey combs through your own style.) (Petrarch 1975b, 1.8.46, emphasis mine)

The crucial set of imagery as regards the third of our primary images—that of filial resemblance—comes once again from Seneca.[6] In a subtle interplay between the presence of the model and its absence, the elusive resemblances with the predecessor invite recognition of the embedded echoes of an ancient author

---

[5]The word "absconde" in Petrarch echoes Seneca's "abscondat" and his notion that our mind "should hide away all the materials by which it has been aided, and bring to light only what it has made of them" ("omnia, quibus est adiutus, abscondat, ipsum tantum ostendat, quod effecit") (Seneca 1991, Epistle LXXXIV, 280–1). (See Kahn [1985, 154–66] on the complexities underlying Petrarch's use of the word "absconde" and on the interplay between concealment and revelation in the *Secretum*.)

[6]"similem esse te volo quomodo filium, non quomodo imaginem; imago res mortua est" ("I would have you resemble him as a child resembles his father, and not as a picture resembles its original; for a picture is a lifeless thing") (Seneca [1991, Epistle LXXXIV, 280–1]).

and, at the same time, conceal such resonances as the poet strives to establish his own distinctive voice through a metamorphic process of recreation and new creation of its sources. The proper distance between model and copy is thereby established, a distance which then gives rise to originality and, more importantly, to superiority over what already exists in the literary tradition. Petrarch's eloquence in treating the image of filial resemblance is persuasive and intensely moving and deserves to be quoted at some length:

> Curandum imitatori ut quod scribit simile non idem sit, eamque similitudinem talem esse oportere, non qualis est imaginis ad eum cuius imago est, que quo similior eo maior laus artificis, sed qualis filii ad patrem. In quibus cum magna sepe diversitas sit membrorum, *umbra quedam* et quem pictores nostri aerem vocant, qui in vultu inque oculis maxime cernitur, similitudinem illam facit, que statim viso filio, patris in memoriam nos reducat, cum tamen si res ad mensuram redeat, omnia sint diversa; sed est ibi nescio quid occultum quod hanc habeat vim. Sic et nobis providendum ut cum simile aliquid sit, multa sint dissimilia, et id ipsum simile lateat ne deprehendi possit nisi *tacita mentis indagine*, ut intelligi simile queat potiusquam dici. (Petrarch 1997b, 23.19.206, emphasis mine)

> (An imitator must take care to write something similar yet not identical to the original, and that similarity must not be like the image to its original in painting where the greater the similarity the greater the praise for the artist, but rather like that of a son to his father. While often very different in their individual features, they have a *certain something* our painters call an "air," especially noticeable about the face and eyes, that produces a resemblance; seeing the son's face, we are reminded of the father's, although if it came to measurement, the features would all be different, but there is something subtle that creates this effect. We must thus see to it that if there is something similar, there is also a great deal that is dissimilar, and that the similar be elusive and unable to be extricated except in *silent meditation*, for the resemblance is to be felt rather than expressed.) (Petrarch 1985, 23.19.301–2, emphasis mine; see Greene [1982, 94–6] to whom I am indebted for his inspiring analysis of this passage and for the resemblances with Seneca which he "subreads" in Petrarch's text)

As this extraordinary passage demonstrates, Petrarch's manipulation of his sources is that of a theorist who is obsessively aware of the fact that style's power of suggestion "turns on compelling images rather than definite concepts," to draw on Pierre Macherey's characterization of style, and that "there is a specifically poetic—rather than logical—rigour which unites form and content," one which derives its "truth" and "coherence" from the complex system of relations between the various components (or images) making up a literary work (Macheray 2006, 64–5). Approached without the knowledge of these components which Petrarch assumes his readers to possess, any literary work will fail to yield up its secrets and will lose immeasurably in richness and resonance; and to neglect these resonances or "umbra quedam" in reading Petrarch's work is not to hear the poetic dialogue between the poet and his predecessors and the underlying interplay between sameness and differentiation (Velli 1995, 34). The "geography of solitude" mapped out by Petrarch in which poetic imitation can take place is thus, as Armando Maggi (2009) writes, characterized by "dialogical solitude," or a "non-alone solitude" ("solitudinem non solam") (180) which involves a "dialogical companionship" (191) with the voices of the past. The identification of the plethora of influences to which a writer is subject has to be done, however, with increasing introspection and self-awareness, in a motion that is highly reminiscent of that of the bees which slowly, laboriously, and in silent meditation gather nectar from which the honey of style is then produced.

The sort of elusive resemblance resulting from this practice of concealment and differentiation as regards repetition and representation is precisely the kind of resemblance to the general tradition that Petrarch wants to create within his poetry. The intent is to continue the tradition but at the same time to change it noticeably with Petrarch now at its head. It is important that this process of generation from old to new, from father to son, has to do not only with what is evident but also with what is concealed: otherwise, the difference between the example and the model would not be interesting. The skill of poetic imitation itself, if it is any good, is always hidden and never speaks its own name—it is either unspoken or spoken quietly, as if under one's breath.

The antiplatonic thrust of such a phenomenon of concealment and difference as regards repetition and representation is so forceful that it deserves to be studied more closely via a comparison of

Petrarch's notion of *imitatio* with that of Plato in *The Republic* (1989). When Plato argues that "if the poet never concealed himself, his whole poetry and narrative would be free of imitation," what he is advocating is pure narrative without the concealment of the presence of its narrating agent or, "pure narrative without imitation" (1989, 30–1). Plato goes on to say that since the imitator is concerned not with the imitation of the essence of reality as it is but with the appearance as it appears,[7] "the art of imitation is far removed from the real, and, it seems, achieves all its results because it grasps only a small part of each object, and an image at that" (1989, 39). What Petrarch aspires to achieve in his imitation of prior works is thus what Plato objects to in all imitative forms, particularly those forms in which concealment plays such a crucial role. In fact, to use Plato's own terminology, what Petrarch strives to "grasp" is precisely "only a small part of each object" or, to draw on Petrarch's own words, that elusive "umbra quedam," but he then proceeds to transform what has been grasped into something new through his own distinctive style. In other words, Plato values exclusively the original and views negatively its declining representations, while Petrarch valorizes the *temporal* progression of any notion of *imitatio* and positively considers each step of the subsequent representation of a model, which, in turn, can be displaced by the imitation itself.[8] For Plato, the imitator lags behind in the normal quest for truth, thereby leading his followers astray instead of educating or informing them. As the power of poetic representation originates in the efficacy of the creation of images, and as those images become more and more convincing, or beguiling, aesthetic appearance takes on a life of its own; but the more this very appearance approaches the simulacrum, or the seemingly perfect re-presentation, the more it diverges from the truth. Instead, for Petrarch, the further removed the imitator's reproduction is from the original, the more successful is the poet's attempt to create his own truth, which, in Petrarch's case, is the truth of the world.

---

[7]For Plato, the artist imitates appearance and is cut off from reality, and consequently, from the truth: "the maker of the image, the imitator, on our view, knows nothing of the reality, but only the appearance" (1989, 42).

[8]For an earlier treatment of the analogy between Plato and Petrarch, see Gloria Lauri-Lucente (2009, 187).

The truth of the world takes us back to the central notion of style. In Petrarch, style is not simply a question of elegance or rhetorical embellishment but rather the attempt to capture in writing the perfection of expression and thus to approach the truth. To put it differently, the transformation of the old into the new takes place not through the individual Petrarch but rather through the individual's style. It is style that provides the format in which the transformation or the metamorphosis of the old form into new form, and thus of old meaning into new meaning, is accomplished. This is why style becomes the subject and not just the medium of Petrarch's verse, as I have suggested in the introductory paragraph of the essay.

The notion of style and linguistic refinement is one that has bedeviled numerous critics, notable among whom in the present context are Thomas Greene, Marco Santagata, and Giuseppe Mazzotta, in that they all discuss this issue at some length with regard not only to the *Canzoniere* but also to the *Familiares* (see Greene [1982]; Mazzotta [1993]; Santagata [1993]). Greene describes Petrarch's style as "a moral style—a texture of feeling, thought, rhetoric, and tone defining itself allusively against a ground of literary tradition" (1982, 96). Santagata extends the questions of morality as well as of literary tradition in terms of their relations to style by turning them into a properly literary/philological question. Commenting on the first book of the *Familiares*, Santagata sees in style the poetics of the fragmentation of the self, or "i frammenti dell'anima," and argues that "the 'rime sparse' are stylistically 'varied,' like the Latin epistles: because varied and unstable is the psychological condition of their author" ("Le 'rime sparse' sono stilisticamente 'varie,' come lo sono le epistole latine: perchè varia, instabile è la condizione psicologica del loro autore") (Santagata [1993, 108, my translation]). Like Santagata, Mazzotta also believes that both Petrarch's reference in the first sonnet of the *Canzoniere* to the collection's "vario stile," as well as his allusion in the opening letter of the *Familiares* to the multiple stylistic registers of the epistolary corpus, express the fragmented style of a fragmented self. However, the important point for Mazzotta is that for Petrarch, "questions of style and composition—paramount to the writer's craft—are crucial to the present understanding of the self, and they embody . . . an ethics of writing" (Mazzotta 1993, 91–2). In other words, style has to do with a "sense of technical and aesthetic rigor" which "reveals the extent to which, for Petrarch, the proper care for language, like the proper care of the mind and the body, can never be neglected" (93). What can be evinced from Mazzotta's analysis is that the sense of style in Petrarch is not just an ethical, moral, or formal question but rather all of these: the style of the tradition, the style of life, the ethical and moral implications of those styles and, most importantly, the style of writing, and especially, the style of writing in the lyric tradition. These elements of style, as it were, create the tradition—the Petrarchan tradition.

To fully appreciate what is at stake in Petrarch's reference to his multiple stylistic registers, we should again look more closely at the opening book of the *Familiares* and the poet's own comments on style, since they are particularly germane to our understanding of Petrarch's notions of tradition, imitation, rivalry, and poetic glory which ultimately all conjoin: "Rursus nec huius stilum aut illius, sed unum nostrum conflatum ex pluribus habeamus" (Petrarch 1997a, 1.8.40) ("Let us write neither in the style of one or another writer but in the style uniquely ours altogether gathered from a variety of sources") (Petrarch 1975b, 1.8.42). This notion obviously has to do with the image of the bees, but it is even more crucial in terms of the bees gathering and producing honey in that the style of the individual guarantees the truth in the form of the metamorphosis of prior tradition into contemporary and future poetic effect. In the same letter, Petrarch goes on to suggest that the bees, however good they are, are not quite as good as their competitors, the silkworms:

> felicius quidem, non apium more passim sparsa colligere, sed quorundam haud multo maiorum vermium exemplo, quorum ex visceribus sericum prodit, ex se ipso sapere potius et loqui, dummodo et sensus gravis ac verus et sermo esset ornatus. Verum, quia hoc aut nulli prorsus aut paucissimis datum est, feramus equanimiter ingenii nostri sortem, nec altioribus invidentes, nec despicientes qui infra nos sunt, nec paribus importuni. (Petrarch 1997a, 1.8.40)
>
> (That writer is happier who does not, like the bees, collect a number of scattered things, but instead, after the example of certain not much larger worms from whose bodies silk is produced, prefers

> to produce his own thoughts and speech—provided that the sense is serious and true and that his style is ornate. But in truth, this talent is given to none or to very few, so that we should patiently bear the lot of our personal talents, and not envy those above us, disdain those below us, or annoy our equals.) (Petrarch 1975b, 1.8.42)

Any affinities with Derrida's description of the silkworm—one of the "Derridanimals of deconstruction"—written more than six centuries later must turn on the motifs of patience and on the return upon oneself, for the contexts are otherwise significantly different (and Derrida does not cite Petrarch) (see Badmington 2007). Indeed, the culture of writing demands the same type of patience that is involved in the culture of the silkworm—laborious, metamorphic, and ultimately revelatory in nature (Derrida 2002). Like the progress of silkworms, whose indefatigable patience turns mulberry into silk in a marvelous process that can barely be discerned, but that can be likened to an "odyssey" culminating in "absolute knowledge," the process of writing makes its way to a specific destination as it slowly and meticulously endows raw material with form (Derrida 2002, 354). For substance must be linked to appropriate form in order to create poetry through style that is, in fact, totally efficacious both in terms of the mind and—here it is crucial for the later Renaissance—in terms of the emotional workings of the heart. Again, though this style may be derived from a variety of sources, and may seem at first to be merely a sign of elegance, it turns out to be a sign of substance as well. As Petrarch writes, "Sed illud affirmo: elegantioris esse solertie, ut, apium imitatores, nostris verbis quamvis aliorum hominum sententias proferamus" (Petrarch 1997a, 1.8.40) ("This much however I affirm, that it is a sign of greater elegance and skill for us, in imitation of the bees, to produce in our own words thoughts borrowed from others") (Petrarch 1975b, 1.8.41–2). It is this question of style in terms of gathering and reproduction that links imitation, meaning, and elegance of the old tradition with the new. Transforming the old tradition into the new is what Petrarch is all about as he writes the *Canzoniere*—renewing poetry within the tradition and creating something that will make its own way into the future under his banner, with all future poets to follow.

While this may seem at first a question of leader and followers, Petrarch frames it somewhat differently by claiming that this is not a question of leadership but rather one of "emulatio" between strong equals. In a letter to Quintilian, Petrarch discusses the envy or "livor" which caused great discord between Quintilian and Seneca:

> Fuit autem tibi *emulatio* non levis magni cuiusdam viri alterius, Anneum Senecam dico; quos etas, quos professio, quos natio iunxerat, seiunxit parium pestis, *livor*; qua in re nescio an tu modestior videare: siquidem nec tu illum pleno ore laudare potes, et ille de te contemptissime loquitur. (Petrarch 1997b, 24.7.242, emphasis mine)
>
> (There was, however, a considerable *rivalry* between you and another great man, Anneus Seneca. Your age, profession, and birthplace joined the two of you but *envy*, that plague among equals, separated you. I know not whether in this matter you might appear the more moderate inasmuch as, while you refrain from praising him fully, he speaks of you with great contempt.) (Petrarch 1975b, 24.7.330, emphasis mine)

The point here is that competition between strong equals is what gives rise to poetic production or, again, the talent of metamorphosing through style is given, as we have seen, "to none or to very few." It is clear in Petrarch that the few or none consist solely of Petrarch the author. His style, his ability to marshal his themes and, in fact, his entire *Canzoniere* make him not the few or none but the one who will lead the tradition.

Style for Petrarch is thus the expressive point at which appropriateness and superiority come together—appropriate for correctness and superiority in terms of competition. Moreover, style is not a means to an end but an end in and of itself because the perfect style will embody the perfect truth. Interestingly enough, that perfect truth involves, as we have seen, not only memory and expression but forgetfulness as well as "willful misreading" (Kahn 1985, 156). As Petrarch says:

> In his quidem discernendis non parvus michi labor oritur; nostrum enim testor Apollinem, unicum etherei Iovis natum, et verum sapientie Deum, Cristum, me nec ullius prede avidum et ut patrimonii sic ingenii alieni spoliis abstinere. Siquid aliter

> inventum erit ac dico, vel in his quos non legi, similitudo facit ingeniorum, de quo epystola ad te superiore disserui, vel in aliis error aut oblivio, de quo nunc agitur. . . . Alioquin multo malim meus michi stilus sit, incultus licet atque horridus, sed in morem toge habilis, ad mensuram ingenii mei factus. (Petrarch 1997b, 22.2.106)
>
> (I have really spent a great deal of time trying to identify my sources; I call to witness our Apollo, the only son of the heavenly Jove and true God of wisdom, Christ, that I have not been eager to plunder, that I have refrained from intellectual as well as from material thefts. If anything contrary to this is found in my works, it results from an intellectual kinship in the case of authors whom I have not read (as I wrote to you in my previous letter) or, in the case of others, from the type of error or forgetfulness that we are now discussing. . . . Otherwise, I much prefer that my style be my own, uncultivated and rude, but made to fit, as a garment, to the measure of my mind.) (Petrarch 1985, 22.2.213)

Again, the lesson here is that one has to develop one's own style. Concealment and forgetfulness come together in the form of expression as "stilus" or writing, after a process of silent meditation through which the poet reproduces in expression the truth of the world, a truth that is no longer a stable, definite truth of medieval allegory but is instead the contingent worldly truth of the world of everyday man as reproduced in poetry through a style that is right because it is effective. This is Petrarch's new tradition that puts poetry into the world and will govern the way that the world is viewed by all of those who read him. Style is the key to this reading and this perception of the world, and it is through Petrarch as the master of style that the substance of his verse will enter his readers. In meditating on how posterity will follow his footsteps, Petrarch, in a journey that takes on the cast of a secularized version of the Dantesque "trasumanar," will transcend through style all the confines previously established by his forebears and carve out a space reserved for no other human except for his own self.

References

Badmington, Neil, ed. 2007. *Derridanimals*, special issue of *Oxford Literary Review* 29(1–2).

Derrida, Jacques. 2002. "A Silkworm of One's Own (Points of View Stitched on the Other Veil)." Translated by Geoffrey Bennington. In *Acts of Religion*, edited by Gil Adinjar, 311–55. New York: Routledge.

Greene, Thomas. 1982. *The Light in Troy: Imitation and Discovery in Renaissance Poetry*. New Haven: Yale University Press.

Jameson, Fredric. 1974. *Marxism and Form: Twentieth-Century Dialectical Theories of Literature*. Princeton, NJ: Princeton University Press.

Kahn, Victoria. 1985. "The Figure of the Reader in Petrarch's *Secretum*." *PMLA* 100(2): 154–66.

Lauri-Lucente, Gloria. 2009. "T.S. Eliot and Eugenio Montale: 'Similar Flowers on Distant Branches?'" *Journal of Anglo-Italian Studies* 10: 173–87.

Macherey, Pierre. 2006. *A Theory of Literary Production*. London: Routledge.

Maggi, Armando. 2009. "'You Will Be My Solitude': Solitude as Prophecy (De vita solitaria)." In *Petrarch: A Critical Guide to the Complete Works*, edited by Victoria Kirkham and Armando Maggi, 179–95. Chicago: University of Chicago Press.

Mazzotta, Giuseppe. 1993. *The Worlds of Petrarch*. Durham: Duke University Press.

—. 2009. "Petrarch's Epistolary Epic: Letters on Familiar Matters (*Rerum familiarum libri*)." In *Petrarch: A Critical Guide to the Complete Works*, edited by Victoria Kirkham and Armando Maggi, 309–19. Chicago: University of Chicago Press.

Petrarch. 1955. *Collatio laureationis*. In *Studies in the Life and Works of Petrarch*, translated by Ernest Hatch Wilkins. 300–13. Cambridge, MA: Mediaeval Academy of America.

—. 1975a. *Collatio laureationis*. In *Opere latine di Francesco Petrarca*, vol. 2. Edited by Antonietta Bufano. 1255–83. Torino: U.T.E.T.

—. 1975b. *Letters on Familiar Matters*. Translated by Aldo S. Bernardo. Vol. 1. Books 1–8. Baltimore: Johns Hopkins University Press.

—. 1985. *Letters on Familiar Matters*. Translated by Aldo S. Bernardo. Vol. 3. Books 17–24. Albany, NY: State University of New York Press.

—. 1997a. *Le familiari*. Edited by Vittorio Rossi. Vol. 1. Libri 1–4 . Firenze: Le Lettere.

—. 1997b. *Le familiari*. Edited by Vittorio Rossi and Umberto Bosco. Vol. 4. Libri 20–4 . Firenze: Le Lettere.

Pigman III, George W. 1980. "Versions of Imitation in the Renaissance." *Renaissance Quarterly* 33: 1–32.
Plato. 1989. *Classical Literary Criticism.* Edited by Donald Andrew Russell and Michael Winterbottom. Oxford: Oxford University Press.
Santagata, Marco. 1993. *I frammenti dell'anima: Storia e racconto nel Canzoniere di Petrarca.* Bologna: Il Mulino.
Seneca. 1991. *Epistles: 66–92.* Translated by Richard M. Gummere. Loeb Classical Library 76. Cambridge, MA: Harvard University Press.
Velli, Giuseppe. 1995. *Petrarca e Boccaccio: Tradizione, memoria, scrittura.* Padova: Editrice Antenore.
Wittgenstein, Ludwig. 2001. *Philosophical Investigations I.* Translated by G. E. M. Anscombe. Cambridge, MA: Blackwell Publishers.

3

Style, rhetoric, and identity in Shakespearean soliloquy

Stuart Sillars

Any attempt to address the issue of style in Shakespeare's plays is essentially bound up with the concept of character, the idea of separate voices interacting, that has become the fundamental approach to the larger dramatic structure, whether performed or read. For too long, the idea of the psychologically valid, consistent, and continuously active individual figure within the plays has exercised a distortive force on the dramatic entity, imposing a whole series of reductive interpretations on the plays when read and in performance. But one can see why: the theatrical text depends on the interaction of a number of separate voices, and within this process the construction of some kind of identity must be somehow important, whether it be in the idea of the construction of the early modern individual, the agency of the subject, or the dialogic imagination. In trying to realize some kind of balance between the plays as aesthetic construct and the plays as a focus for human, if not necessarily humanist, empathy, I want to argue that the concept of style, as conceived ideologically and theoretically within Shakespeare's own period, is fundamental. And I will also suggest that this concept is surprisingly close to much more recent ideas of individual subjectivity as both involving the intersection of a range of performative discourses and as something constant only in its repeated reformulation through a series of acts of language. To put it another way: "In the post-structuralist analysis, subjectivity is not a single, unified presence but the point of intersection of a range of discourses, produced and re-produced as the subject occupies a series of places in the signifying system, takes on the multiplicity of meanings language offers" (Belsey 1985, 188). In quoting this passage I draw together the chronological extremes, the early modern and the postmodern, with which this essay engages. At the same time, its presence acknowledges one of the starting points of my discussion. To it should be added the work of Alan Sinfield, Judith Butler, and that of a number of earlier writers—earlier by decades and centuries—in my endeavor to peel away some of the layers in the palimpsest of character criticism and so reveal an alternative actuality of the dramatic text. Bringing together these two temporally remote eras is a risky business, and always involves cross-inflections of the one with the other. But the exchange will I hope go some way toward suggesting that the idea of a stable and continuous personhood, in actuality as well as in the dramatic text, was as little evident in the sixteenth century and before as it is today, and that the concept of style, especially as revealed in the soliloquy, is fundamental to this assertion.

Despite the fact that the soliloquy has repeatedly been untimely ripped from its larger textual corpus by anthologists, critics, and performers, it is not, of course, an isolated textual element. And here a larger, equally troublesome, relationship emerges, that between the style of the textual passage defined by a speech-prefix, and that of the individual author-function generating the whole of which it is part. In attempting appropriately to reinstate the soliloquy, we are forced to confront again a familiar question: who is speaking? In addressing this issue I shall be arguing that the soliloquy is always a dialogue, in which its speaker engages not with the other roles of the text but with a series of theoretical, ideological, aesthetic, and educative conventions, a series of voices present to the contemporary auditor or the reader—contemporary, that is, to the time of the plays' composition. And moving back still further from the moment of the soliloquy, I shall address the question of change or growth within these styles over the span of the whole canon, an area that has aroused no little interest of late, demonstrated most rigorously in the work of Russ McDonald (2006) and Gordon McMullan (2007).The progression, I will argue, has much to offer in suggesting a way through the intellectual maze presented by the relations between style, text, and state of the subject. As the canon of the plays develops, this dialogue is one in which these other voices are progressively contested and the idea of subjectivity advanced with greater complexity. The result is the paradox that psychological penetration becomes greater at the same time as the artifice of literary and theatric construction becomes more evident. Or, to put it in the words of a much earlier voice, as rich in ambivalence then as today, what is achieved is "an artificiall construction of the mynd." The voice is that of Thomas Wilson, in *The Arte of Rhetorique*, first published in 1553 (1553, fol. 1r).

The word "style" itself appears 14 times in the plays of Shakespeare. In *Love's Labour's*, Berowne introduces his reading of a letter by Don Armado by saying "Well, sir, be it as the style shall give us cause to climb in the merriness" (1.1.200).[1] And so it proves: the letter is full of exaggerations, embellishments, and strained parallels that in themselves cause great and satirical mirth. Later in the same play, Boyet comments on a second letter of Armado's, "I am much deceived, but I remember the style" (4.1.96). The two uses occur in a play which makes—well, makes play—with the idea of the suitability of language to a range of communicative and rhetorical purposes, not only in the written words of Armado but in his speech and, at a different level and in another kind of misapplication, in the language of Holofernes. In *All's Well That Ends Well*, Lafew makes a similar fine distinction between ranks and languages when he asks "what is count's man. Count's master is of another style" (2.3.195). But such applications are not the sole preserve of the comedies. In *2 Henry VI*, Gloucester attacks "the poor King Reignier, whose large style / Agrees not with the leanness of his purse" (1.1.101–2). Perhaps the most directly satiric use of the word comes in *I Henry VI*, when La Pucelle makes sport with a long list cataloging prisoners according to their rank and once again rejects its inappropriate wording:

> Here's a silly-stately style indeed!
> The Turk, that two and fifty kingdoms hath,
> Writes not so tedious a style as this. (4.7.72–4)

---

[1]All quotations from Shakespeare's works have been taken from Shakespeare 1997.

These usages, and the others for which they stand representative, share some essential features. All are concerned not with style as an entity in itself, but with its appropriateness to situation or rank. Often, this relates to a manner of language affected in writing, not speech, that is read aloud before or after the satirical attack. The link between style and rank is present in other, slightly different comments, most directly the withering question addressed to Suffolk in *2 Henry VI*: "Am I a queen in title and in style, / And must be made a subject to a duke?" (1.3.48–9). Here, "style" refers to a manner of behavior fitting to a person of a specific rank, a concept that underlay many aspects of Tudor social structure and is constantly explored and exploded within the plays.

Lest this be thought a simple assertion of a return to order beloved of critics in the anxious wake of Tillyard, there is a larger thrust: it is that not only the individual assuming this style, but style itself and what it stands for, that are being satirized (Tillyard 1943). In *Much Ado*, Benedick replies to Margaret's demand "write me a sonnet in praise / Of my beauty" (5.2.5) by saying he will do it "In so high a style, Margaret, that no man living shall come over it" (5.2.6–7). The riposte contains an elaborate compliment, but it also comically undermines the hyperbole of lovers' language—the very language demonstrated, and exposed to similar ridicule, by Armado in *Love's Labour's*.

In all these examples, the writing discussed is an attempt to assert the writer's identity, and in the exchanges such identity is rejected as invalid. It is a debate in which the failure of language lies at the root—and the word *lies* here nicely suggests the slipperiness of the attempted act of identity construction through words. But it is not only the identity of the other that is being destabilized. Since the speakers are themselves assuming another identity, that of the role they, as actors, are presenting, the whole notion of personhood in theater is undermined, and we are placed in a position analogous to the present-day reader witnessing a debate about the multiple deferral and constant inconstancy of the subject when asserted through language. In this instance, the "compelling illusion" of stable identity, and its production through a series of linguistic moments that, in the argument of Judith Butler (1990, 271), become speech acts, can be seen to move across boundaries of gender and be applicable, albeit in a variety of ways, to any acts of identity constitution through language. I use the word *role* here quite deliberately, to avoid the more prevalent *character*, and also to emphasize the importance of the origins of the word in the roll of paper on which the part was written. In all these situations, the words satirized come from a written object: but so, at an earlier level, do the words in which they make their attacks, so the double artifice, and double insecurity, of style in role/roll is a constant presence. All of this suggests that the very notion of style is a way in which the duality—at the very least the duality—of the performative text is signaled to the auditor, an auditor who in Shakespeare's theater would have been fully aware of the complexities of linguistic utterance and the importance of "plainnesse," a quality repeatedly stressed by Thomas Wilson, Thomas Eliot, Roger Ascham, and the other arbiters of rhetoric and form.[2]

There is another use of the word in one of the plays that takes the significances further. It occurs in Amiens's response to Duke Senior in *As You Like It*. The Duke has just delivered his "Sweet are the uses of adversity" speech (2.1.12–17), which culminates in his assertion that in their retreat the courtiers will find "Sermons in stones, and good in everything." Amiens replies:

> Happy is your Grace
> That can translate the stubbornness of fortune
> Into so quiet and so sweet a style. (2.1.18–20)

Which is just what it isn't, of course. The Duke's speech begins with what sounds remarkably like one of the sentences given to students of rhetoric as the starting point of a writing exercise—"Sweet are the uses of adversity." As it nears its ending, it includes a metaphor that is similarly derivative: adversity, "like the toad, ugly and venomous, / Wears yet a precious jewel in his head" (2.1.13–14). As editors of the play have long told us (see, for example, Latham 1975, 30), the toad is described in like terms by Lyly in *Euphues*, and draws on a line in Pliny's *Historia Naturalis*, an expression of exactly the kind students were taught to memorize and imitate. It then moves to assert that the courtiers will find "sermons in stones," and, as its climactic point "good in everything," the metaphoric level moving from a familiar parallel toward a weaker,

---

[2]For example, Wilson (1553, 164–5) has a section titled "Plainessse, what is it."

if more individual one, to the final absence of metaphoric invention. The speech is almost a pre-echo of the confused utterance of Starveling who, as moonshine, finds his efforts to explain his props repeatedly interrupted by the stage audience, and can only conclude in exasperation:

> All that I have to say is to tell you that the lanthorn is the moon, I the man i'th'moon, this thorn bush my thorn bush, and this dog my dog. (5.1.257–9)

It seems, then, that the Duke's speech is a failed attempt at a rhetorical exercise. It can hardly be seen as demonstrating a style "so quiet and so sweet;" this, and the fact that Amiens's response blatantly ignores the concept it struggles to convey, and is itself couched in a level of obsequiousness expected in the very court whose values the Duke claims to have rejected, undermines both of the speeches and reveals "style" once more as a sign of affectation and indecorum. And all of this, of course, takes place within a fable itself enacting another fable, the pastoral, a literary genre always already a parody: the listener is consequently invited to engage with the speeches, and their styles, on multiple yet intertwining ironic and referential levels.

The Duke's speech and Amiens's response bring together elements common to all the appearances of the word "style" in the plays and point toward the larger significances they contain about style the concept. All function by bringing together questions about the use of language, the rank of the speaker, and the situation of utterance. A further issue is shown most directly in the *As You Like It* passage: the whole series of textual intersections, with writings classical and recent, theoretical and theatric, in poetry and prose, in which such passages participate. That the educated members of the audience would recognize many of the allusions, and the rhetorical exercises in which they are placed, enriches their comic effects and emphasizes again the circumstance that the speakers are themselves engaged in a rhetorical, as well as theatric, performance.

From these forces, and their multiply destabilizing effect on the concept of style, I would like to move to another dimension that in a sense underlies them all, but is more directly associated with the soliloquy, its relation to the complete play and the idea of Shakespeare's progression of style. This is the rhetorical figure known as ethopoeia. This figure, and the practice of its composition, entered the grammar school curriculum through a number of texts by classical writers. One was the *Institutio Oratoria* of Quintilian; another, more widespread, was the Greek *Progymnasmata* of Aphthonius, often in a version translated into Latin in the early sixteenth century by Agricola. Discussing a series of orders of writing and the methods used for their production, this was used as the basis of composition exercises for those at the higher levels of study. We may, I think, safely assume Shakespeare's knowledge of the practice: in 1944 T. W. Baldwin delightfully exploded the myth of *William Shakespere's Small Latine and Lesse Greeke* by using the quotation as the title of a book exploring Shakespeare's use of classical sources—a book that extends to two volumes and over 1,500 pages. The more recent *From Humanism to the Humanities* by Anthony Grafton and Lisa Jardine (Grafton and Jardine 1986, 133) provides a useful definition of what ethopoeia consists of—"a highly emotionally-charged, first person speech." In the Greek text, Aphthonius gives a single example: the situation in which Niobe speaks after the death of her children. As Grafton and Jardine point out, this is the speech alluded to in *Hamlet* in the reference to Gertrude as "Niobe, all tears" (1.2.149) on the death of old Hamlet, so it seems quite clear that Shakespeare was, somehow and to some degree, aware of the technique from this source, and used it as a shorthand to convey an emotional state to part of his audience.

But there is an ambivalence central to the theory and craft of ethopoeia, which is central also to the recurrent relation of the word itself to the identity of the speaker in Shakespeare's use of the device. In introducing the practice as an exercise, Quintilian defines it as "*imitatio morum alienorum*" (2001, 68). *Morum* is the accusative form of the noun *mos, moris*. In the *Bibliotheca Eliotae*, the Latin dictionary compiled by Sir Thomas Eliot and published in 1545, the word is translated as "a manier, a condicion, also custome" (s.v. "ethopoeia"); in the dictionary by Thomas Thomas of 1587, it is similarly "a manner, fashion, guise, or behaviour, a custome, an order, a condition" (s.v. "ethopoeia"); and in my own shabby yet faithful Latin dictionary of 1830, *Tyronis Thesaurus*, it is again "a manner, way, fashion or custom, temper, humour, or nature" (Crakelt 1830, s.v. "ethopoeia"). It is in this sense that the word today is most familiar, in the lament, beloved of academics of a certain age, "O tempora o mores," meaning "O times, O customs."

In the translation of Donald A. Russell, the most recent Loeb edition, however, Quintilian's phrase is given as "With the representation of characters of others" (Quintilian 2001, 68). Similarly, the only English translation of the Greek of Aphthonius, made in the early 1950s by Ray Nadeau, heads the section of the manual "Concerning a characterization" and introduces the "Words such as those Niobe might utter after her children were murdered" as "A Model Characterization" (Nadeau 1952, 278). Contrast this with a passage from Richard Rainolde's *The Foundacioun of Rhetorike* of 1563, the closest thing to an Elizabethan English translation of Aphthonius-Agricola, which also includes references to Quintilian. "Ethopoeia is a certaine Oracioun made by voice, and lamentable imitacion, upon the state of any one." And further, "Ethopoeia is that, whiche hath the person knowne: but onely it doth faigne the manners of the same, and imitate in Oracioun the same." And again: "Quintilianus saieth, that Ethopoeia is a imitacioun of other meane manners" (Rainolde 1563, Fol. xlix)—and here, it seems, Rainolde is offering a direct translation of Quintilian's Latin, given above.

Imitatio mores alienorum: imitacioun of other meane manners: concerning a Characterization. My point is this: somewhere between the Greek and Latin texts, the idea of ethopoeia has slipped from the imitation of a "manner, way, fashion" to the personation of a living being or character. It is worth recalling here that "character" as a substantive to define the psychological independence of an individual is first recorded in the *OED* in a quotation from *Tom Jones*, first published in 1749—ironic in itself that a picaresque should be the origin of a term subsequently used of a stable personhood. That particular attribution may not be trustworthy, of course, but it is nonetheless a valuable hint, that "character" was neither a concept of personality nor a valid translation of *mos* at the time when Shakespeare was writing.

If to this we add the force of the repeated uses of the word *style* in the plays as a way of revealing falsity, a question begins to form itself around what happens in soliloquy. Is a revelation of stable personhood being presented, or an exploration of manner—an instance within a single continuous and consistent human entity—or a generalized response to a specific situation? The pedagogic texts all present ethopoeia as an exercise in recounting the response to a situation, not an imitation of personhood. If this is the case, then the rhetorical-stylistic device works counter to the concerns of character, and the implications are deep—perhaps nowhere other than in the play *Hamlet*, which has for so long been dominated by discussions about its place as the origin of the humanist individual within its existential dilemma. Recently Margreta de Grazia (2007) has refuted this in her *Hamlet without Hamlet*; and I am particularly struck by a comment made during a lecture by the Indian scholar Supriya Chaudhuri; "Hamlet is a succession of textual instances" (2009). Style in ethopoeia, it would seem, reinforces such readings. Moreover, the effect of falsehood implicit in the uses of the term throughout the canon further undermines the notion of identity construction implicit in many recent stances to soliloquy. And this perhaps is the ultimate complexity: if the application of style is a pretence, then in undermining it in speeches of individual roles the dramatist is both ironizing the aesthetics of his own profession and forcing the careful auditor to remember that what she is seeing or reading is not an actuality, but a counterfeit in both the early modern and the present-day senses of the word. In such a way is the true effect of theater achieved—and, ironically, a suggestion of a later and more insecure idea of identity, with all its postmodern anxieties and multiplicities, is at the same time implied. But there is a difference: it is not that one man in his life plays many parts, but that the whole concept of his being one man is dissolved.

If we approach style in this way, allowing that it may be freed from questions of personality, how does it affect the place of the individual soliloquy within the individual play, and then the changing concept of style as the canon moves on? The answer may be approached by looking at three soliloquies that demonstrate different features of the form, which can with some assurance be placed within different periods of the canon. The first is from *3 Henry VI*, and is spoken in the role of the king after his defeat at Towton.

> This battle fares like to the morning's war
> When dying clouds contend with growing light,
> What time the shepherd, blowing of his nails,
> Can neither call it perfect day nor night. (2.5.1–4)

O God! Methinks it were a happy life
To be no better than a homely swain,
To sit upon a hill, as I do now,
To carve out dials quaintly, point by point,
Thereby to see the minutes how they run—
How many makes the hour full complete
How many hours brings about the day,
How many days will finish up the year,
How many years a mortal man may live.
When this is known, then to divide the times—
So many hours must I tend my flock;
So many hours must I take my rest;
So many hours must I contemplate;
So many hours must I sport myself;
So many days my ewes have been with young;
So many weeks ere the poor fools will ean;
So many years ere I shall shear the fleece:
So minutes, hours, days, weeks, months, and years
Pass'd over to the end they were created,
Would bring white hairs unto a quiet grave.
Ah, what a life were this! How sweet! How lovely! (2.5.21–41)

The rhetorical formations here are so tightly structured that they assume the form of a schematic diagram—a flow-chart, almost. The situation is established in time, with the reference to the battle's ebb and flow as a contention between light and dark, itself a classical borrowing familiar to the audience from its use in Homer and in several earlier English writers before Shakespeare. The moment of place is then made clear, with the molehill on which the king sits. And then the meditation—the fourfold "How many" balanced against the matching "So many," then a threefold "So many" that links days, weeks, and years before a further line that completes the fourfold structure and gathers all of the divisions of time, before a final couplet and concluding statement of regret. The situation of the king wishing he were a commoner is again a standard form; but one that is worth revisiting later in the canon in a startling transformation, in the situation when the role of Henry V itself assumes another role as common soldier before the battle of Agincourt, a sophisticated game with the ideas of identity and theatric personation.

In *3 Henry VI*, though, this statement of order within the role of a shepherd acquires its force through the situation in which it is presented, and the identity of its speaker abruptly changed. Order has collapsed in the defeat of the king: the king discusses a new kind of order. It is another kind of symmetry, balancing those of the speech itself; but it is also a heavy irony: the order is obsessive within a situation that is apparently the ideal of one who is supposed to enforce and embody order, but for whom and around whom order has collapsed. The irony is amplified by the speech's use of a generic artifice, the pastoral romance, a fiction in which order is illusory. The speech reveals the failure of rule through the inadequacy of its metaphorical and conventional alternative, ironized by the extreme rhetorical order that is its armature. At the same time, the very use of the ethopoeic convention is modified, so that the passage conveys not a response to a situation but a series of longings—a failure of rhetorical discipline that matches the other kinds of failures. Here the compound valency of the speech is revealed. It is a statement of individual response, an act of momentary subject-construction, and an engagement with the rhetorical convention of ethopoeia that works through a version of pastoral. In this sense, the soliloquy presents a dialogue not with other roles but with convention. As a result, style is shown as a fundamentally dual, slippery, and altogether untrustworthy medium whose counterfeit nature defines the constant inconstancy of personhood.

My second example comes from the final act of *Richard II*, in the role of the now deposed king.

> I have been studying how I may compare
> This prison where I live unto the world;
> And, for because the world is populous
> And here is not a creature but myself,
> I cannot do it. Yet I'll hammer it out.
> My brain I'll prove the female to my soul,
> My soul the father, and these two beget
> A generation of still-breeding thoughts,
> And these same thoughts people this little world,
> In humours like the people of this world,
> For no thought is contented. The better sort,
> As thoughts of things divine, are intermix'd
> With scruples, and do set the word itself

Against the word,
As thus: "Come, little ones"; and then again,
"It is as hard to come as for a camel
To thread the postern of a small needle's eye."
Thoughts tending to ambition, they do plot
Unlikely wonders: how these vain weak nails
May tear a passage through the flinty ribs
Of this hard world, my ragged prison walls;
And for they cannot, die in their own pride. (5.5.1–22)

What is immediately striking here is not an elaborate rhetorical geometry but instead an apparent struggle between orator and oratory. Earlier, failure was suggested by over-elaboration; here, it is presented through wrestling with forms to find an appropriate metaphorical language for the situation. This is not a response to a situation—"This prison where I live"—in the strict Aphthonian sense of reflections on past, present, and future feeling appropriate to it. It is instead an attempt to regularize the situation through a rhetorical device, a struggle to compose the metaphor, in the manner prescribed by Thomas Wilson as an "Allegory" or "Similitude" (1553, 157). Like the *3 Henry VI* passage, it interrogates the strict practice of ethopoeia, but in a new and different way. Whereas we might read the earlier speech as a successful exemplum of a complex rhetorical exercise being used as a way of avoiding a specific situation, it is hard to read this later one as anything but a complex failure in the effort to confront one. We may be moved by both of them because of the failures they present; but it is our response to a manipulation of tropes and conventions that causes this, not an engagement with a consistent and stable individual.

There is another element here that relates the speech both to earlier uses of the word *style* in the plays and to the larger concept of role and character. Throughout the play, the language of the role of the King is associated with hyperbole and exaggerated comparison. In returning from France, there is an implied comparison with the sun, "the searching eye of heaven" (3.2.37); in descending from the walls of Harfleur, the speaker uses the words "Down, down I come, like glist'ring Phaëthon" (3.3.178). This has led some to see the search for outlandish metaphor as a feature that defines the character of Richard in its consistency. But here again the play as a whole evidences the other kind of undermining seen in the shorter allusions to style: repeatedly, similar metaphors are presented in the role of Bullingbrook as ways of satiric destabilizing. Between the two lines just quoted, the sun metaphor is turned around, when Richard is compared to "the blushing discontented sun" (3.3.63). Those who choose may see this as the greater skill of Bullingbrook as a rhetorician; considered in the larger stylistic frame of the play as a whole, the stress is far more on a debate about the construction of kingship through language that again undermines the notion of aggrandizement through *style*.

This move to the play as a whole is enhanced by another feature of the speech that functions at yet another level in revealing an element often seen as a key feature of Shakespeare's rhetorical style: the speech moves rapidly from one metaphoric vehicle to another. It begins with the familiar gender relation between mind and soul, and then shifts to two Biblical texts—"suffer the little children" and the camel passing through the eye of a needle—which in turn suggests the idea of the speaker's nails tearing through the prison walls, and then becoming the slaves to fortune, which are like beggars in the stocks. Critics from Caroline Spurgeon (1935) and Wolfgang Clemen (1951) onwards have drawn attention to this method of metaphoric progression in the plays, and there is no need to discuss or exemplify it further. But it demonstrates well a further issue of style within a dramatic frame: that of the complex and insoluble question of who is speaking, the dramatist or the constructed role-in-situation. The question suggests a further, and seriously disruptive, question in addressing Shakespeare's style: to what level is the text a ventriloquial construction, in many voices, and to what extent a single utterance? It is an insistent question, to which I shall return.

Consider now the final speech, made by the figure of Leontes at the close of the second scene of *The Winter's Tale*.

Exeunt POLIXENES, HERMIONE, and Attendants

Gone already!
Inch-thick, knee-deep; o'er head and ears a fork'd one!
Go, play, boy, play: thy mother plays, and I
Play too, but so disgrac'd a part, whose issue
Will hiss me to my grave: contempt and clamour
Will be my knell. Go, play, boy, play. There have been,

(Or I am much deceived) cuckolds ere now;
And many a man there is (even at this present,
Now, while I speak this) holds his wife by th'arm,
That little thinks she has been sluic'd in's absence
And his pond fish'd by his next neighbour, by
Sir Smile, his neighbour: nay, there's comfort in't,
Whiles other men have gates, and those gates open'd,
As mine, against their will. Should all despair
That have revolted wives, the tenth of mankind
Would hang themselves. Physic for't there's none;
It is a bawdy planet, that will strike
Where 'tis predominant; and 'tis powerful, think it,
From east, west, north and south; be it concluded,
No barricado for a belly. Know't;
It will let in and out the enemy
With bag and baggage: many thousand on's
Have the disease, and feel't not. How now, boy! (1.2.185–207)

The stage direction is an invention of Nicholas Rowe in his 1709 edition: there is none in the Folio, the only authoritative early text. That's interesting. It suggests that this be played very much within the acting convention of the time, as a soliloquy that allows the individual actor to display his talents to the full. Restoration and early-eighteenth-century performance was more concerned with individual recitation than interacting, and the insertion gives full scope to the actor here—and the words prompt all kinds of emphases and gesturings to reveal the lubricious horror with which they are spoken. Already, then, in the insertion of the stage direction, a major decision has been made about what is going on in this passage. I make the point largely in passing, but also to show that the pull toward the actualization of role into person was already powerful at the start of the eighteenth century, and enacted not only on stage but in the printed text, in this case to the extent that most modern editions follow Rowe and print the direction with only minor annotation.

The speech can certainly be read, and performed, as an immediate and appalled initial response to a situation, and in this regard it is an extension of ethopoeic practice. But it is quite a remote extension. The language is full of fractures and convolutions: it turns back on itself, becomes its own theme in exploring its own doubleness, most particularly in the awful force of the word "play." If the speech has any vestige of the ethopoeic, it is in the location firmly, and continuously, in the present: it moves beyond the example of Niobe's self-examination in Aphthonius toward a present-continuous dynamic of conceptual uncertainty, linguistic internalization, and moral generalization, all way beyond the limited rhetorical tropes used in *3 Henry VI*. At the same time, this process might be seen as an extension of the rolling metaphors seen in the *Richard II* speech, where one figure sparks off another, to give an associative pattern rather than a sustained logical growth or conceptual parallelism. And yet, this linguistic fracture, and the sudden, unexplained and inexplicable outburst of jealousy that it reveals, can be seen as a moment of extreme and grave psychological insight, one of the most incisive, baffling and yet deeply resonant in the whole canon. How do these two elements function together? The question is at the root of the role-character opposition.

Related to it, I think, is another: how do all three of these passages align with the larger structures of which they are part, and how do they contribute to this different, more structural, aspect of style? That speeches of this kind have been erected into a separate species known as the soliloquy, and have been anthologized and individually performed and studied, implies that they are distinct from the greater forms they help to construct. This may be explained in several ways. We may take the straightforward option of saying that they demonstrate the onset of a true conception of the individual, a foretaste of Althusserian agency, the presentation of an individual voice astray in the wilderness of external actuality. But this is too simple. It overlooks the engagement that the passages demonstrate with the rhetorical theory of ethopoeia, the practice that flows from it, and the traditions with which they are in dialogue. It also neglects the subtle play of stylistic devices between speaking roles that I touched on in the discussion of *Richard II*, where a particular chain of linguistic association passes, like the gold chain in *The Comedy of Errors*, between one role and another. Yet the irony is that, at each moment of such possession, in the stylistic immediacy of ethopoeic invention, these passages invite the audience to become involved with the emotions generated by the situation and develop a sympathy, if not quite an empathy, with the speaker. To accept this as a genuine ambivalence rather than an unfortunate paradox is to approach more closely the response of an experienced auditor or reader of Shakespeare's time, as yet mercifully free of the Romantic notion of character. And to say that we are allowed in some measure to share feelings of a performer within a specific situation is a long way from asserting that we empathize with a sequentially convincing identity, continuous throughout the play. The engagement is carefully controlled, in the same way, but on a much larger scale, as the earlier, briefer signposts warning us to mistrust "style" in written language or formal speech.

Within this frame—where the moment of situational perception is not anchored to person but is, instead, a stylistic exercise drawn from a manual of rhetoric—we may find a suggestive parallel in eighteenth-century opera and oratorio. The form is structured through a sequence of arias, each introduced by a recitative that establishes situation, that then engenders a single complex of mood. Elaborate codes for this expression, known as the practice of *affektenlehre*, were well known—a complex of the specific tonalities, intervallic progressions, melodic shapes and rhythmic patterns, each having its own associative significance, deployed to provide a tonal analogue to the emotional state of the figure in response to the prescribed situation. The examples spread across nation and genre: "*Che faro senza Eurydice?*" from Gluck's *Orfeo ed Eurydice*, Dido's lament from Purcell's *Dido and Aeneas*, the arias of the Evangelist from the Bach passions—all these convey feeling through codes shared between composers, performers, and listeners. They are separate, but work as a series of statements that together produce a response of feeling as much as of aesthetic engagement. Perhaps this is a valid analogy for the larger effect of the soliloquy within the complete play, employing as it does a range of rhetorical devices in response to a situation. There is engagement with feeling, but not identification with person, alongside a recognition of the way in which the codes are employed and modified through the individual aesthetic identity of the composer.

This returns us to the larger question of style within Shakespeare's plays as something that transcends ethopoeic techniques and rhetorical devices, and the extent and nature of its change through the canon from the earliest plays through to the notional "late style." In discussing the three passages I have suggested what Russ McDonald has demonstrated with infinitely greater subtlety and depth—that there is in the canon a progression away from received formal rhetorical devices toward a far greater flexibility. Does this suggest that Shakespeare becomes less concerned with the formal devices of the ethopoeic method as the canon grows?[3] Certainly, we can say that the style, the way that the words are moved around on the page or in aural space, changes radically from the first to the last. The shift mirrors the larger discontinuities of the last plays—the mingling of genres, caesurae of event, the use of narrated rather than presented action, and other departures from earlier sequences. The shift is parallel to the protean forms and abrupt shifts found in the late quartets of Beethoven. But this is only one aspect of what might be termed a late style.

The changes suggest features associated with Mannerist art—and, indeed, Murray Roston has suggested this in a long discussion of the possible parallels in stylistic development between Shakespeare and Renaissance painting and sculpture (1989, 239–75). The association may be helpful in suggesting a parallel between contortions of form and extremes of feeling. The very fracture of the last plays gives greater prominence to moments of ethopoeic invention as situational sharing, and the moments themselves, of which the speech from *The Winter's Tale* is a fine but by no means rare example, reveal through their own faultlines a greater psychological depth. If we forget the construction of independent character as a developmental actuality in the plays, it is possible to see a movement toward a freer language, a rejection of earlier *style*, toward an immediacy that vigorously reinvents the "plainnesse" advocated as the aim of all rhetoric by Thomas Wilson and the rest. At the same time, the broken structures act against the presentation of continuous, stable personhood; the last plays extend ethopoeia, but along its situational, not its characterizing, axis. That we persist in seeing them as interactions between actual people, who have lives between the acts, is a distortion that we ourselves apply, having looked through Stanislavskian spectacles, whereas the actuality is arguably that the plays' linguistic forms allow us to be moved by soliloquies, while seeing not actual people genuinely moved but highly professional counterfeits of moments of such feeling. The result is that the plays are most convincing when their artifice is at its greatest, when style is a matter

---

[3]It is easy, but reductive, to see this as a shift toward a romantic individualism of characters.

of pretence, with the end of arousing and reflecting on feeling, not to feel directly itself.

Once this becomes feasible for the late plays, its principle may be folded back over the rest of the canon. Ethopoeic moments acting as revelations of situation may be just as effective in the earlier plays, albeit that their appropriation of other voices, other traditions and practices may give them different inflections from what might be termed the irregular directness of those at the end of the canon. Seeing them in the more isolated, more fragmentary manner in which the last plays are constructed suggests their qualities of human insight within their qualities of style. Sorting out how to conceptualize this balance between the aesthetic and the human, the mannered and the innate, though, has inevitably posed problems for modern, and postmodern, critical readers. Discussing the linguistic-dramatic construction of Desdemona, Olivia, and Lady Macbeth, Alan Sinfield attempts "to exemplify a way of reading in which speech and action in a fictional text may be attributed to characters—understood not as essential unities, but as simulated personages apparently possessing adequately continuous or developing subjectivities" (1992, 78). Yet he offsets against this "a textual organization in which character is a strategy" (78). His conclusion is that "subjectivity is itself produced, in all its complexity, within a linguistic and social structure," which I take to mean that the discontinuities of textual practice themselves mimic and deepen those of human identity. Other critics would see the avoidance of stable developmental identity as the postmodern understanding of a basic existential state, the random sequence of performative acts I mentioned earlier, when referring to Judith Butler's argument that it is only from such moments that the "compelling illusion" of personhood is constructed. In performance, the work of Christian Billing in attempting to produce the plays in a pre-character mode is an extension of these practices onto the stage, an equivalent perhaps of musical performances in mean-tone tuning rather than equal temperament, and just as difficult to achieve.[4]

If it is possible to reconcile these positions, then the performative aspects of the ethopoeic method, and the stylistic operations that it involves, stand as something remarkably significant. Instead

[4]This practice is discussed in Billing, forthcoming.

of moments of shared feeling that reveal the true nature of individual character, they become the raw materials from which identity is constructed, while imposing a distance that allows an analytical response in the perceiver. And this is the irony which I offer as a way of drawing together the complexities of style, rhetoric, and individuation that are a constant presence within any reading or performance of the plays. In offering fragmented moments of situational response, the plays of Shakespeare present the discrete elements from which personhood is constructed, not a continuous analogue of stable or developmental character. The use of rhetorical devices, held up for trial on the grounds of affectation or falsity through the disparaging use of the word *style*, becomes a metaphor of this process, not a depiction of its result. And within this is contained not only a mistrust of the process of self-definition through appropriation of language, but an undermining of the whole process of theater—a version of Diderot's paradox of acting, that it is most convincing when most pretentious.[5] And here I return to the use of the word style in the plays themselves—as an accusation of assumption, of impropriety, of counterfeiting. The artifice of style, and the artifice of dramatic language, are both exposed as counterfeits: but the word itself has powerful driving ambivalences, suggesting a positive imitation—the resonance of Renaissance *imitatio* is important here—as well as darker associations of illicit reproduction. This suggests that the power of the language, and the psychological insight of the new art, can exist simultaneously, in a new paradox of acting. The convincing presentation of moments of deep feeling, toward which I have suggested the canon moves, in a progression from more rigid rhetorical forms, offers itself as something very close to the revelation of character. The parallel with postmodern notions of identity, understood in the broad sense of subjectivity in process, is therefore perhaps rather closer than we might think. However closely these approach the idea of identities repeatedly suffering reinvention through social pressure and circumstance, they do not reject the possibility of some kind of identity within each moment. And here, perhaps, in Shakespeare, is

[5]For example, "A man who, having learnt the words set down for him by the author, fools you thoroughly, whether in tragedy or comedy" (Diderot 1883, 39); "Perhaps it is just because he is nothing that he is before all everything. His own special shape never interferes with the shapes he assumes" (53).

the subtle, supple way in which role becomes character, the roll of paper on which the actor's part is written being transformed into a metaphor of actual identity. Sorting out the nature of each separate moment in performance, to avoid the fallacy of continuous character, is the task of the onlooker or reader; and making sense of that most troublesome of notions, the style of words and delivery, as Shakespeare signals in his use of the word *style*, remains as intriguingly complex today as it was in the Elizabethan theater.

References

Baldwin, T. W. 1994. *William Shakspere's Small Latine and Lesse Greeke.* 2 vols. Urbana, IL: University of Illinois Press.

Belsey, Catherine. 1985. "Disrupting Sexual Difference: Meaning and Gender in the Comedies." In *Alternative Shakespeares*, edited by John Drakakis, 166–90. New York: Routledge.

Billing, Christian. Forthcoming. "Rehearsing Shakespeare: Alternative Strategies in Process and Performance." In *Shakespeare Bulletin* 30(4), edited by Christian Billing. Baltimore: Johns Hopkins University Press.

Butler, Judith. 1990. "Performance Acts and Gender Constitution: An Essay in Phenomenology and Feminist Theory." In *Performing Feminisms: Feminist Critical Theory and Theatre*, edited by Sue-Ellen Case, 270–82. Baltimore: Johns Hopkins University Press.

Chaudhuri, Supriya. "Shakespeare and the Art of Lying" (Presented paper, Indian Institute of Advanced Studies, Simla, October 2009).

Clemen, Wolfgang. 1951. *The Development of Shakespeare's Imagery.* London: Methuen.

Crakelt, William and Rev. M. G. Sarjant. 1830. *Tyronis Thesaurus; or, Entick's Latin-English Dictionary*. London: Rivington et al.

De Grazia, Margreta. 2007. *Hamlet Without Hamlet.* Cambridge: Cambridge University Press.

Diderot, Denis. 1883. *The Paradox of Acting.* Translated by Walter Herries Pollock. London: Chatto and Windus. Originally published as *Paradoxe sur le comédien: Ouvrage posthume.* Paris: A. Sautelet, 1830.

Eliot, Thomas. 1545. *Bibliotheca Eliotae Eliots Librarie.* London: Thomas Berthelet.

Grafton, Anthony and Lisa Jardine. 1986. *From Humanism to the Humanities: Education and the Liberal Arts in Fifteenth- and Sixteenth-Century Europe.* London: Duckworth.

Latham, Agnes, ed. 1975. *As You Like It*. The Arden Shakespeare. London: Methuen.

McDonald, Russ. 2006. *Shakespeare's Late Style*. Cambridge: Cambridge University Press.

McMullan, Gordon. 2007. *Shakespeare and the Idea of Late Writing: Authorship in the Proximity of Death*. Cambridge: Cambridge University Press.

Nadeau, Ray. 1952. "The *Progymnasnata* of Aphthonius in Translation." *Speech Monographs* 19: 264–85.

Quintilian. 2001. *Quintilian: The Orator's Education*, vol. 4, books 9–10. Edited and translated by Donald A. Russell. Cambridge, MA: Harvard University Press.

Rainolde, Richard. 1563. *A Booke Called the Foundacioun of Rhetorike*. London: Ihon Kingston.

Roston, Murray. 1989. *Renaissance Perspectives in Literature and the Visual Arts*. Princeton, NJ: Princeton University Press.

Shakespeare, William. 1997. *The Riverside Shakespeare*. 2nd edn. Edited by Blakemore Evans et al. Boston: Houghton Mifflin.

Sinfield, Alan. 1992. "When is a Character not a Character? Desdemona, Olivia, Lady MacBeth, and Subjectivity." In *Faultlines: Cultural Materialism and the Politics of Dissident Reading*, 52–79. Oxford: Clarendon.

Spurgeon, Caroline. 1935. *Shakespeare's Imagery and What It Tells Us*. Cambridge: Cambridge University Press.

Thomas, Thomas. 1587. *Dictionarium Linguae Latinae et Anglicanae*. Cambridge: Thomas Thomas.

Tillyard, E. M. W. 1943. *The Elizabethan World Picture*. London: Chatto and Windus.

Wilson, Thomas. 1553. *The Arte of Rhetorique, for the use of all suche as are studious of eloquence. . . .* London: Richard Grafton.

4

Style and history in Diderot and Winckelmann

Saul Anton

Style is history. That has been the constant of modernity since the eighteenth century, when the traditional humanist understanding of style grounded in the rhetoric of persuasion—a *lexis*, states Aristotle, needed because "it is not enough to know *what* we ought to say, we must also say it *as* we ought" so that "persuasion can be produced from the facts themselves"—gave way to an aesthetic understanding of style as the expression of history, the index of a specific time and place (Aristotle 1941, 3.1435).[1] The history of this development is well known, and it conditions the rise of the academic disciplines of literary and art history in the nineteenth century, as well as the twentieth-century avant-gardes and contemporary neo-avant-gardes.

It is nonetheless worth briefly recapitulating some of this history. One can begin with Voltaire's neoclassical vision of the "century" of Louis XIV as an era of "great men, the fine arts and *politesse*" (Voltaire 1957, 1,299, my translation) and as "the century which most approaches perfection," as an early instance of the claim that the arts are an expression of a specific historical time and place (617). The nineteenth century takes Voltaire's vision of seventeenth-century France a step further by overturning his view that this history is one of the perfection of an ideal of beauty, that

[1]All italics in quotations are those of the author quoted unless otherwise indicated.

it is, in other words, a history that takes the form of French classicism, even as it holds onto his understanding of the arts and beauty as expressions of a specific historical moment. In "The Painter of Modern Life," Baudelaire upholds the modern ideals of the historical, the transitory, and the contingent, even though he is unwilling to jettison the classical altogether: "Beauty is made up of an eternal, invariable element, whose quantity it is excessively difficult to determine, and of a relative, circumstantial element, which will be, if you like, whether severally or all at once, the age, its fashions, its morals, its emotions" (Baudelaire 1995, 3). Baudelaire's elevation of the transitory and the historical—emblematized by his celebration of the modern city in *Les Fleurs du mal*—is a poetic analogue of the attempt to develop a general theory of style by art historians such as Heinrich Wölfflin and Alois Riegl that could serve as the basis of the history of both the fine and the decorative arts: "To *explain* a style then can mean nothing other than to place it in its general historical context and to verify that it speaks in harmony with the other organs of its age" (Gombrich 1998, 136).

In the twentieth century, the idea of style as an expression of history is radicalized by more than one thinker. One can invoke, perhaps most obviously, Walter Benjamin's conception of the dialectical image, as a limit concept of style, the critique of the historicist understanding of style in the name of a radical understanding of it as the pure possibility of historical revolution or change (Benjamin 2006, 389–400). Closer to Benjamin than is generally recognized is Clement Greenberg, who saw the avant-garde as the transformation of Western history and the historical progress it had proclaimed since the Enlightenment into an essentially aesthetic phenomenon, the index of historical rupture and revolution. In the 1939 article "Avant-Garde and Kitsch," the American critic argued that the avant-garde's retreat into formal innovation and change—that is, into *stylistic* innovation—ought to be understood not as a bourgeois gesture, but rather as the only viable form of historical revolution:

> The revolution was left inside society, a part of that welter of ideological struggle which art and poetry find so unpropitious as soon as it begins to involve those "precious" axiomatic beliefs upon which culture thus far has had to rest. Hence it developed that the true and most important function of the avant-garde

> was not to "experiment," but to find a path along which it would be possible to keep culture *moving* in the midst of ideological confusion and violence. (Greenber 1961, 5)

One could cite many more examples of the intimate relation between style and history in modern and contemporary cultural discourse. Yet this relation itself has a history, of course, that goes back to the Enlightenment. More specifically, perhaps, it can be traced to the eighteenth-century emergence of antiquarianism, art history, and the "salons, the cafés, the clubs, and the periodicals" that constituted, as Roger Chartier has pointed out, a "tribunal of aesthetic criticism" that functioned as a living and practical horizon of public reception and judgment, and, consequently, of a historical modernity and contemporaneity (Chartier 1991, 21–2). Of these, perhaps the most prominent and important were the Salon exhibitions of painting and sculpture held biannually at the Louvre beginning in 1737. A brave new world in which social classes mixed freely, according to Thomas Crow, they represented the development of a "completely secular setting . . . for the purpose of encouraging a primarily aesthetic response in large numbers of people" (Crow 1985, 3; see also Chartier 1991, 21–5). Significantly, the French Royal Academy conceived the Salon from the beginning as both the public institution of art and the institution of the art public. In 1699, in moving the Academy to the Louvre, where the first public Salons of living painters had been organized by Colbert in 1673, Jules Hardouin-Mansart, the *Surintendant des Bâtiments*, set out to "renew the former custom of exhibiting their works to the public in order to receive its judgment and to foster that worthy competition so necessary to the progress of the fine arts" (quoted in Crow 1985, 37). In this way, the Salon was an actual historical horizon for the Enlightenment, a public sphere that sought to extend the seventeenth-century "Republic of Letters" to society as a whole via the mechanism of aesthetic experience and taste. Such an extension implies a double program: both the creation of an actual viewing public who visits the exhibitions and, insofar as such a public becomes identified with works of art and their perfection, the transformation of the classical concept of style grounded in the rhetoric of persuasion into the aesthetic expression of history, the *work* of a specific time and place.

Yet this aesthetic conception of style does not entirely leave behind the traditional idea of style as persuasion. The immediacy of the aesthetic appreciation of visual works of art required the development of a critical discourse capable of asserting the historical value of aesthetic experience. Along with the tens of thousands of visitors that the Salon would receive by the 1760s, it also gave rise to a new journalistic art writing and criticism that served as the medium of the new public. Between 1737 and 1789, in the name of the perfection of art, critics, journalists, and other literati published over 150 pamphlets and reviews addressed both to the Academy and to the general public in newspapers and journals (Crow 1985, 6). Although one often thinks of this new critical public as the foundation of our own modernity, in fact, it was clearly an extension and realization of the classical program laid out by Mansart. In his *Salon de 1763*, for example, Diderot pays homage to this new classical vision of the art public in an opening invocation of Colbert, the celebrated minister of Louis XIV who refounded the Royal Academy of Painting and Sculpture in 1661 and presided over the first exhibition of the works of living painters in 1673: "Forever blessed be the name of he who, by instituting this public exhibition of paintings, excited emulation amongst artists . . . [and] put off for us the decadence of painting by more than a hundred years, perhaps, and made the nation more educated and discerning in this area" (Diderot 1984a, 179, my translation).

Formulaic and ceremonial, this passage nevertheless clearly affirms the Academy and the Salon exhibition as foundations for a classical model of culture delicately balanced between artists and audiences, production and reception. Such a classical vision presumes that the arts are subject to an indefinite "perfectibility" through the competitive and critical conditions of their institution. Here, perfectibility is an ongoing critical task intended to sustain and reproduce a living cultural era through the mechanism of the kind of "tribunal of aesthetic criticism" described by Chartier.

Unsurprisingly, Diderot's *Salons* have long been emblematic of the emerging bourgeois public and the modern art public. In Michael Fried's *Absorption and Theatricality: Painting and Beholder in the Age of Diderot*, they represent the founding texts of a phenomenological conception of painting, that is, of a modern pictorial—and thus explicitly aesthetic rather than poetic or theatrical—conception of painting first realized by Jacques-Louis David.[2] Yet Diderot's comments in the passage above from the *Salon de 1763* also show that the "tribunal of aesthetic criticism" conceived as a living, breathing historical horizon of culture was not entirely untheorized. In fact, although he invokes Colbert, the passage also registers his skepticism about the classical vision of the Academy and the dream of sustaining art's perfection through the creation and preservation of public taste. Diderot invokes the perfection of painting above, but only to weigh the possibility of its mortality and historicity. Painting is historical by virtue of public taste, he suggests, yet in the quotation above this also implies the very possibility of its decline. Moreover, by the time Diderot writes the *Salon de 1767*, the dream of achieving and sustaining a classical historical present, finely balanced between genius and taste—a classical modernity balanced between the production and reception of art—gives way to an explicit recognition of the impossibility of doing so: "When does one see the birth of critics and grammarians? Right after the century marked by genius and divine productions. Those centuries are eclipsed never to reappear. . . . Method, when there's no longer any genius" (Diderot 1995a, 114, translation modified). The question of how the French School might avoid decadence and decline is no longer, so to speak, "academic." The relation between art and its criticism is now presented in temporal terms. Genius and taste now

---

[2]According to Fried, Diderot is the first to theorize a modern conception of painting that actively concerns itself with its formal and material elements as a visual medium, that is, with what the painting *looks* like and how, as a *pictorial* object, it engages and constitutes the *look*. Diderot is the first to recognize and champion, Fried claims, the development of scenes of "absorption" in eighteenth-century genre painting by Chardin, Jean-Baptiste Greuze, and others. With the absorptive image, the viewer's presence in front of the painting is negated by the refusal of any of the figures in the painting to return his or her gaze, and this new "beholder," constituted by the painting's refusal to acknowledge his presence, is the visual analogue of Diderot's literary style of critical description, which begins from the premise that his reader is not really there and, for the same reason, seeks to reproduce the work as a pictorial image in the latter's mind's eye. The result, for Fried, is the "the creation of a new sort of object—the fully realized *tableau*—and the constitution of a new sort of beholder—a new 'subject'—whose innermost nature would consist precisely in the conviction of his absence from the scene of representation" (Fried 1980, 104).

belong to distinct eras whereas, in 1763, Diderot still appeared, at least on the surface, to entertain the possibility of a symbiotic relation between the two.

Diderot, moreover, is hardly the only Enlightenment figure aware of the question of art's historicity and its potential decline. Salon criticism of the period is deeply concerned that the style we know today as Rococo had corrupted the vigor of classical French history painting, and calls for a return to the *Grand goût* were regular and unceasing. This ongoing obsession with decline is also an important impetus to the emergence of neoclassicism. In his 1755 *Reflections on the Imitation of Greek Works in Painting and Sculpture* (*Gedanken über die Nachahmung der Griechischen Werke in der Malerei und Bildhauerkunst*), Johann Joachim Winckelmann, the German antiquarian still regarded as one of the inventors of art history, asserted not only the historical fact of a classical era in the Hellenic age of Greece, but also argued that Hellenic sculpture represented nothing less than the historical instance of the perfection of art:

> The only way for us to become great or, if this be possible, inimitable, is to imitate the Ancients. What someone once said of Homer—that he who admires him has learned to understand him well—also goes for the artworks of the Ancients, especially those of the Greeks. One must become as familiar with them as with a friend in order to find their statue of Laocoön just as inimitable as Homer. (Winckelmann 1987, 5; see Potts 1994)

This well-known passage has numerous implications that can't all be explored here. For my purposes, what is important is that for Winckelmann, Hellenic Greece represents the unique historical perfection of an ideal of beauty. Hellenic Greece was the historical *event* of style, the aesthetic expression of history, but only because its climate created the historical possibility of the realization of the ideal (see Hartog 2005, 84–5; Décultot 2000; Potts 1982, 377–407). In linking art to climate in this manner, Winckelmann is able to assert, in effect, that style *is* history, and history first becomes historical by becoming classical, that is, it becomes the realization in art of the ideal of natural beauty in a specific time and place (see Ferris 2000, 16–51). Neoclassical style, in other words, is never merely one style among others. It is, rather, something of an absolute notion of style in and through which art and history are said to take place in and through one another.

More significantly, however, Winckelmann is not content simply to wait around for the return of the classical ideal. He sets out to bring about its rebirth—the imitation of "the inimitable"—by means of the critical description of works such as the *Apollo Belvedere* and the *Laocoön*. Winckelmann, in other words, does not see art history in the way that it is still largely practiced, that is, as a scholarly account of the variation of style in time and an explanation of the sources and causes of this variation. Rather, he sees critical description as inherently linked to the historical production of art. In a 1757 letter to Johann Georg Wille, an engraver who lived in Paris and who also knew Diderot, he writes: "How can one paint and describe the *Apollo*?" (cited in Winckelmann 2006a, 36, my translation). The answer was to find a style in language that could match the sublimity of the original, and, of course, such a sublime style did not come easily. As Élisabeth Décultot has shown, Winckelmann obsessively worked and reworked the descriptions that would make up the bulk of the *History of the Art of Antiquity*, even after its publication in 1764. In the "Manuscript of Paris" dated 1756–7, for instance, one of three versions of a description of the Apollo Belvedere which appear in the *History of the Art of Antiquity*, Winckelmann identifies a sublime descriptive style with the very possibility of the rebirth of the Greek ideal in the modern era:

> I undertake to describe here a work that was conceived by a powerful mind capable of elevating itself above matter, and was realized by a hand destined to produce superior beings. Begin by penetrating mentally into the empire of impalpable beauties and immerse yourself in it in order to prepare yourself to contemplate it. Gather the ideas of celestial poets and try to make yourself the creator of a celestial nature. Once you have produced a statue in yourself and created a more perfect form than your eye has seen, only then go to the statue of this divinity. (Winckelmann 2006a, 122–3)

In other words, it is a matter not merely of scholarship but of repetition. A sublime style of description would not merely study and describe Hellenic art, it would translate the ideal of natural beauty that it represents into the means of its rebirth. I am undoubtedly moving too quickly here, but it is clear that sublime critical description is, for the German scholar, sublime history—the very possibility of *making* history in the form of art. It is in this sense that in the preface to the *History of the Art of Antiquity*, Winckelmann announces that he understands history not merely as the narrative of artistic styles over time—still today our own everyday understanding of the discipline of art history and one that he also pioneers—but rather as a "system": "The history of the art of antiquity that I have endeavored to write is no mere narrative of the chronology and alterations of art, for I take the word *history* in the wider sense that it has in the Greek language and my intention is to provide a system" (Winckelmann 2006b, 71).

The system Winckelmann envisions requires a model of critical description capable of *making* history by remaking art, for only in this way can it articulate the origin of art in and *as* history. Such an origin is implied by the fact that Winckelmann wishes to produce a system which will take as its "principal object the essence of art" (Das Wesen der Kunst ist in diesem sowohl, als in jenem Teile, der vornehmste Endzweck), an essence now defined no longer as an eternal ideal but rather as the aesthetic expression of the ideal in and as history (Winckelmann 1934, 9, my translation). Whether or not one agrees with Winckelmann's neoclassical taste for Hellenism, the point in this particular instance is a methodological one. The return of Greece, as Winckelmann conceives it here, becomes possible because he has produced the critical template according to which art, through its critical description, becomes the medium in which history takes place (see Barbe and Pigeaud 1995 on Winckelmann's invention of art history).

Translated in January of 1756 in the *Journal d'étranger*, Winckelmann's *Reflections* played an important role in the emergence of antiquity as a critical point of reference in Parisian Salon criticism, in particular in the debates about Carl Van Loo's *Sacrifice d'Iphigénie* at the Salon of 1757 that were the occasion for Diderot's first public comments on the Academy's exhibitions.

It is well known that Diderot was one of Winckelmann's earliest and most astute readers. Although the former's *Salons* have been understood almost uniquely in belletrist terms, his *Salons* of 1765 and 1767, as well as the 1766 *Essais sur la peinture*, are published in the immediate wake of Winckelmann's 1764 *History of the Art of Antiquity*, which would not be translated until 1766, but parts of which appeared in various journals much earlier.[3]

Diderot's admiration of the German scholar, however, was hardly uncritical.[4] Quite significantly, he names Winckelmann in the *Salon de 1765* in the section devoted to sculpture, and compares him to none other than Don Quixote and his *frère-ennemi*, Jean-Jacques Rousseau (see Bukdahl 1984, 9–10; Seznec 1959, 103–5):

> I'm fond of fanatics, not the ones who present you with an absurd article of faith and who, holding a knife to your throat, scream at you: "Sign or die," but rather those who, deeply committed to some specific innocent taste, hold it to be beyond compare, defend it with all their might . . . calling on everyone they meet to either embrace their absurd view or to avow that the charms of their Dulcinea surpass those of every other earthly creature. Such a one is Jean-Jacques Rousseau . . . Such a one is Winckelmann when he compares the productions of the ancient artists with those of modern artists. What doesn't he see in this stump of a man we call the *Torso* [of Apollo]? . . . Ask him if it's

---

[3]Indeed, the reception of Diderot's *Salons* in the past two centuries has focused almost entirely on their stylistic verve. For Romantics such as Charles Nodier, for example, Diderot's style was the very embodiment of Imagination, "a style as spontaneous as the imagination, as independent and infinite as the soul, a style that lives upon itself and in which thought has been incarnated in the verb" (cited in Trousson 1997, 99, my translation). In his 1995 introduction to the first comprehensive English translation of the *Salons*, for instance, Thomas Crow asserts that "the best introduction to Diderot the critic of art is to transpose to the realm of ideas his own praise of Vernet in 1765. . . . It's impossible to describe his compositions, they must be seen" (Crow 1995, xix).

[4]Jacques Chouillet argued, quite correctly, that Diderot and Winckelmann shared a fundamentally aesthetic understanding of art. However, at issue here is the historical significance of the aesthetic experience that each attempts to embody in description (see Chouillet 1973, 486–7). Jean Seznec also points to Diderot's connections to Winckelmann and his milieu through his friendship with Grimm, but recognizes his reserve for the former's idealization of ancient Greece (see Seznec 1957, 103–5).

> better to study the antique or nature, without the knowledge and study of which, without a taste for which ancient artists, even with all the specific advantages they enjoyed, would have left us only mediocre works: The antique! He'll reply without skipping a beat; the antique! . . . And in one fell swoop a man whose intelligence, enthusiasm, and taste are without equal betrays all these gifts in the middle of the Toboso. Anyone who scorns nature in favor of the antique risks never producing anything that's not trivial, weak, and paltry in its drawing, character, drapery, and expression. Anyone who's neglected nature in favor of the antique will risk being cold, lifeless, devoid of the hidden, secret truths which can only be perceived in nature itself. It seems to me one must study the antique to learn how to look at nature. (Diderot 1995a, 1.156–7)

The comparison here of Winckelmann (and Rousseau) to Cervantes's deluded hero makes clear Diderot's skepticism regarding the former's vision of antiquity and the historical origin of art. The *philosophe* clearly does not share the antiquarian's conception of Hellenism. Rather, he upholds the value of nature *against* that of antiquity, and demotes the latter from an ideal moment of artistic perfection to a pedagogical aid. Antiquity should be studied not because it is the historical realization of ideal beauty to be repeated, but rather as an example of how to look at nature, that is, as a model of visual description and representation.

Diderot makes the same point in the 1766 *Essais sur la peinture*, a text he wrote as a theoretical addendum to the *Salon de 1765*. In this text, he insists on the absence of an ideal of natural beauty, which implies that one should also refuse the Academy's hierarchy of the arts, that is, the classical distinction between history and genre painting, the representation of exemplary actions and the representation of objects such as people, landscapes or still-lifes. Against both, which historically depended on ideals of action or natural beauty, he insists on the rendering of natural forms and bodies in their historical actuality: "There would be no mannerism, in either drawing or color, if nature were scrupulously imitated. Mannerism derives from teachers, from the academy, from drawing schools, and even from the antique" (Diderot 1995a, 1.196). In other words, nature is less an unchanging ideal than an infinitely varied set of possibilities possessing no ideal form.

More crucially, however, Diderot's refusal of antiquity as an ideal of beauty and its historical perfection is also the explicit subject of his introductory comments to the *Salon de 1767.* Although he is speaking to Grimm, it is clearly Winckelmann, whose 1764 *History* had appeared in French the year before, whom he is addressing: "And if the Antique had not existed, how would you proceed? Listen to me, then, for I will try to explain to you how the ancients, who had no antiquities, proceeded" (Diderot 1995a, 2.68). Antiquity was only able to achieve what it did precisely because it lacked a model for beauty, an antiquity of its own. Crucially, the refusal of antiquity here is also accompanied by an explicit turn away from the stylized literary renderings in the *Salon de 1765*: "Don't expect me, my dear friend, to be as rich, various, wise, mad and fertile this time as I've been in previous Salons. Exhaustion is setting in" (Diderot 1995a, 2.3). Instead of literary verve, Diderot promises precise prosaic descriptions and sober critical judgment: "But I will try to compensate what's lacking in the way of digressions, insights, principles, and reflections with the precision of my descriptions and the equity of my judgments" (Diderot 1995a, 2.16).

Diderot thus simultaneously takes up the challenge of Winckelmann's desire to develop a sublime style of critical description and rejects its premises in order to articulate his own, quite different understanding of the relation between the aesthetic dimension of painting as a visual art and history. To understand his conception of critical description, we need to begin by looking at an oft-cited passage of the same *Salon de 1763* in which Diderot announces what has long been regarded as the literary ambition of his art criticism. He writes that he will produce a "variety of styles that respond to the variety of brushes" (une variété de styles qui répondit à la variété de pinceaux) (Diderot 1984a, 181, my translation). Continuing, it would appear, the *Encyclopédie*'s systematic substitution of concrete, empirical knowledge in place of a priori ideas and normative ideals of verisimilitude and natural beauty, Diderot proposes to "respond" to the art on view at the Salon, thus affirming the role of the public in art. Two years later, however, in his preliminary address in the *Salon de 1765* to Melchior Grimm, his friend and the coeditor of the *Correspondance littéraire*, the newsletter in which the *Salons* would appear, Diderot expands this descriptive program in the following way: "I'll describe the paintings for you, and my description will be such that, with a little imagination and taste, you'll be able to envision them spatially, disposing the objects within them more or less the way I saw them on the canvas" (Diderot 1995a, 1.26, translation modified).

Although it is subtle, the shift that takes place between 1763 and 1765 is crucial. In addition to faithfully recording and "responding" to the diverse painterly styles of the Academicians—their *pinceaux*—Diderot here announces a vivid literary mode of description that would allow his readers to "see" in their mind's eye the visual image depicted by the painter. In addition to responding to the material and formal attributes of the works, Diderot will now re-present the pictorial image depicted by the work. He will produce an "imitation" in language of the painter's imitation of a literary text—that is, of the exemplary actions and events that made up the literary source materials of classical history painting.

Take, for example, Diderot's account of Francesco Guiseppe Casanova's now-lost history painting, *Une marche d'armée*, in the *Salon de 1765*. In order to render this potentially exemplary tableau, Diderot begins with a highly stylized description conceived as a sequence of clearly rhetorical questions in which he simultaneously conveys the scene of the painting and wonders about the possibility of ever being able to fully describe it. I will here cite only the beginning and end of a very long paragraph:

> This is one of the most beautiful, most picturesque machines known to me. What a handsome spectacle! What grand, beautiful poetry! How can I transport you to the foot of these rocks that touch the sky? How can I show you this broad-beamed bridge supported by rafters, thrown from the summit of these rocks towards this old château? How can I give you an accurate idea of this château, of the crumbling antique towers that compose it and of the other vaulted bridge that unites and separates them? . . . But perhaps, while despairing of summoning up in your imagination so many animate and inanimate objects, they're there and I did it; if such is the case, God be praised! But this doesn't exhaust my obligations. Allowing Casanova's muse and

> mine to catch their breath, let's examine his work a bit more objectively. (Diderot 1995a, 1.83)

Diderot here describes the various elements of the scene without telling us anything about how these elements are situated and what they actually look like. At the end of this passage, he is not yet finished and there remains further work to be done. He thus announces the need for a second, more "objective" description and thereby underscores the limitations of a literary representation of the work. After first describing the landscape and the general disposition of the army, what is still needed is an account of how the objects depicted are located in space and in relation to one another. Yet even this is insufficient. It is simply impossible to render the scene of Casanova's painting. A critical description of the work will never be complete: "Imagine around this hill, on which rises the château, all the incidents characteristic of military camps, and you'll have Casanova's picture; it isn't possible to enumerate all these incidents, their variety is infinite; and what I sketched in the opening lines should suffice" (Diderot 1995a, 1.84).

Diderot thus performs the way in which a linguistic description of a visual work of art encounters its limit in the infinity of detail implied by pictorial representation, both at the level of content and the level of form. In the face of this infinity, Diderot must content himself with simply *designating* what he cannot describe. Even the best description is merely a "sketch" that could never represent the myriad details of the painting or the variety of its technical and formal style, the *faire* to which he was, in 1763, so eager to respond (see Beaujour 1981 for a useful and related discussion of description).

Diderot thus simultaneously describes Casanova's tableau and reinscribes the epistemological limits of description, thereby marking the limits of a classical understanding of ekphrasis as both a critical method and the rhetorical paradigm of history painting understood as the depiction of the highest and most expressive moment of a narrative action. At the outset, his conception of critical description is double: it is divided between an attention to visual "form" and "content." It aims to reverse engineer the machine of classical literary painting, but what this reversal reveals is not the analogy of the literary and the pictorial—of poetry and painting—but rather the simultaneous necessity and impossibility of such an analogy. It reveals, in other words, a fissure in the general theory of description that undermines the very possibility of art and its public working in harmony to produce and sustain a classical style.

It would require more space than I have here, but one could show that this divergence is present throughout the *Salon de 1765*, where, in fact, it conditions Diderot's celebrated renderings of the paintings he had seen at the Louvre. With it, Diderot effectively ruins, so to speak, classical literary painting, because it reveals that the theory of ekphrasis that binds the representation of nature and objects to history in order to create a narrative scene, is riven at its descriptive core. He ruins the identity of language and image that underwrites the genetic understanding of description at the core of classical aesthetics —and the Horatian analogy of *ut picture poiesis* in which humanism had long expressed it. This is because only if classicism understands ekphrasis as an account of the process of a work's production—invention, composition, expression, etc.—can it sustain the latter's prescriptive and systematic aesthetics and the possibility of perfectibility at the heart of a classical theory of style (On this, the literature is vast. See, for example, Lee 1967). Diderot's ekphrasis, by contrast, makes the reader "see" the work in his or her mind's eye as a unified, simultaneous image, yet the virtual repetition of such an act of seeing is neither systematic nor genetic. It is mimetic, aesthetic, and fragmentary. At the same time, Diderot's account of Casanova's painting clearly marks its own limits as an aesthetic representation of the work. Ultimately, critical description is language that *tells* the reader about the visual work of art. It is unable to virtually mediate the aesthetic experience of the Salon and its public because it is unable to repeat the work in its simultaneity and totality. Description may call up the image of the work in the reader's mind and metaphorically transport the latter to the Salon, but such a representation is never a single, complete, and perfect aesthetic object that can embody an ideal of beauty (even if such an ideal, it should be noted, is none other than the mimetic, realistic description of the world). Description remains a fundamentally sequential, analytic, and prosaic process that can convey what has been seen part by part, detail by detail, aspect by aspect, without the hope of ever producing a total image. The aesthetic, here, implies the fragmentation of the work, not its realization as an index of history, a moment of perfection.

Diderot thus deploys the aesthetic and pictorial powers of description, but he does so less to achieve a classical perfection than to suspend the prescriptive mode of classical aesthetics and the dream of a historical contemporaneity that depends on the possibility of such a perfection. His reader, a virtual one who is never present at the Salon, is thus a public only insofar as his critical judgment is suspended rather than constituted in and by description. One might say, then, that the aesthetic mediation of art through critical description becomes a reflection on the limits of such a mediation, whether one is speaking about the classical present of the works at the Louvre Salon or the historical past of Hellenism. Consequently, the possibility of art arises here not in the repetition of the work but rather in the absence of the ideal as an object of critical description and elevation.

This is clearly the case in the celebrated set pieces that Diderot devotes to Jean-Baptiste Greuze, J.-H. Fragonard, and others in the *Salon de 1765*, where, in each instance, he separates the task of describing the scene from that of describing the formal and technical realization of the scene, its "faire." In his account of Fragonard's *The Grand Priest Corésus sacrifices himself to save Calirhoé* in the *Salon de 1765*, which he writes as a fictional dialogue between himself and Grimm and a humorous rewriting of Plato's allegory of the cave, Diderot claims to have dreamt that he had seen the events depicted in the painting on what can only be described as a cinematic screen visible in the cave (see Bonnet 1995). Moreover, he insists at the outset that he cannot talk about the painting, which won the Academy's prize that year at the Salon, because, presumably, he has not seen it: "It is impossible for me to talk to you about this painting; you know that it was no longer at the Salon when the incredible stir it created summoned me there" (Bonnet 1995, 141). Yet immediately after insisting on this impossibility, he goes on to give an account not only of the heroic and tragic moment of noble self-sacrifice that Fragonard had chosen according to the principles of classical history painting, but also of the events leading up to it.[5]

[5]Grimm confirms that, in fact, Diderot first elaborated his *rêve* standing in front of the painting. See Lojkine's (2007, 351) citation of Grimm.

Under the sign of the Platonic allegory, we are given to read a description not supported by an act of seeing. Instead, "Diderot" recounts the events in the scene leading up to the young priest's self-sacrifice based on a dream, while "Grimm" describes the painting's formal qualities based on his visit to the Louvre. In thus separating the narrative and descriptive modes, Diderot clearly implies that the unity necessary to the classical ideal and its sublime moment of exemplary action can never be more than a "dream" recounted and designated in a description. In fact, he makes an ironic allusion to the French classical sublime in his account of the cave: "In the midst of this tumult . . . I heard the god, or perhaps the subaltern knave behind the canvas say: 'She must die, or another must die in her place'" (Lojkine 2007, 143, translation modified). In this ironic allusion, Diderot is referring to a famous line from Pierre Corneille's *Horaces* that had come to exemplify the French classical sublime. It is a line in which an aging father calls for his disgraced son's death: "qu'il mourût" ("may he die"). By suggesting that it may instead be a moment of cheap, mechanical artifice, a deception, Diderot casts cold water on the aesthetic simultaneity and intensity of emotion presumably realized in sublime poetic verse.

In this way, Diderot clearly deflates both Winckelmann's vision of critical description as a means for the "sublime" repetition of antiquity and the French classical ideal of the exemplary action and moment of history, which represented the pinnacle of the Academy's hierarchy of the arts and, by extension, the basis of a classical vision of contemporaneity and of a historical present sustained and reproduced through the critical mediation of artistic production and public taste. In fact, as we have already seen, if the *Salon de 1765* mocks the possibility of a sublime critical description, the *Salon de 1767* systematically rejects the possibility that such description can serve as a medium for history, the return of Hellenism. Moreover, the famous "Promenade of Vernet," in which Diderot narrates a country outing that takes the reader through seven paintings by Joseph Vernet, is not merely intended to translate paintings into literature or vice versa. Rather, precisely because Winckelmann's Hellenism was founded on the idea that Greece was a historical realization of the ideal of natural beauty—a product of climate—Diderot takes up Vernet's landscape paintings as seven "sites" of history rather than of a pastoral ideal of an eternal and unchanging natural beauty and climate. He begins with a landscape that promises natural beauty, but by the seventh site, Diderot confronts us with the historical reality of time as a force of fragmentation rather than continuity. Here again, a complete exposition of the movement of Diderot's text requires far more room than I have here, but one can begin to gain a sense of how Diderot interprets landscape painting as the locus of history rather than of natural beauty and climate by considering the seventh and last "site" which depicts a scene of shipwreck, death, and ruin: "The flames from the ship illuminated the surrounding area, and the inhabitants of the region had been drawn to the shore and the rocks by this terrible spectacle, from which they averted their eyes" (Diderot 1995a, 2.68).

The stark difference between Diderot's understanding of painting as a fragmentary expression of history and Winckelmann's neoclassical historicism should be clear. Whereas, for Winckelmann, ruins are a site for an act of critical description that enables the rebirth of antiquity, here, the presumed unity and perfection of the past as a unified moment is clearly presented as a critical *fiction*, an effect of description imposed upon the broken fragments and shards of a historical world that is never unified or self-same. Vernet's landscapes are "natural histories" that challenge Winckelmann's historicism by demonstrating the way in which the historicity of art is a function of its critical description; paradoxically, therefore, the Promenade refuses the elevation of aesthetic experience into a medium of historical representation or repetition, precisely because landscape registers a historicity that escapes representation, that leaves nothing but fragments and ruins. Description implies the decomposition of the unity of the work or the object through sober and precise observation, a decomposition that itself allegorizes the historical fragmentation of the works of the past, their ruin, in time. Not by accident, when Diderot arrives at the work of the ruin painter Hubert Robert later in the *Salon de 1767*, it is, in fact, such a "poétique des ruines" that he will set out to sketch. In his account of Vernet, nature's beauty is already an expression of the fragment. The six sites of his "Promenade," therefore, ought to be seen as laying out, one after another, a description governed not by simultaneity but rather by the succession that characterizes linguistic discourse. History in art is the fictional domain in which objects are made to appear one at a time like words on a page or paintings arranged on a wall.

This is counterintuitive. We are accustomed to think of history as a succession of simultaneities, and we tend to believe that the aesthetic experience provided by works of visual art establishes, maintains, and represents the unity of a historical moment, whether such a moment is a distant past, the present of the Enlightenment public sphere, or our own era of "contemporary" art. The "aesthetic tribunal" that Chartier invokes as the actually existing sphere of Enlightenment is thus, for Diderot, not the aesthetic production of modernity as a present visible and knowable to itself, but rather a process of critical decomposition and analysis in which the idea of history embodied by both history and genre painting is revealed as the fiction of a historical moment modeled on the simultaneity and unity of the visual image. Critical description, in Diderot's *Salons*, is the analysis and decomposition of the image of history as a moment, a past possessing the unity and anatomy of a work.

In contrast to Hardouin-Mansart's dream of a classical public sustaining a classical art, then, Diderot's public is constituted in the act of reading and writing in which the "dream" of the classical is recognized as an ideal projected by the very movement of description in both the visual work of art and its criticism. Paradoxically, however, such a vision of history should be seen neither as depriving aesthetic experience and style of a historical role nor certainly as a return to an Aristotelian vision of style as persuasion. The sober critical style Diderot announces in the introduction to the *Salon de 1767* as a critical analogue of the ruin and the fragment, that is, of prosaic description, might rather be understood as the realization of a genuinely historical style, provided however, that by such a style one pretends neither to see art as the representation of a historical moment nor as an event of history. Rather than offering historical determination, critical description constitutes a historical present as the perpetually open possibility of further description, and therefore, of a future still-to-be constituted public and modernity. It is this opening of the space and possibility of the future—an *à venir* to use a phrase coined by Jacques Derrida—that Diderot's conception of critical description aims to secure as the genuine historical task of art and of a modern understanding of style.

References

Aristotle. 1941. *Rhetorica (Rhetoric)*. In *The Basic Works of Aristotle*. Edited by Richard McKeon. Chicago: University of Chicago Press, 1325–454.

Barbe, Jean-Paul and Jackie Pigeaud, eds. 1995. *Winckelmann et le retour à l'antique, Actes des entretiens de La Garenne-Lemot I, 9–12 juin 1994*. Nantes: Université de Nantes.

Baudelaire, Charles. 1995. *The Painter of Modern Life and Other Essays*. Translated by Jonathan Mayne. London: Phaidon Press.

Beaujour, Michel. 1981. "Some Paradoxes of Description," in *Yale French Studies* 61: 27–59.

Benjamin, Walter. 2006. *Selected Writings*, vol. 4. Cambridge, MA: Harvard University Press.

Binoche, Bertrand, ed. 2004. *L'Homme perfectible*. Paris: Champ Vallon.

Bonnet, Jean-Claude. 1995. "Diderot a inventé le cinema." In *Recherches sur Diderot et l'Encyclopédie*, vol. 18, 27–33.

Bukdahl, Else-Marie. "Introduction." In Diderot. 1984b. *Salon de 1765*, edited by Else Marie Bukdahl and Annette Lorenceau, 3–11. Paris: Hermann.

Chartier, Roger. 1991. *The Cultural Origins of the French Revolution*. Translated by Lydia G. Cochrane. Durham, NC: Duke University Press.

Chouillet, Jacques. 1973. *La formation des idées esthétiques de Diderot, 1745–1763*. Paris: Armand Colin.

Crow, Thomas. 1985. *Painters and Public Life in Eighteenth Century France*. New Haven: Yale University Press.

—. 1995. "Introduction." In *Diderot on Art*, vol. 1, translated by James Goodman, ix–xx. New Haven: Yale University Press.

Décultot, Élisabeth. 2000. *Johann Joachim Winckelmann: enquête sur la genèse de l'histoire de l'art*. Paris: Presses Universitaires Françaises.

Diderot, Denis. 1984a. *Essais sur la peinture; Salons de 1759, 1761, 1763*. Edited by Gita May and Jacques Chouillet. Paris: Hermann.

—. 1984b. *Salon de 1765*. Edited by Else Marie Bukdahl and Annette Lorenceau. Paris: Hermann.

—. 1995a. *Diderot on Art*. Translated by James Goodman. 2 vols. New Haven: Yale University Press.

—. 1995b. *Ruines et paysages: Salon de 1767*. Edited by Else Marie Bukdahl, Michel Delon, and Annette Lorenceau. Paris: Hermann.

Ferris, David. 2000. *Silent Urns: Romanticism, Hellenism, Modernity*. Stanford: Stanford University Press.

Fried, Michael. 1980. *Absorption and Theatricality: Painting and Beholder in the Age of Diderot*. Chicago: University of Chicago Press.

Gombrich, Ernst. 1998. "Style." In *The Art of Art History*, edited by Donald Preziosi, 150–63. Oxford: Oxford University Press.

Greenberg, Clement. 1961. *Art and Culture*. Boston: Beacon Press.

Hartog, François. 2005. *Anciens, modernes, sauvages*. Paris: Galaade.

Lee, Rensselaer. 1967. *Ut Pictura Poiesis: The Humanistic Theory of Painting*. New York: W. W. Norton.

Lojkine, Stéphane. 2007. *L'Œil révolté: les Salons de Diderot*. Paris: Actes Sud.

Potts, Alex. 1982. "Winckelmann's Construction of History." *Art History* 5(4): 377–407.

—. 1994. *Flesh and the Ideal: Winckelmann and the Origins of Art History*. New Haven: Yale University Press.

Preziosi, Donald, ed. 1998. *The Art of Art History*. Oxford: Oxford University Press.

Seznec, Jean. 1959. *Essais sur Diderot et l'antiquité*. Oxford: Oxford University Press.

Trousson, Raymond, ed. 1997. *Images de Diderot en France: 1784–1913*. Paris: Honoré Champion.

Voltaire. 1957. *Œuvres historiques*. Edited by René Pomeau. Paris: Gallimard.

Winckelmann, Johann Joachim. 1934. *Geschichte der Kunst des Altertums*. Vienna: Phaidon.

—. 1987. *Reflections on the Imitation of Greek Works in Painting and Sculpture*. LaSalle, IL: Open Court.

—. 2006a. *De la description*. Edited and translated by Élisabeth Décultot. Paris: Editions Macula.

—. 2006b. *History of the Art of Antiquity*. Translated by Harry Francis Mallgrave. Los Angeles: Getty Research Institute.

5

Nietzsche, style, body

Douglas Burnham

Style in its relationship to *underlying* content or meaning is a problem that has for centuries been bound up with discussions of mind and body and, ultimately, truth and falsehood also. Nietzsche, too, casts his treatments of style in this mould—but as we shall see, in a way that is more complex and interesting than it at first appears.[1] There seem to be two opposed ways of evaluating the relationships among style, content, mind, and body.

Either mind is the proper possessor of content, concept, meaning, true form, substance, communication, or essence; and body is the contingent, the obscuring, accidental form, mere appearance or surface, mere style. For just the most famous examples, we find the discussions of poetic drama in the *Ion* or in the *Republic*, where the artist captures only the apparent materiality of something, not its inner idea—and, moreover, does so in a way as to appeal to and excite the bodily passions. Again, see *Poetics* where Aristotle comments that "the writings of Herodotus could be put into verse" without that altering its true historical substance (1987, 51a36ff.). Neither of these examples is as clear-cut as one might like, though. For Plato is one of philosophy's most consummate stylists, and the *manner* in which he writes itself self-consciously

[1]Many thanks to Dr Melanie Ebdon and Dr Martin Jesinghausen with whom I have previously collaborated on the topic of Nietzsche. In forging ahead on my own, I of course make myself fully responsible for anything daft (see Burnham and Ebdon 2009; Burnham and Jesinghausen 2010a; Burnham and Jesinghausen 2010b).

bears philosophical *meaning*; while Aristotle, in the same text, will discuss style in much less trivial ways as at the heart of communication and poetic effectiveness. Both of these complicating features (style as performance, style as effective communication) will also turn up later and aide us in understanding Nietzsche's concept of style.

Or mind is a secondary phenomenon, an echo or herald of the body, falsely elevated above and distinguished from body; and thus style is the direct expression of the living body and indeed is materially continuous with body. Style is therefore prior to content in the sense that content is a spiritualization, or rendering abstract, of style or that (body, world) that is most immediately related to style. This second alternative has brought us closer to Nietzsche, to be sure. However, just as there were complications with the accounts of Plato and Aristotle above, so will there be with Nietzsche. The purpose of this paper is to explicate the nature and function of the concept of style in Nietzsche's work and how it develops from early to later work. This chapter will have three parts: first, a discussion of Nietzsche's treatment of life and style in the period of *The Birth of Tragedy* and *Untimely Meditations* (i.e. in the early 1870s); second, a focus on the particular concept of will to power, which is developed in the late 1870s and early 1880s, and how this development complicates and enriches the earlier treatment; third, a narrowing down of the focus to a small handful of themes—masks, wandering, and parody—which will illustrate the mature account of style.

The problem of style in early Nietzsche

"On Truth and Lying in an Extra-Moral Sense" (Nietzsche 1999c) is the obvious place to start—although, as we shall see, also misleading. Here, Nietzsche describes language as a constant falling away, through forgotten metaphor (and through abstraction which, Nietzsche claims here, is also metaphor) from the affection-states of the living body. Although, to be sure, Schopenhauer's metaphysics hovers nearby, we can approach this description of body and language as a straight-forward materialist realism. These affection-states or stimuli are the most immediate objectification of the will; higher level objectifications such as concepts or words originate in and only carry truth value *through* these states (they may have other values, such as the communicative, classificatory, and above all pragmatic). The possibility of a more fundamental access to truth lies in the reactivation of metaphor so as to reverse its effects; this can happen in poetry or, above all, in musical drama. At a certain point, Nietzsche's general name for this possibility is style. The proper function of style is the reconnection of language with the body and, ultimately, with the Will.

In 1873, in notes for the first *Untimely Meditation*, which is a rather poorly judged attack on David Strauss, Nietzsche writes of Strauss and those who praise him: "They relate (*verhalten*) to style the same way they relate to art; they relate to art the same way they relate to life; namely: commonly, superficially, weakly (*gemein, oberflächlich, weichlich*)" (1988, VII.27.16; Nietzsche 1999d, 160, translation modified). This is a complex, extended analogy. Obviously important for our purposes is the implied link between style and art: style evidently occupies something like the same role within culture as art. However, still more important here is the ground of the whole analogy in a conception of life. What is at stake in the Straussian "relation" to style or art (and unfortunately we cannot pursue exactly what Nietzsche believes this is) is a similarly "common" (implying vulgar or base), meek or superficial relation to life. This immediately raises the question of what it could mean to have a "relation" to life. Can we infer that the Straussians are themselves, as types of human life or as living beings, common, superficial, and weak? Or does Nietzsche mean to characterize how they understand or treat life, whether in themselves, in others, as a whole, or as a concept? Or—and this is the most attractive option—perhaps Nietzsche means *both* of these? One of the things it means to be alive is to have a relation to life. Both of the above alternatives are modes of life's "expression." "Culture," Nietzsche thus writes in the first *Untimely Meditation*, "is, above all, unity of artistic style in all the expressions of the life of a people" (1997, I.1.5).

Within the contemporary "pseudo-culture of the cultured philistine" style is "the absence of anything offensive—*but anything truly productive is offensive*" (Nietzsche 1997, I.11.49). "Offensive," we can presume, not just because it violates the established norms, but because it does so from out of a different and opposed mode of life and relation to life. "With instinctive unanimity, they [the Straussians] hate all *firmitas* because it bears witness to a healthiness quite different from theirs" (I.11.52). Thus they are forced to "invert the nature and names of things" (I.11.53). The restoration of a proper relation to style will require a revolution within the organic sphere. Style manifests the living body's health (or disease), a subclass of a people's health or disease. Again, style is access to the inner nature of this body and of this health. In this idea of inversion (anticipated already in Socrates' inversion of the relation between consciousness and instinct), however, should we hear a simple turning upside down (Nietzsche 1999a, 13.65–6)? Or, perhaps, we should hear an anticipation of the more complex analysis of the inter-relation of apparent oppositions (as in the first few sections of *Beyond Good and Evil*)?

That question applies most generally to the turning upside down of the content/style distinction with which we began. This simple inversion of the traditional priority of content over style underestimates the complexity of Nietzsche's position. The note "On Truth and Lying" (1999c) may have been an obvious place to start, but perhaps it is a little too obvious. The note combines a sophisticated treatment of the general functions or games of language with a remarkably crass linear naturalism (words are metaphoric displacements of bodily states) in the treatment of semantics and virtually no account of syntax at all (see Derrida 1982). The latter is corrected to some degree in "The Dionysiac World-View" (1999b—another unpublished note from the period) and in the treatment of melodic line, harmony, and dissonance in *The Birth of Tragedy*. Here, we will not have opportunity to discuss problems of syntax at all, although there is an important analogy with the themes of masks and wandering to which we will turn in the last part of this chapter. We shall confine ourselves to correcting the former simplification (the naturalism of semantics); this requires also that we look to *The Birth of Tragedy*.

The mind-body dualism that seems replicated in "On Truth and Lying" leads many readers of *The Birth of Tragedy* to the mistake of confusing Apollo and Socrates, that is, to interpret Nietzsche as asserting that Socratism is a diseased or degenerate Apolline drive. The result of this mistake is an overly Hegelian reading of Nietzsche's early philosophy (Heidegger is among the most prominent interpreters who appear to fall into this trap. See Heidegger 1981). On such a reading, tragedy is viewed as a synthesis of two antithetical art drives, while in Socratism, this dialectical logic has become constipated, incapable of reaching resolution. Nietzsche himself employs something like this misreading strategically, as a hyperbolic correction of the early text, in the "Attempt at Self-Criticism," which is a new "preface" to *The Birth of Tragedy* written for the 1886 edition. A main point of Nietzsche's self-critique is that in those youthful days he was not yet fully equipped to follow the imperatives of the instinctive maenadic voice of the Dionysiac that had already gripped him and was trying to speak through him (1999a, 1.3). Thus, he tries to over-correct the more balanced treatment of the original book. To be sure, Nietzsche's position changed in part because he recognized that the early configuration of drives *resembled* the Hegelian model. But as we will see, the "Attempt" ignores the fact that Nietzsche's account in *The Birth of Tragedy* already surpasses the simple dualisms of which its author accuses it; and moreover, the preface exaggerates by playing down the productive possibilities of *The Birth of Tragedy*'s complex juggling of positions.

Let us try to restore the balance from within *The Birth of Tragedy*. Nietzsche does discuss what happens if the Apolline does not make clear its appearance-status: the "effect" is "pathological" (1999a, 1.16). But that is quite different from an assertion that the Apolline *itself* (as opposed to its effect) is ever pathological—which is what this misreading of the book would require him to assert. Thus, we should not be surprised when Nietzsche writes unequivocally that Socrates is "an altogether newborn daemon" (1999a, 12.60). He even considers just this point significant enough to include it in his brief summary of the book written much later in 1885–6, and it is alluded to again in the corresponding discussion in *Ecce Homo* (1987, XII.2.110; 2003, 80–2). Socratism, then, is a *third* cultural drive. It is neither Apolline, Dionysiac, nor a modification of either, one that gradually takes hold of Greek sensibility from Sophocles onwards. The defining feature of Apollo, Nietzsche makes clear in the early sections, is appearance that knows itself as appearance (thus the famous example of the dream that wishes to carry on dreaming). The Apolline is a cultural drive to create forms, understanding these forms *both* as beautiful, powerful, effective, *and* as objectifications of, and constituted from out of, the underlying fluid surge of will. Perhaps we should say that the

Apolline is a phenomenological rather than a naïve natural attitude (see Sallis 1991). The defining feature of the Socratic drive, however, is that it is intrinsically incapable of such an attitude; it defines itself and its world in a way as to render this awareness rigorously impossible. Here, we claim that the eruption of Socrates into philosophical culture is the historically novel introduction of the modern distinction between mind and body. Prior to this advent, the Apolline could not be understood either as mere matter masking a fundamental truth, nor a "false content" which would interfere with the Dionysiac mode of life. Instead, the Apolline is the *means by which* the Dionysiac can become culture. It follows that, if we try to understand the concept of style by employing the mind-body distinction—even as an analogy—then this understanding must fail with respect to the pre-Socratic notion of style that Nietzsche pursues in *The Birth of Tragedy*. Thus also, this pre-Socratic notion will evade the overly simplistic description of semantics discussed above and outlined in "On Truth and Lying." In particular, the naturalism that posits for every semantic unit an underlying truth at the level of bodily affect gives way to a poetics (or a music) which can reactivate metaphors, allowing them to remain language while (knowingly, ironically) "speaking" in a transformative manner of the Dionysiac, where the latter is no more to be identified with a set of bodily affects than with an individual human being.

Now, all drives are intrinsically relational (i.e. in struggle *vis a vis* other drives, or obstacles). However, the Socratic drive is both endlessly optimistic (it recognizes no obstacle to itself) and also demands that it be recognized as universal (it recognizes no other drives—indeed, not even recognizing itself as a drive and its products as cultural forms). Although incapable of internalizing the fact, Socratism as a drive nevertheless remains relational, and in fact must work with respect to the materials (i.e. the cultural forms) at hand. Thus, Socratic culture will comprise a *misinterpretation* of the existing metaphysics of culture. So, Dionysus-like cultural forms are interpreted simply as emotion; Apollo-like cultural forms are interpreted as logic. Historically, Nietzsche argues, both these original art drives are subsequently either marginalized or repressed. Dionysus becomes the property of cults. Apollo's fate is worse: the Apolline drive suffers a kind of living death, only allowed to appear if it can successfully masquerade itself as something else. Nietzsche's metaphor for this is particularly striking.

Under conditions of the dominance of Socratism, the Apolline has *sich verpuppt*, "it cocoons itself away" (1999a, 14.69). The cocoon is a shield of Apollo, and a refuge in the face of Socratic culture—it is womb, coffin, fortress, disguise. Mention of the Apolline then virtually disappears from the text of *The Birth of Tragedy* until near the end as, encased, Apollo prepares himself for a future transfiguration, for an emergence under conditions of modernity. The resurgence of the Dionysiac drive (described at the end of the book) does not in turn rescue Apollo, but rather is conditional upon the latter, too, having (first or already) emerged from its long pupation. Thus, in the last section of *The Birth of Tragedy*, Nietzsche argues that if in the present day we are seeing in the works of Wagner a rebirth of tragic culture, then "Apollo, too, must already have descended amongst us, concealed in a cloud" (1999a, 25.116). The descent from clouds is an extraordinary triple allusion: first to the *deus ex machina*—a plot and stage contrivance that Nietzsche had already criticized Euripides for employing; second to Aristophanes' play, which lampoons Socrates; and finally to the emergence of Apollo from the cocoon. The modern triumph over modernity that Nietzsche predicts, then, is the reincorporation of the Socratic drive into productive and self-knowing relations with the Greek art drives. Thus, earlier, Nietzsche prophesied the figures of the "music-making Socrates," or science realizing itself as art (1999a, 15.75). This would be Apollo absorbing and transforming a de-universalized scientific culture (as in the early Greek period it absorbed myth), becoming thereby the symbolic means of Dionysiac expression while also not being other than what it is (i.e. still being in some sense "science").

Nietzsche makes the point nicely in a note from late 1874. What is important here is to listen to the voice in which he is writing. It is a mock-naïve voice, chiding itself: "how can one possibly consider style and the manner of presentation to be so important! It is really only a matter of making oneself understood." He then continues, as if this voice were partially reconsidering its position: "But, admittedly, that is no easy matter, and it is very important. Just think (what) a complex creature the human being is: how infinitely difficult for him to truly *ex*press himself! Most human beings remain trapped inside themselves and cannot get out" (1988, VII.37.8; 1999d, 385–6). This miniature drama *enacts* the point. We have a contrast between an individual form of life and the mode of language available to it. The latter serves the current communal mode of life and its health, reducing in the process of communication all modes of life to the one. Following the linear naturalism model—and the direction the ironic, naïve voice seems to be indicating—might the solution be a private language for distinctive affective states? But that would be neither expression nor even language. Style is more important than content, but not because of a simple inversion of the traditional content/style valuation. Rather, style designates that aspect of language in use whereby language can be re-enchanted, so that its expressive possibilities—and especially its possibility of *changing something* in an intersubjective setting—exceed its strict semantic possibilities.

A proper understanding of the relationship between the Apolline and the Socratic, for our purposes, makes clear that the account of style even at this early stage of Nietzsche is more complicated than a simple reversal of the traditional account. The reciprocal dependence of the Apolline and Dionysiac, then, cannot be mapped straightforwardly onto the relation of style and content, or mind and body. That dependence "names," but above all tries to *bring about*, a mode of human life which, under specific historical conditions (which include a range of discursive practices), is alienated neither from becoming nor from language, history, or culture. The Apolline names the "detour" that is essential to the Dionysiac. The *essential detour*—this is for Nietzsche the basic problem of style and, indeed, of philosophy.

The exteriority of will to power

Five years later in the late 1870s, things have changed—although, as we shall see, the conclusions remain surprisingly similar. The temptation to a materialist realism, and to what we called a linear naturalism of language, has passed. Will to power, even if understood as a grounding metaphysical claim, is an intrinsically evasive ground. That is, there is no perspective-neutral position from which such a claim could be inspected, or demonstrated true. The delightful paradox is that it could be a metaphysically grounding claim only for a certain form of life, that form of life whose instincts and spiritualizations are aligned to the nature of the will to power and, for this reason, is also most aware of the perspectival nature of its claims. Similarly, there is now no simple recourse to the truth of the body (its actual, material affective stimulation). Our relationship to the real is mediated "all the way down," so to speak, because the real itself is always already relational (it is will to power). All this is well known, and any detailed explication of the will to power is far beyond the scope of this chapter. Instead, we will focus down onto the notion of style. What has not changed in later Nietzsche is the importance of style, its expressivity of the health and development of life, and its significance for understanding the task that is cultural production and especially philosophy.

Relationality gives us our clue. This is a theme already apparent in the period of *The Birth of Tragedy*, particularly as we saw in the notion of drive. Drives always exist relationally, in "contest" with other drives. The will to power offers a much more thorough-going treatment of relationality, and specifically brings into play the structure of what we shall call, following Kant, "exteriority." The genesis of this notion of exteriority lies in Kant's "Transcendental Aesthetic" and, again, in the second part of *The Critique of Judgement* (Kant 2000, B66–9; 1998, 408–9; see also Burnham 2004, especially chapters 2 and 3). Another important antecedent is in eighteenth- and nineteenth-century attempts to think about matter, and then also space and time, in terms of what would later be called "fields"; of particular importance for Nietzsche was Boscovich (see, for example, Whitlock 1996). In Nietzsche's own career the point of genesis is very early: we have extended notes for a dissertation (dating from the late 1860s) on the organism as exterior form, which is based precisely on those sections of the third *Critique;* and, moreover, the concept is evident in the famously dense "time-atom" fragment from 1874 (Nietzsche 1999d, 147–51). However, it is only later with the will to power that Nietzsche finds a way to make the structure of exteriority the fundamental principle of his thought. So, what is meant by "exteriority"?

In Kant, intuitions are characterized by being *exterior*, in contrast to concepts that are *interior*. The distinction has to do with constitution. As a presentation, a concept may enter into relations with and be affected by other concepts, but it always has a prior core content; similarly, its objects are understood as entities that exist prior to their relations (as, for example, substances). Intuitions are presentations that are originally "nothing but relations" (Kant 2000, B66). Nor can relations themselves be considered as types of objects, that is, as interiors (the relation of cause to effect, for example). The domain of intuition is a relational field or a continuity of situation that is prior to the constitution of *things* (of any type) that are in relation; determination is always from the *outside* of any *inside*.

For Nietzsche, however, this is not merely a formal structure, for it describes the dynamics of the will to power. Will to power is a striving to express power. It should not be understood as a substantial or material interior that seeks "power," moving from out of itself. Nor again can the relation be hypostatized as if it could be isolated and studied. For example, early Nietzsche appears to fall into such a trap in using the terms "virtue" or "drive." To be sure, for the earlier Nietzsche the drive is disembodied. Sophocles qua individual entity does not *have* a drive, rather, the drive operates through him, and to that extent it is a pure active relation and not a thing. Nevertheless, a drive has an identity that it *brings to* a situation. By contrast, the "identity" or "content" of the will to power at any point (what it strives to express in having power) is constituted by its position with the field. For example, at *Zarathustra* (Nietzsche 2005b) "On the Thousand and One Goals," the virtues celebrated by a historically located people are a product of history, geography, climate, and so forth. Neither the people nor the virtues preexist the situation, and it follows that such virtues not only are different from those esteemed by their neighbors, but positively make no sense to them. (Thus, as we said above, will to power is an "intrinsically evasive" ground.) A transcendent virtue would be one that posits itself as an interior and is thus indifferent to situation; a transcendent account of virtue would be one that is able to understand or evaluate virtue separately from situation (and is thus distinguished from genealogy). Accordingly, at *Zarathustra*, "On the Three Evils," we get a careful distinction between, on the one hand, the impossible, transcendent "weighing of the world" in the dream sequence—which would be to arrive at laws of the constitution of virtues that were akin to mathematical laws of nature—and, on the other, a weighing that is carried out only "humanly well" (2005b, III.10.1.163).

Weighing "humanly well" means to explicate as generally as possible, from within situations, the values that arise out of situations. For example, at *Genealogy of Morality*, Nietzsche analyzes the words for good and evil in various languages; he finds that they all come back to "the same conceptual transformation" (1998, I.4.12). Yet, this "rule" is stated only two sections after Nietzsche accused the "historians of morality" of thinking "essentially ahistorically" by anachronistically projecting back their contemporary principle of utility. The rule of transformation would thus fall into the same trap, unless we notice that Nietzsche introduces it as a "quiet problem" which "addresses itself selectively to but a few ears"—Nietzsche's more historical history is no longer anything like an objective history (1998, I.5.13). So, weighing "humanly well" means two things. First, it means the activity of evaluating and reevaluating, that explication from within that we suggested above. But second, it means that such an evaluation is necessary—that is, it itself is a vital tool for the expression of will to power and the transformation of modes of life. "Spirit," Nietzsche writes, "is the life that itself cuts into life" (2005b, II.8.90); and thus "experimenting with knowledge it [the body] elevates itself" (2005b, I.22.2.67). It is important for us to notice that this structure by which objectifications of the will to power transform themselves (and others) by way of the detour of the spiritual is very similar to the "essential detour" structure that we observed in the early Nietzsche.

The problem of expression which we discussed above with respect to the 1874 note has been absolutely generalized. No longer do we have a trapped, minimal Cartesian subject, seeking expression but frustrated by a common language. Nor, correspondingly, do we have a listener or reader who must see through the compromised expression to the absolute particularity of the expressed. The real of the body of the speaking (or listening or reading) subject, is constituted from out of its exteriority. For example, the *very first thing* Zarathustra says upon his descent from the mountains is immediately subjected to retraction or modification, as the teacher is seen in the process of becoming a teacher (Nietzsche 2003b, Prologue.2.10). Indeed, the self is exterior even to itself. Thus, in *Zarathustra*, Nietzsche replaces the language of the subject pole with a host of voices in interior dialogues and dramas (e.g. in the sections called "On Friendship," "The Stillest Hour," or the two Dance Songs [II.10 and III.15]). These dramas are either of self-overcoming (in which case, if we can talk about the identity of the self at all, then that identity lies outside of itself) or resistance to self-overcoming (identity lies in the negation of, or presumptive transcendence to, that which lies outside of itself). Will to power, conceived of as the prior relation of expression, means that expression *constitutes the expressed*, for both the speaker and the listener. What is said, and how, are aspects that arise from the situated drama of the will to power. Likewise, reading constitutes the reader, in the sense that the fundamental function of language is not to deliver this or that content, but to overcome (or, perhaps, to preserve) a mode of life: "whoever writes with blood wants to be learnt by heart" (2003b, I.7.32). What Zarathustra brings down the mountain, then, is not a teaching, not even a teacher, but a health: a mode of life that is aligned to will to power and thus does not react against exteriority or becoming. Summing up this account, Nietzsche writes: "A philosopher: this is a person who constantly experiences, sees, hears, suspects, hopes, and dreams extraordinary things; who is struck by his own thoughts as if from outside, from above and below, as if by *his* type of events and lightning bolts" (2002, 292.174).

Given this, though, what happens to Nietzsche's concept of style?

Parodies, masks, wanderings

For Nietzsche in his earlier period, style is what we called above the "essential detour." This means several things. First, style has a more immediate connection to a mode of life and ultimately to the will to power than any concept or other shared cultural form. Second, however, it means that style does not entail that it is in itself a more fundamental or truthful type of *content*. This is because style is not in simple opposition to content, and thus also does not fall neatly into associated distinctions such as body and mind. We countered the temptation to read early Nietzsche in this way by explicating a more viable interpretation of the Apolline function in *The Birth of Tragedy*. Third, instead, style designates the possibility of a *re-enchantment* of language so as to realize its expressive possibilities and above all its possibilities for the transformation of life forms. Nietzsche employs the reciprocal dependence of Apollo and Dionysus to understand this re-enchantment.

Now, elsewhere, Martin Jesinghausen and I argue that there is preserved for Apollo a vital role in later Nietzsche, since the will to power in language *does* achieve itself, momentarily, as the expressed (Burnham and Jesinghausen 2012). Or, more generally, the will to power as relation is an exteriority which has, as a necessary moment, the will to form. It must constantly achieve itself as an interiority (a form of life, cultural form, virtue, a speaking subject, the stillness of beauty, etc.), only to then surpass or destroy that form. For example, returning to *Zarathustra*, virtues are raised up as models for a people, but the full attainment of that virtue would also be to surpass it toward revolution or the constitution of a new people. In "The Way of the Creator," Nietzsche describes this play of creation and destruction with the dramatic rhetorical question: "What does he know of love who did not have to despise precisely what he loved!" (2005b, I.17.56). In later Nietzsche, then, the Apolline is a *moment of* the Dionysiac will to power. This is what Nietzsche signals at the end of *Beyond Good and Evil* in writing that Dionysus' "mastery includes an understanding of how to appear" (2002, 295.175). "Appearance" is the signature concept of Apolline, and it is seen here as a moment "included" in Dionysus. The fact that the Apolline is to be found in the later work gives us reason to suggest that Nietzsche's understanding of style also remains in its broad outline unchanged—although it certainly will be generalized and radicalized in a way consistent with the exteriority of will to power. We will pursue this generalization and radicalization by way of exploring the philosophical significance of three self-evidently Nietzschean styles.

It is difficult to miss the parodic elements in Nietzsche: mocking portraits or assumed voices of types and individuals. All forms of satire generally are of interest here, but parody has the additional feature of involving the production of an *other* voice and the style of that voice. It is significant, though, that Nietzsche's brand of parody does not assume a parod*ist*, behind the scenes writing the jokes and free to be transparently serious *with himself*. Rather, parody is for Nietzsche always in part self-parody. This in turn is only possible if one does not oneself have a fixed voice or style. The object of parody might be an aspect of Nietzsche (e.g. the scholar, the invalid), a past Nietzsche (the "positivist" Nietzsche of the mid-1870s is a common target, as is the Wagner-worshiper), a possible Nietzsche (the figure of the Shadow in *Zarathustra* might be interpreted as an anxiety about Nietzsche/Zarathustra's future). Thus the higher men in *Zarathustra* Book IV may be parodies of Schopenhauer, Wagner, and others, but are *also* parodies of Nietzsche. After all, some of the poems put into the mouth of the parodic figures there he considered among his best work, and planned to republish as part of *Dithyrambs of Dionysus*. Likewise, throughout the book, Zarathustra is not immune from parody or, more broadly, satire ("On Passing By" with its figure of "Zarathustra's Ape" is an obvious example, and the sexually naïve Zarathustra of "Young and Old Little Women" is certainly another). Likewise, Nietzsche's portrait of Wagner in *The Wagner Case* is also a kind of self-portrait. (In *Ecce Homo* he says this explicitly about "Wagner in Bayreuth," although of course that does not involve significant parody.) Now, Nietzsche is by no means the only literary figure who has fun at his own expense by portraying himself with voices or behaviors that archetypally belong to others; less common, however, is to conceive of self-parody as methodological necessity.

Not taking oneself too seriously is Nietzsche's description of a "lightness" that is counterpart to the "spirit of heaviness"—thus also the frequent images of dancing or flying. The "spirit of heaviness" variously embodies a range of anti-life cultural forms, such as religious asceticism, pessimism, nihilism, or philosophically significant affects such as pity, shame, or the sense of disgust that might arise from the thought of eternal recurrence. This lightness is a sign of health, broadly speaking, but it is also a *method*. The first methodological rationale behind self-parody is as a kind of antidote to anything that serves to prevent the ascent of life, which holds back or smothers life. But in order for that to be the case, there must be something intrinsically correct or at least inescapable about such life-denying modes of life; they must be a part of Nietzsche's thought rather than simply opposed to it. Otherwise, one could simply counteract such serious (but erroneous) positions with more seriousness—or at least the method behind parody would not require *self*-parody. Nihilism or pity cannot be simply idiotic, then, but must have a structural necessity. Nietzsche's thought includes these positions or affects because it is not itself a position but rather a drama of self-overcoming; self-parody is part of the constituting movement of this drama. Thus, the speaker and the object of self-parody here are neither "I" nor another. Rather, both emerge from a relation-between, a spiritualization of the fundamental dynamic of exteriority. That is, parody is an enactment of the constitution of I and other as subject positions or identities. The second methodological rationale, then, is that only through parody (and activities of expression like parody) does there come to be, even for Nietzsche, a content that can be called "Nietzsche," "Nietzsche's philosophy," or, for example, "Nietzsche's critique of Schopenhauer." Thus, in this surprising way, style as the essential detour still serves Nietzsche's early project of an authentic culture by being a mechanism of the constitution of form (especially, a culture or a people *as* a form— Zarathustra's "chosen people").

While parody appears primarily as a style or mode of writing, it is important that we broaden the notion of style away from conceiving it exclusively as a phenomenon of language. The wanderer, our next theme, requires this broadening, for it concerns how one lives one's life and relates to cultural or social situations. The wanderer carries considerable symbolic significance for Nietzsche, standing in among other things for his oft-professed untimeliness (the genuine critical distance he has from his milieu, even and especially when in the mode of mask he uses it against itself), and for his personal and professional life and stateless status. Wandering, we suggest, should be seen as a style of living or a style of thinking that might also be the meaning of such a life or thinking.

Zarathustra is a wanderer, of course; the first sentence of the Prologue tells us about how he left "his home and the lake of his home" (2005b, Prologue.1.9). When this opening section was first given at the end of the original edition of *The Gay Science*, Nietzsche names the lake (Lake Urmi), which gives definite content to the notion of "home." This in turn implies that at a certain point Zarathustra *started* to wander. But that name is deleted in *Thus Spoke Zarathustra*, indicating that the figure of Zarathustra does not *become* a wanderer, but is so from the beginning. Likewise, the narrative of the book has Zarathustra wandering from cave in the mountains to the flatlands, and back, several times. But by its nature, wandering cannot be a state of being, as if there were a transcendent subject that wandered through history and geography and indifferent to it all. We have already observed, in Part II above, that the first public sentence of Zarathustra is immediately retracted or modified. Wandering thus also designates what above we called the drama of self-overcoming, which is the primary "content" of Nietzsche's thought. This drama begins as the relationality of exteriority, and then realizes itself, always provisionally, as for example "being a teacher in this town," "with these disciples," or "on this ship." This wandering also comprises a symbolic attempt to catch up with oneself, or to become whole (the theme of wholeness is made explicit in "On Redemption"). For example, in the Prologue, Zarathustra's conscious insight about the dead tightrope dancer is some distance behind what his body *already knows*; or again, comically, in Part 4, section 9, where Zarathustra tries to run *away* from the Shadow, while also running *after* the Voluntary Beggar; or finally, the whole of the first half of Part 4 where Zarathustra scrambles all over "his" mountains looking for the one he believes to be in distress, not realizing that the call of distress is actually multiple. The notion of wandering is neatly encapsulated at the beginning of Part 3, section 7. Zarathustra is once again heading back to his cave, but does not, or can not, go there directly. Instead, he wanders "slowly" through "many peoples and towns" (2005b, III.7.152). Wandering, then, names a style of living or thinking that returns us to the idea of style as the "necessary detour"—it is a method of inhabiting a series of methods. Wandering, considered as a style of living and investigation, is the individual counterpart to Nietzsche's idea of the coordination of methods: "*All* sciences are henceforth to do preparatory work for the philosopher's task of the future" (1998, I.17.37).

Let us turn, finally, to the theme of masks. We are familiar with the sudden changes of color and attitude in Nietzsche's prose. Nietzsche is now the scholar, now the historian, anthropologist, philologist, psychologist, "Devil's Advocate," social commentator, confessor, visionary, nihilist, hyperbolic satirist, musicologist, now the jester. Again, there is not a central, coordinating voice—not even in his letters or notebooks, which keep up the strategy. One way of understanding such apparently uncoordinated diversity is the notion of "mask." A mask, in Nietzsche, is a historically specific discourse, method or role, employed perhaps as a disguise of one's true purpose, or as a means to an end, a mode of engagement with one's contemporaries, or a stage in a process of development. However, for Nietzsche, a mask is never simply put on deliberately—that is, it is not a fully conscious strategy or lucid deception belonging to a transcendent subject. Nor is the mask something that could simply be taken off—removing the mask would be removing oneself from historical conditions, again a transcendence. Instead, removing the mask means overcoming the situation within which the mask became necessary. Thus, it is neither strictly speaking a true nor a false appearance. In *Ecce Homo* Nietzsche writes: "It is clever of me to have been many things and to many places so I can become one thing,—can come to one thing. For a long time I even *had to* be a scholar" (2005a, 115). This "cleverness" is not the cleverness of calculation but rather the historical and cultural sensitivity that generates masks.

Beyond Good and Evil develops the idea of masks in several passages. Section 40, for example, begins "Whatever is profound loves masks" as if the mask were a choice, even a luxury, that protects the profound spirit from his or her milieu (2002, 40.39). However, as the analysis progresses, Nietzsche subsequently removes the idea of choice in favor of "instinct," then speaks of "necessity," and finally ends up with the involuntary: the masks grow, accreted from the outside, even if the "profound spirit" does not so desire. The mask, though, is not exclusively a phenomenon of language; rather, akin to our treatment of wandering above, we have to think about the mask of a style of investigation or even a style of living. To be sure, in such a mask there is not a total investment in the metaphysical implications of a method—for example, one can take on the role of philologist without also taking on the standard assumptions about subjectivity, knowledge, or history. In other words, one is not *simply* a philologist, but neither is one merely putting on an appearance. As *Beyond Good and Evil* winds to its close, Nietzsche elaborates further. Section 278 is a dialogue; the first voice questions the "wanderer" who is like a "sounding lead that has returned to the light"; the second voice responds by asking for "Another mask! A second mask!" Obviously, on one level, this repeats the notion of a mask as something voluntary and essentially defensive in nature; that is, something that is put on to protect one from the inquisitiveness of others. But notice that the wanderer here does not assume a mask, but requests one from the other; the mask comes from the outside. Moreover, he does not ask for a mask, but for *another* mask—it follows that the activity of plumbing the depths, and perhaps even being the wanderer, was *already a mask*. Far from just a withdrawal from the drama of overcoming, the desperate cry for another mask is a determination to carry on, and to do so in this or that style. Again, then, we have the idea of mask as positive (not merely defensive) method, one arising from out of the exterior historical situation and the discourses and attitudes that organize that situation, and one that intervenes in that situation in order to further a transformation. However necessary the mask is at a certain point, it also finds itself recognized as contingent, though only with respect to *other* masks that will have to arise in my continual becoming.

What, then, have we learned with this brief tour of some of Nietzsche's styles? First of all, there seemed to be good reason to extend the concept of style beyond a simple question of the use of language. This is a natural outgrowth of the concern with style as transformative practice. In the later Nietzsche, style refers to the "how" of a mode of life, insofar as it has a transformative aspect with respect to life. Writing style is just one, albeit important, aspect. Thus, as we discussed at the beginning of this chapter, for Nietzsche we can neither simply invert a traditional evaluation of the relationship of style and content or meaning (because a style of life is neither style nor content in a conventional sense), nor can we correlate it to the relationship to body and mind (because the evaluation of a style of life is rooted in body only insofar as it also takes the essential detour through spiritualizations: methods, philosophy, parodies, and masks).

Second, the will to power, understood as a dynamic structure of exteriority, entails that what we think of as content or meaning—for example, Zarathustra's teachings—are not given or even discovered, but coming to be within a relational situation. What we think of as style (e.g. parodic writing or the philological method considered as a mask) is no less a product of progressive constitution. Nevertheless, style does have a certain priority (though not a simple inversion, as we at first thought). This priority is again of the necessary detour. Earlier, we talked about the re-enchantment of language so that its expressive possibilities are not limited to its semantic possibilities. In the later, broadened notion of style, the same holds. A method or mode of living adopted as a mask or as a moment of a wandering is—by virtue of the mask or wandering —not restricted by its standard parameters of communicability or metaphysical commitments, but gains new expressive and ultimately transformative possibilities.

References

Aristotle. 1987. *Poetics*. Translated by Richard Janko. Indianapolis: Hackett.

Burnham, Douglas. 2004. *Kant's Philosophies of Judgement*. Edinburgh: Edinburgh University Press.

Burnham, Douglas and Martin Jesinghausen. 2010a. *Nietzsche's "The Birth of Tragedy."* London: Continuum.

—. 2010b. *Nietzsche's "Thus Spoke Zarathustra."* Edinburgh: Edinburgh University Press.

—. 2012. "Of Butterflies and Masks." In *Nietzsche and Phenomenology*, edited by Andrea Rehberg, 33–52. Cambridge: Cambridge Scholar's Press.

Burnham, Douglas and Melanie Ebdon. 2009. "Philosophy and Literature." In *The Continuum Companion to Continental Philosophy*, edited by John Mularkey and Beth Lord, 238–58. London: Continuum.

Derrida, Jacques. 1982. "White Mythology." In *Margins of Philosophy*, translated by Alan Bass, 207–71. Chicago: Chicago University Press.

Heidegger, Martin. 1981. *Nietzsche: The Will to Power as Art*. Translated by David Krell. London: Taylor and Francis.

Kant, Immanuel. 1998. *The Critique of Judgement*. Translated by Werner Pluhar. Indianapolis: Hacket.

—. 2000. *The Critique of Pure Reason*. Translated by Werner Pluhar. Indianapolis: Hacket.

Nietzsche, Friedrich. 1988. *Kritische Studienausgabe*. Edited by Giorgio Colli and Mazzino Montinari. Berlin: Walter de Gruyter.

—. 1997. *Untimely Meditations*. Edited by Daniel Breazeale. Translated by R. J. Hollingdale. Cambridge: Cambridge University Press.

—. 1998. *On the Genealogy of Morality*. Edited and translated by Maudemarie Clark and Alan J. Swensen. Indianapolis: Hackett.

—. 1999a. *The Birth of Tragedy*. In *The Birth of Tragedy and Other Writings*, edited by Raymond Geuss, translated by Ronald Speirs, 1–116. Cambridge: Cambridge University Press.

—. 1999b. "The Dionysiac World View." In *The Birth of Tragedy and Other Writings*, edited by Raymond Geuss, translated by Ronald Speirs, 117–38. Cambridge: Cambridge University Press.

—. 1999c. "On Truth and Lying in a Non-Moral Sense." In *The Birth of Tragedy and Other Writings*, edited by Raymond Geuss, translated by Ronald Speirs, 141–53. Cambridge: Cambridge University Press.

—. 1999d. *Unpublished Writings from the Period of* Unfashionable Observations. Translated by Richard T. Gray. Stanford: Stanford University Press.

—. 2002. *Beyond Good and Evil.* Edited by Rolf-Peter Horstmann and Judith Norman. Translated by Judith Norman. Cambridge: Cambridge University Press.

—. 2003. *Writings from the Late Notebooks.* Edited by Rüdiger Bittner. Translated by Kate Sturge. Cambridge: Cambridge University Press.

—. 2005a. *The Anti-Christ, Ecce Homo, Twilight of the Idols and Other Writings.* Edited by Asron Ridley and Judith Norman. Translated by Judith Norman. Cambridge: Cambridge University Press.

—. 2005b. *Thus Spoke Zarathustra.* Translated by Graham Parkes. Oxford: World's Classics.

Sallis, John. 1991. *Crossings: Nietzsche and the Space of Tragedy.* Chicago: University of Chicago Press.

Whitlock, Gregory. 1996. "Roger Boscovich, Benedict de Spinoza and Friedrich Nietzsche: The Untold Story." *Nietzsche-Studien* 25: 200–20.

6

Crimes against fecundity: Style and crime, from Joyce to Poe and back

Jean-Michel Rabaté

The human embryo in the womb passes through all the evolutionary stages of the animal kingdom . . . Every age had its style, is our age alone to be refused a style?

—Adolf Loos, "Ornament and Crime" (1908)

Le style, c'est l'homme même

Wittgenstein revisited a well-known motto in a fragment dating from 1949 when he jotted down twice, "Le style c'est l'homme." "Le style c'est l'homme même" (1980, 78):[*] He adds: "The first expression has a cheap epigrammatic brevity. The second, correct version opens up quite a different perspective. It says that a man's style is a *picture* of him" (78).[1] The notion of *description* might send us back to an older discussion opposing Bertrand Russell to the younger Wittgenstein, but this is not the route I want to follow here. I would like first to pay attention to the

[*]A previous version of brief parts of this chapter appeared in Rabaté 2007.

[1]All italics in quotations are those of the author quoted unless otherwise indicated.

redoubling of a *selfsame self* that finds a corroboration, a proof, or a clue in an *x* that confirms that it is indeed "himself" or "herself." Quite often, Wittgenstein takes *style* in a dismissive sense, as evinced by an earlier statement from 1939–40: "Even a work of supreme art has something that can be called 'style' [Stil], something too that can even be called 'mannerism' [Manier]" (37). He prefaces this by saying: "*They* have less style than the first speech of a child" (37). Who is this "they"? A note tells us that it refers to mannerist artists, whose imitative mode fits the comparison with a child's speech. Such negativity does not spare Wittgenstein's own philosophical works and includes his own style, as judged by himself: "My style is like bad musical composition" (39). This stresses the particular musicality of his philosophical language, revealing moreover a disparaging modesty. These tensions find a resolution in the often quoted paragraph:

> I think I summed up my attitude to philosophy when I said: philosophy ought really to be written only as a *poetic composition*. It must, as it seems to me, be possible to gather from this how far my thinking belongs to the present, future or past. For I was thereby revealing myself as someone who cannot quite do what he would like to be able to do. (Wittgenstein 1980, 24)

The line from this that is often quoted out of context, "Philosophie dürfte man eigentlich nur dichten," which could be translated as "Philosophy should be written only as poetry," takes on a nostalgic ring if we understand it as the regret of a "stylist" who seems aware that he has fallen short of his higher expectations. Indeed, there is a latent contradiction between the philosophy of everyday language in which so many plural language games are to be observed and the perfect epigrammatic quality of the statements of the *Tractatus*: "Die Welt ist alles, was der Fall ist"—"The world is everything that is the case" (1990, §1).

Theory in general appears caught up in this dilemma: we face either an endless exploratory discourse that unfolds in the hope of acquiring new insights and new concepts, or the cryptic and arresting grandeur of philosophemes that can be quoted and commented, but fail to reveal their meaning immediately. What do I mean by *philosopheme* here? It could be defined as any little phrase similar to those mentioned by Samuel Beckett's character Malone ("I know these little phrases that seem so innocuous and once you let them in, pollute the whole of speech" [1991, 193]).[2] They function as theoretical tags, quotable one-liners from famous authors, mottos, and aphorisms that can be mentioned independently of their original context. They are typified by characteristics of form: they tend to be dense, paradoxical, oxymoric even. In their best shapes, they are arresting *sentences* avoiding mere *sententiousness.*

Their brevity and notable structural parallels are two additional features. They are closer to maxims or to lines of poetry that one can memorize easily than to *concepts.* I'll provide a short list to exemplify this: "Die Sprache spricht" (Heidegger), "Tout autre est tout autre" (Derrida), "Cogito ergo sum" (Descartes), "Le coeur a des raisons que la raison ne connaît pas" (Pascal), "Rose is a rose is a rose" (Stein), "Je est un autre" (Rimbaud), "Les non-dupes errant" (Lacan), "Verum Ipsum Factum" (Vico), "Rien n'aura eu lieu que le lieu" (Mallarmé), "O my friends, there are no friends" (Aristotle, translated by Derrida), "Wo Es war, soll Ich werden" (Freud), "D'ailleurs c'est toujours les autres qui meurent" (Duchamp), "Ubi nihil vales, ibi nihil velis" (Geulincx) and, finally, "Le Style c'est l'homme même" (Buffon). One could multiply examples, but the number of these sentences, potentially great, is not infinite. They all evince several characteristics: a notable syntactic compression (see Tufte 2006), a high dependence on a language's amphibologies that renders literal translation quasi impossible (which is why they are often memorized in the original), and a tantalizing ambiguity that somehow attracts commentaries that proliferate all the more given the impossibility of a direct translation.

If we agree that these sentences, by condensing styles of thinking and styles of expression, mummify for eternity the monumental cadavers of their authors, it is because they function above all as clues. As clues, they call up a whole context, which has to be rethought through and through as process; it is a process of thought, no doubt, but at times, a whole lifestyle is implied (can we quote Heidegger without evoking the snowy slopes of the Feldberg, the Spartan but cozy hut in Todtnau, the inspiring trees of the Black Forest?). This follows from Wittgenstein's main insight

---

[2]Samuel Beckett, *Malone Dies,* in *Three Novels, Molloy, Malone Dies, The Unnamable,* New York: Grove Press, 1991, p. 193.

when he revisits Buffon's famous saying. Since "Style is the man himself"—individuality is captured in a description. Style provides a link between a rational level and the *musical* aspect of a way of thinking depending from the author's body. Therefore, style is what affects an audience most, because it is a marker of extreme singularity, while leading to a whole system, like an ethics of language. Style triggers an infinite investigation if we stress less the formal qualities than the process at work. It is to this aspect that I want to turn now. Moving from Joyce to Poe, I will try to use a certain type of detection via clues that send the literary sleuth or the *stylistician*-turned-detective on the right track. In the end, one might have to pose the question of an essence of style. And when I will suggest that it has something to do with crime, this will be an allegorical and hyperbolic way of speaking about death, negativity, and destruction.

I will want to treat style suspiciously by posing questions that any detective would ask a suspect, which will make me negotiate between the literary and the forensic. I will begin by examining the "Oxen of the Sun" episode of *Ulysses*, a difficult episode in which we see Joyce romping through the various histories of English style. It is a good episode to tackle if one really means to understand what style is. When I taught this episode in the seventies, I would use Wolfgang Iser's groundbreaking 1972 work, *The Implied Reader* (1974). Now I add to Iser's approach concepts found in Jacques Rancière's work. It is possible that their approaches to style are complementary. In 1972, Iser defined style as the imposition of a cultural "form" on reality, which led him to affirm that Joyce's play with styles had a strong ethical component. For Iser, Joyce's ultimate meaning was a critique of the illusion that language and reality will ever coincide. His language games constantly varying styles would alert readers to the constructed nature of reality. More recently, Rancière links the aesthetics of style with ethics and politics, which entails a different emphasis. In *Mute Speech* (2011),[3] Rancière starts from the contradictions that he sees in formalist approaches so as to connect a new aesthetic regime defined by the autonomy of style and its domination over all other concerns, to efforts toward a democratic liberation that frees

[3]I owe a lot to friendly discussions with Gabriel Rockhill, who wrote an excellent Introduction (Rockhill 2011) to this translation of *Mute Speech*.

one from all constraints. For him, then, style will be defined by a new rapport between subjectivity and the power to express, which in the end brings us back to issues of ethics and politics.

Since my focus is on the "Oxen of the Sun" episode, I will pay attention to Joyce's conceit in elaborating this episode within Homeric parallels. I would like to combine Iser's and Rancière's approaches while keeping in mind the equation posited by Joyce between the art of stylistic variation, an art that he pursues systematically throughout "Oxen of the Sun," with what he calls "the crime committed against fecundity" (1957, 139). This last phrase refers to the fact that the scene takes place in a maternity hospital where Mrs Purefoy is giving birth to a baby. Meanwhile, Stephen Dedalus, Leopold Bloom, and several other medical students chat irreverently about conception, coition, contraception, and other themes pertaining to sexuality and obstetrics. Joyce famously said that his main idea was "the crime committed against fecundity" when we use birth-control. I found myself asking: what are we slaughtering with Joyce when we play games with style? Did Joyce want to kill literary clichés only, or was he launching a more ambitious program such as a new view of language, caught both in its evolutionary function and as leading back to universal history? This led me to broaden the issue of style, since style is always a synecdoche revealing a whole vision. And finally this brought me to a more delicate question: I had to assess whether Joyce's novel, not the author himself, with all we can learn on his life, beliefs, prejudices, and foibles, could be called *pro-life*, that is, opposed to abortion, or pro-choice? Had he remained a Catholic at heart, or did he allow free play to unleash styles that would assert the domination of writing—Derrida's "dead letters" (see 1987, especially 124–39) hidden inside a French letter, as it were—in its urge to conquer everything? Since I had almost reached an impasse, I had to move around Joyce and look at other models, and in order to leave room for a less anxious and more spacious problematization, I found myself moving back and forth between Joyce and Poe. I decided to insert my Joycean musings into Benjaminian analyses of Poe's famous tale of "Marie Roget," a move I justified by paying closer attention to the gothic qualities of Joyce's style in "Oxen of the Sun."

To make better sense of these peculiar combinations, I will begin with two anecdotes. The first one dates from the mid-nineties, from a time when I had just moved to Philadelphia. One evening, I accompanied two female friends to a demonstration supporting a local family-planning facility that had been threatened by anti-abortion activists. We marched for a while in the streets of downtown Philadelphia with a crowd of people chanting slogans. After an hour or so, there was a lull in the chanting and a tired silence followed songs and slogans. A sudden inspiration seized me, and I shouted: "James Joyce, Pro-Choice!" To my astonishment, the entire group repeated it. For a while, we were all walking around City Hall chanting "James Joyce, Pro-Choice." This was my only moment of political triumph in North America. Even if I was proud of my contribution at the time, doubts came creeping in soon after. Hadn't Joyce described the argument of "Oxen of the Sun" as being underpinned by the idea of "the crime committed against fecundity by sterilizing the act of coition" (1957, 139)? Was James Joyce really or simply "pro-choice"? Should one have to choose in this case, or could one leave the issue undecided, as most scholars who have worked on "Oxen of the Sun" tend to do?

The second anecdote comes from my experience as a pedagogue teaching *Ulysses*. A few years ago, I had reached "Oxen of the Sun" and was discussing a passage that I always find hilarious, the mock-epic evocation of food and drink displayed in the waiting room of the maternity hospital. Here is the passage:

> And there were vessels that are wrought by magic of Mahound out of seasand and the air by a warlock with his breath that he blases in to them like to bubbles. And full fair cheer and rich was on the board that no wight could devise a fuller ne richer. And there was a vat of silver that was moved by craft to open in the which lay strange fishes withouten heads though misbelieving men nie that this be possible thing without they see it natheless they are so. And these fishes lie in an oily water brought there from Portugal because of the fatness that therein is like to the juices of the olivepress. (1986: 14.146–53)

I asked my students what this evoked for them. They seemed embarrassed, and then one asked: "Are they in a bathroom? Flushing floating turds?" I shook my head. Another: "Are they squashing olives in a printing press?" A third one: "Frying fish for dinner?"

None of them was able to understand the literal meaning of the passage. I tried to help them: "Think of sardines in a can." "Sardines in a can?" What was that? They were not sure. Not only had they not been able to recognize what Joyce had obliquely depicted (glass bottles and headless sardines in oil) but they claimed that the notion of a sardine can was outlandish. Their grandparents might have eaten that, a long time ago. It dawned on me that a sardine can was as archaic for them as telephones with wires, those tangled "strandentwining cables" mentioned by Stephen. Their story was confirmed when I heard that in April 2010 the last American cannery had closed: no sardine can would ever be produced in the United States. And then I didn't make things easier when I told my students that sardines had to be headless not only because that was the way they were prepared, but because Joyce was establishing a correspondence with the earlier stages in the development of the embryo. Headless sardines refer to the period when the fetus is a blob floating in amniotic fluid. The discussion made me aware not only of my age but also of the hermeneutic difficulties facing "Oxen of the Sun." Styles as they are foregrounded in this episode are only perceived as such when recognition patterns implying some competence are set in motion. Without this minimal competence, the succession of styles is not recognized. There is a learning curve entailed by stylistic recognition, and it begs the reader's participation, even more, a whole education. In fact, as I hope to show, the topics of style, obstetrics, and forensic science, and beyond that, scientific or neo-scientific discourses on generation(s), are intimately connected.

Indeed, the scholarship on the "Oxen" episode is equally divided between two types of approaches. One is concerned with debates on sexuality (Richard Brown) or birth-control (Mary Lowe-Evans). In *James Joyce and Sexuality* (Brown 1989) and *Crimes Against Fecundity: Joyce and Population Control* (Lowe-Evans 1989), we do learn a lot about the material that Joyce had read, about his position in the debates of the time, but no mention is made of the stylistic devices used to present these problems. The other approach is more textual or genetic. In Robert Janusko's canonical *The Sources and Structures of James Joyce's Oxen* (1983), we discover Joyce's literary sources and his reliance on compilations—George Saintsbury's 1912 work, *A History of English Prose Rhythm*, above all—but the political or ideological problem is all but avoided.

This is the time to go back to Wolfgang Iser's exemplary reading of "Oxen of the Sun." It is to be found in *Der Implizite Leser: Kommunikationsformen des Romans von Bunyan bis Beckett* (1972), published in English as *The Implied Reader: Patterns of Communication in Prose Fiction from Bunyan to Beckett* (1974). With this book, Iser launched a phenomenological approach to literature in English. It was founded upon a central claim, that the act of reading is implied by any literary work. This led him to argue that it is this implied reader who discovers how a text signifies, how it presupposes and programs its reception. Any reader will thus learn to read herself or himself via an interactive hermeneutic process. Joyce's episode provided an important example in this phenomenological approach: here was a text that seemed to need the participation of the reader, even if it could not be taken for granted.

In the chapter devoted to Joyce, Iser began by quoting Eliot's "Ulysses, Order and Myth" (1970) essay so as to examine the problems posed by the idea of a continuous parallel between myth and the present time. He concluded that myth could not provide ready-made solutions, only new potentialities, and that the process of interpretation must be engaged with each time by new readers. This corresponded to the fact, observed by most commentators, that every chapter of *Ulysses* tends to be written in a different style. The relation between the world and literary language had become more complex since Einstein; important critics like T. S. Eliot and Hermann Broch emphasized this. Thus, it is style that emerges as the central topic, as the hero even, in "Oxen of the Sun." This is the episode in which Joyce forces his readers to be aware of the shaping function of art by foregrounding his linguistic manipulations.

Following insights provided by Goldberg's *Classical Temper* (1961), Iser began his reading with a critique of Stuart Gilbert's (1963) canonical introduction to *Ulysses.* Gilbert had stated that Joyce wished to create a parallel between the sequence of period styles and the development of the embryo. For one thing, this reading was too serious and missed the comedy running through the chapter, defined by a great sense of fun when we see the degree of deformation brought about by each style (Iser 1974, 187). Iser analyzed a few examples, including the sardines in olive oil, and concluded: "This incongruity between style and object is apparent all through the series of imitation from one century to the other"

(189). Incongruity is the key-word in his careful readings. It leads to another principle: given this constant stylistic variation, one could perceive that "each style reveals a latent ideology, constantly reducing the reality to the scope of individual principles" (190). For Dickens, love is seen as peace and bliss, for Bunyan it ushers in a moral or Christian allegory, while for Carlyle a consideration of love is pretext for a quasi-Nietzschean affirmation of life, life overcoming everything. We have thus reached a perspectivist ethos since each style defines a point of view:

> [T]he predetermined, predetermining nature of all style is demonstrated quite unmistakably through the individual variations. The judgment inherent in each style creates a uniform picture of the subject presented, choosing these elements of the given reality that correspond to the frame of reference essential to the observation. (191)

A second conclusion can be drawn: if style reproduces only one aspect of reality and not reality itself, then style is closer to a distortion of reality. Joyce uses parodies, that is, stylistic caricatures of the major writers of English literature, to highlight that we'll never know really what love, say, is, but only what it was for Malory, Bunyan, Addison, Carlyle. . . . It would be idle to try to assign a truth-value to all the statements of the characters who voice such widely divergent theories about sexuality, reproduction, and contraception. Style would thus be shown to have failed in its attempt to provide a truthful picture of life. This is linked with a major principle that the essential characteristic of style is that it imposes a grid on an essentially formless reality (we are back to Eliot's contention here). Hence, there is no objectivity, since, ultimately, all styles are determined by the historical conditions that shape them. However, this is not a nihilistic position either. Here is how Iser concludes:

> While the theme of this one chapter is love, the theme of Ulysses itself is everyday human life, and the stylistic presentation of this varies from chapter to chapter, because it can never be grasped as a whole by any one individual style. Only by constantly varying the angle of approach is it possible to convey the potential range of the "real-life" world, but in literature the "approach"

> is what gives rise to the style. By constantly changing the style, Joyce not only conveys the preconditioned, one-sided nature of each approach but also seems to set both object and observer in motion, thus accumulating an assembly of mobile views that show the essential expansiveness of reality. In this sense, "The Oxen of the Sun" epitomizes the technique of the whole novel. The sequence of styles brings out the one-sidedness of each and the constant expansion of the object. (194)

Indeed, we know from Joyce's various schemata that the "organ" for the episode is the "womb" while its technique is "embryonic development" (Gilbert 1963, 38). One can apply the four-fold type of reading launched by Dante about his own *Commedia* in his letter to Can Grande (1995). Here we would have, first, a literal level that could be explicated as follows. This is the first time Bloom and Stephen actually sit together and engage in some social rapport. Bloom visits the maternity hospital of Holles street to see how Mrs Purefoy is doing. After three days of labor, she will finally give birth to a son (one of the rare "events" of *Ulysses*). Meanwhile Dixon, Lynch, Madden, Crotthers, Stephen, Lenehan, and Costello are drinking and Bloom sits there with them for a while. Then Buck Mulligan and Bannon appear. Finally, after a thunderstorm, the baby is born, and Stephen suggests they all leave to go to a pub.

This would be followed by a moral level, corresponding to the following point of view, as exposed by Joyce: "the idea [is] the crime committed against fecundity by sterilizing the act of coition" (1957, 139). This would be enacted by the cynical banter of the young men who variously deride the idea of reproduction and also engage in a series of pseudo-scientific discussions about embryology and heredity. Doctor Horne is Helios whose oxen are slaughtered by the medical students' witty barbs.

Then there would be the allegorical level. The text embodies the growth of the fetus by progressing through nine months (Joyce's drawings). The first is represented by alliterative Anglo-Saxon prose; the second by Middle-English prose; the third by medieval prose like that in *Le Morte d'Arthur.* The fourth by Elizabethan prose; the fifth by Milton's Latinate prose; the sixth goes from Burton and Browne to Pepys via Bunyan. The seventh month is illustrated by eighteenth-century wits and the birth of realism, Defoe,

Swift, Sterne, and Burke; the eighth by gothic novels, Dickens and Newman, and the ninth extends from Thomas Carlyle to modern slang.

And finally, there is the anagogical level. The series of English styles is either giving birth to the language of the future, a new prophetic tone in an American idiom, or destroying the very concept of style as such (much as music is destroyed—for Joyce and Bloom, if not necessarily for the reader—at the end of "Sirens") and leading to a "writing degree zero," such as was announced by Roland Barthes (1977)—the utopia of being able to write without style, Beckett's own post-Joycean dream.

It is when addressing the fourth level that *Mute Speech* (2011), Rancière's study of the evolution of nineteenth-century literary styles, from Balzac to Flaubert, Mallarmé and Proust, is most helpful. In his fast-paced survey, Rancière implicitly criticizes current accounts of modernism by looking at a longer history of genres and of the rules that govern representation. In the classical poetics of representation since Aristotle, fables, understood as the arrangement of an action, belonged to genres defined by conformity with the subject represented. These rules would de determined by the nature of the action and defined the regime of representation. Rancière stresses that the literary productions of the representative system are not necessarily conservative. The same sets of rules can express the hierarchical structures of monarchy, but also help the promulgation of a new republic, or even allow for the emergence of socialist aspirations in the middle of the nineteenth century, when workers attempted to give voice to their longings and frustrations (see also Rancière 1991). However, the ancient hierarchy of *inventio* over *dispositio* and *elocutio* is destroyed once the modern principle of equality, the famous *indifference* of style to its topic or subject that comes to the fore with Flaubert, becomes the norm.

The main issue is the way in which these categories impact on what Rancière calls the "distribution of the sensible" (partage du sensible) (see especially, 2006, 12–45) proper to the poetics of expressivity. The change happened in the middle of the nineteenth century. The representative system was founded on the subordination of the material side of the arts (*elocutio*) to the intellectual side (*inventio*). Hence, Victor Hugo's 1831 novel *Notre-Dame de Paris* provides an example of the collapse of the poem as it was understood within the representative order. In a series of superb analyses, Rancière (2011, 52–61) shows that Hugo's novel is in fact a prose poem; by a process of contamination, Hugo shows how style petrifies when it expresses the stones of the cathedral. The hierarchical relationship between the intellectual and the material is undercut by the unleashed power of the written word. Such a material language overthrows the stable hierarchy of earlier poetics. Hugo launches the principle of modernity: hierarchical fiction yields to language as such, and *style* is caught up in a material mode of functioning of language. When *elocutio* frees itself from *inventio*, or the choice of subject matter that had formerly governed it, it ushers in a new power of expression which animates objects in a new performativity. Hugo's inspired prosopopeia returns style to the matter of linguistic expression.

I cannot rehearse the minute close readings provided by *Mute Speech* and will only summarize some of its conclusions. One main conclusion is that the old regime controlling the distribution of genres will be overthrown with the rise to power of the novel. The novel contains in seed the principle of the equality of represented objects and subjects. Thus the principle of decorum is negated by a purely expressive language that abolishes *styles* in a total indifference of literature to the subjects represented. With the abolition of genres, *style* becomes *pure style* or, as Flaubert would say, it becomes an absolute manner of seeing things. There are no more beautiful or ugly topics, and Joyce, in that matter, appears truly as Flaubert's direct disciple (see Baron 2012).

This model of writing corresponds to the modernist unleashing of style as an absolute. Given this new anarchic freedom, one cannot distinguish between style as elevated speech and the plurality of spoken idioms. This changes the very notion of performative speech: it escapes from the space of the theater, previously reserved for persuasive rhetoric, and moves to the novel. The novel will henceforth be the site of a democratic letter endlessly wandering in the world without having any privileged place. This disturbing nomad roaming in the fields of meaning reconstitutes its place in the world of letters by going back to an ideal genealogy. This genealogy will in Joyce's case entail the entire rewriting, albeit mocking and systematically parodic, of the tradition of English styles. It exemplifies a new poetics in which silent things and hitherto disenfranchised subjects can take on a language of their own. They create a whole new system of signs through which the expressive regime holds sway, underpinning a principle of lability or translatability in all the arts.

Flaubert had collapsed the two principles of romantic poetry: the principle of the indifference of style before subject matter and the principle of the virtuality of a language that is inherent in all things. The danger of this attitude is that the principle of indifference risks destroying the principle of poetic difference. A little like Bouvard and Pécuchet at the end of the eponymous novel, the writer seems condemned to undo art as a principle of distinction in the world, thereby disappearing in the idiotic chatter of the alienated masses. This is the drama that is reenacted at the end of "Oxen of the Sun," when we hear only gibberish, and what is more, an American-inflected medley of slangs.

The tension between the principle of the necessity of language and the principle of the indifference of style would have underpinned all the literary disputes from the end of the nineteenth century to the present. For Rancière, literature is fundamentally torn between the spirit and the letter (Rockhill 2011, 16–19).[4] The breakdown of the subordination of *elocutio* to *inventio* does not lead automatically to formal experimentation. Instead, *elocutio* finds itself split between the expression of that which gives birth to speech—that is, spirit—and the equality of subject matter facing the indifferent power of the letter. For Rancière, literature at the end of the nineteenth century is caught between extremes: the generalized poetics of life that engulfs poetry in spirit and the prose of the world that dissolves spirit into the immanent plane of exchangeable letters. Such a contradiction between spirit and letter is productive, it generates original attempts to deal with incompatible principles. Literature is rejuvenated by its effort to absorb the clash between the hierarchical dictation of the spirit and the egalitarian and neutral space of letters. While noting that this problematic owes much more to the thought of Derrida than is acknowledged, it is in this productive tension that I would want to situate Joyce's hesitation between fecundity and sterility as replayed allegorically

---

[4]I am indebted to Rockhill's excellent summaries (2011, 16–19).

by the politics of birth-control in Ireland first and then in the whole world.

One of main consequences of Rancière's work is that he forces us to abandon for good Walter Benjamin's almost glib opposition between an aestheticization of politics typical of fascism and a politicization of aesthetics (2006, 269–70) provided by leftist programs, as in Brecht's political plays. For Rancière, if the aesthetic realm is directly political, it is because it creates a new distribution of the sensible. Are we so far from Iser with Rancière's categories? In a sense, yes, since what has changed is the way in which we connect literature, aesthetics, and politics. Rancière sees in the distribution of the sensible the result of an aesthetico-political operation. This *partage du sensible* should also be, in the context of Joyce's "Oxen of the Sun," gendered or even feminized. One is tempted to rephrase the concept of *partage* (sharing) with that of parturition, a real or metaphorical giving birth to presence and the world as represented and expressed, a *parturition* of the sensible. In other words, Joyce would be suggesting in this episode (as well as in all of *Ulysses*, but more radically so, obviously, here) that the distribution of the sensible depends less from a male or phallic gesture of cutting, dividing, and then sharing out to all, than from a feminine process that ends up by giving birth to reality as we know it. This is why, for Joyce, and also for Flaubert before him, literary creation had to be understood as a parturition of style. There would be a direct link between Stephen's amateurish villanelle in *A Portrait of the Artist as a Young Man*—"O! In the virgin womb of the imagination the word was made flesh" (Joyce 1968, 217)—and the no less virgin poet of "Oxen of the Sun": "In woman's womb word is made flesh but in the spirit of the maker all flesh that passes becomes the word that shall not pass away" (1986, 14.292–93).

Le style c'est la femme même

All this has been well summed up by Genevieve Abravanel when she wonders why such a gestation has to lead us to a present idiom dominated by American-English slang. She notes that what Jennifer Levine has called one of "the most obviously subversive episodes" in *Ulysses* is a "linguistic prank" in its parodies of the evolution of literary styles from Anglo-Saxon to the present day (2010, 165). She continues:

> Set in a maternity hospital and riddled with images of gestation and development, the episode serves as an allegory for the organic, changeable character of the English language. Joyce's use of a gestation model is particularly powerful here because it implies that the chapter will end with birth and thus with something greater than the developmental stages that have come before. It is therefore especially striking that this episode should end with American English. Yet why does Joyce's gestating English language ultimately deliver up American slang? (165; see also Abranavel 2012)

Her answer is simple but I believe irrefutable: it is a "conceit that undermines the structures of value that privilege Ben Johnson and Shakespeare over bawdy American curse words," since Joyce may be seen "turning even more starkly to American content to reflect upon the globalism and imperialism of the modern age" (2010, 159). Thus, even though Joyce ascribed to Bloom the function of a "spermatozoon" in "Oxen," this role should be seen in the context of the general scheme of the organs in *Ulysses*. By providing an organ for each chapter, Joyce places the narration within the body, but nowhere else is this body so clearly seen to be made up of language. In this case, it looks as if Leopold Bloom's diegetic role as an empathetic observer of the feminine body was meant to present him embodied in the text through a schematic "womb." Bloom's rare and cautious statement in the midst of carousing students is his way of experiencing his participation in a birth process. He approximates the interiority of a female perspective. In "Oxen of the Sun," Bloom's *logos spermatikos* transcends its diegetic function and becomes united with Stephen presented as an "embryo philosopher" (1986, 14.1295). The convergence of males fascinated by the feminine process of parturition allegorizes the body of the text and merges into the fluid component in this embryonic sequence. The physical birth and the birth of language allegorize the process of writing. When Joyce unfolds and parodies the history of literary styles, Bloom and Stephen blend in the nine sections that follow Joyce's womb-schema. Finally, a new language is born, the language of the present and even the future. It entails also the new American idiom—spoken by Poe . . . Poe, who forces us to look at the site of literature not only as that of a new parturition, but also as that of a crime. Could it be that the two notions are intimately connected?

We now need to return to the quandary of a *pro-life Joyce* and a *pro-choice Joyce*. We will be armed with what we have gained from the theoretical discussion. We can reformulate the question in this way: was Joyce trying to kill literary clichés in order to give birth to a new language, or was he demonstrating his mastery over language and being playful, telling a story in a highly stylized manner, via the conceit that the evolution of literary language is similar to the evolution of a human fetus? Or was he suggesting, twisting the old motto, that "Le style, c'est la femme même"? If the conflation of literary style and femininity had to be made, why did he need the idea of a *crime*? Who was the object of the murder, who perpetrated it?

Rancière exhibits, through a typically—almost parochially—French cultural history, the genealogy of the new "indifference" of style to its object; a similar evolution leading to the principle of *indifference* had also been the object of the Victorians' investigations, even if they put a different stress on the principle. What they invented was the treatment of murder stories as a species of documentary drama that can be enjoyed for the thrills they offer without paying heed to moral issues. In this bracketing off of ethics lies the root of *aesthetics*. We may remember that the term of *aesthetics* was introduced into English for the first time as a translation from the German of Kant and Schiller by Thomas de Quincey in his famous essay "On Murder Considered as One of the Fine Arts" (2006). The first of the two essays, which established de Quincey's name among British humorists and even gained for him a place in André Breton's *Anthology of Black Humor* (1997), states that murder has two handles. It can be seized by the moral handle (which we can leave to priests and judges) or by the esthetic handle (used by everyone else). That esthetic handle turns murder into a spectacle and allows us to treat it purely *aesthetically*. The victim has been killed and cannot be resuscitated: let's just see whether this can make a good or a bad show. De Quincey's narrator considers at some length the murderer Williams, who had slaughtered two entire households, as a genius, an inimitable *artist* of murder. His crimes have to be assessed as works of art, and have set higher standards for forthcoming murderers. They all have been *signed* with his own personal stamp for posterity.

Thus, de Quincey tells us, via Kant, that murder is not a crime when it is art. The autonomy of aesthetics means that the work of art simply turns into its own reality. The point is less that art will *kill* reality in order to assert its own laws than that it becomes self-reflexive, its significance bounded by the deployment of its formal procedures, an active bracketing out of other worldly concerns that acknowledges the legislation of no human or divine tribunal. De Quincey attempts to found this articulation of ethics and aesthetics on a distinction between action and contemplation. His central argument is that as long as we can do something to prevent a murder or help a potential victim, we must act—this is the realm of ethics. Should we happen to come too late when the murder has been committed, then we must be allowed to enjoy the crime scene as pure spectacle. However, such a clear-cut distinction between a *before* and an *after* moment simplifies the issue or misleads us. What makes murder stories thrilling is that there is a style in murder—an amusing passage of "On Murder" consists in having the members of the "Society for the Encouragement of Murder" (2006, 8) assess certain criminals' styles and compare them with those of Dürer and Fuseli (30–1). A detective will use a similar stylistic expertise to catch find the perpetrator. He will also add an intellectual element of ratiocination that is lacking in de Quincey's sadistic hedonism.

Le style, c'est le crime même

Poe's faith in the powers of ratiocination facing riddles and mysteries is the counterpart of his belief that the most poetic topic in the world is the death of a young and beautiful woman. Dupin's rationalism intervenes as the intellectual opposite of the gothic clichés and romantic necrophilia displayed in "The Raven." Poe's equivalence of love and death is grafted onto the popular coupling of madness and genius, the productive interaction between feminine irrationalism and male intellect, all of which intertwined in a conflict between subjective chaos and an artificially imposed social order (see Rabaté 2007, 101–10).

One recurrent reference in Benjamin's *Arcades Project* (1999) is Régis Messac's book *Le "Detective Novel" et l'influence de la pensée scientifique* (1929). Messac insists on Poe's centrality for the genesis of the genre he studies, which is the detective novel, a novel characterized by the process of *detection*. A detective comes on stage after a murder, and takes up the ancient art of examining traces, originally left by thieves or animals. What happens there is not unlike embryology: the temporal sequence is reversed by intellection since a forensic examination retraces a criminal gesture from the intention to its consequences, the murder. Any murder or crime will be reduced to signs that will be interpreted in the right order until the identity of the culprit is revealed. This paradigm derives from the art of observing traces in the sand, grass, or streets, and then of reconstructing what has taken place. This is cognate with the art of looking at animals when they run or eat in order to assess their qualities or defects, thus also with the pseudo-science of physiognomy, which had its heyday with Johann Kaspar Lavater. Fundamentally, the progress of *detection* corresponds to a burgeoning scientific spirit that came to maturity with the Age of Enlightenment. However, since the emergence of Dupin and Sherlock Holmes, everyone speaks of *deductions* in order to describe the ratiocinative process aimed at reconstructing the criminal's actions, whereas this ought to be called more properly *inductions*.[5] However, everything that has been called *stylistics* so far could fall under the general heading of the ancient *physiognomy.*

Poe's Dupin stories founded the genre of the detective novel. Overall, the quest is a quest for the legibility of signs, even when they resist. Thus "The Man of the Crowd" begins and ends famously with the German sentence "*er lässt sich nicht lessen*" (he does not let himself be read) (Poe 1983, 481). This tale looks like the story of detection. At the end, the narrator abandons his pursuit of the wanderer, this anxious London flâneur, and renounces to learn the desperate old man's secret. Poe suggests that it is as well, since our "little garden of the soul" (in reference to the *Hortulus Animae* of Grünninger, a sixteenth-century prayer book alluded to in the tale's last sentence) contains far worse nightmares than the teeming horrors of the world around us. "The Man of the Crowd" repeats the

[5]A footnote (Messac 1929, 34) states that the book's idea came from the surprise caused when this point was made by a philosophy teacher in 1913.

pattern of "The Purloined Letter." We follow a circuit devoid of any content, a circular displacement from legitimate addressee to the intervening minister who steals the object, until Dupin steals it again, and gives it back while leaving a duplicate in the same place. We will never be privy to the contents of the letter, in the same way as the few elements we learn about the "man of the crowd" are too sketchy to create a consistent portrayal. What remains of the usual trappings of the gothic genre is muted; what counts is to produce a pure blueprint, a scheme, a simple pattern—crime is defined in a metaphysical perspective as the source of opaque signs that request an interpretation.

Poe is a sentimentalist in love with melodrama, but one who, like Freud, wishes to be rational about his own enjoyment, especially when real life provides an equivalent to his thesis that "The death . . . of a beautiful woman is, unquestionably, the most poetical topic in the world" (1969, 170). Poe recognized such a scandal when he saw one, as he did in the newspapers of 1841, with the tantalizing *fait divers* provided by the demise of young and beautiful Mary Rogers in New York. Walter Benjamin summed it up thus:

> The original social content of the detective story was the obliteration of the individual's traces in the big-city crowd. Poe concerns himself with this motif in detail in "The Mystery of Marie Rogêt," the most voluminous of his detective stories. At the same time this story is the prototype of the utilization of journalistic information in the solution of crimes. Poe's Detective, the Chevalier Dupin, works not with personal observation but with reports from the daily press. The critical analysis of these reports constitutes the rumor in the story. (1977, 43)

Dupin, like Poe, is a reader of local newspapers. Like Joyce, they relish mystery stories in almanacs, sensational pamphlets, and the tidbits of the penny press. Hence the length and repetitiveness of this tale, the only one that comes close to an authentic police inquiry—the irony being, of course, that the investigation fails. Dupin's strategy is to find his way through a printed maze, conflicting accounts discussing a highly visible murder. It is a paper trail that he will superimpose on the map of the city. Needless to say, he will not succeed in this quest.

A degree of hermeneutic undecidability is added by Poe's decision to transpose the *fait divers* to Paris. His Parisians cross the Seine in ferry-boats, the children who discover the young woman's clothes gather sassafras bark (Poe 1983, 198; Messac 1929, 349). Baudelaire excuses these blunders and notes that Poe never pretended to have been in Paris—it is only an allegorical translation. In fact, Mary Rogers, the "beautiful cigar girl," had been found in the Hudson river after having been apparently sexually molested in the summer of 1841. She becomes Marie, a Parisian *grisette,* in Poe's tale. Suspects had been named: Daniel Payne, who was to marry her, but committed suicide out of grief in October 1841. Another, John Morse, was apprehended but cleared himself when he proved that he had been on Staten Island at the time, and not in Hoboken, where Mary's body was found (see Srebnick 1995; Stashower 2006). It is under the pretence of rational calculations of probabilities that the opening pages of "The Mystery of Marie Rogêt" make a bold assumption. The death of Marie was a murder: "The atrocity of this murder (for it was at once evident that murder had been committed), the youth and beauty of the victim, and, above all, her previous notoriety, conspired to produce intense excitement in the minds of the sensitive Parisians" (Poe 1983, 171).

The tale was serialized in three issues of the *Ladies' Companion* in 1842 and 1843. Poe assumed that there was a single murderer, a man with whom Mary had a date; the murderer would then have been killed by a local gang. The idea combined two hypotheses developed by the penny press that attributed the crime either to a jilted lover, or to a collective rape by a notorious gang of New York. Yet Poe was not sure that his conclusions were right. He delayed the publication of the third installment, and then revised the text for his collected *Tales* of 1845. Later revisions made room for another hypothesis, namely that Mary had not been gang-raped or murdered by a jealous suitor, but had died after an abortion. The publication of his *Tales* in 1845 was contemporary with a new abortion law. Well-known abortionists like Madame Restell had been named in connection with the death of Mary. In November 1842, a certain Mrs Loss, who owned a roadside inn near where the corpse was found, made a deathbed confession, connecting Mary's death to a botched abortion. She becomes Madame Deluc in Poe's story. And this might not have been Mary's first abortion, since we have heard of a previous suspicious disappearance. One year earlier, Mary's many admirers had been "thrown into confusion"

(Poe 1983, 171) by her absence from the cigar shop. Indeed, the police were in the process of starting an official investigation when she mysteriously reappeared "in good health, but with a somewhat saddened air" (171) or with "a slight paleness" (192). She resumed her work without giving any explanation, but soon after left her job to help her mother manage their boarding house. The place did not have a great reputation. Mary seems to have behaved just like Polly, the loose and pretty daughter of Mrs Mooney in Joyce's story "The Boarding House" (1954). As in the *Dubliners* tale, she was hoping to entice men of some means and had got at least one promise of marriage as a result.

Poe's "mystery" started with an unverified assumption: since this did not look like an accident, since it was not a suicide, then this must have been a murder. Like every riddle, it has to find a solution. Symptomatically, Poe wrote that there was "nothing *outré*" (1983, 180) in this murder, by which he means that it did not come up to the gruesome violence of the two women's deaths—their throats slashed by razors, one body stuffed in a chimney—of "Murders in the Rue Morgue." In consequence, Poe surmised that this enigma would be easy to solve. It turned out differently. The deciphering of a mass of press documents led to an intractable illegibility. Indeed, one might say of Mary's story that *sie lässt sich nicht lessen*. This is why Poe has to insert qualifications. He writes: "if murder was committed on her body" (1983, 181), and adds: "There might have been a wrong *here*, or more possibly; an accident at Madame Deluc's" (1983, 200). Later, he grants equal probability to competing theses: "either a fatal accident under the roof or Madame Deluc or a murder perpetrated in the thicket of the Barrière du Roule" (1983, 203–4). However, these later modifications do not prevent him from looking for clues of murder as he still seems intent on finding one or several guilty parties, of "tracing to its *dénouement* the mystery which enshrouds her" (1983, 206).

Poe's programmatic delusion is evident when we look at the police reports that he quotes. They mention "brutal violence" (1983, 174) but cannot be explicit about details of a very intimate nature. Like the newspapers' accounts, Poe's analysis is both precise and purposefully vague:

> In the outer garment, a slip, about a foot wide, had been torn upward from the bottom hem to the waist; but not torn off. It was wound three times around the waist, and secured by a sort

> of hitch in the back. The dress immediately beneath the frock was of fine muslin; and from this a slip of eighteen inches wide had been torn entirely out—torn very evenly and with great care. It was found around her neck, fitting loosely, and secured with a hard knot. (1983, 174)

Since the "slip" was not used to strangle her to death, the clean cut in the inner garments is not compatible with a savage rape performed by inebriated gangsters or with the murderous act of a single man. Poe's sagacity is at fault here—one reason that has been adduced was that it might bring suspicion to the plausible father of a first aborted fetus, his friend John Anderson. Besides, all the evidence mentioning screams of terror and a gang of mischief-makers came from "Madame Deluc" or her friends who had an interest in diverting suspicions from what took place in the house.

In the last pages of his tale, Poe still sticks to the hypothesis of a collective murder, but adds that one should take into account "coincidences" and "important miscalculations" (1983, 207). His wish to use reason and rule out chance occurrences seems at odds with the facts. In the end, Poe appears as a duped Dupin, since far from solving the riddle, he has added to the chronicle of Marie's demise another layer of commentaries that are as full of holes as the rest. The contradictions between his praise of the sleuth's search for clues and his rationalist "induction" come to a head when the detective appears blinded by an excess of evidence. To be true, the facts in the case of Mary's death were, from the start, tainted by melodrama—all the elements were combined: a promiscuous young woman, whose corpse is washed ashore, the disappearance of a local beauty whose entourage counted at least three or four persons who had reasons to want to murder her. . . . The popular press did not wait for Poe to invent the "mystery" of Mary Roger's death. From the start, it was couched in the stuff of popular epics, dated gothicism, and urban melodrama. Dupin's superb rationalism is the reverse of tired journalistic clichés. Poe's romantic exchange between love and death was grafted on a popular culture that loved murdered *grisettes,* mad geniuses, and pipe-smoking detectives. But the real upshot of the young woman's murder was a tightening of the antiabortion laws, and the creation of a more efficient police force in New York.

This interaction is parallel to a drift toward a modernity marked by everyday life in big, bustling metropoles like London, New York, or Paris. Thus Poe's confusions and equivocations will have to be brought closer to our definitions of the modern spirit. This is what motivated Walter Benjamin in his *Arcades Project*. One could take Benjamin as a guide who would show that, in the process, Poe's ratiocinative and ruminating detective needs to acquire a more *modern* sense of style. The evolution will entail a high degree of stylization that will bring style as a concept very close to parody. For this process to be perfected, Poe will have to be relayed by Lautréamont's systematic and cold-blooded delirium. Poe's sentimentalism verging on kitsch will be replaced by a deliberate recycling of kitsch as a literary medium. This sketches Ducasse's aesthetic program, one that successfully integrates stylistic tensions by heightening them. Ducasse chose popular melodrama as the literary site that he would occupy more as an army does with an enemy's land, with massive amounts of destruction and by inflicting as much pain as possible, than by gentle colonization. This is the site that he set out to warp and pervert by blending the positivism of the rationalist tradition with excessive gothic features. In doing this, he radicalized the link between melodrama, crime, and *fait divers*. Poe was one of his models, although he more often pillaged Ponson du Terrail's endless feuilletons. His decision to copy and invert popular crime stories in the *Songs of Maldoror* (1978) was parallel to what he did in "Poésies" (1978): this sequence of quotes from moralists like Pascal and Vauvenargues was made up of sentences whose meaning he inverted and negated. Lautréamont, a figure of excess, would lead to Surrealism; Breton and his friends relished his concerted outrage against good taste, stylistic distinction, morality, and aesthetics.

Ducasse specialized in the outré style that he absorbed from the feuilletons. It allowed him to reach climaxes of gratuitous horror. This happened in the third book of the *Songs of Maldoror*, a section that shocked even Water Benjamin. For Benjamin, Lautréamont was one of the three anarchists (the other two are Dostoevsky and Rimbaud) who detonated literary bombs all at the same time. They transformed the Romantic praise of evil into a political weapon. In this passage, we first meet a crazy old crone who dances along the road. A stranger enquires about her, and she pulls out a roll of paper on which she has consigned the sad story of her life. She reads to him the account of her daughter's murder. The stranger reads the text. It describes how the lovely and innocent little girl is violently raped by Maldoror. Having finished, Maldoror then commands his dog to bite her to death. Not obeying the order, the bulldog imitates his master and rapes the girl once more. To Maldoror's surprise, she is still alive. Then Maldoror unleashes his devastating furor:

> He takes an American penknife from his pocket, consisting of twelve blades which can be put to different uses. He opens the angular claws of this steel hydra; and armed with a scalpel of the same kind, seeing that the green of grass had not yet disappeared beneath all the blood which had been shed, he prepares, without blenching, to dig his knife courageously into the unfortunate child's vagina. From the widened hole he pulls out, one after one, the inner organs; the guts, the lungs, the liver and at last the heart itself are torn from their foundations and dragged through the hideous hole into the light of day. The sacrificer notices that the young girl, a gutted chicken, has long been dead. (1978, 129–30)

The old woman who had narrated this concludes that she believes that the maniac rapist was insane. Because of that, she forgives him. The stranger almost faints, then comes to. He was none other than Maldoror himself, who had returned to the scene of his crime although he had forgotten it. Ducasse adds sarcastically, "how habit dulls the memory!" (1978, 130). The paroxystic passage ends quietly, with a strange quiver sending up the mock pastoral tone of the beginning: "He will not buy a bulldog! . . . He will not converse with shepherds! . . . He will not sleep in the shade of plane-trees! . . . Children chase after her and throw stones at her, as if she were a blackbird" (130). The tone is Yeatsian in its elegiac suggestion of deepening shades that will veil, quite conveniently, the gruesome transgression.

Songs of Maldoror exploits popular genres like the feuilleton narrating the exploits of invincible criminals, adding surreal gore in the tradition of the Grand Guignol plays, which attracted the crowds along the grands boulevards of Paris (the meticulously documented site of the adventures of Maldoror) in which torrents of fake blood would spout at the least provocation. The mixture of melodrama and inflated rhetoric undermines itself and produce a dark poetry of pulp gothic. This verbal pop art *avant la lettre* bridges the gap between an older, debased mass culture and a new sensibility attuned to linguistic excess, jarring metaphors, and the parody of conventional morality. Maldoror revisits both the English gothic tales and the French *romans noirs,* adding grotesque twists that mimic convulsive hysteria in language. At the same time, he makes fun of Romantic aspirations to a recollection in tranquillity by means of an immersion in bountiful Nature. Since Nature means crime, as Sade and Baudelaire knew there is no peace to expect from it. Like Rimbaud, Ducasse has read Baudelaire and has absorbed the distilled spirit of Sade. Benjamin writes, commenting on Baudelaire's sadism:

> Nature, according to Baudelaire, knows this one luxury: crime. Thus the significance of the artificial. Perhaps we may draw on this thought for the interpretation of the idea that children stand nearest to original sin. Is it because, exuberant by nature, they cannot get out of harm's way? At bottom, Baudelaire is thinking of parricide. (1999, 240)

Ducasse was a systematic literary parricide who managed to dispatch his immediate predecessors, Baudelaire and Poe above all. He also created a poetic style that opened new doors of perception for André Breton and the Surrealists. The most direct forms of address accompany the most bizarre images clamping together incompatible levels of style. This new hybrid style provides an equivalent of the Parisian arcades sung by Aragon and memorialized by Benjamin: they are outmoded, sooner or later condemned, already ruined from within. The remnants of another age, they contain the seeds of the future, announce new forms of change and exchange. Benjamin, who noted: "The arcades as milieu of Lautréamont" (1999, 847), knew that Isidore Ducasse had first lived near Passage Vivienne and then died in a small room at 7, rue du Faubourg Montmartre. "Go and see for yourself, if you do not believe me" (De Lautréamont 1978, 245).

What is new in Ducasse's writing is that he explicitly quotes popular genres, reclaims their debased style and cheap sensationalism for serious poetry while making a show of pithy condensation: "in a tale of this sort . . . there is no occasion for diluting in a godet the shellac of four hundred banal pages. What can be said in half-a-dozen pages must be said, and then, silence" (De Lautréamont 1978, 240 [translation modified]). Like Joyce's *Ulysses*, Lautréamont's poem condenses countless interminable dime novels. By giving birth to such a monstrously magnificent abortion of an older literature, Ducasse and Joyce accomplished what Duchamp and Breton were aiming at, the reconciliation of high modernism with popular culture.

Samuel Beckett condensed the issue I have been grappling with in a pithy formula: "Mr Joyce does not take birth for granted, as Vico seems to have done" (1972, 8). Admittedly, Beckett is discussing *Finnegans Wake* and not *Ulysses*; yet I believe that this insight applies to Joyce's entire oeuvre. At least since the *Portrait*, we have learned to superimpose the notion of a developing style with the organic account of the embryonic development of a soul. "The soul is born, he said vaguely, first in those moments I told you of. It has a slow and dark birth, more mysterious than the birth of the body" (Joyce 1968, 203). Indeed, Joyce does not take birth for granted—this is how he puts a distance between his writing and the biological metaphors that it appeals to. Not to take birth for granted means that one will not hold it as sacred, and perhaps, not even as *natural*. Joyce was neither an eighteenth-century physiocrat nor a Catholic pro-life supporter. His ambition was to examine critically the conditions of possibility of the gift implied in the verb "granted." Then and only then can one "take" something or nothing out of the process of writing.

Beckett was evidently the heir of Joyce's and Poe's meanderings through style considered as crime and destruction. This is why he famously decided to write in French in order to write "without style" (1993, 48). He made that fateful decision in the fifties, just at the time when Roland Barthes was advocating the *Nouveau Roman* as a *blank* writing. Its pure writing would be writing without literature and without style. He made his position very clear in *Writing Degree Zero* (1977), a book with which Rancière's *Mute Speech* is often in dialogue. More recently, Ben Hutchinson has investigated the conflicted links between the main modernist writers and the concept of style in his brilliant *Modernism and Style* (2011). I can only pay homage to his magnificent synthesis. Among all the writers he examines in his survey of all those who identified style with crime, none has gone further than Beckett in "worsening" (1983, 27, 29) language so as to pave the way for a new subjectivity, capable of resisting in spite of all. This program had been explained quite early by a minor character in his first play, *Eleutheria*. The speaker is Doctor Piouk, who has found a solution to solve the problems of the human species.

> Dr. Piouk: I would ban reproduction. I would perfect the condom and other devices and bring them into general use. I would establish teams of abortionists, controlled by the State. I would apply the death penalty to any woman guilty of giving birth. I would drown all newborn babies. I would militate in favour of homosexuality and would myself give the example. And to speed things up, I would encourage recourse to euthanasia by all possible means, although I would not make it obligatory. Those are only the broad outlines. (1996, 44–5)

No doubt, listening to this, we can only assert, as Madame Krap does in her reply: "I was born too early" (1996, 45). When style and crime coincide, this is when we discover that we were always born too early . . .

References

Abranavel, Genevieve. 2010. "American Encounters in *Dubliners* and *Ulysses*." *Journal of Modern Literature* 33(4): 153–66.

—. 2012. *Americanizing Britain: The Rise of Modernism in the Age of the Entertainment Empire*. Oxford: Oxford University Press.

Baron, Scarlett. 2012. *Strandentwining Cable: Joyce, Flaubert, and Intertexuality*. Oxford: Oxford University Press.

Barthes, Roland. 1977. *Writing Degree Zero*. Translated by Annette Lavers and Colin Smith. New York: Hill and Wang.

Beckett, Samuel. 1972. "Dante . . . Bruno. Vico. Joyce." In *Our Exagmination Round his Factification for Incamination of Work in Progress*, 1–22. London: Faber and Faber.

—. 1983. *Worstward Ho*. London: John Calder.

—. 1993. *Dream of Fair to Middling Women*. New York: Arcade Publishing.

—. 1996. *Eleutheria*. Translated by Barbara Wright. London: Faber and Faber.

Benjamin, Walter. 1997. *Charles Baudelaire: A Lyric Poet in the Era of High Capitalism*. Translated by Harry Zohn. London: Verso.

—. 1999. *The Arcades Project*. Translated by Howard Eiland and Kevin McLaughlin. Cambridge, MA: Harvard University Press.

—. 2006. *Selected Writings,* vol. 4. Edited by Howard Eiland and Michael W. Jennings. Cambridge, MA: Harvard University Press.

Breton, André. 1997. *Anthology of Black Humor*. Translated by Mark Polizzotti. Los Angeles: City Lights Books.

Brown, Richard. 1989. *James Joyce and Sexuality*. Cambridge: Cambridge University Press.

Dante. 1995. *Epistola a Can Grande*. Edited by Enzo Cecchini. Firenze: Giunti.

De Quincey, Thomas. 2006. "On Murder Considered as One of the Fine Arts." In *On Murder*, edited by Robert Morrison, 8–34. Oxford: Oxford University Press.

Derrida, Jacques. 1987. *The Post Card: From Socrates to Freud and Beyond*. Translated by Alan Bass. Chicago: The University of Chicago Press.

Eliot, T. S. 1970. "Ulysses, Order, and Myth." In *James Joyce: The Critical Heritage*, vol. 1, edited by Robert H. Deming, 268–71. London: Routledge.

Gilbert, Stuart. 1963. *James Joyce's Ulysses*. Harmondsworth: Penguin Books.

Goldberg, Samuel Lois. 1961. *The Classical Temper: A Study of James Joyce's Ulysses*. London: Chatto and Windus.

Hutchison, Ben. 2011. *Modernism and Style*. New York: Palgrave Macmillan.

Iser, Wolgang. 1974. *The Implied Reader*. Baltimore: Johns Hopkins Press.

Joyce, James. 1954. "The Boarding House." In *Dubliners*, 74–84. New York: The Modern Library.

—. 1957. *Letters of James Joyce,* vol. 1. Edited by Stuart Gilbert. New York: The Viking Press.

—. 1968. *A Portrait of the Artist as a Young Man*. New York: Viking Critical Library.

—. 1986. *Ulysses*. Edited by H. W. Gabler. New York: Vintage. (References give chapter and line number.)

Lautréamont, Comte de (Isidore Ducasse). 1978. *Maldoror and Poems*. Translated by Paul Knight. London: Penguin.

Lowe-Evans, Mary. 1989. *Crimes Against Fecundity: Joyce and Population Control*. Syracuse: Syracuse University Press.

Messac, Régis. 1929. *Le "Detective Novel" et l'influence de la pensée scientifique*. Paris: Honoré Champion.

Poe, Edgar Allan. 1969. *Poe's Poems and Essays*. London: Dent.

—. 1983. *Complete Tales and Poems*. London: Penguin.

Rabaté, Jean-Michel. 2007. *Given: 1° Art, 2° Crime: Modernity, Murder and Mass Culture*. Brighton: Sussex Academic Press.

Rancière, Jacques. 1991. *The Nights of Labor: The Workers' Dream in 19th Century France*. Translated by John Drury. Philadelphia: Temple University Press.

—. 2006. *The Politics of Aesthetics*. Translated by Gabriel Rockhill. London: Continuum.

—. 2011. *Mute Speech*. Translated by James Swenson. New York: Columbia University Press.

Rockhill, Gabriel. 2011. "Introduction. Through the Looking Glass: The Subversion of the Modernist Doxa." In Rancière, *Mute Speech*, 1–37. New York: Columbia University Press.

Srebnick, Amy Gilman. 1995. *The Mysterious Death of Mary Rogers: Sex and Culture in Nineteenth-Century New York*. Oxford: Oxford University Press.

Stashower, Daniel. 2006. *The Beautiful Cigar Girl: Mary Rogers, Edgar Allan Poe and the Invention of Murder*. New York: Dutton.

Tufte, Virginia. 2006. *Artful Sentences, Syntax as Style*. Cheshire, CT: Graphics Press.

Wittgenstein, Ludwig. 1980. *Culture and Value*. Translated by Peter Winch. Chicago: University of Chicago Press.

—. 1990. *Tractatus Logico-Philosophicus*. London: Routledge.

7

Style and arrogance: The ethics of Heidegger's style

Chris Müller

Introduction: Style and the desolation of responsibility

There is an ethical dimension to style. Even more so if a style of thinking is under consideration, as it is when encountering, for instance, the idea that "questioning is the piety of thought" (Heidegger 2004c, 40).[1] This is the concluding line of Martin Heidegger's "The Question Concerning Technology." How are we to understand these words, which come from a thinker notoriously reluctant to answer questions? Heidegger's well-documented elusiveness about his involvement in Nazism was matched by an unwillingness to respond directly to questions posed about his critiques of science, technology, and ethics. The emphasis on questioning in Heidegger's assertion suggests that *answering* is not part of the piety he is advocating. It is questioning, and not answering, that is attributed with a redemptive quality: "The closer we come to the danger

---

[1]I would like to thank James Corby, Mareile Pfannebecker, and Laurent Milesi for their comments and encouragement.

Unless otherwise indicated translations are my own, as my argument requires the most literal rendition of the German original. All italics in quotations are those of the author quoted unless otherwise indicated.

[*Gefahr*], the more brightly the ways begin to shine into that which rescues [*Rettende*] and the more questioning we become" (Heidegger 2004c, 40). Heidegger intrinsically connects the task of becoming ever more questioning, or rather, of being ever more involved in a certain *style* of questioning, to a promise of salvation. "Rescuing," as Heidegger explains, says "more" than "grabbing hold of that which is threatened by its demise." The term, as it is elaborated, denotes the process of "bringing" something "into [its] essence" (32).

In *The Jargon of Authenticity*, probably the most famous published reaction to Heidegger's style, Theodor Adorno rebukes the "archaic tone" with which this more "essential" and "simpler" mode of questioning human existence is promised: "whether questions are essential can be judged, at best, only after answers are provided" (1973b, 52). Questioning without providing answers, and even responding to concrete suffering by alluding to the abstract question of being, is seen as the height of arrogance. Not only is Heidegger's writing style seen as symptomatic of the person, but more worryingly for Adorno, it also offers a template which others might follow. By focusing on the essence of man rather than the concrete "conditions which were made by men," Heidegger's style, according to Adorno, not only "releases one" from the duty of responding to the issues of the day, but also allows one to dismiss their contemplation as a vulgar enterprise (60). A political and moral stance is replaced, as Adorno puts it, by a "linguistic attitude [*sprachliche Haltung*] of which ambiguity is the medium" (12–13; translation modified; see Adorno 1973a, 421). Adorno outlines an ethical dimension of style in order to demand a *stylistic* responsibility of the writer. Style is meant to reflect intentions clearly and not to obscure them. If this is not achieved, then style may give rise to a jargon that does not merely erode the ethical responsibility of the writer, but also that of the reader: "whoever is versed in the jargon does not have to say what he thinks, does not even have to think it properly" (9).

Heidegger's own understanding of the ethical dimension of style is diametrically opposed to Adorno's. *Letter on Humanism*, the first publication after the war, opens with a reflection on language which implies that the suffering of the war is ultimately caused by our treatment of language: "The desolation [*Verödung*] of language that is proliferating quickly and is taking place everywhere does not merely emaciate the aesthetic and moral responsibility in the usage of language. It stems from the danger to the essence of man" (Heidegger 2000a, 10). The term *Verödung*, which I have translated as "desolation" above, brings this passage into context with an often overlooked strand of Heidegger's later thought, in which he coins the term "desertification [*Verwüstung*]" to describe the (material) effects of the mode of thought he calls *Vorstellung*, which he sees as the West's prevalent mode of thinking ever since Plato's conception of thought as the formation of representative ideas. The image of a growing desert is employed to give urgency to the task of "fundamentally unlearning what [thinking] has been up to now" (Heidegger 1997, 5) by turning to a contemplation of the relation of language and the human. The stakes, according to Heidegger, could not be higher: an appropriate style is not merely a matter of moral responsibility. It may even "rescue [*retten*]" the human from the danger posed to its essence.

The stylistic inventions of Heidegger's later thought, his use of conversations, and his ever more poetic language resist the notion that language is an instrument of communication. Heidegger uses his writing style to question the very demand Adorno retrospectively places upon him. It is here that I would like to introduce a reading of the term *arrogance*. As a compound of *ad* and *rogare*, *arrogance* is intrinsically connected to the problematic of questioning. In Latin it can literally mean both "to put to question" and "to be beyond questioning." It is with this double meaning in mind that I propose to approach the question of Heidegger's style. The moment Heidegger sets out on his path toward a renewal of thought, the semblance of arrogance becomes an increasing concern, but also one of the resources of his writing style. The term *arrogance* (*Überheblichkeit*) is carefully deployed to counter the impression that he is "elevating himself too far"—the literal translation of the German term. However, arrogance is also employed to raise an ethical concern which could not be illustrated otherwise, since the "danger to the essence of man," metaphorically disclosed by the idea of a growing desert, is, as I outline, fundamentally connected to the question of style. Adorno's charge that Heidegger is placing himself "beyond questioning" by means of a stylistic device would thus be countered by the suggestion that this very charge is a symptom of the conception of language which is being "put to question." I argue that the relation between what Heidegger calls the instrumental (technical) aspect of language and what he sees as its poetic ground can provide an insight into the ethical dimension of style. I will approach this question by focusing on *Verwüstung*, a term which is commonly employed to suggest "destruction," since it is here that Heidegger's "arrogance" is most apparent.

Verwüstung first appears in Heidegger's penning of a fictional conversation between two prisoners of war. The "Evening Conversation" is dated May 8, 1945, but was only posthumously published. On the day of Germany's capitulation, when large parts of Europe lay in ruins, Heidegger has the younger interlocutor say: "The desertification which we mean has not just existed since yesterday. Neither does it exhaust itself in the visible and tangible. Also, it can never be calculated by adding up acts of destruction and the loss of human lives, as if desertification were merely a result of this [destruction]" (2007a, 207).[2] This position informs the stance reiterated in several of Heidegger's postwar writings. The forgetting of being (*Seinsvergessenheit*), which is perpetuated by the mode of thought Heidegger calls the formation of representational ideas (*Vorstellung*), is seen as the direct but hidden cause of the World Wars. This notion is brutally encapsulated in the lines with which Heidegger signs the "Evening Conversation": "[written] on the day the world was celebrating its victory and did not yet realize that for centuries it had already been the victim of its own uprising [*Aufstand*]" (240). This comment, a reference to the technological and scientific progress which has enabled the rise of the West, poignantly illustrates Heidegger's arrogance.

The first part of this essay will show how desertification is a critique of *Vorstellung*. According to Heidegger, this mode of thought, which secures itself against an object of representation, assumes that the object of its evaluation can ultimately be understood and mastered. The knowledge so obtained enables a "calculating-acting" (Heidegger 2000a, 10) which has improved the quality of life. Heidegger claims that this tangible effect has not only affirmed the validity of representational thought, but has

---

[2]In *What is Called Thinking?* (Heidegger 1997, especially 10–24, 60–70) the concept of desertification is developed in discussion of Nietzsche's sentence "'the desert is growing, woe to him [*weh dem*], who harbours [*birgt*] deserts within.'" In this earlier formulation, however, Nietzsche's sentence is not alluded to directly.

also left its overall conception of being unquestioned. It is this forgetting of (the question of) being at the heart of *Vorstellung* which Heidegger addresses with the concept of *Verwüstung*. The visually evocative image of a growing desert is used to give his earlier writings, in which the question of being (*Seinsfrage*) is posed, a more overtly critical edge.

For Heidegger, the omission of the question of being is most manifest in the conception of language which underpins representational thought. Following the rationale of Hölderlin's line "'where there is danger the saving power grows also'" (Heidegger 2004c, 32), Heidegger analyzes *Vorstellung* in order to develop an alternative style of questioning. It is only through the "unlearning" of representational thought that its reorientation can be attained. This necessarily involves the transformation of the style by which thinking operates through a reconception of its relation to language. If one sticks to the assertion that "questioning is the piety of thought," one might say that, for Heidegger, content and justification answer rather too willingly by hiding the fact that they are nonetheless linguistic constructions.

The ethics Heidegger develops in his later works, I suggest, can only be hinted at stylistically, since "that which heals [*Heilende*] never lets itself be represented in statements [*aussagenden Sätzen*]" (Heidegger 2007a, 231). This leads to a style of employing language which actively attempts to counteract the diagnosed process of desertification. In Heidegger, the *how* of language, the manner in which it speaks and is employed, has precedence over its *what*, the determinable content which can be summarized and translated. The refusal to write an instructive ethics does not refuse instruction as such, but rather the mode of its delivery. This task is warily announced in the "Evening Conversation": "It is going to be most difficult to show desertification to those afflicted *without arrogance* and to give them advice—without the slightest trace of dictation [*Bevormundung*]—on the long reflection required to become familiar with desertification as an event that lies beyond human guilt and expiation" (216; emphasis mine). This quotation reiterates that instructing explanations must be avoided, but it also introduces a stance prevalent in Heidegger's postwar texts which seems to suggest that the events of the war are to be considered beyond the realm of human guilt. Heidegger's insistence that the war is a mere symptom of "the danger to the essence of man" constituted by the essence of modern technology is heavily criticized by Adorno; the suspicion is never far away, as Anson Rabinbach elaborates, that this line of argument is merely an attempt to "philosophically excuse" an involvement in Nazism (1997, 99). It is, however, not this question that I am interested in when I use the term arrogance, since any judgment on whether Heidegger's style of thinking is ethical is already intrinsically connected to the *ethical aporia* of style which I will outline in the second part of this essay. I will show that the term arrogance, which is part of the fabric of the project of "unlearning" representational thought, is a mark of responsibility as much as irresponsibility. In conclusion, I will draw out this paradox, which is opened by Heidegger's writings.

The question of being as a question of style

"'When are you going to write an ethics?'" This question—allegedly posed by a "young friend" 20 years earlier—is recounted by Heidegger in his first publication after the war (2000a, 45). Rather than answering the question with a program outlining "how man . . . ought to live in a fitting manner," the question's call for an ethics is seen as symptomatic of a "perplexity [*Ratlosigkeit*]" about how man should live (45; see also Brandner 1992, 13–19). This perplexity is conceptualized in the recurring theme of an "urgency for housing [*Wohnungsnot*]," a homelessness of which bombed out cities are a consequence, and not a cause (Heidegger 2004a, 156; Heidegger 2004b, 181–2).[3] In the "Evening Conversation" desertification is conceived as a "malice" which is "not evil in the sense of the moral badness of its supposed originators." It cannot be averted—as the older interlocutor continues his explanation—by "moral indignation, even if expressed by a worldwide public" (2007a, 209). On the contrary, as the dialogue continues, it is feared that moral indignation will further cast the question of being into oblivion, thus consolidating desertification.[4]

---

[3]Adorno's response to this notion can be found in Adorno 1973a, 33–5.
[4]For the main markers of Heidegger's "gesture of defiance" (Rabinbach 1997, 115) in view of the moral response to the war, see Rabinbach 1997, 113–17.

The question about ethics is repeated only to indicate that its demand will not be answered. Heidegger rather turns to the contemplation of the "originary" term *ethos*, described as follows: "*ethos* means residence [*Aufenthalt*], the place of dwelling. The word names the open region in which the human dwells. The openness of its residence lets that appear which approaches the human in its essence and—arriving in such a manner—resides in its proximity" (Heidegger 2000a, 46). *Verwüstung*, as I understand it, is an allusion to this notion of *ethos*; it describes a retreating "openness." Thus Heidegger takes ethics literally. For him, the term describes the already defined and historically determined dwelling space into which one is thrown. The ethical determination of man as a "*homo humanus*" is resisted, because it conceals the relation of language and being (Heidegger 2000a, 11). For Heidegger, the human's dwelling space is not ethics in the shape of moral knowledge, but language. As he famously puts it, "language is the house of being. The human lives in its dwelling" (2000a, 5). After the war, the question of dwelling, already central to *Being and Time*, is explicitly turned into a question of language.[5]

Language, however, does not merely denote the expression of words. For Heidegger, *it* is the very possibility of sense and meaning. This circumstance is maybe best illustrated as the already-felt presence of being, the "understanding of being" which is a prerequisite of expression in the first place.[6] The axiomatic line "*die Sprache spricht* [language speaks]" (Heidegger 2007b, 12) indicates that *it* speaks, even when it is not employed: "The human would not be human, were it denied to it to speak incessantly in an '*it is*' [and to do this] from anywhere, to anything, in multiple variations and mostly by not bringing anything to word [*unausgesprochen*]" (241).[7]

---

[5]Heidegger (2006a, 54) writes, "'I am' means: I dwell, reside by . . . the world, with which I am intimate [*vertraut*] as being such and such."

[6]"We do not *know,* what [the term] 'being' says [*besagt*]. But already when we ask: 'what is "being"?' we stand [*halten uns*] in an understanding (*Verständnis*] of the 'is' without being able to fix conceptually [*begrifflich*] what the 'is' means" (Heidegger 2006a, 5). The fact that being is already understood is thus approached as a linguistic problem: the term "is" conceals a question which cannot be put to *word.* It is this inability, which calls on us to speak. Derrida (1982, 175–205) provides a detailed reading of the particular linguistic problem the term "being" represents.

[7]See also Heidegger 1993, 112: "only because the human can say: 'it is,' can it also say 'I am,' and not vice versa."

For Heidegger, language is the experience of the call of being, "the opening," as Jean-Luc Nancy puts it, "of and to sense" (2003, 186). This call is always already fashioned—its opening delimited—by a speakable language and the epistemic frameworks informing it. The call of being cannot be apprehended in isolation but is always experienced concretely through discernible entities (and thoughts). Language discloses *how* the call of being *is heard*, how entities are apprehended and brought into relation. By opening us to the word, language as this "hearing" is the *ethos* of the human.

This originary openness, however, is *necessarily* forgotten and lost. This loss is not a lack but the very condition of speech: "We can actually only speak a language, speak of and about something, because in its everyday usage, language does not bring itself to word, but rather holds itself back in itself. Where then does language itself come to word as language? Curiously there, where we cannot find the right word for something that concerns, attracts, besets or rejoices us" (Heidegger 2007b, 161). In the prewar writings, this phenomenon of being left without words describes a "naked" apprehension of being, an experience of passivity in which one is forced to realize that one "is and has to be" (Heidegger 2006a, 134–5).[8] This is also the moment in which the hold of linguistic expression is most markedly felt. By consigning one to silence, the call of being forces one to realize that *it* is speaking, that the self-evidence and transparency of linguistic expression can "break open" (134). The phenomenon of forced silence is given preference in *Being and Time* because it *emphasizes* the disclosedness [*Erschlossentheit*] of sense and meaning (190–1). It can be contemplated only because one is already in its sway. Stripped of words one has to realize that one must live with the limited sense one can make, that one is bound to the words one can employ and understand, that one is part of *a necessarily delimited* and thus *styled ethos*, in which the meaning of being has already been set-out (*ausgelegt* that is, interpreted).

The sentence *die Sprache spricht* is, as I read it here, a development of the line "*Dasein is its disclosedness*" (Heidegger 2006a, 133). The term *Erschlossenheit* illustrates the simultaneous "openness"

---

[8]In *What is Metaphysics?* (2007c, 35) Heidegger writes that "anxiety shatters the word for us." The same rationale underpins the discussion of the call of conscience, which calls only in silence (Heidegger 2006a, 267–301).

and "closedness" of being in the immediacy of experience.[9] Since entities are always concretely experienced, the immediacy of sense and meaning conceal a historicity which already shapes the manner in which they are apprehended. "Dasein is the *manner* of its disclosedness" would therefore be a more appropriate translation in this context, since it emphasizes the *primacy* of the *how* of disclosedness over the *what* of its expression. For Heidegger, the world is not made up of *content*—the entities and circumstances our words describe—but of *style*, which here denotes the specific manner in which these entities are *found already translated* into sense and meaning. One already apprehends a significance, which means that *the question of being is a question of style, not of content*. The *how* of signification determines the entity signified.

Verwüstung, desertification, can be situated at the heart of this question of style. It describes the actualization of an unhomely force which has its root in the very unhomeliness of being outlined above. The "naked" call of being forces its own conceptualization. Unhomeliness is therefore the very essence of language. "Man dwells poetically" (Heidegger 2004b) in language—as Heidegger famously reads Hölderlin's words—since it is this anguished feeling of unhomeliness which forces one to seek a measure.[10] For Heidegger, the poetic dimension of language is thus concerned with the groundlessness and immeasurability of being which the descriptive dimension of language necessarily conceals. The moment language is merely conceived as a descriptive tool, employed to *find* and not *seek* a measure, an autopoietic process is set in motion which gradually "drives [*fährt*]" knowledge down a path determined by the very mode in which being is evaluated. For Heidegger, this instrumental conception of language sets in motion a distinctly Western style of conceiving being which styles the human and shapes the planet, and forces it out of its home: "Man behaves as if *he* was the sculptor and master of language,

[9]*Erschlossenheit* is derived from *schliessen* which means "to close." *Erschliessen* describes the process by which a stretch of land, for example, becomes accessible through the creation of an infrastructure, and has thus been "opened up," or "made accessible." Literally, however, the term describes the opposite, namely a process of locking down (see Heidegger 2006a, 222).

[10]David Michael Kleinberg-Levin (2005, especially xvii–xliv, 21–61) draws out the implications of Heidegger's essay in a detailed reading.

whereas *it*, however, remains the ruler over man. Maybe it is before all else the inversion of *this* power relation incited by man, that drives his essence into the unhomely [*Unheimische*]" (2004a, 140). The instrumental conception of language thinks of being as preexisting its presencing in thought; being itself is conceived to exist *beyond the realm of style*. It is the thing styled by thought. Therefore, it is seen to have a necessary cause beyond it. The more the human is conceived as the center from which an objective observation of nature can emanate, the more the world is shaped and transformed by one possible response to the call of being.[11]

In the *Zollikon Seminars* Heidegger quotes from Descartes's *Discours de la méthode* to emphasize that "science is bent to '*turn us into masters over nature and to turn us into its proprietors*'" (2006b, 136). Far from being neutral then, the objectivity of science is, in Heidegger's understanding, based upon the inherently adversarial style of thinking he calls *Vorstellen*. By *placing* the object of thought *in front* of itself—a process which the term *Vor-stellen* denotes literally—representational thought already assumes a mastery over the object of its thought. Heidegger elaborates in "Überwindung der Metaphysik" that the notion of the human informing Descartes's call for a representational method "places everything at its disposal [*zu-stellen*] and so places itself in opposition to other things" (2004d, 70). Heidegger is here playing on the literal meaning of the words *Vorstellung* and *Gegenstand* (object, literally, that which stands against) in order to emphasize a destructive potential which is unleashed as soon as mastery over the object of evaluation is assumed. In pursuit of Descartes's dream, the progress achieved commits ever further "to *one* way [*eine Art*]" (Heidegger 2004d, 60) of conceiving being while also unleashing the oppositional and adversarial potential which, for Heidegger, links representation to material violence.

[11]Heidegger's concern is well summed up by Kleinberg-Levin (Levin 2005, xxxii): "If philosophy has from its inception been determined by the belief that we differ from the other animals in having a measure (*ratio*) to live by, and in having thereby a *maßgebende* capacity, an ability to give or manifest measure, then, for Heidegger, the urgent question for our time concerns the fateful reduction of this measure to calculation, *Rechenschaft*, a measure totally determined by an economy in which technologization and commodification must prevail."

It is here that an insight into the inner workings of the essence of modern technology, the *Ge-stell*, can be gained.[12] In German, the term *stellen* can denominate the process of posing a question: "a question put to me" is "*eine mir gestellte Frage.*" If I subsequently seek to answer the question, the epistemological frameworks informing it will also provide (*stellen*) the parameters of a permissible answer. The answer is merely "extracted [*herausgefördert*]" in response to the challenge (*Herausforderung*) posed by the *Ge-stell.* This is famously demonstrated in the example of the power plant and the landscape (Heidegger 2004c, 19). The ability to harness electricity not only *poses the question* of its use, but also the challenge of generating it. Scientific and technological progress responds to this demand, but at the same time it thoughtlessly transforms the way the human relates to the world. The term *herausfordern* thus describes an epistemological challenge which demands the extraction of resources which, in turn, also transforms "the human (into) the most important 'raw material'" and object of investigation (Heidegger 2004d, 88). Through this challenge the meadow reveals itself as a reservoir of coal, the human a reservoir of labor and a source of scientific data. The tangible and epistemological infrastructure which gradually accumulates creates a debt which determines how one can live. It continuously issues further challenges: the power plant may reveal itself as a polluter and become unsustainable; it may demand its replacement. The human is thus ever more at the beck and call of technology which, through its "demand" for solutions, begins to speak for the human.[13] The things supposedly mastered begin to "pursue us [*nachstellen*]" and *dictate how* and *why* questions

[12]It is worth recalling Heidegger's famous definition of the essence of modern technology here: "The mode of revelation, which dominates modern technology, does now however not unfold itself in a bringing forth in the sense of *ποίησις* [*poiēsis*]. The mode of revelation that acts within modern technology is a challenging [*Herausforderung*] that puts the request [*Ansinnen*] to nature, to supply energy that can be extracted [*herausgefördert*] and stored" (Heidegger 2004a, 18).

[13]This is maybe most poignantly summed up in the lecture series *The Ister* (1993, 53–4) held in 1942: "What distinguishes modern technology, is that it is no longer merely a 'means' which is standing in the 'service' [*Dienst*] of another, but that it unfolds its own trait of dominance [*Herrschaftscharacter*]. Technology itself demands [*fordert*] for itself and from within itself, and it develops its own mode of discipline and its own mode of conceiving victory [*Bewusstsein des Sieges*]."

can be posed (see Heidegger 2004c, 22).[14] In the greatest silence, as Heidegger puts it, language, the supposed tool, has made an instrument of us.

This process is poignantly encapsulated in Heidegger's brief discussion of *Sprachmaschinen*, "language-machines." In *Parmenides*, Heidegger states, "it is no coincidence that the modern human writes 'with' the typewriter [*Schreibmaschine*, literally, the writing-machine] and 'dictates' (the same word as 'poetry [*Dichten*]') 'into' the machine" (1992, 119).[15] Since language is conceived as a mere vehicle of meaning, a delivery system of content, it follows that the machine dictates its own mode of poetry which should smoothen and accelerate this process:

> [Since] it disturbs the speed of reading, a hand-written letter is today old fashioned and unwanted. Mechanical writing deprives the hand of its rank in the realm of the written and degrades the word to a vehicle of communication. Further, mechanical writing has the advantage that it conceals hand-writing, and therefore the character. Written by the machine [*in der Maschinenschrift*] all humans look the same. (Heidegger 1992, 119)

I have taken the liberty of translating *Maschinenschrift* in the way that I have in order to emphasize that for Heidegger, the typewriter acts as a metaphor for the actualization of the instrumental conception of language. Heidegger is quick to dismiss the negative tone of his words by emphasizing the inevitability of the writing-machines, as these are merely a tangible consequence of having forgotten that it is language as the possibility of sense which discloses being, and not the human. For Heidegger, a thoughtlessness resides at the very heart of representational thought. It has mistaken the disclosedness of being, the access to meaning granted through our dwelling in language, to be the access to being itself, and not merely to its conception. For Heidegger, the measurability of being which language enables has gradually turned into a

[14]The most extensive discussion of the pursuing and demanding character of modern technology is discussed in Heidegger 2005, 46–67.

[15]See Kleinberg-Levin (2005, 208ff.) for an alternate reading of this passage, and an outline of some of the reactions it has prompted.

destructive form of poetry and an impersonal calculation dictated by modern technology.

It is this *technological poetry* that is announced by the term *Verwüstung*. A desert is concealed at the outset of the Western tradition to "then draw everything into itself" (Heidegger 2007a, 212). The printing press and typewriter are merely stages of a process in which the world becomes *calculable* by one measure (object-oriented representation); a measure, however, granted not by the human, but by the unfolding "machine" of language. In 1957 Heidegger offers a compelling description of this process: "The conception of language as an instrument of information is pressing into the ultimate today. . . . One knows that in connection to the construction of the electron-brain not only calculating machines are built, but also thinking—and translating—machines. All calculation in a narrow, as well as broader sense, all thought and translation, move [*bewegen sich*] in the element of language. Through these machines the *language-machine* [*Sprachmaschine*] has actualized [*verwirklicht*] itself" (2002, 133–54; 148–9). For Heidegger the actualization of the machine transforms the poetic speaking of language, language as the originary "measure taking" of being into an impersonal calculation.[16] The language-machine entails a confrontation with one's value, average life-expectancy, and biological composition. One is challenged and enthralled by a plethora of information, while remaining unwittingly interpellated by the individuating call of being.

In the eyes of the language-machine, however, "all humans look the same."[17] One is forced into an evaluative framework (*Ge-stell*) which has already set the parameters of one's life. One's bank balance, communicated through a mechanically generated letter, autonomously provides information about one's *credit* or *debt*. The particular writing-machine at work in my example points toward monetary value as a pertinent example of a fundamental

---

[16] An etymological comment seems fitting here. The term "*bewegen*" (to move) that Heidegger employs is derived from gothic *vigan* meaning "to weigh," "to take measure." *Deutsches Wörterbuch*, s. v. "*bewegen*."

[17] It is in this sense that the desert "can coincide with the achievement of a highest standard of living as well as the organization of uniform state of happiness for all humans" (Heidegger 1997, 11).

indebtedness to the language-machine. Monetary value has become inseparable from the calculating, trading, and betting machines which enable instantaneous flow and calculation. The hold of this particular machine needs little elaboration and it seems that Heidegger's diagnosis is not far off: "the semblance that the human is mastering the language-machine can be superficially preserved. The truth will probably be that language will start to employ [*in Betrieb nehmen*] the language-machine and so will master the essence [*Wesen*] of man" (2002a, 149). The spatial, geographical metaphor of the growing desert is the visual marker of this evolving machine. For Heidegger, the systematic evaluation and calculation which underlines *Wissenschaft* in all fields is, as Kostas Axelos (1966) demonstrates, inseparable from the language-machines of modern technology. What sets modern science (in Heidegger's sense) apart, is that its *modus operandi* is not merely a "discovering of knowledge [*Wissen-schaft*]" but also a *safeguarding of one style of disclosure* through huge investment in a convoluted form of labor. It is here that the full implications of desertification come to light. It describes a *gradual narrowing down of the possible horizon of questioning*, an erosion of the multiple manners in which being can be conceived.

Style as ethics: The task of seeing in thinking

An arrogant tone is, as I argued in the Introduction, one of the resources of Heidegger's writing style. This willful arrogance is apparent in the famous sentence "science does not think," to which Heidegger immediately adds the words: "this is a goading [*anstößig*] sentence," and notes that this "character" is intended (1997, 4). An arrogant tone is thus employed "to put to question." This has hopefully been made sufficiently apparent in the first section, in which I have tried to preserve the negative tone which Heidegger's critique of modern technology overtly conveys. Yet, at the same time, this arrogant tone is employed to introduce a style of thinking designed to bring the *unthought* dimension of thought to light. Desertification is thus not merely contemplated, but is also *acted against*, by means of stylistic invention.

Heidegger opens *Letter on Humanism* with a famous discussion of the relation between thought and praxis. Thought is at the heart of all action, all praxis (*Handeln*). It is the action of *making* sense. In response to this passage, Nancy outlines that for Heidegger "thinking (and/or poetry) is not an exceptional form of action, the 'intellectual conduct' to be preferred to others, but what, in all action, brings into play the sense (of being) without which there would be no action" (2003, 175). This *making* of sense thus exceeds mere fabrication and evaluation. Thinking, as the opening toward sense, first *lets* being be. With regard to ethics this means, as Nancy puts it, that "human conduct" is first a "conduct of sense": the manner in which sense is arrived at—the manner in which sense presences itself—fashions human conduct and the image one can have of oneself (175). This stance informs the concept of desertification discussed in the first section. The "not yet [*noch nicht*]" of thought diagnosed at the outset of *What is Called Thinking?* (Heidegger 1997, 2) can be seen as a direct response to the question of ethics which Heidegger chooses to repeat after the war. What is required is a mode of thought which distinguishes itself by a non-adversarial, that is, non-object-related style of thinking. This is summed up in "Die Kehre" in an often quoted passage: "Before [answering] the always next and singularly pressing question, what should we do? [We must consider the question] *How must we think?*" (Heidegger 1962, 40). The way to transform human conduct is not through an instructive content but through a reconsideration of the relation between language and thought.

The most explicit elaboration of this task can be found in "Das Ende der Philosophie und die Aufgabe des Denkens," in which Heidegger argues that his thought is involved in the sole task of posing the question "in which learning"—and with it thinking—"can prepare its own transformation" (2000b, 66–7). Aware of the arrogance of such a stance he writes:

> Is there not an arrogance speaking here, that wants to elevate itself above the greatness of the [previous] thinkers and philosophers? This suspicion is pressing. However, it is easily disposed of. . . . It [my thinking] is lesser than Philosophy. Lesser also because of the circumstance that in this thinking it must be prohibited even more so than it already was in philosophy to have as well

a direct, or an indirect effect on the technically and scientifically cast public of the industrial age. (2000b, 66)

This noninterventionist stance, this emphasized abstinence from seeking to influence the public is Heidegger's intervention. It is in this sense that "questioning" and not answering "is the piety of thought." However, the advice Heidegger is so cautious not to provide in the form of dictation is given in the form of a style that seeks to unlock the speaking of language in an exemplary manner. And it is here that Heidegger inevitably has to fall in line with the very notion of ethics he so skillfully seeks to deconstruct. Heidegger's "ethics" is not given in the form of a program or moral reflection, but it nevertheless operates programmatically at the level of language. This leads to texts which need to be supplemented with a commentary on how they should be read. At times, they even open with a direct demand to discount their content: "when thinking tries to pursue something that has claimed its attention, it may happen that on the way it undergoes a change. It is advisable therefore, in what follows to pay attention to the path of thought rather than to its content" (Heidegger 2003, 3).

Rather than formulating an instructive content, Heidegger thus employs an instructive style. This observation is by no means a criticism of Heidegger's thought, but it does imply that he seeks to "rescue" the human essence by liberating it from the program of representational thought. The opening footnote to *Letter on Humanism*, in fact, announces the emergence of an "other language [*andere Sprache*]" (Heidegger 2000a, 5) designed to counter the rampant "desolation" of language diagnosed in the same text. I read the footnote as an oblique reference to a passage from Goethe Heidegger was fond of: "'in every-day life [*gemeinen Leben*] we scrap by with language in a makeshift manner, because we only describe superficial relations. As soon as speech turns to deeper relations, then *another language* takes place immediately, the poetic one'" (Heidegger 2002a, 149; emphasis mine). The other language is thus the poetic language of thought which is concerned with the *unanswerable*, but already *answered*, question of being. The language of *Vorstellung* which is preoccupied with the representation of entities and its ceaseless drawing up of *conclusions*, is countered by a writing style which intends to underscore that language, as the *opening* toward sense, is a "letting see [*sehen lassen*]"[18] of entities rather than being a mere instrument for their determination. In accordance with the meaning Heidegger attributes to *technē* and *poiesis*—both Greek terms denote a process of production, that is, a making (of sense)—a technical and a poetic dimension of language are not only uncovered, but also set against each other (Heidegger 2004c, 16). Whereas the former for Heidegger points to the arrogance of an assumed mastery, the latter is seen as the mark of a *Gelassenheit*, an expression of humility in the sight of the question of being. The arrogant tone is thus understood as a gesture of humility which would save the human from the danger of representational thought; yet it is precisely here that a paradox begins to emerge to which I will gradually turn my attention.

In a speech that was broadcast in 1975, Heidegger repeats the Goethe passage quoted above and draws a strong distinction between the instrumental and poetic dimension of language. He maintains that the question of being requires "a new method of thinking . . . a praxis—as one might say—of seeing in thinking" (Rüdel and Wisser 1975; for a transcript see Wisser 1998, 425–50). This "praxis" is key to the "advice" he did not want to give in the form of "dictation." He seeks to prompt the emergence of a different conception of thought and language through the manner in which the words change and assume a meaning not present at the outset of the reading. Consequently, his words cannot directly be translated into content or into another language since their content is an *affect*, the forced experience of being at the mercy of language. The poetic mode thus emphasizes the impossibility of translating the question of being into a stable conception. Following his paths of thought, the "voyage" (*Er-fahrung*) on them should lead to a new consideration of what it means to "be passively driven" (*ge-fahren*) along a path determined by the conception that language merely represents a communicable content (Heidegger 2007b, 159; 170). The fundamental axiom—it is language that speaks and not the human as such—has to be experienced. It cannot be mediated by the means of description.

---

[18] Heidegger draws out this rationale by means of a shaky etymology through which "*sagen* [to say]" means: "to show, to let see, hear and appear" (Heidegger 2007b, 252–6).

This is the task which Heidegger sees encapsulated in Nietzsche's sentence about the growing desert. It is the "pathword [*Weg-Wort*]" which does not just illuminate a danger but "in its saying traces and clears a path" toward thought (Heidegger 1997, 61). In the short piece "Sprache und Heimat," we can find the underlying rationale of Heidegger's "advice": "we are granted rescue only then and there, where the danger is first seen in its entirety, where we have experienced the power [*Macht*] of the dangerous ourselves and acknowledged it as something that *is*" (2002b, 157). The implications of the negative tone of Heidegger's critique of modern technology can be contextualized here. Since the "danger" of desertification ultimately has its origin in the instrumental conception of language which is invited by language itself, it is the "power" of language that must be experienced. As was already the case with the inclusion of the "young friend's" question in *Letter on Humanism*, a negative tone is willfully played upon only to later indicate that it should not be heeded. An analogous strategy informs the term *Verwüstung*. Heidegger intervenes against the negative tone the term cannot fail to convey by stating that his argument does not belong to the "chorus of voices that disparage modern Europe as sick, and our age as on the decline," and is "neither pessimistic nor optimistic" (1997, 12–13; see also 58). The guiding assertion of the text which seemingly laments the "*not yet*" of thought—it is "*thought-provoking* [*bedenklich*] *that we are not yet thinking*"—is yet a further example of this strategy of playing upon the negative tone or connotations of a term (Heidegger 1997, 2).

The term *bedenklich*, then, which Heidegger seeks to distance from its immediate meaning ("worrying") in order to emphasize a verbal meaning ("that which *gives* to think," and thus lets thought be learned [Heidegger 1997, 2]) is only one of the many examples in which the accustomed tone of a term is preserved—*precisely because it is misleading*—in order to force its meaning into a new direction.[19] This is the paradox I wish to elaborate upon in conclusion: does Heidegger not expressly make use of language as an *instrument* to attain its "other" *noninstrumental* dimension? Do

[19] We have already encountered several examples in the course of this essay (*Gefahr*, *Vorstellung*, *Gegenstand*). Eric Nelson (2008, 411–35, 414) elaborates well on this point with regard to the "ethically-charged and inflected language" of the early works.

his frequent instructions on how his texts should be read not have to presume that language is also a vehicle of communication? At the outset of *Letter on Humanism* Heidegger states that the "liberation of language [*Befreiung der Sprache*] from grammar into a more originary realm of essence is held open [*aufbehalten*] for thinking and poetry" (2000a, 6). Heidegger's attempt to reach what Goethe called a "deeper" (poetic) realm of language by means of style is from the outset dependent on the perversion of grammar and accustomed meanings. This praxis does not only require the frequent interjection of direct instructions, but also achieves its very effect only by holding on to the accustomed meanings while refashioning them. The more Heidegger seeks to liberate the untranslatable aspect of language, its poetic dimension of a "saying (seeing) of being," the more he is forced into translation, circumscription, and thus communication. This inherent connection of *technē* and *poiēsis* is no doubt one of the driving factors of Heidegger's thought. How else could desertification be the product of a style of thinking? How else could it be averted through the reconception of the tool (language) by which it unfolds?[20] Heidegger, as we have seen, has no other alternative but to reproduce the violence of representation which he seeks to counteract, since this violence is the very "secret [*Geheimnis*]" by which language already houses its speaker.[21] Rather than succeeding in distancing itself from this machine, Heidegger's thought moves toward its formulation. The very style by which this liberation from the technical is sought, prepares the reformulation of the relation between the human and technology. In the wake of Heidegger, human existence is conceived to unfold not despite its turn toward the programmatic, but rather *because* of this turn toward it (*pro-gramma*). Style is poetic, but the very singularity and immediacy which this notion conveys is already a mark of the language-machine Heidegger begins to formulate.

---

[20] This aspect of Heidegger's conception of language is discussed at length in the first volume of Bernard Stiegler's *Technics and Time* (1998, 204–6).

[21] Heidegger's stance that "it is not technology that is dangerous" but that its threat consists in the secret nature of its "essence" implies that seeing the "secret [*Geheimnis*] of [technology's] essence" could grant access to a different relation to—and conception of—being (Heidegger 2004a, 29). The German term *ge-heim* (secret) with its allusion to the home is mobilized against the un-homely violence unleashed by the instrumental conception of language. It is in this sense that the "danger" also harbors that which "rescues."

In *Of Grammatology* Jacques Derrida calls this originary violence of representation "arche-writing" and famously describes it as "the nonethical opening of ethics" (1997, 140).[22] The ethos of language is thus the very calculating machine which inevitably catches our hand(s) since it demands that we style *its* words, be it with a pen or through a printer's ink. Style is thus the mark of an arrogance which has forced one to take hold of words as if they were one's own. If we recall the Latin root of the term arrogance, then one can *put it to question*, only by placing it *beyond questioning*; only by also being complicit with it. This arrogance, then, liberates the hand only by binding it. The machine evolves because it lets itself be formed and shaped, but can never be held at a distance. As a consequence, one necessarily has to "hold oneself above it [*über-heben*]" the very moment one is dragged into it. Adorno, despite clearly raising the ethical dimension of style and offering an incisive critique of Heidegger's conduct in his specific context, seems to see style as a diversion from immediate expression. In doing so, however, he points toward an aporia which he seems unable to accept: "whoever is versed in the jargon does not have to say what he thinks, does not even have to think it properly. The jargon takes over this task and devalues thought" (Adorno 1973b, 9). Following Heidegger one can ask whether there is a word that is not already part of a jargon; whether it is ever possible to simply say what one thinks, as if one were not already protected and determined by words and conceptions which one cannot own and did not invent. Style, then, is the mark of the innumerable modes of "devaluing" thought by which thinking actually takes place. It can never be purely or essentially human. When Adorno suggests that Heidegger writes "without the print even blushing" (1973b, 130), he rather stylishly gives a possible definition of style, recast as the meaning envisaged in this essay. Its arrogance would be that it shamelessly offers the illusion that it is us alone who are writing and responding. In doing so it allows us to forget, as it might be put in the wake of Heidegger, just how much the human hand is caught in the machine. It is because of Heidegger, and especially his style, that the silent movement of the machine has also prompted the reformulation of the question of ethics.

---

[22] The link between arche-writing and style is further discussed by Laurent Milesi in this volume.

References

Adorno, Theodor. 1973a. *Gesammelte Schriften Band 6: Negative Dialektik; Jargon der Eigentlichkeit*, ed. Rolf Tiedermann. Frankfurt: Suhrkamp.

—. 1973b. *The Jargon of Authenticity*. Translated by Knut Tarnowski and Frederic Will. New York: Routledge & Kegan Paul.

Axelos, Kostas. 1966. "Ein Gespräch über Wissenschaft." In *Einführung in ein künftiges Denken*, 91–9. Tübingen: Max Niemeyer.

Brandner, Rudolf. 1992. *Warum Heidegger keine Ethik Geschrieben hat*. Wien: Passagen Verlag.

Derrida, Jacques. 1982. "The Supplement of Copula: Philosophy Before Linguistics." In *Margins of Philosophy*, translated by Alan Bass, 175–205. New York: Harvester Wheatsheaf.

—. 1997. *Of Grammatology*. Translated by Gayatri Spivak. London: John Hopkins University Press.

Heidegger, Martin. 1962. "Die Kehre." In *Die Technik und die Kehre*, 37–47. Stuttgart: Klett-Cotta.

—. 1992. *Gesamtausgabe Band 54: Parmenides*. Frankfurt: Vittorio Klostermann.

—. 1993. *Gesamtausgabe Band 53: Hölderlin's Hymne* "Der Ister." Frankfurt: Vittorio Klostermann.

—. 1997. *Was heisst Denken?* Tübingen: Max Niemeyer.

—. 2000a. *Über den Humanismus*. Tübingen: Niemeyer.

—. 2000b. "Das Ende der Philosophie und die Aufgabe des Denkens." In *Zur Sache des Denkens*, 61–80. Tübingen: Niemeyer.

—. 2002a. "Hebel der Hausfreund." In *Aus der Erfahrung des Denkens*, 133–50. Frankfurt: Vittorio Klostermann.

—. 2002b. "Sprache und Heimat." In *Aus der Erfahrung des Denkens*, 155–80. Frankfurt: Vittorio Klostermann.

—. 2003. *Identität und Differenz*. Stuttgart: Klett-Cotta.

—. 2004a. "Bauen Wohnen Denken." In *Vorträge und Aufsätze*, 139–56. Stuttgart: Klett-Cotta.

—. 2004b. ". . . dichterisch wohnet der Mensch." In *Vorträge und Aufsätze*, 181–99. Stuttgart: Klett-Cotta.

—. 2004c. "Die Frage nach der Technik." In *Vorträge und Aufsätze*, 9–40. Stuttgart: Klett-Cotta.

—. 2004d. "Überwindung der Metaphysik." In *Vorträge und Aufsätze*, 67–95. Stuttgart: Klett-Cotta.

—. 2005. "Die Gefahr." In *Bremer und Freiburger Vorträge*, 46–67. Frankfurt: Vittorio Klostermann.

—. 2006a. *Sein und Zeit*. Tübingen: Niemeyer.

—. 2006b. *Zollikoner Seminare*. Frankfurt: Vittorio Klosterman.

—. 2007a. "Abendgespräch in einem Kriegsgefangenenlager in Russland zwischen einem Jüngeren und einem Älteren." In *Gesamtausgabe Band 77: Feldweg-Gespräche*, 201–40. Frankfurt: Vittorio Klostermann.

—. 2007b. *Unterwegs zur Sprache.* Stuttgart: Klett-Cotta.

—. 2007c. *Was ist Methaphysik?* Frankfurt: Vittorio Klostermann.

Kleinberg-Levin, David Michael. 2005. *Gestures of Ethical Life: Reading Hölderlin's Question of Measure After Heidegger.* Stanford: Stanford University Press.

Nancy, Jean-Luc. 2003. "Originary Ethics." Translated by Duncan Large. In *Finite Thinking*, edited by Simon Sparks, 172–95. Stanford: Stanford University Press.

Nelson, Eric. 2008. "Heidegger and the Questionability of the Ethical." *Studia Phenomenologica* 8: 411–35.

Rabinbach, Anson. 1997. *In the Shadow of Catastrophe.* Berkeley: University of California Press.

Rüdel, Walter and Richard Wisser, dirs. 1975. *Im Denken Unterwegs*, dir. Baden-Baden: Südwestfunk. Videocassette (VHS).

Stiegler, Bernard. 1998. "The Instrumental Condition." In *Technics and Time, 1*, translated by Richard Beardsworth and George Collins, 204–6. Stanford: Stanford University Press.

Wisser, Richard. 1998. "Martin Heidegger: Im Denken Unterwegs: Ein Film von Richard Wisser und Walter Rüdel. Drehbuch." In *Vom Weg-Charakter des Philosphischen Denkens*, 425–50. Würzburg: Könighausen und Neumann.

8

Style is the man: Meillassoux, Heidegger, and finitude

James Corby

Correlated style

Quentin Meillassoux's *After Finitude*, published in French in 2006 and translated into English in 2008, calls for a new style of philosophy, one that rejects the limiting legacy of Kantian critical philosophy and reinstates knowledge of the absolute as the proper aim of philosophical inquiry. It is a message that echoes loudly throughout the book, from the first paragraph, where Meillassoux makes it clear that "what is at stake . . . is the nature of thought's relation to the absolute" (2008, 1), to the final line where he enjoins us to "reconcile thought and absolute" (128).

The boldness of Meillassoux's project has attracted a significant amount of attention and commentary, much of which astutely notes that Meillassoux's call for change is no less remarkable stylistically, aesthetically and formally signaling the substantial philosophical rupture it advocates. Alain Badiou, in the preface to *After Finitude*, comments on the "astonishing force" (Meillassoux 2008, vii) of Meillassoux's arguments and on his "particularly lucid and argumentative style" (viii). Peter Hallward notes the book's "trenchant force," calling it "exceptionally clear and concise, entirely devoted to a single chain of reasoning" (2008, 51). Simon Critchley, in a review published in the *Times Literary Supplement*, observes that "there is something absolutely exhilarating about Meillassoux's argument," commenting that "although his style of presentation can turn into a sort of fine-grained logic-chopping worthy of Duns Scotus, the rigor, clarity and passion of the argument can be breathtaking" (2009).[1]

The principal target upon which Meillassoux trains this forensic gaze is what he terms "correlationism," which he identifies as "the central notion of modern philosophy since Kant" (2008, 5). Meillassoux explains:

> By "correlation" we mean the idea according to which we only ever have access to the correlation between thinking and being, and never to either term considered apart from the other. We will henceforth call *correlationism* any current of thought which maintains the unsurpassable character of the correlation so defined. Consequently, it becomes possible to say that every philosophy which disavows naïve realism has become a variant of correlationism.[2] (2008, 5)

Such thinking results in what Meillassoux calls "the correlationist circle," "according to which one cannot think the in-itself without entering into a vicious circle, thereby immediately contradicting oneself" (2008, 5). Correlationist thinking, of course, has developed its own particular stylistic traits with which it is often associated. Identifying markers range from the ubiquity of the prefix "co-" (which Meillassoux calls "the grammatical particle that dominates modern philosophy, its veritable 'chemical formula'" [5–6]) and the term "always already" (another "essential locution" according to Meillassoux [7]) through to the dense styling of deconstructive writing, which

[1]Gabriel Riera (2008) also comments on its "clarity and consistency." Graham Harman (2011, 9) refers to Meillassoux's "precision labors that resemble the work of a gem cutter." Meillassoux's desire for clarity and precision is manifested, most noticeably, in the frequent use of examples and recourse to summary.

[2]On a stylistic note, it seems quite extraordinary that in a short anti-correlationist paper entitled "Time Without Becoming" (2008), presented at Middlesex University, Meillassoux should use the decidedly correlationist phrase "according to me" no fewer than ten times!

sets out performatively to counter the naïve faith in objectivity that arguably is manifested in the profound and widespread cultural and artistic investment in realism and the fidelity of representation, as well as in the confidence in demonstration and observation characteristic of the sciences. Such linguistic strategies suggest a desire to foreground the essential finitude of any given perspective insofar as that perspective is indissociably imbricated in a self or a world or a multiplicity of signifying systems that can never accede to the sort of self-coincidental transparency that might make an objective, noncorrelational grasping of the world-in-itself possible. The correlationist, then, is a type of relativist for whom nothing is true, justified, or as it is *simpliciter.*[3]

In the twentieth century, the "two principal 'media' of the correlation," Meillassoux writes, "were consciousness and language" (2008, 6). An inability to transcend either one of these (or both) restricts philosophy to an exploration of how things are *for us* rather than how things are or might be *in themselves*. The finitude of our perspectival grasp of the world, one might say, *infects* or *deforms* everything that we know or can claim to know.[4] It should not be surprising that philosophy and, latterly, theory have often reacted to this situation by animating various forms of broadly romantic thought (aporetic thinking, tropes of marginality, borders, alterity, fideism, revolutionary suspension of law, and so on) since this interdiction against absolute knowledge was established in philosophy by Kant's Copernican turn, where it encountered strongest resistance in the emerging romanticism of Friedrich Schlegel and Novalis. Behind this, Meillassoux sees the return of a religious impulse:

> The end of metaphysics, understood as the "de-absolutization of thought," is thereby seen to consist in the rational legitimation of any and every variety of religious (or "poetico-religious") belief in the absolute, so long as the latter invokes no authority beside

---

[3]Although "correlationism" is not referred to by name, for the broader context see Williams (2001, 220–9).

[4]Maurice Merleau-Ponty (1973, 60, 61), quoting André Malraux, suggests that style might be thought of as a "coherent deformation." This idea is explored in relation to twentieth-century art and literature by Carbone (2010, 33–47).

> itself. To put in other words: *by forbidding reason any claim to the absolute, the end of metaphysics has taken the form of an exacerbated return of the religious.*[5] (2008, 45)

Absolute knowledge—that is, knowledge of how things are in themselves—is claimed, in the modern era, by science and mathematics, and philosophy is deemed no longer capable of accounting for knowledge that purports to be independent of and unaffected by human existence. This correlationist position has, Meillassoux thinks, served only to stymie and embarrass philosophy. *After Finitude* sets out his attempt to lead philosophy back out once again to "the great outdoors, the eternal in-itself, whose being is indifferent to whether or not it is thought" (Meillassoux 2008, 63), "that outside which [is] not relative to us" (7). He describes this noncorrelated realm as possessing the "independence of substance." It is a "*glacial* world . . . in which there is no longer any up or down, centre or periphery, nor anything else that might make of it a world *designed* for humans" (latter emphasis mine). Revealing the influence of his former mentor, Alain Badiou, Meillassoux suggests that it is only by means of modern mathematized science that "the world manifests itself as capable of subsisting without any of those aspects that constitute its concreteness for us" (115).

An account of how Meillassoux intends to lead philosophy out of the correlationist circle, and an evaluation of whether he can to any degree be considered successful, are beyond the scope of this chapter. Nor would they be strictly relevant, since the primary interest here is Meillassoux's premise that correlationism is a mistake to be overcome, and the peculiar *manner* or *style* in which (and, as I will argue, *by* which) *le grand dehors* or the absolute or the unconditioned might be considered out of bounds for us. It should then gradually become clear why it might be thought that it is precisely an inattention to matters of style that constitutes *After Finitude*'s most radical and provocative stance, one that risks rendering it as distant and as ultimately irrelevant as that glacial realm of the absolute to which it aspires.

When Meillassoux talks about the world beyond the correlationist circle as possessing "the independence of substance," and suggests that it is "capable of subsisting without any of those

---

[5]All italics in quotations are those of the author quoted unless otherwise indicated.

aspects that constitute its concreteness for us," we might feel prompted to think of the Aristotelian conception of substance. In the *Categories* Aristotle famously defines a substance as that which is neither predicable of anything nor present in anything as an aspect or property of it (1995, 2a10). Substances remain self-identical through change (4a15–20). Aristotle distinguishes substances from all other things, which are merely accidents of substances and exist as aspects, properties, or relations of substances (1b25–2a1). If Kermit the Frog is a substance, then the fact that he is green would be classed as an accident. Meillassoux, however, in drawing our attention to Locke's distinction between primary and secondary qualities (while acknowledging the prior existence of that distinction in Descartes), seems to feel more at home with British empiricism which, of course, in many respects constituted a rejection of the tradition of Aristotelian Scholasticism. This is perhaps not insignificant. For Locke, primary qualities are those that are "utterly inseparable from the Body [i.e. material object]" (1979, 134), namely, "Solidity, Extension, Figure, Motion, or Rest, and Number." Secondary qualities—"Colours, Sounds, Tasts, *etc.*"—in contrast, "are nothing in the Objects themselves, but Powers to produce various Sensations in us" (135). Thus, Kermit has a definite physical shape, but he is green only insofar as an idea of his greenness is produced in our minds.

We might be inclined to think that it is largely such secondary qualities or Aristotelian accidents that make the thing what it is ("constitute its concreteness") "for us" (Meillassoux 2008, 115). The implication of this is that such aspects and properties must be considered peripheral or even extraneous to any absolute conception of something. They are just the way we dress up the bare world of substances or primary qualities. Any attempt to grasp the world absolutely, then, would involve, as it were, *undressing* the *clothed* world of experience. Only then would we be able to step outside of the correlationist circle. However, under the influence of Berkeley, Hume's critique of this standard theory of the qualities apparently puts paid to any such possibility. Hume collapses the distinction between primary and secondary qualities by arguing that both are experienced through the senses and are, as such, matters of perception. Merely on the evidence of the senses, therefore, there cannot be any justification for imposing a distinction between two orders of qualities on the basis that one inheres in objects and the other inheres in the relationship between subject and object (Hume 1983, 192–3). Moreover, Hume shows that what Locke took to be primary qualities can only be known to us through so-called secondary qualities (229). Clearly, on this view, the notion of something like substance in an Aristotelian sense cannot be anything but cognitively empty. We appear, therefore, to be fully contained within the correlationist circle, the clothed world "designed for humans," by humans, in the act of perception.[6] Ironically, though, Meillassoux's attempt to break out of the correlationist circle arguably leads him away from Hume's skeptical empiricism and back toward Aristotle. Humean skepticism and post-Kantian correlationism allow him to argue that the facticity of human experience is universalizable. This then provides him with something that, ironically, might be said to approximate, albeit very abstractly, Aristotelian substance. For Meillassoux, that which "remain[s] self-identical through change" is the very possibility of radical change implied by a factical, correlationist view of the world. The glimpse beyond correlationism offered by this rather subtle argument is encouragement enough for Meillassoux to call for the distinction between primary and secondary qualities to be reinstated: "*all those aspects of the object that can be formulated in mathematical terms can be meaningfully conceived as properties of the object in itself.*" His thesis is that these "mathematizable properties of the object" are, unlike the sensible, free from the constraint of "the subject's relation to the world" (2008, 3).

But before we allow ourselves to be carried along by Meillassoux's breathtakingly bold argument, let us pause here and look a little more closely at what he is proposing we cast aside. How might we understand this clothed, finite, relative, or relational realm that exists only and, at least in the post-Kantian tradition, irrecusably for us? Styling this question somewhat differently, one might ask: *in* what *manner* and *by* what *manner* are we excluded from absolute knowledge? Accidents and substance may be a familiar philosophical pairing, but perhaps its even more familiar relation, the common hendiadys *style and substance*, might be a more promising way of approaching these questions. Thus understood, the world-for-us would be the world *styled* by us, the world disclosed

---

[6]The notion that perception stylizes is prominent in the work of Merleau-Ponty (1973, 58–61).

in the human style; in dressing up the bare substance of the world, we, as human beings, style the world according to our own style or styles.

Correlationism, then, would be viewed as the de-absolutization of knowledge but the absolutization of style, rendering substance (i.e. the in-itself) secondary to, and thus conditioned by, the manner or style by which it is taken up into cognition. This is not just *any* style, of course. For there to be a relatively coherent common experience of the world, and yet for that experience not to be absolute, there must be some shared sense in which *we* cannot help but style the world as we encounter it, rendering it and any knowledge of it relational to ourselves. A human styling, in other words. So although correlationism presents some form of human styling as the absolute condition of knowledge, such styling is, in Meillassoux's terms, factical rather than absolutely necessary. In other words, for the correlationist, forms of thought (such as, for Kant, "space and time as forms of intuition and the twelve categories of the understanding" [Meillassoux 2008, 38]) can only be described, not deduced as a matter of absolute necessity. So whereas they might be said to hold for everyone (they are "fixed" [39]) and as such constitute a fact, "we cannot think why it should be impossible for them to change, nor why a reality wholly other than the one that is given to us should be proscribed *a priori*" (40). Meillassoux's response to correlationism involves recognizing and endorsing "the non-facticity of facticity" (79), that is, the necessity or absoluteness of contingency implicit in the correlationist's position. That the de-absolutization of knowledge produces its own absolute—absolute contingency—is, Meillassoux suggests, "the faultline that lies right at the heart of correlationism; the one through which we can breach its defenses" (59). As Ray Brassier puts it,

> to absolutize facticity is to assert the unconditional necessity of its contingency, and hence to assert that it is possible to think something that exists independently of thought's relation to it: contingency as such. In absolutizing facticity, correlationism subverts the empirical-transcendental divide separating knowable contingency from unknowable facticity even as it strives to maintain it; but it is thereby forced to acknowledge that what it took to be a negative characteristic of our relation

> to things—viz., that we cannot know whether the principles of cognition are necessary or contingent—is in fact a positive characteristic of things-in-themselves. (2007, 67)

The facticity endorsed by correlationism that Meillassoux forces against itself, then, requires that there be the possibility that how the object is in itself might well be entirely different to how it appears styled by us and, moreover, how it appears to us is not guaranteed to remain the same. This is, of course, in keeping with Hume's revision of the theory of the qualities, but it is also implied in calling the human way of encountering the world a "style": it has often been claimed that for anything to be a style or styled, there must be alternative possibilities. Stephen Ullmann, for instance, writes:

> There can be no question of style unless the speaker or writer has the possibility of choosing between alternative forms of expression. Synonymy, in the widest sense of the term, lies at the root of the whole problem of style. (1957, 6)

E. H. Gombrich (1968, 353) has argued that style exists against a "background of alternative choices." Berel Lang (1987, 178) suggests that "style presupposes choice," meaning that "only where there are two styles is there one," and that "this is a condition both for the detection of style and for its existence." This is echoed by Leonard B. Meyer (1987, 21) who, in defining style, suggests that it "*results from a series of choices made within some set of constraints*." The emphasis on choice in these quotations might strike us as a little problematic in the context of the analogy with correlationism as it is easier to think of this type of correlation as factical rather than both factical *and* optative, but as I hope will become clear when we turn to Heidegger, it need not be so. Setting that aside for a moment, though, we can conclude that style is changeable, plural, and never necessary. Absolute knowledge—that is, knowledge of the glacial, nonhuman world—would therefore be styleless, and any form of scientific or mathematical knowledge claiming to be absolute in this sense would, literally *of necessity*, be styleless. Human being, one might even say, is made manifest, in all aspects, as style, and moreover, that *styling* is the horizon beyond which post-Kantian philosophy has deemed itself incapable of thinking. Would it be too flippant to conclude that Buffon was right? Style *is* the man?

Would this not be too conveniently styled a conclusion to have any substance? Should we not, perhaps, be wary of what Wittgenstein called the "cheap epigrammatic brevity of the phrase" (2006, 89)?[7] Peter Gay, in his book *Style in History*, suggests that "Buffon's epigram has a beautiful simplicity that makes it both possibly profound and certainly suspect" (1988, 3). But the idea that man, that is, the human, is tied in some fundamental way to style or to something like style has, over the ages, resonated with enough writers, thinkers, and philosophers to give us pause and invite us to wonder whether the idea might indeed be one of substance as much as it is of style. Cicero, in the *Tusculan Disputations*, attributes the idea to Socrates.[8] In 1589, long before Buffon, George Puttenham, in *The Arte of English Poesie*, declares "stile, the image of man" (1869, 161).[9] Robert Burton, in *The Anatomy of Melancholy*, says, "It is most true, *stilus virum arguit*, our style bewrays us" (2001, 27).[10] Pascal, in the *Pensées*, anticipates Buffon when he suggests that "custom is our nature" (1995, 125; 1963, 419) and that when we "see a natural style we are quite amazed and delighted, because

---

[7]Wittgenstein (2006, 89) is keen to point out that "style is the man" ("le style c'est l'homme") is in fact a misquotation which should read "style is the man himself" ("le style c'est l'homme même"). He interprets the latter as possessing much greater significance than the abbreviated version.

[8]"Now we wish it [life] to be supremely happy and our view is confirmed by Socrates' well-known conclusion. For this was the way in which that leader of philosophy argued, that as was the disposition of each individual soul so was the man; and as was the man in himself so was his speech; moreover deeds resembled speech and life resembled deeds" (1945, V.16.47).

[9]"And because this continuall course and manner of writing or speech sheweth the manner and disposition of the writers minde, more than one or few words or sentences can shew, therefore there be that haue called stile, the image of man [*mentis character*] for man is but his minde, and as his minde is tempered and qualified, so are his speeches and his language at large, and his inward conceits be the metall of his minde, and his manner of vtterance the very warp and woofe of his conceits" (1869, 160–1).

[10]"It is most true, *stilus virum arguit*, our style bewrays us, and as hunters find their game by the trace, so is a man's genius descried by his works; *multo melius ex sermone quam lineamentis de moribus hominum judicamus* (we can judge a man's character much better from his conversation than his physiognomy); 'twas old Cato's rule. I have laid myself open (I know it) in this treatise, turned mine inside outward" (2001, 27).

we expected to see an author and find a man" (1995, 215; 1963, 675). Arthur Schopenhauer says that "style is the physiognomy of the mind" (2004, 11).[11] Edward Gibbon limits the reach of the claim a little when he asserts that "style is the image of character" (1900, 1). Walter Pater argues that far from reducing style to the subjectivity of the individual, the notion that "style is the man" locates man "not in his unreasoned and really uncharacteristic caprices, involuntary or affected, but in absolutely sincere apprehension of what is most real to him." In this sense, Pater holds, style is "impersonal" (2008, 23–4). Freud adjusts the phrase to his own needs and declares that "style is the history of the man" (Reik 1973, 223).[12] Jacques Lacan begins *Écrits* with Buffon's phrase but finds its modification to "style is the man one addresses" more appealing, though entirely expectedly he worries that "man is no longer so sure a reference point" (2006, 3). Deleuze, intriguingly, asserts that "style is not the man, style is essence itself" (2000, 48). Philippe Lacoue-Labarthe suggests that style is "*confession* itself" (1998, 166). Berel Lang speaks of "the native connection between style and person" (1987, 182). Stanley Cavell, discussing Wittgenstein's brief remarks on the phrase, suggests that the "insight of the aphorism is . . . that every handling by the man (of an impulse or circumstance) is a signature, or a sketch that needs no signature for its attribution" (2004, 32). Jacques Derrida playfully, if obliquely, refers to the phrase in *Spurs* (1979, 57) and draws attention to it again in "On Style" (Derrida and Cixous 2010, 201). The idea pervades much of Merleau-Ponty's work, most notably *The Prose of the World* (1973), where he explores the idea that our way of perceiving or being-in-the-world is shaped by human style (see also Linda Singer 1998). For one reason or another, the

[11]Significantly, given the argument of this chapter, he goes on to say: "A man's style shows the *formal* nature of all his thoughts—the formal nature which can never change, be the subject or the character of his thoughts what it may: it is, as it were, the dough out of which all the contents of his mind are kneaded" (2004, 11–12).

[12]Reik says: "Freud once varied the saying 'Le style, c'est l'homme' to 'Le style, c'est l'histoire de l'homme'" (1973, 223). Elsewhere, Reik writes: "Freud revised the well-known maxim to 'Style est l'histoire de l'homme'. By that maxim he did not mean merely that literary influences fashioned the style of the individual, but that the development and experiences of an individual do their part in moulding his style" (1942, 19).

notion that man is intimately related to style has long captured the imagination and continues to resonate to this day.

However, while it is no doubt curious that the connection between style and the human has proved so enduring, this rather odd rag-bag collection of names and assertions remains more intriguing than illuminating. In the second part of this chapter, therefore, I would like to suggest, by means of a reading of Heidegger, that by indirectly leading us to think about style and styling as perhaps being indissociable from human being in some way, Meillassoux can be understood as having brought us to an insight that might serve to redeem the "cheap epigrammatic brevity" of the phrase "style is the man." An exploration of this will in turn, I hope, help focus with a certain degree of urgency questions about whether Meillassoux is, in principle, right to want to move philosophy away from its correlationist preoccupation.

Dasein styles

The idea provoked by Meillassoux's attack on correlationism is that man might be considered an inherently styling creature, imprinting his signature on everything that can be known or experienced, styling it in such a way that knowledge or experience is inextricably tied (i.e. correlated) to him. Human being, thus understood, would be a style of being that essentially styles being and, as such, should be considered a sort of *styling-being.* This notion of styling, it seems to me, is of fundamental importance to Heidegger's analysis of Dasein, though he articulates it differently. Heidegger's word for this styling or designing is *entwerfen*, which is usually (and appropriately) translated as "to project." Accordingly, in Heideggerian contexts, *Entwurf* tends to be translated as "projection."

Heidegger discusses projection and projectedness in chapter V of *Being and Time*, "Being-in as such." A way of understanding what Heidegger is trying to get at with this notion of "being-in" might be to think of it as that which *ties* "a subject present-at-hand" (einem vorhandenen Subjekt), that is, man understood as substance, to an "Object present-at-hand" (einem vorhandenen Objekt), that is, the world understood as substance (1998, 170; 1967, 132). From Meillassoux's perspective, then, it would be the very correlation that gets in the way of absolute knowledge, the unavoidable human *style* that obscures and deforms substance. Meillassoux calls this "weak correlationism," the primary example of which, he suggests, is Kantian critical philosophy (see 2008, 30–5). Heidegger, however, goes much further than this. To think of the "being-in" as the between of the subject and object, as I have just suggested we might, is, Heidegger thinks, misleading since that would imply that "being-in" is secondary to and thus dependent upon "two things that are present-at-hand." As Heidegger points out, "to assume these beforehand always *splits* the phenomenon asunder," thus giving rise to traditional problems of mind-world dualism. "What is decisive for ontology," Heidegger writes, "is to prevent the splitting of the phenomenon [die Sprengung des Phänomens vorgängig zu verhüten]" (1998, 170; 1967, 132). It is to this end that Heidegger conceives of human being as Dasein, the basic state of which is characterized by an essentially "*unitary* phenomenon" he calls being-in-the-world (In-der-Welt-sein) (53/78). It is, broadly speaking, this "*belonging* together [*Zusammengehörigkeit*] of man and Being" (Heidegger 2002, 28–38; Meillassoux 2008, 8, 50) that Meillassoux has in mind when he speaks of "strong correlationism" (35–42), the model of correlationism he most trenchantly opposes.[13]

Heidegger characterizes the style of Dasein's "being-in," that is, the manner of its existence, as "thrown projection" (geworfener Entwurf). Although they are ultimately indissociable in Dasein's being, both aspects of this "essentially twofold structure" serve a particular function in allowing Heidegger to avoid giving an account of Dasein that would split the phenomenon asunder (1998, 243; 1967, 199). Thrownness overcomes the traditional notion of "a subject present-at-hand" and projection allows Heidegger to do without the idea of an "Object present-at-hand." Together, as they are properly thought of as belonging, they are constitutive of Dasein's being. However, in order to try to shed more light on the possibility of a deep association between human style and being suggested by Meillassoux's criticism of correlationism—and, more

[13]"It is this strong model of de-absolutization that we are going to have to confront, since this is the model that prohibits most decisively the possibility of thinking what there is when there is no thought" (Meillassoux 2008, 36). Besides Heidegger, Meillassoux marks out Wittgenstein as a major proponent of strong correlationism (41–2).

explicitly, by Buffon's apparently throwaway epigram—we must momentarily bracket thrownness to focus on projection as a form of styling.

Heidegger presents Dasein as a being whose own being "is an issue for itself" (1998, 182; 1967, 143). It is possessed of "understanding," where "understanding" signifies a "competence" in relation to "the kind of Being which Dasein has," which is always a "potentiality-for-Being" (182–3/143). Understanding, then, is the inherent familiarity that Dasein has with its possibilities. Understanding, thus construed, forms one of the two existential elements that make up Dasein's "Being-in" (the other, "state-of-mind," we will come to in a moment). Heidegger calls the structure of this understanding that discloses Dasein's own possibilities *projection* (Entwurf). Dasein's understanding, then, is the projection of its own possibilities *as* possibilities. Recalling that this projective understanding is an important constitutive part of Dasein's being—being which is always a "Being-in-the-world"—it becomes apparent that a defining characteristic of Dasein's existential style of being is a projecting (styling) that projects (styles) Dasein and its possible styles (insofar as Dasein *is* its possibilities [185/145]) upon the world that can be experienced.

Projection, as Heidegger puts it in *The Fundamental Concepts of Metaphysics*, can therefore be understood as "*the fundamental structure of world-formation*" (1995, 362). Dasein is its possibilities and its possibilities shape, order, and style its world. Dasein's existential styling "has no object at all, but is an *opening for making-possible*" (1995, 364). Understanding does not "grasp thematically" its possibilities. As projecting, or styling, the understanding of Dasein "is the kind of Being of Dasein in which it *is* its possibilities as possibilities." Dasein, then, is not a static number of grasped possibilities or styles; it is constituted by an active projecting or styling that means it is "constantly 'more' than it factually is" (1998, 185; 1967, 145). It is *in* (ontically) and *as* (ontologically) this styling-opening that Dasein is able to become (or fail to become) what it is. To become what it is, Dasein must project itself onto one of the existentiell possibilities before it (the possibility of being a teacher perhaps or a mother or a mechanic), thereby taking a self-understanding stand on its being (where its being is its possibilities). In taking a stand on its being in this way, Dasein becomes what it is insofar as it is, in its being, a projectional understanding of itself as its possibilities, and the *choosing* of one of the existentiell styles available to it amounts to a confirmation of this. In other words, one can say that in taking a stand on its being, Dasein becomes what it is because it *is* a becoming-what-it-is, precisely insofar as it is a projective, styling entity. For Dasein to fail to become what it is, it simply has to fall into one of its possibilities, neglecting to take a stand on its being, not taking up its "ownmost possibility," which is the styling of itself and, thus, of its world (68/42).

This does not mean that the Dasein that acknowledges its existence as a projecting, styling being (i.e. *authentic* Dasein in Heidegger's terminology) can style itself however it pleases. The freedom that it recognizes in the possibilities available to it as a projecting, self-understanding entity, are conditioned and finite. Projective Dasein is emphatically not some untethered cogito. Projection is just one element of Dasein's being; the other equiprimordial element, as mentioned earlier, is *thrownness*.

If projection describes the nature of Dasein's understanding, thrownness describes the originary manner of Dasein's finding of itself (*Befindlichkeit*) in the primordial disclosure of its being-there (1998, 172; 1967, 134). The ontic correlates of this "attunement" or "disposedness" are, Heidegger suggests, our everyday moods.[14] We are simply thrown into moodedness[15] and this indicates, Heidegger thinks, a deep, comprehending attunement to the world which is Dasein's originary *befindlichkeit* (1998, 172–9; 1967, 134–40; 1995, 67). Attunement eludes any attempt we might make to grasp it. It is always "there" as a given, that "there" into which Dasein finds itself thrown, and our only access to it is not cognitive but affective.[16] As Heidegger puts it, the "pure 'that it is'" of Dasein

[14]*Befindlichkeit* has proved itself to be virtually untranslatable. Two of the more felicitous renderings are "attunement" (Heidegger 1996) and "disposedness" (Blattner 2009). It is generally agreed that Macquarrie and Robinson's (Heidegger 1998) translation of the term, "state of mind," is deeply problematic and misleading. Other renderings include "disposition," "situatedness," "affectedness," "so-foundness," and "attuned self-finding" (see Polt, 1999, 65, n.41).

[15]"A mood assails us. It comes neither from "outside" nor from "inside," but arises out of Being-in-the-world, as a way of such Being" (Heidegger 1998, 176/136).

[16]". . . the possibilities of disclosure which belong to cognition reach far too short a way compared with the primordial disclosure belonging to moods, in which Dasein is brought before its Being as 'there'" (1998, 173/134).

in its thrownness shows itself in moods, "but the 'whence' and the 'whither' remain in darkness" (1998, 173; 1967, 134).

As such, then, Dasein's mooded attunement functions as a sort of *originary styling*, a styling over which ultimately Dasein has no control.[17] This might be likened to the way an artist can never fully *know* her style insofar as it is coextensive with herself as signature.[18] This style of attunement ultimately determines one's grasp upon the world, limiting and conditioning the possibilities that are available. It is disclosive, it positions us as styled beings and, as such, it delimits the range of styles we might adopt. This, of course, takes us back to projection and makes clear why it is indissociable from our thrownness. Dasein is thrown—styled, one might say—*as a styling being*. Understood in this way, style is central to Dasein's existential constitution as "thrown projection" (1998, 188; 1967, 148): its projectedness (its nature as a styling being) is thrown (styled) and its thrownness (its styledness) is projected in the various possible stylings available to it.[19] It is this constitution of Dasein's being that makes it essentially temporal.

As I have briefly suggested, however, it is by no means assured that Dasein will take up the challenge of its existence as thrown projection. To fail to take responsibility for one's projected

---

[17]It might be possible for us to change or alter our mood, but one cannot change the fact that we are mooded creatures: "Factically, Dasein can, should, and must, through knowledge and will, become master of its moods; in certain possible ways of existing, this may signify a priority of volition and cognition. Only we must not be misled by this into denying that ontologically mood is a primordial kind of Being for Dasein, in which Dasein is disclosed to itself *prior to* all cognition and volition, and *beyond* their range of disclosure. And furthermore, when we master a mood, we do so by way of a counter-mood; we are never free of moods" (1998, 175/136).

[18]Here one might recall Derrida's declaration, "I am blind to my style," and his claim that his style is that which for him "never will have been present" (1982, 296). Elsewhere he says: "I would be the last one to be able to see my style, in a way" (Derrida and Cixous 2010, 201).

[19]Heidegger calls Dasein understood as thrown projection "enigmatical" (*rätselhafter*) (1998, 188; 1967, 148). Critchley (2002, 159) analyzes Heidegger's various suggestions that Dasein's being is enigmatic and argues for an interpretation of *Being and Time* that locates an "*enigmatic apriori*" at the heart of Dasein's being-in-the-world "that eludes phenomenological manifestation." Critchley goes on to draw out the political implications of this interpretation. In my interpretation, as will become clear, this "enigmatic apriori" is style—style is the enigma of the human.

stylings, or, even worse, to become detached from the very possibility of taking a stand on one's existence in this way, is, to put it colloquially, to let go of life's rudder, to do simply *the done thing* as though of necessity. The very antithesis of style, then. It is precisely this stylelessness that Heidegger has in mind when he speaks of "inauthenticity" (*Uneigentlichkeit*). It is a failure to take a stand on one's being which amounts to a disowning of one's existence as a styling being that projects possibilities onto the world, the resulting loss of style serving to impose a *de facto* necessity on one's way of life. In essence, then, stylelessness—both existential and existentiell—would be Dasein's failure to acknowledge and affirm its *being-there*. As such, disowning one's existence as a styling being reduces life to an atemporal "sequence of 'nows'" (1998, 474–80; 1967, 422–8; see also 374/326) lived through the idle talk and choices of *das Man* (the One or the They), and sustained by suppressing the discomforting thought of one's death (295–6/252; 303/259).

But it is precisely because one's own death has the capacity to be discomforting that Heidegger presents it as the key to reclaiming one's authenticity as a styling being. Heidegger writes that "our everyday falling evasion *in the face of* death is an *inauthentic* Being-*towards*-death. But inauthenticity is based on the possibility of authenticity" (1998, 303; 1967, 259). What, then, would an authentic understanding of one's death amount to? Death cannot be grasped, Heidegger suggests, if we view it as an impersonal event or actuality. Rather, it must be grasped as an existential possibility, one that shapes our life, one that we can either affirm or disown (304/259–311/267). Death, however, cannot be considered simply one possibility among many, not least because it seems to resist any attempt to think of it as something we could take up *as* a possibility. In what sense is it *our* possibility if we cannot actualize it *in* our own life? As Wittgenstein expresses this ancient idea, "Death is not an event in life: we do not live to experience death" (2009, §6.4311). And yet, that we will die is of course certain. It is, Heidegger writes, "the certain possibility of death" (1998, 309; 1967, 264), our "ownmost possibility" (304/259). Death, then, might be considered our impossible possibility, our relation with the nonrelational or indefinite (304/259–60; 307–8/262–4). What, though, would be an authentic understanding of *this*, our ownmost possibility? Death cannot exist as a possibility for us on an ontic or existentiell level, and yet it is only on that level that it can be grasped as a possibility at all. How, then, does death show up for us as a possibility that is ours? Heidegger's answer is as "*Being towards death*" (277/234). But what would that be? Dasein's anticipation of its end, its awareness of the possibility of the impossibility of its possibilities, animates and reinvigorates its sense of its own potentiality.[20] Death as that which cannot be outstripped is the horizon against which all of our possibilities show up *as* possibilities.[21] An anticipation of death discloses one's life as a whole and affirms the nonnecessity of one's life on both an existential and existentiell level. Reacquainting us with the thrown-projected temporality of our existence, this intimation of death prompts us to take a stand on our being. We are lifted out of our inauthentic, unthinking absorption in the world

[20]This is of course precisely what Levinas rejects as the "supreme virility" (1987, 70) of Heidegger's authentic being-towards-death, going so far as to link this "virility of a free ability-to-be" (1998b, 207), this "proud virility" "contingent upon that unadulterated 'mineness' [*Jemeinigkeit*]" (1998d, 226) that Levinas sees as a willful indifference to the other, with Heidegger's involvement with National Socialism (1998b, 207). Contra Heidegger, Levinas suggests that "my mastery, my virility, my heroism as a subject can be neither virility nor heroism in relation to death" (1987, 72). Death is not so much the possibility of impossibility as the impossibility of possibility (see Levinas 1997, 70, n.43; 1988, 235; Blanchot 1995, 70) and, as such, it signals the "the limit of the subject's virility" (Levinas 1997, 74). This "end of virility" (Levinas 1997, 73) announces "the impossibility of having a project" (74). Death, then, for Levinas, is the relation with an absolutely other that "we cannot assimilate through enjoyment" (74). "My solitude," he writes, "is thus not confirmed by death but broken by it" (74). This suggests a movement beyond "the ontology of Heidegger's *Dasein*" (1998c, 131) toward a recognition of the relationship with the other and, in particular, with the other's death: "Death is the death of other people," Levinas writes in relation to Albertine in Proust's *À la recherche du temps perdu*, "contrary to the tendency of contemporary philosophy, which is focused on one's own solitary death" (1996, 103). Thus (though the implications of this cannot be explored here), for Levinas the human being receives a prior ethical styling by means of a felt responsibility in the face of the death of the other (see, in particular, 1998b, 217; 1992, 84; 1998a, 173).

[21]Reiner Schürmann, interpreting *Being and Time*, writes: "Death is that horizon of projection within which all projects are made possible. Any possibility that can positively be seized by Dasein has Being-towards-death as its ground" (Critchley and Schürmann 2008, 102). He goes on: "Being-towards-death is that moment coming upon Dasein in which the annihilation of futurity is possible, is lived as a potentiality" (102).

and become aware of our potential to style our own existence. As Heidegger puts it: "Being-towards-death is the anticipation of a potentiality-for-Being of that entity whose kind of Being is anticipation itself" (1998, 307/262). Our relation to death, then, is manifested and affirmed specifically in our styling existence *as* styling existence. To forget death is to abandon style and become unfree. In choosing one possibility among a number, we style, we choose life, but a life that is, however gradually, ending. Our style is our finitude; finitude is our style.

Style: Our impossible possibility

To conclude, we might say that the source, the site or, better, the point of human being is the very same source or point of style. But one must also say at this point that there is neither human being nor style (one might think of this through the ambiguity of the French word *point*, as in *point d'eau*). In relation to human being, Heidegger calls this Dasein's enigma, but it is also, I want to say, the enigma of style: it is the blind-spot and source of both. And as Heidegger himself puts it in his book on Nietzsche, "everything named in the word 'style' belongs to what is most obscure" (1991, 124). For Dasein to become what it is (i.e. a styled-styling being) it must understand itself, quite literally, as pointless: that is, factically thrown into being and nonnecessary—already styled by attunement in the finding of itself, and styling in its awareness of its being-towards-death. We might imagine the point of a stylus pressed onto paper—*point de style.* As style emerges, the point of style, the site of that originary touch, is lost and rendered irrecoverable. Style, like human being, is never punctual, never *in time.* Rather, it is the trace and the tracing of time. It is our opening and our closing: it is the cut that exposes us and the mark of an irremediable wound that we bear. Derrida, we might say, was right: it is here, in style, that "*I* loses itself" (1982, 296). Style, in other words, *is* the man.

Which, to take us back to where we began, is why to see this, our radically conterminous style, as an impediment to be overcome, as Meillassoux evidently does, should be considered an error of judgment. As others have suggested, Meillassoux's position might perhaps suffer from a confusion of the ontological and the epistemological, but I have offered no such argument.[22] Nor have I attempted to refute his proposed escape route out of the correlationist circle. The absolute is all very well, it's just not *for us*, one might somewhat facetiously say. Rather, what I have attempted to set out is a defense of a particular, strong correlationist position through the question of style, showing why it might be considered to have the very strongest claims on our philosophical attention.

If my Heideggerian reading of style holds, to forget style would be to lose our grip on human being. In a fascinating passage from Franz Fischer's *Zeitstruktur und Schizophrenie* that Merleau-Ponty quotes in *Phenomenology of Perception*, mental breakdown is associated with meaninglessness, atemporality and, explicitly, a loss of style (2004, 329–30).[23] My underlying worry is that if philosophy abandons style—style that, as I have argued, is constitutive of our relationship to the phenomenal life-world and, thus, of meaning—the bleak prospect we would have to consider, waiting for us *after finitude*, is the possibility of this human breakdown being played out at the level of the humanities. Indeed, might this radical, institutional devaluing of human stylings in all their various forms be something that we are already beginning to witness? The systematic dismantling of key areas of the humanities in the United Kingdom and the United States during the financial crisis that began in 2007 could certainly be diagnosed as symptomatic of just such a coming *stylelessness*.[24] But if philosophy does come to judge Kant's Copernican turn as a grievous error, as Meillassoux

---

[22]The suggestion that Meillassoux's indictment of correlationism depends upon the mistaken equation of epistemological limitations with ontological claims about the world has been put rather persuasively by Hallward (Mackay 2007, 444–5; Hallward 2008, 54–5). Adrian Johnston (2011, 95, 97) makes a similar point. Nathan Brown (2011, 142–3), on the other hand, defends Meillassoux against the suggestion that he confuses the epistemological and the ontological.

[23]As we have seen, meaninglessness, atemporality, and loss of style are, from a Heideggerian perspective, all associated with Dasein's failure to become what it is. This too would be a kind of breakdown in which, in David Couzens Hoy's words, Dasein "become[s] disconnected from itself" (1993, 181).

[24]This devaluing of style, which, I would argue, has facilitated the closure of Philosophy at Middlesex and drastic cuts to French, Italian, Russian, Classics and Theater at Albany, State University of New York, and countless other cuts and closures, has typically been justified in terms of value for money and efficiency, both of which are, unsurprisingly, judged from the perspective of free-market capitalism.

suggests it should (and, arguably, much of it already does and has done so for a very long time), then perhaps this might serve to clarify the role of so-called theory within the humanities. Its critical attentiveness to all aspects of human styling and its advocacy of the unsurpassable correlatedness of meaning suggest that if we are looking for an appropriate discursive site from which to resist the loss of style, theory—which currently appears rather exhausted and aimless—might turn out to be it, disclosing what might be found to be, in every sense, theory's proper style.

References

Aristotle. 1995. *The Complete Works of Aristotle: The Revised Oxford Translation*. Edited by Jonathan Barnes. 2 vols. Bollingen Series. Princeton, NJ: Princeton University Press.

Blanchot, Maurice. 1995. *The Writing of the Disaster*. Translated by Ann Smock. Lincoln NE and London: University of Nebraska Press.

Blattner, William. 2009. *Heidegger's Being and Time*. London: Continuum.

Brassier, Ray. 2007. *Nihil Unbound: Enlightenment and Extinction*. New York: Palgrave Macmillan.

Brown, Nathan. 2011. "The Speculative and the Specific: On Hallward and Meillassoux." In *The Speculative Turn: Continental Materialism and Realism*, edited by Levi Bryant, Nick Srnicek, and Graham Harman, 142–63. Melbourne: re.press.

One might argue that the lack of a general appreciation of the inherent value and centrality of the arts and humanities must, at least to some degree, be attributed to the arts and humanities' failure to take seriously the importance of preaching more widely and insistently their cloistered practices, evangelizing in favor of style both inside and outside of the academy, that is. A new militancy has begun to emerge, however, and many leading academics have protested angrily against the closures, helping prevent cuts at several institutions, most notably at Liverpool, Keele, Greenwich and King's College London, in the UK. In response to the situation at Albany, Jean-Luc Nancy (2010) wrote a public letter indignantly mocking the absurdity of what he all-too-clearly portrays as a coming stylelessness: "Someone needs to invent a kind of instruction that is, first, strictly monolingual—because everything can be translated into English, can't it?—and also one from which all questioning (for example, of what 'translation' means, both in general and in terms of this or that specific language) has been completely eliminated. A single language alone, cleansed of the bugs of reflection, would make the perfect university subject: smooth, harmonious, easily submitted to pedagogical control" and, one might add, styleless.

Burton, Robert. 2001. *The Anatomy of Melancholy*. New York: New York Review Books.

Carbone, Mauro. 2010. *An Unprecedented Deformation: Marcel Proust and the Sensible Ideas*. Translated by Niall Keane. New York: State University of New York Press.

Cavell, Stanley. 2004. "The *Investigations*' Everyday Aesthetics of Itself." In *The Literary Wittgenstein*, edited by John Gibson and Wolfgang Huemer, 21–33. New York: Routledge.

Cicero, Marcus Tullius. 1945. *Tusculun Disputations*. Translated by J. E. King. Cambridge, MA: Harvard University Press.

Critchley, Simon. 2002. "Enigma Variations: An Interpretation of Heidegger's *Sein und Zeit*." *Ratio* 15(2): 154–75.

—. 2009. "Back to the Great Outdoors." *Times Literary Supplement*, February 28.

Critchley, Simon and Reiner Schürmann. 2008. *On Heidegger's* Being and Time. Edited by Steven Levine. London: Routledge.

Deleuze, Gilles. 2000. *Proust and Signs*. Translated by Richard Howard. Minneapolis: University of Minnesota Press.

Derrida, Jacques. 1979. *Spurs: Nietzsche's Styles*. Translated by Barbara Harlow. Chicago: University of Chicago Press.

—. 1982. "Qual Quelle: Valéry's Sources." In *Margins of Philosophy*, translated by Alan Bass, 273–306. Brighton: Harvester Press.

Derrida, Jacques and Hélène Cixous. 2010. "On Style (A Question to H. Cixous and J. Derrida)." Translated by Laurent Milesi. In *The Portable Cixous*, edited by Marta Segarra, 199–206. New York: Columbia University Press.

Gay, Peter. 1988. *Style in History: Gibbon, Ranke, Macaulay, Burckhardt*. New York: Norton.

Gibbon, Edward. 1900. *The Memoirs of the Life of Edward Gibbon with Various Observations and Excursions*. Edited by George Birkbeck Norman Hill. London: Methuen.

Gombrich, E. H. 1968. "Style." In Vol. 15 of the *International Encyclopedia of the Social Sciences*, edited by David L. Sills, 352–61. n.p.: Macmillan and Free Press.

Hallward, Peter. 2008. "Anything is Possible." *Radical Philosophy* 152: 51–7.

Harman, Graham. 2011. *Quentin Meillassoux: Philosophy in the Making*. Edinburgh: Edinburgh University Press.

Heidegger, Martin. 1967. *Sein und Zeit*. Tübingen: Niemeyer.

—. 1991. *Nietzsche: Volumes One and Two*. Translated by David Farrell Krell. San Francisco: HarperCollins.

—. 1995. *The Fundamental Concepts of Metaphysics: World, Finitude, Solitude*. Translated by William McNeill and Nicholas Walker. Bloomington: Indiana University Press.

—. 1996. *Being and Time*. Translated by Joan Stambaugh. Albany, NY: State University of New York Press.

—. 1998. *Being and Time*. Translated by John Macquarrie and Edward Robinson. Oxford: Blackwell.

—. 2002. *Identity and Difference*. Translated by Joan Stambaugh. Chicago: University of Chicago Press.

Hoy, David Couzens. 1993. "Heidegger and the Hermeneutic Turn." In *The Cambridge Companion to Heidegger*, edited by Charles B. Guignon, 177–201. Cambridge: Cambridge University Press.

Hume, David. 1983. *A Treatise of Human Nature*. Oxford: Clarendon Press.

Johnston, Adrian. 2011. "Hume's Revenge: À Dieu, Meillassoux." In *The Speculative Turn: Continental Materialism and Realism*, edited by Levi Bryant, Nick Srnicek, and Graham Harman, 92–113. Melbourne: re.press.

Lacan, Jacques. 2006. *Écrits: The First Complete Edition in English*. Translated by Bruce Fink. New York: Norton.

Lacoue-Labarthe, Philippe. 1987. "Looking for the Styleme." In *The Concept of Style*, edited by Berel Lang. 174–82. Ithaca, NY: Cornell University Press, 1987.

—. 1998. "The Echo of the Subject." Translated by Barbara Harlow. In *Typography: Mimesis, Philosophy, Politics*, edited by Christopher Fynsk, 139–207. Stanford: Stanford University Press.

Levinas, Emmanuel. 1987. *Time and the Other*. Translated by Richard A. Cohen. Pittsburgh, PA: Duquesne University Press.

—. 1988. *Totality and Infinity: An Essay on Exteriority*. Translated by Alphonso Lingis. Pittsburgh, PA: Duquesne University Press.

—. 1992. "Ethics as First Philosophy." Translated by Seán Hand and Michael Temple. In *The Levinas Reader*, edited by Seán Hand, 76–87. Oxford, MA: Blackwell.

—. 1996. "The Other in Proust." In *Proper Names*, translated by Michael B. Smith, 99–105. London: Athlone Press.

—. 1998a. "Diachrony and Representation." In *Entre Nous: On Thinking-on-the-Other*, translated by Michael B. Smith and Barbara Harshav, 159–78. New York: Columbia University Press, 1998.

—. 1998b. "Dying For. . . ." In *Entre Nous: On Thinking-on-the-Other*, translated by Michael B. Smith and Barbara Harshav, 207–18. New York: Columbia University Press, 1998.

—. 1998c. "Nonintentional Consciousness." In *Entre Nous: On Thinking-on-the-Other*, translated by Michael B. Smith and Barbara Harshav, 123–32. New York: Columbia University Press, 1998.

—. 1998d. "The Other, Utopia, and Justice." In *Entre Nous: On Thinking-on-the-Other*, translated by Michael B. Smith and Barbara Harshav, 219–22.

Locke, John. 1979. *An Essay Concerning Human Understanding*. Oxford: Clarendon Press.

Mackay, Robin, ed. 2007. *Collapse: Philosophical Research and Development, Volume III*. Falmouth: Urbanomic.

Meillassoux, Quentin. 2008a. *After Finitude*. Translated by Ray Brassier. London: Continuum.

—. 2008b. "Time Without Becoming" (Presented Paper, Middlesex University, London, May 8, 2008). http://speculativeheresy.files.wordpress.com/2008/07/3729-time_without_becoming.pdf.

Merleau-Ponty, Maurice. 1973. *The Prose of the World*. Translated by John O'Neill. Evanston: Northwestern University Press.

—. 2004. *Phenomenology of Perception*. Translated by Colin Smith. London: Routledge.

Meyer, Leonard B. 1987. "Towards a Theory of Style." In *The Concept of Style*, edited by Berel Lang, 21–71. Ithaca, NY: Cornell University Press.

Nancy, Jean-Luc. 2010. "Albany: An Open Letter from Jean-Luc Nancy." *Printculture*, October 19. www.printculture.com/item-2708.html.

Pascal, Blaise. 1963. *Oeuvres complètes*. Edited by Louis Lafuma. Paris: Seuil.

—. 1995. *Pensées*. Translated by A. J. Krailsheimer. London: Penguin.

Pater, Walter. 2008. *Appreciations: With an Essay on Style*. Rockville, MD: Arc Manor.

Polt, Richard. 1999. *Heidegger: An Introduction*. Ithaca, NY: Cornell University Press.

Puttenham, George. 1869. *The Arte of English Poesie*. London: Murray and Son.

Reik, Theodor. 1942. *From Thirty Years with Freud*. London: Hogarth Press and The Institute for Psychoanalysis.

—. 1973. *Fragment of a Great Confession: A Psychoanalytical Autobiography*. Westport, CT: Greenwood Press.

Riera, Gabriel. 2008. "Review of *After Finitude: An Essay on the Necessity of Contingency*, by Quentin Meillassoux." *Notre Dame Philosophical Reviews*, October 12, 2008. http://ndpr.nd.edu/news/23797-after-finitude-an-essay-on-the-necessity-of-contingency/

Schopenhauer, Arthur. 2004. *The Art of Literature*. Translated by T. Bailey Saunders. Mineola, NY: Dover.

Singer, Linda. 1998. "Merleau-Ponty on the Concept of Style." In *The Merleau-Ponty Aesthetics Reader: Philosophy and Painting*, edited by Galen A. Johnson, 233–44. Evanston, IL: Northwestern University Press.

Ullmann, Stephen. 1957. *Style in the French Novel*. Cambridge: Cambridge University Press.

Williams, Michael. 2001. *Problems of Knowledge: A Critical Introduction to Epistemology.* Oxford: Oxford University Press.

Wittgenstein, Ludwig. 2006. *Culture and Value.* Translated by Peter Winch. Malden, MA: Blackwell.

—. 2009. *Tractatus Logico-Philosophicus.* Translated by D. F. Pears and B. F. McGuinness. London: Routledge.

9

Style in communication: The hip swing of Hélio Oiticica's *Parangolés*

Fiona Hughes

My aim in this chapter is to explore the role played by style within communication.[1] By *communication* I am referring to our everyday expression of ideas, feelings, and emotions to each other through language, gestures, and other sensible signs, not the expression of an internal subjectivity to other subjects similarly engaged in the expression of *their* subjectivities. Communication is a shared project through which meanings are instituted both by delving within and by going beyond personal perspectives. For instance, an artwork communicates and we need not assume that we must trace this back to a unitary origin in the subjective intentions of an artist. Moreover, I am not presupposing that communication always, or even often, achieves what we might imagine it achieves, or, when it is successful, that the meanings it conveys are transparent or identical for all participants. Even when communication fails, however, a process of communication has occurred. Indeed,

---

[1]I have benefited from comments by Neil Cox, among others, in response to a presentation of this chapter in the Department of Art History and Theory at the University of Essex. I am also very grateful to Ariane Pereira de Figueiredo of *Projeto Hélio Oiticica* in Rio de Janeiro for her tireless helpfulness on many details. Particularly, I would like to thank James Corby for the insight and good judgment he has exercised throughout the preparation of the final version of this chapter.

if communication did not sometimes fail, it could not succeed, because it would have become an automatic transfer of information. I will not give a general theory of communication here, although were I to do so I would emphasize its dynamic process and not only its conditions of possibility or its results. I start from the phenomenon of our self-understanding as communicating with one another within everyday life. This understanding can be deceptive but not, perhaps, to the extent that we can deceive ourselves that we have a project of communicating. It is within this horizon that I intend to focus on the relation between style and meaning in communication.[2]

In the first section I discuss a difficulty that I claim arises for theory in addressing the relation between style and meaning within communication. In speaking of theory, I am principally concerned with philosophical theory, although I believe the problem I point out is not restricted to philosophy and is significant for other types of theory. I argue that this arises from a general feature of theory, namely, that it aims to capture a quarry. I use this expression in order to leave open the precise way in which theory may seek to pin down its object, for instance, in clarifying, in making precise, in explaining, in determining, as well as in uncovering and laying forth as a phenomenon and so on. I am not suggesting that all of these goals are equivalent, but rather that, when indeterminacy is not ruled out, each of these strategies masters or husbands indeterminacy, even in making it apparent. A project of disambiguation is, therefore, intrinsic to theory and is exercised either directly or indirectly. While many philosophical theories overtly aim at disambiguation, others such as deconstructive theories (in philosophy, but also in literary theory) aim to bring out the pervasiveness of ambiguity. However, even these theories implicitly offer a disambiguation of ambiguity at a meta level insofar as they make a claim for the phenomenon of ambiguity. My idea is that theory encounters problems when its quarry is indeterminate, even when it embraces

---

[2]I am not here offering even the beginnings of a definition or a theory of either meaning or style, although I am, of course, engaged in examining them within a theoretical framework. Perspectives that emerge *could* inform a theory of meaning. For instance, I mention in passing that the artist Hélio Oiticica whom I will be discussing later in this chapter, holds that the color white has meaning and I suggest that his *Parangolés* express meanings intertwined with the culture of a community.

that indeterminacy. The species of quarry I have in mind in this discussion is a relation and I will suggest that the indeterminate character of relations makes them elusive for theoretical inspection. In the second part, I turn to an alternative form of reflection—artistic reflection—that may, in collaboration with theory, help to illuminate matters.[3] Instead of giving a general account of what it means to talk about artistic reflection, I turn to one artist in whose work—I would suggest—we find a sustained activity of reflection expressed in artistic projects. In particular, his works offer an experiment in relations and, more precisely, in the relation between meaning and style. Hélio Oiticica developed a number of different artistic styles, culminating in an art-form that operates as stylized performance in the everyday world. Some of these works are wonderful colored capes or *Parangolés,* often worn by samba dancers. These "inventions," as Oiticica puts it, combine painting with performance, communicating at many different levels and yet defying any determinate meaning (Ramírez 2007, 17). I will make use of a Brazilian concept that captures the spirit of these dancing paintings. *Jogo de cintura*—hip sway—expresses rhythmic flexibility in samba, in *art football,* and in the Brazilian martial art of *capoeira.* My idea is that Oiticica's *Parangolés* communicate through opening up the possibility of communicating. In particular, I suggest they communicate possible meanings through presenting a genesis of style: I call this *communicative style.* My aim is to show that consideration of Oiticica's *Parangolés* helps illuminate the relation between style and meaning not only in the communication of these particular artworks, but also more generally.

Style in communication and the limitations of theory

My thesis—one I cannot vindicate other than retrospectively and indirectly through what follows—is this: style is not simply opposed to meaning, nor are the two indifferent to one another. Style stands in relation to meaning, even in extreme cases where a

[3]So, artistic reflection acts as a supplement to rather than a replacement for theory.

stylized intervention appears to abandon any meaningful content whatsoever or, contrastively, where style appears to break down. I am trying to get at the way in which style and meaning relate within communication. Relations, however, are slippery and hard to pin down. This is due, mainly, to their being transitions where one thing becomes another *and* where one thing becomes itself and not the other.[4] Therefore, we should not expect that it will be easy to identify or analyze the point of intersection between style and meaning. *Any* relation is hard to pin down. The relation between style and meaning is not any different and may even be a particularly difficult case.

My focus in this chapter is style in communication with an accent on the *in*. Style *in* communication is the style that is part of the overall project of communication and not a separable part of that communication. But the other side of the coin is that we cannot take the style out of communication—either in practice or in theory—and still have communication. Style is a part of the whole that is communication and when we examine style in communication, we should take that wider horizon (particularly, meaning) into account. The whole that is communication can hold together in many different ways. On some occasions the relation between the constituent parts of communication may be harmonious, while on others it may be dysfunctional. By this I mean that the different parts relate to one another in a difficult and problematic fashion—rather like a dysfunctional family—but they do still hang together, even though the relating is painful and even destructive. (My claim that there is always a relation between style and meaning is thus not limited to harmonious or even to successful communication.[5]) So when style tries to escape from meaning, it does so as an act of rebellion against the *status quo*. Style never loses its connection to the meaning conditions of communication, even if it succeeds on the surface in escaping from them. Communication communicates

[4]In the *Critique of Pure Reason* Kant presents imagination as allied both with the spontaneity of thought and with sensibility. This, in my view, is not evidence for confusion or for disingenuousness but is, rather, an expression of the relational status of this third capacity. Imagination, insofar as it acts as a mediating term, makes possible both the distinctiveness and the connectedness of the faculties of understanding and sensibility. See Hughes 2007, especially, 112–68 and 169–206.

[5]The distinction is necessary because communication can be disharmonious and yet successful.

something: content and meaning are communicated, however stylized, elliptical, ironic or incoherent they may be.

In practice, within actual communications, it is often hard to be aware of the element of style, never mind highlight the point of contact between style and meaning. Mostly, we simply get on with communicating and let style intersect with meaning without worrying about it unduly. Nevertheless, the problem of the relation between style and meaning is not absent within everyday life. All of us experience instances when we ask ourselves if what we want to say has been successfully communicated, and when we do so we will be aware on some occasions, at least, that our difficulty has arisen from the *way*, or style, in which we have tried to express something.

Even for the individual who lives her life *as* style, there will be moments of hesitation and also failure, where her style threatens to break down or does not work. At such moments there is an interruption in style *and* in the meanings embedded within it. If she is to recover poise in her style, she must discover resources in addition to those that have informed her practice up until that point. Here reflection would allow new perspectives to be uncovered and style to recover its ability to orient a life. Such moments in the breakdown of style typically reveal the ongoing relation between style and meaning that is the condition of any life whatsoever. Why do I want to adopt or maintain *this* style? The question can only be answered in conjunction with—though not exhaustively determined by—a reflection on the meanings that will be released by this style rather than others.

Theory, I would argue, has a distinctive problem in focusing on the relation between style and meaning, which is lived and, as a result, always somewhat elusive and even ambiguous. This is true by token of relations lying at the interstices of objects, persons, and theoretical positions. Theory—however subtle, self-aware and self-undercutting—tries to pin things down. Even when a theory does not aim at the Cartesian gold standard of clear and distinct ideas, it aims at mastery of its material. A theory may identify, and even aim to dwell within, the proliferation of ambiguity and elusiveness of its subject matter, but at another level it seeks to capture or identify the patterns it describes.[6] To this extent I would suggest that

[6]Deconstruction, at its best, recognizes and investigates the impossibility of escaping the theoretical voice.

there is inevitably a goal of disambiguation in any theory. Even the type of theory that claims that ambiguity is pervasive within artworks, in life and, indeed, in theoretical works must *qua* theory aim to control ambiguity at a meta level insofar as the latter is asserted as a phenomenon. It is not in principle impossible that theory may find within its own resources a way around this difficulty. However, my contention is that the goal of mastery implicit within theory makes sustaining an insight into the relational *as relational* difficult without help from another source. Later in this section I will discuss two philosophers who address the issue of style and meaning within a theoretical perspective, but I will also suggest that doing so leads them to occupy in an uncanny fashion the limits of theory.

I have characterized theory as a project of pinning down its objects or of disambiguation.[7] But what theory is this and whose is it? Representatives of the dominant style of philosophizing within the Anglo-American world might agree with my characterization as far as it goes, although many would think it too weak in that I have not said that theory aims to establish truth, nor that it will do so by methods that are rigorous or, even, analogous to the principles and procedures of science. But philosophers working within other traditions of philosophy might think the characterization of theory I have given is too strong. Does it really make sense to say that a Derrida, a late Heidegger, or a Nietzsche seeks to disambiguate? Even some versions of philosophical theory, it may appear, fail to conform to and, indeed, resist the role I have attributed to theory. The case might be even more striking if we turn to other types of theory, for instance, literary theory. While there have been and no doubt still are literary theorists who would be happy to describe their work as one of disambiguation, there are many more who would not.[8] Although in this discussion I will restrict my focus to the limitations of philosophical theory, a field for which I have some competence to speak, I hope my account will strike resonances for those working across a range of theoretical disciplines.

Disambiguation—or the project of disambiguating where possible—is a necessary human potentiality that theory takes up in a

[7]The emphasis is on *project*. I am not suggesting that theory succeeds in purging itself of ambiguity.

[8]This is particularly relevant in the light of the disciplinary orientation of many of the chapters in this volume.

focused manner. A problem arises only in that the project of pinning down something as such and such a thing may appear to be a task capable of achieving an absolute goal. And such an assumption arises insofar as there is an anticipation of *getting it right* in any theory. Indeed such an assumption is structural for any theory, even for those that qualify as heuristic. And this assumption implicitly suggests that there could be a final control of ambiguity, at least at the level of the theoretical voice's presentation of it as a phenomenon. But what if the phenomenon under examination is not only temporarily resistant to disambiguation, but is in its very nature ambiguous? In other words, what if the experience of the phenomenon requires an experience of its ambiguity? When we encounter such a phenomenon, do we simply give up theory? This is not necessary because within theory we can recognize the limitations of theory. We can gesture toward—even if we cannot fully determine—the point at which theory has to stop or where it fails. And at this point we can *either* take theoretical limitation as a theme for theory *or* we can try to develop a conversation between theory and another form of reflection, which acts as supplement not correction, in the hope that a new insight will emerge.[9] In both cases theory survives, although it does so through an acceptance of its limitations.

What I take to be clear is that theory cannot simply give up on the resistance to disambiguation and claim that it is not theory's problem.[10] Of course, some problems are pseudo-problems, which lead us astray. We should examine potential problems for their authenticity and necessity with the greatest rigor at our disposition and unveil those that are not really problems at all. But the nature of a problem is to resist solution, at least for a period of time. If theory's reaction is to deny the validity of a problem just because it is problematic, then we should be suspicious, as that would risk excluding the sort of problem that initially intrigues the theorist as

---

[9]In the first case the theorist may bring out the role played by disambiguation within her theory. However, even this will lead to a further level of disambiguation, now practiced as meta-critique. (This is in contrast to the first meta level of reflection, that of the theoretical voice.)

[10]This is addressed to theories for which total disambiguation is a meaningful goal. A problem for theories that, on the other hand, embrace ambiguity is addressed in the paragraphs preceding this.

a theoretical problem, but resists our ability as theorists to find a solution for it. It is not just that at some later stage another theorist will come along and achieve what we cannot presently grasp, but that there is something about the nature of the theoretical position that makes these problems arise, and yet they are resistant to solution within the theoretical perspective. We might say that such questions lie at the limit of theory's relation to itself. And the particular problem that I am suggesting falls under this category is that of the relation between style and meaning in communication.

One should, however, now ask: *does* theory have a problem in establishing the relation between style and meaning? The answer I will give here, as previously mentioned, will be with respect to philosophical theory, although I hope it may supply the beginnings of a more general account. Philosophy divides between those who take style seriously and those who consider style external, at best, and perhaps even antithetic to philosophical concerns—they being mainly Analytical philosophers, although this is not true of all such philosophers, especially if we are prepared to include Wittgenstein within that category. For those who consider style as external or antithetic to the proper procedure of philosophy, there is no problem with the relation between style and content because only the latter counts (as far as they are concerned).[11] However, I would claim that it comes back to haunt even their positions because of the intrinsic relation between style and meaning in *any* communication.[12] For those who take style seriously, meaning only arises in relation to style. Nietzsche is a particularly striking example of this, for one cannot get his point without engaging with his style.[13] Nietzsche's strategy is to expand the horizon of theory, so that the undercutting of theory emerges within it, thus setting the scene for

[11]In this discussion I am not using *content* in a technical philosophical sense as propositional content, that is, something that can be judged. When I talk of *content* I am pointing to what a communication is *about*. While a content (used in this way) may not yet have a meaning, a meaning must always express some content, which may be real, imaginary, novel, or impossible.

[12]In saying this I am taking a position that I cannot defend here, namely, that there is continuity between philosophical discourse and everyday discourse. My view is that philosophy is a particular distillation of the reflective possibilities within everyday discourse.

[13]Nietzsche regularly teases his readers with statements or positions that cannot be taken at face value. We have to be aware of the style of their pronouncement and the context in which they arise if we are to begin to understand their sense.

various deconstructive strategies that came later. Nietzsche does not do what I am proposing to do, that is, to set theory in relation to something other than itself so that another style of reflection enters into discussion with theory. I am not suggesting that the approach I am putting forward for consideration here is preferable to Nietzsche's. I am suggesting that moving theory into a conversation with another approach beyond its horizon opens up different insights from the strategy of investigating shifts between different perspectives *within* the theoretical perspective. Getting a grip on the relation between style and meaning is *always* difficult for philosophical theory, while doing so within the limits of pure theory alone is particularly uncanny. It is as though we were chasing our own tails, for the problem I am outlining is one where theory has to confront its own limitations. What makes the situation even more difficult is that it is exactly theory's strength in mastering its subject matter that gives rise to its weakness in addressing the relational in general and the relation between style and meaning in particular. While, in principle at least, theory has the resources to approach this problem, in practice it may be easier to sustain reflection through the intermediary of another, that is, through taking on an alternative perspective in collaboration with, not as an alternative to, theory.

One of the most successful attempts to address relations from within a theoretical perspective is offered by Maurice Merleau-Ponty, particularly in *The Visible and the Invisible*. The *chiasm* or reversibility is a figure of relation (Merleau-Ponty 1968, 130–55; 1964c, 172–204). My left hand touches my right hand, which is touching a thing. In its relation to the thing, the right hand is experienced as active, while in relation to the left hand it is passive (133–4/176–7). We can extend Merleau-Ponty's investigation of bodily relations.[14] My perception can change if my body's intervention in the world changes. Now it is my left hand that touches the thing and my right hand that touches my left hand. Not only can my right hand be both active in relation to the thing and passive in relation to my left hand, but the direction of the activity-passivity axis can be reversed. This is, I would suggest, the reciprocal structure of relations, even though the reciprocity

[14]Merleau-Ponty does not develop his account in this way, which is, however, consistent with the spirit of his investigation of the *chiasm*.

between two members of a relation can all too easily settle down into a situation in which one side conserves and does not simply temporarily occupy the dominant position.

Merleau-Ponty came to believe that the approach he had taken in *The Phenomenology of Perception* (1945; 1962) prevented him from uncovering the nature of perception. He considered that he needed a completely different approach and style of writing if he was going to get to the deepest roots of seeing, touching, hearing, and thinking. The development from the *Phenomenology* to *The Visible and the Invisible* is a shift of style in the interests of an advance in the expression of meaning. This shift happens within Merleau-Ponty's philosophy, while stretching philosophy to its limits. Philosophy becomes so much broader than previously, with the result that many philosophers would consider his later work no longer really philosophy. However, Merleau-Ponty, like Nietzsche before him, was more interested in following philosophical questions where they took him, rather than abiding by the already-established boundaries of the discipline. The exploration of the *chiasm* is a theoretical investigation of the relation between passivity and activity within perception. In taking up this task, theory is expanded so that in trying to pin down its elusive subject matter, philosophy no longer has—nor cares about having—a firm grasp of its own identity.

But at the same time as Merleau-Ponty was developing this self-undercutting theoretical approach, he approached the same quarry from a different direction. From *The Phenomenology of Perception* on, Merleau-Ponty worked with and through examples. In his late work "Eye and Mind" (1964a), in particular, the example is not a mere illustration of an already existing theory: the example becomes the medium within which the examination of a theoretical point is pursued. For instance, he pursues a phenomenological insight into the way in which color and line make each other visible through a discussion of the artistic treatment of color and line in some paintings by Klee and Matisse (1964a, 182–5; 1964b, 71–7).[15] Theory has gone outside itself and finds its verification in a conversation with an alternative, artistic, way of reflecting on the world. The approach I will take in my discussion today

[15]The plates in the French edition are of Matisse's *Baigneuse aux cheveux longs* (1942) and Klee's *Park bei Lu* (Lucerne) (1938).

is strongly influenced by this way of opening up theory not just within its own boundaries, as we have already seen in Nietzsche and the Merleau-Ponty of *The Visible and the Invisible,* but also to an exchange with an alternative and quite differently structured style of reflection. I want to initiate a conversation about the overlapping of style with meaning in communication and the interlocutors in that conversation will be, on the one hand, a theoretical perspective and, on the other, a distinctive but equally reflective artistic perspective. (I say *equally* here not to suggest that they are the same and certainly not to claim that I can measure them. I am, instead, insisting that, within both theory and artworks, there is an unlimited activity of reflection and that there is no good reason to conclude that theory alone is capable of reflection.)

I cannot rule out a priori that a solution to the problem I have diagnosed will be provided. However, I do not anticipate the dissolution of the problem, nor do I think it likely. Why? Because no definition, however comprehensive, can wholly pin down the precise moment when style becomes meaning. We can point to, describe and partially explain, but we can neither dissolve nor fully determine the relation between style and meaning, which is, in the first instance, experienced or lived. We can identify with some effort necessary conditions for a relation, but it is much more difficult to grasp the dynamic or process and shifts in the balance of a relation. The relation between style and meaning is a transition, a liminal moment, and as such is resistant to the theoretical approach and its project of disambiguation. However, to say that theory has a problem with focusing on the relational status of relations is not to say that the alternative perspective—art—has the solution. Any progress that we may make in our exploration of the conjuncture between meaning and style in communication would require our occupying the uncanny territory that hovers around the limits of theory.[16] This is not to say that we should give up on theory. In this essay, a reflection on those limits will arise from an exchange between theory and an alternative form of reflection—in the interstices between them—not in art alone.[17]

[16] I have suggested that this can be pursued either within theory or by co-opting an accomplice with an alternative form of reflection.

[17] Oiticica wrote many texts alongside his visual works, but I will not consider the relation between his two forms of production here.

I hope it is at least clear that it is worth considering the question of the relation between meaning and style and that theory has a problem in grasping that relation. I now want to move the theoretical understanding of the problem onto another terrain. I want to take it on holiday or, at least, let some fresh air—or *life*—pass through it.[18] I am going to turn to the second part of my title.

The hip swing of Hélio Oiticica's *Parangolés*

Hélio Oiticica is one of the best-known twentieth-century Brazilian visual artists. He died prematurely, aged 42, in 1980. In the mid-1960s, Oiticica began to develop a way of working that took the artwork out of the gallery into the life-world. In earlier works a desire to motivate the artwork with the perceptual qualities of a living being was already evident. In the *Metaesquemas* (1957–8), for example, shapes that would have been happy in a formally abstract composition are set free in such a way that they almost dance over the canvas.[19] Oiticica's aim in these works seems to be to liberate space so that the canvas becomes a lived environment and not merely a formal or abstract context.

There can be little doubt that at this stage Oiticica was inspired—as he was throughout his career—by Mondrian. Instead of seeing Mondrian as a painter of abstraction, the mid-twentieth-century Brazilian avant-garde—of which Oiticica was a very young but nevertheless influential representative—saw the Dutch painter as taking the artwork out of the gallery into the world. Particularly important was Mondrian's idea of the relation between the work and the work-space or atelier, where the artwork was alive within an environment of production, in contrast to the museum where he felt the artwork lost its conditions of production and its vivacity. And central for the Brazilian reception of Mondrian were his *Boogie Woogie* paintings, of which the two

[18]As theory is a possibility within life, my intention is not to invoke a polarity but to remind theory of its roots in life.

[19]For plates of the *Metaesquemas*, see Ramírez 2007a, 147–72. See especially plates 31 and 32 on page 151.

best-known are *Broadway Boogie Woogie* (1942–3) and the unfinished *Victory Boogie Woogie* (1942–4).[20]

I would suggest that it is not at all coincidental that these works are explicitly inspired by the modernist architecture and street-planning of New York, as well as by jazz. Brazil has a love affair with modernism and, in particular, with modernist architecture and town-planning, as evidenced by the extremely important role played by architects such as Oscar Niemeyer and by the designer and landscape gardener Roberto Burle Marx in the country's late-twentieth-century cultural history. But if Brazil is in love with modernism, the country's relation with music goes even deeper. Music flows in the life-blood of Brazil and, importantly, the sort of music that is most Brazilian is one that demands a response in dance. Brazil is well known for its *bossa nova* and, of course, for its samba. But this is only the tip of the iceberg, for there are as many Brazilian styles of music as there are regions, and even those forms of music that have been imported from elsewhere are given a particular Brazilian twist in their reception. So, Brazilian rock is *Brazilian* in style. If Brazilian music is anything to go by—and it would not seem unreasonable to suggest that music can give us important insights into Brazilian culture in general—then not only style, but the development of a plurality of styles is characteristic of Brazil. The country offers a polyphony of styles.

Mondrian's New York *Boogie Woogie* paintings dance to the rhythm of Boogie Woogie.[21] What could be merely formal shapes on a canvas, cavort and shimmy in a colorful, noisy display.[22] And, as I have already suggested, Oiticica's *Metaesquemas* also dance. Their tune, too, is syncopated, but it has a less frantic rhythm inspired by *bossa nova* and samba.[23] The shapes in these paintings

---

[20]See Oiticica's comment on the relation between Mondrian's paintings and the workspace cited in Ramírez 2007a, 22. See also plate of *Victory Boogie Woogie* with some of Mondrian's *Wall Works* on page 23.

[21]Boogie Woogie is a fast style of jazz, influenced by blues and especially popular in the 1930s and early 1940s.

[22]That this is an interpretation is, I trust, clear. But I would argue that, while any account of an artwork should start with what we perceive in it, none can entirely escape what we think about it.

[23]Later works by Oiticica express the new wave of post-Bossa, *Tropicalia*, which took its name from Oiticica's exhibition at the Whitechapel Gallery in London in 1969.

no longer inhabit even the animated grid of the Mondrian canvas. The spatial organization of Oiticica's canvases is more relaxed and more off-beat. Mondrian was already working not only with shapes, but with the relations between shapes, which appear to vibrate. Oiticica makes spatial relations even more visible, by attracting the eye to the spaces between the forms, which appear as if they could be about to shift position. We are invited to look at the spaces into which the forms might move.[24]

Forms in Oiticica's *Metaesquemas* stand at an angle to one another.[25] They move in not yet established ways and swing their hips. In saying this I am introducing a concept that is important for Brazilian self-understanding: *jogo de cintura*.[26] We can translate this as *hip swing* or, more literally, as *waist play*, so long as the waist is understood to be moving in concert with the hips. The idea is not restricted to dancing the samba, although the image clearly owes a lot to what can be learned from the experience of dancing. The idea is that any undertaking requires hip movement, that is, the ability to move, adapt, respond and, most importantly, to enjoy improvising. Picture the very mobile, classical Brazilian style of playing football—which Brazilians call *art football*—and you will get a sense of the idea.

After the *Metaesquemas*, Oiticica moved the canvas away from the wall and then out into the room in, for instance, the *Bilaterals* (*Bilaterais*) (1959) and the *Spatial Reliefs* (*Relevos Espaciais*) (1960) (see Phelan 2007, 73–103, especially 81–5). At each stage of the development of his style of artistic presentation, the work becomes less of an object and more of a provocation for a response from—or a relation with—the spectator. In the same movement, spectators are transformed into *participators*, which perhaps they always already were, potentially at least, even in the *Metaesquemas* because of the way in which space becomes mobile or dynamic in those paintings.[27] If the canvas hangs at a small distance from the

---

[24]My sense is that at this period Oiticica was interested in the non-spaces or negative spaces between shapes and the way in which these in-between spaces make possible the relation or movement within the formal composition.

[25]I am thinking in particular of two *Metaesquemas* from 1957. See Ramírez 2007a, 151, plates 31 and 32.

[26]I am grateful to Rodrigo Duarte and Myriam Avila for introducing me to this concept.

[27]Oiticica talks of a "participator [*participador*]," for instance, in "Notes on *Parangolé*" dating from November 25, 1964 and May 6, 1965. See Figueiredo 2008, 172.

wall as in the *Inventions* (*Invenções*) from 1959 to 1962, viewers are made aware of the relation between the canvas and the wall and, at the same time, of the spatial relation in which they themselves stand to a two-dimensional flat surface.[28] We no longer take the surface as a neutral or invisible base on which an image is presented.[29] If the artwork now moves out into the exhibition space and hangs in open space, as in the *Bilaterals* which, as their name suggests, are two-sided works and are suspended on nearly invisible monofilament line, our involvement with the work becomes spatial in a more complex way (Ramírez 2007a, 191–8, plates 96–101; see also Phelan 2007, 82). This is also true of the *Spatial Reliefs* which are folded so as to be reminiscent of origami (2007a, 200–17, plates 102a–20b). Not only has the work become three-dimensional, even if, as Wynne Phelan suggests, the third dimension is very thin, but we are now required to walk around the work if we are to perceive it.[30] We cannot simply stand in front of a canvas, for there is no longer a front and a back nor indeed sides, except in relation to our own perspective. These works are the first beginnings of Oiticica's move into the field of installation, a direction that is developed further in the *Nuclei* (*Núcleos*) from 1960 to 1963, which create architectural spaces by hanging panels in the center of a gallery space (Phelan 2007, 85–94; see also 245–59, plates 159–62c).

Among the *Nuclei* are a group of works called *Penetrables* which, as their name suggests, can be entered either in fact or in the imagination, thus extending the role of the participator-spectator's contribution to the artwork. One of these is a maquette for an

---

[28]See Phelan 2007, 80–1: "The *Inventions* include an important structural component. Small wood-strip frames are attached to the central back portion of the panels. These invisible platforms elevate the painting slightly, approximately one centimeter away from the wall. A line of shadow forms in the space between the wall and the painting. This elegant strategy dissolves the edges of the panel form and launches color into space. In profile, these works present a thin edge of color accented by dark negative space."

[29]Another intriguing aspect of Oiticica's moving beyond the frame is that on the reverse side of these canvases are to be found faint pencil inscriptions with the details of the technical entry and paint sample for the top layer of color. See Phelan 2007, 94–5.

[30]Phelan (2007, 82) says that they are "only slightly three-dimensional" but that they also form "a dark line of negative space between" the panels that back onto one another.

architectural maze, called *The Hunting Dogs Project* (1961) (see Phelan 2007, 98).[31] A maze only counts as such if there is someone who finds herself within and who moves around a spatial puzzle. Oiticica considered such projects works even when they remained models (see Ramírez 2007a, 369). Full-size versions of some of these have been constructed in recent times.[32] *Tropicalia* (1968), *Éden* (1969), and *Cosmococa* (1973–4) are large-scale built environments or installations constructed under Oiticica's direction and, since then, have been reconstructed on a number of occasions (Ramírez 2007b, 17–24). The erstwhile viewer has no choice but to wander around these spaces and does so without a guidebook. There is no beginning and no end, although there are many beginnings and many odd endings. For instance, in *Tropicalia* we enter into a shanty-style hut and find ourselves turning a succession of corners, penetrating what appears, again, to be a maze. Finally, we pull aside a curtain and find a television always switched on and showing whatever is currently broadcasting.

In this discussion I am interested in some particular works—or as Oiticica considered his projects, "inventions"—where a style of communication develops that goes beyond the architectural relation between artist/designer and participator.[33] In an architectural work, the form is designed by the architect, even though it will be transformed by the practice of its users. No doubt the architect may invite a dynamic transformation of the built form by its inhabitants. But even allowing for such anticipation of participation by the inhabitants of the building, architectural planning requires that the final plans determine the construction of the building. In some of Oiticica's works, such as the *Parangolés* (1964–79), the

---

[31]There are also later maquettes such as *Magic Square* (1977) (Ramírez 2007a, 332, plates 222–3).

[32]While *Hunting Dogs* remains a "utopian project" (Figueiredo 2008, 110), *Magic Square* has been constructed in New York, in Rio de Janeiro (See Ramírez 2007a, 333–5) and, more recently, at Inhotim in Minais Gerais, Brazil.

[33]Although there is a particular series of Oiticica's works with the title *Invençoes* (1959–62), he thought of others of his three-dimensional works as "inventions." See 1979 interview with Ivan Cardoso: "my aim was to trigger states of invention" (Quoted by Ramírez 2007b, 17). For an interview with Ivan Cardoso see Favaretto 1992, 47.

relation between form and content/material or form and use is radicalized beyond the limits of the architectural model.[34] Even architectural works, such as *Tropicalia*, may have already moved back to the prior and more indeterminate stage of the architectural sketch.[35] In all of these inventions, the work takes on form in so far as it is explored or used by a participator who now becomes a collaborator.[36]

My particular interest is in some of the *Parangolés* and my suggestion is that they offer a perspective for reflection on the relation between style and meaning. The title *Parangolé* is usually reserved for a particular group of works that started to appear in the mid-1960s, comprising capes, banners, and tents.[37] But Oiticica also used the term more broadly to apply to a style of artistic production, and one of the works I will consider belongs to this broader sense of *Parangolé* (Figueredo 2008, 181).[38] Oiticica took painting away from a flat surface and into an environmental space in order to address the relation in which the viewer (later participator) stands to the artwork. Although the *problem* almost certainly started out as that of the relation of the elements of the work in space, as we can see in, for instance, the *Metaesquemas*, this concern already implicitly implies a question about the relation between viewer and work, because only for a viewer does the question of the spatial relation of the shapes arise. A question about the internal spatiality of paintings becomes one about the relations or

---

[34]These, more than the earlier architecturally oriented works, help us understand Oicitica's claim that what he makes is music. See note 46.

[35]I owe this idea of the architectural sketch to Lesley Graham.

[36]See, for instance, *Basin Bólide 01* (1965–6), a basin of earth equipped with rubber gloves inviting us to dig our hands into the contents of the basin (Ramírez 2007a, 292–3, plate 189). See also Figueredo 2008, 188, cited below in note 49.

[37]So while I have referred to the *Parangolés* as capes, they are also banners, tents, and flags made out of jute, plastic bags, painted or printed fabrics and sometimes including painted or stenciled texts. They are intended to be used or worn by the viewer.

[38]In a journal note from July 1966, Oiticica writes: "[*Parangolé*] is much more than a term to define a series of characteristic works (the capes, banners, and tent); *Parangolé* is the definitive formulation of environmental antiart." The word "*parangolé*" is a slang term in Rio de Janeiro that refers to a range of events or states including idleness, a sudden agitation, an unexpected situation, or a dance party. See Dezeuze 2004, 58–71, in particular, 59. On Oiticica's epiphany on the productiveness of the concept, see Ramírez 2007a, 373.

interstices between art and life.[39] I will suggest that an important way in which the *Parangolés* offer a reflection on life and on art is by highlighting the genesis and potential breakdown of style. Tellingly, these artworks simultaneously uncover emergent meanings, suggesting the interconnection of meaning and style within life more generally.[40] Style brought to our attention as pregnant with meaning is what I call communicative style.

Communicative style is related to but is not the same as communication.[41] In communication something is communicated and the

---

[39]Ramírez 2007b, 17. Ramírez remarks that one way in which Oiticica stepped outside acceptable limits was through "the impulse to take art to its limits in order to materialize his vision of a new 'state of invention' that blurred the perceived division between art and life."

[40]Oiticica kept journals in which he examined many of the ideas he was engaged with in his works. These journals are a rich source for those trying to understand those works. In this discussion, however, I try to understand the works starting from their presentation as such, rather than from the artist's writings. I intend to engage with the journal entries in further work on Oiticica. I consider that both approaches offer points of entry into the works while resisting the view that the words of artists—however reflective they may be (and Oiticica was unusually verbally reflective)—provide the code-breaking key for their visual productions. Were I to take Oiticica's writings as key for interpreting the significance of the artworks, I would have to address his apparent resistance to the very notion of style. On the rare occasions when he introduces the notion, he does so in a negative tone. In a conversation with the film-maker Ivan Cardoso, during the making of the film *H.O.*, Oiticica says: "the existence of style is no longer possible" (Figueirido 2008, 31). However, the specificity of his rejection of style is, I think, clarified by the way he continues this thought: "the existence of a unilateral, departmentalized form of expression such as painting is no longer possible." His rejection is of style as something exclusive and determinate. Painting can, in Oiticica's view, no longer be a style of artistic expression that excludes other styles such as architecture, film and, even, music. This also seems to be the point of his claim that "'style' does not exist" in a note from November, 11, 1979 (see Figueirido 2008, 278). I will suggest that Oiticica's works display an alternative pre-understanding of style as in formation or in the process of breaking down. In contrast to his infrequent and negative remarks on style, the journals often mention "meaning." I cannot here enter into an analysis of the way in which the concept of meaning functions for Oiticica, but exemplary of his innovative use of the term, is his view that each color—for instance, white—has a "meaning" (see, for instance, a note from 1960 cited in Figueirido 2008, 137 and also 37–8).

[41]*Communicative style* is my expression. There are a few occasions when Oiticica introduces communication in his journals (see, for instance, Figueirido 2008, 124; Ramírez 2007a, 257). It is clear that he thought of communication as *dialogue*, especially that between spectator and work (Ramírez 2007a, 257). It is also, I would suggest, clear that he thought his works aimed at communication, so long as we do

activity of communication is normally perceived as secondary to meaning. Any communication has a certain style, but this is not usually in the forefront of our awareness when we are communicating. As I have already suggested, we can become aware of style, when, for instance, we realize that the way we are going about things is undermining our attempt to communicate. Communicative style is distinguished by operating explicitly at the level of style and opens up possibilities of meaning, without the precise signification of those communications being determined or completed.

I am suggesting that communicative style is principally to be found in artworks—I say *principally* because it is at least possible that someone could achieve communicative style in the way they live their life. However, we would then be inclined to say that life has become an art-form. Yet, there is an important way in which ordinary communication can display an approximation to communicative style. Think of a conversation in which the exchange freely develops without any discernable constraint. The conversation is no longer anchored in projects or criteria external to it—although these will still play a part as the medium within which the conversation develops. Conversation becomes playful in its structure, open-ended in its development, and self-sustaining in its motivations. In such a case, each participant is willing to embrace an open development of meaning and is not intent on determining the outcome of the exchange according to a preexisting agenda. I would also suggest that when a conversation takes off in this way, we can become aware of the form or pattern—we might say the stylistic frame—of the conversation quite differently from the normal case. This awareness can be rather uncanny, which is not surprising as we become aware of this background condition for any communication. Style as a horizon for communication shoots into the foreground and disturbs our perspective on what we are about. Actual conversations tend to do this, at best, in fits and starts. And

---

not assume that communication is something *ready-made*. (See my comments at the outset of this chapter.) The sense in which communication is at issue in this article is that of conversation, which is close to dialogue, although I have not chosen that term because of its binary connotation. The conversation I discover within Oiticica's works is not only a two-way transmission between work and participant, but also a complex exchange between multiple works and participants within a dynamic and developing environment.

although even a rare conversation that at least approximates to this ideal can be a joyous experience, it also has something of the vertigo of flying, or, at least, of dreaming of flying. The higher we fly in a conversation—that is the more we escape external constraints—the greater chance that we will become aware that something may go wrong and that our parachute might fail. Nevertheless, without some improvisation and style, conversations, dialogues, and intellectual investigations are moribund, because their introductory or initial conditions determine the outcome—or the limited outcomes—of the exchange. No innovation in science, philosophy, culture, or living arises without an open play of communication both with others and as internal reflection. We have to be able, metaphorically speaking, to move around a subject and see it from angles we had not previously even dreamt of.[42]

When conversations attain the freedom I have just described, they approach what I am calling communicative style. I am not saying that all open-ended conversations fully achieve this or, indeed, that they are artworks, although I would not rule out that some conversations could count as such. I am saying that *some* artworks display features of the freedom that is necessary as a possibility for the meaningfulness of a conversation. All conversations have some style whether we are aware of this or not: communicative style is style *as* communication. By this I mean that an artwork can display the act of communicating when style is in genesis and at the birth of meaning. When we try to achieve meaningfulness in art, in science, or in life, we need to follow a path that is *there*, yet not already drawn.[43] Artworks such as Oiticica's are capable of existing in the medium of communicative style, whereas our conversations, as well as scientific and philosophical experiments, are usually counterbalanced or anchored by a project or set of commitments that stops us from merely floating in the realm of ideas.[44] For this reason, the communicative style of Oiticica's art educates our understanding of our own communicative projects.

---

[42]Just as Oiticica's *Bilaterals* and *Spatial Reliefs*, for instance, force us to move around them.

[43]Oiticica's *Tropicalia* presents paths that we follow without any determinate order. We find the way as we go along.

[44]My hunch is that the idea of communicative style would be helpful for addressing a range of artworks.

The Brazilian expression I mentioned earlier can help us explore communicative style further. In any undertaking that aims to be more than a repetition, we need *jogo de cintura*—hip sway or hip play. The suggestion of dance is not at all accidental, but the metaphor does not refer to any musical movement whatsoever. Courtly dance would not sustain the image the expression evokes. Only some sorts of dance require that the center—or low center—of the body is moved in a flexible way. Again, this would not be true of Irish dancing where, although great mobility of the legs and feet is required, the upper body must be kept totally still, while the arms remain stiffly straight at one's sides. If the upper body is static and the lower body is mobile, the central axis of the body is not fluid. Hence there is no *jogo de cintura*.[45] I would not go so far as to say that samba is the only dance with hip movement, but it is a style of dance for which *jogo de cintura* is imperative.[46] My suggestion, in short, is that dance is an important metaphor for understanding communicative style. I am not embarrassed to use metaphors to further my discussion, as will have been clear from my discussion so far. Such a concept as communicative style will be difficult to pin down. It is unlikely we will be able to do so solely using logical permutations of concepts. Images will be necessary and metaphor is an extremely important element in our repertoire of self-understanding.

What can we make of this kinetic metaphor? Communicative style displays *jogo de cintura* in the sense that it displays and emphasizes the flexible activity out of which genuinely productive communication may arise. Communicative style highlights a hinge within communication. Hinges or transitions within relations arise between one interlocutor and another, between one idea and another, between what has already been said and what might possibly be said next. The particular hinge under examination here is that between style and meaning. I have suggested that although such transitions are to be found in everyday conversations, they are

---

[45]The popular *River Dance* displays rather more flexibility than the traditional style of Irish dancing, but is still focused on the lower body. However, there is *jogo de cintura* in the Irish sport of hurling!

[46]Oiticica thought that rock music was extremely important for inaugurating a style of dance that does not follow rules (see, for instance, Figueirido 2008, 37–8; 277–8).

not usually evident to us. This is why artworks displaying communicative style are so important. Just as *jogo de cintura* suggests an activity emanating from a central axis around the hips and giving kinetic balance to the whole body, communicative style displays a balancing activity between constituent forces in communication, revealing the emergence of meaning in conjunction with the genesis of style.

The *Parangolés* are *artworks* that have entered into dance.[47] This highly accomplished visual artist, who could easily have pursued an international career as a painter or installation artist, chose to move his efforts into the field of dance. He came to think of dance as a medium in which the relation between artwork and the reception of art could be particularly productively addressed. The communicative possibility of the artwork is set free in the medium of dance. But this does not mean that he chose dance rather than the other arts. The fabulous capes—*Parangolés*—preserve an architectural attention to structure, but also focus on color in a way that is reminiscent of painted surfaces. At the same time, these are canvases for wearing, for going out into the world and for communicating in the free spontaneous exchange of the samba experience. We might also talk of a carapace, a skin, or a membrane between the wearer and her world or, as Oiticica suggested on several occasions, a shelter (see, for instance, Figueirido 2008, 173). These metaphors, in various ways, evoke not a boundary that closes off inside from outside, but rather a limit that allows the wearer to inhabit and move around the outer space. The dancer, wearing the *Parangolé*, is a kinetic painting or sculpture weaving patterns in an environment. In fact, she contributes to the construction of an environment, which is also a tradition. This environment, expressed in a culture and bearing meanings both for its members and for observers, is one of the conditions of communication. And as all of this is accompanied by music and has the quality of street theater, we can see the *Parangolé* as a radical reworking of

[47]In 1979 Oiticica wrote: "I have discovered that what I make is MUSIC and that MUSIC is not 'one of the arts' but the synthesis of the consequence of the *discovery of the body*" (see Figueirido 2008, 277, also, 37). We could only begin to understand this claim, I would suggest, through a thorough exploration of the importance of dance for the *Parangolés*. In particular, it would be important to investigate how music can be seen as an expression of the synthesizing activity of the body.

the classical nineteenth-century notion of the *Gesamtkunstwerk* (see Figueirido 2008, 181). Whereas Wagner saw opera as combining all the arts in one total expression, the performance of the *Parangolés* is an explosion of different levels and styles of expression in an event that resists totality—at least the sort of totality that is final. Expressiveness is released by the resistance to conclusions. The seduction of possible communication is opened up by *not* trying to achieve any particular communication or, at least, by not pursuing it to a singular conclusion. Style opens up the possibility of meaning without establishing any particular meaning: but, crucially, the style that is capable of doing so is itself aware of its own development and the problematic status of its identity.[48] Style in genesis becomes visible in a kinetic balancing—*jogo de cintura*—with the birth of meaning. This is what I understand by communicative style.

I am thinking here, in particular, of two sequences from the film *H.O.* (Cardoso 1979). The first of these sequences shows some members of the Mangueira Samba School, dancing informally and wearing brightly colored *Parangolés*.[49] The scene is shot in daylight on a street and on a rooftop in the Mangeira *favela*. The accompanying samba music has a heavy, rhythmic drum beat. We see a succession of dancers, including a man wearing a white, red, and pale yellow *Parangolé* made out of cloth, followed by a woman wearing another cape in red and green cloth, then another man wearing one in red plastic, yet another wearing one made out of red and green cloth panels inscribed with "*incorporo a revolta* [incorporate the revolt]" and, finally, a man wearing tight swimming trunks and a blue plastic cape. He gyrates to the Rolling Stones's "Sympathy for the Devil." The dancers move freely and with obvious enjoyment. Their movements are much less choreographed than they would in Carnival. While they are clearly conscious of the camera

[48]See Figueirido (2008, 32) where Oiticica decries seeing art as supplying meanings and signifying structures. This does not entail, however, that meaning is not at issue, only that it is not to be found or interpreted in the works. On page 188 he speaks of the participator's act of digging the earth in the *Basin Bólide*, suggesting that this "already constitutes the meaning of the work." Meaning is not an already established content that determines an interpretation. Meaning arises from or perhaps, even, *is* an activity.

[49]This sequence follows the title "veja-se MORRO DA MANGEIRA" ("See Mangeira Hill").

and of their own activity, they try out steps with an air of easy experimentation.

Style is in genesis here in an unforced manner, but so too is meaning. The performance shows the *Parangolé*-wearing dancers instituting new practices. I am suggesting that the latter qualify as emergent meanings. The meanings are dance steps, which are practices embedded within wider practices and, ultimately, within a community.[50] The performance is not a merely formal act and gives an admittedly indeterminate insight into the lives of the participants. This, I would argue, is visible in the performance and is a necessary constituent of the project Oiticica developed in conjunction with the Mangeira Samba School. Theory only comes along afterwards and points to what is visible. As yet, the meanings that constitute the significance of the evolving style are not established or determined. They will remain undetermined so long as they are part of the *Parangolé* performance and are not yet, for instance, included in a choreographed Carnival routine. If we can accept that cultural practices qualify as meanings, then this sequence of the film presents us with emergent meanings. In conjunction with this, through the spontaneity and general *joie de vivre* of those practices, we can discern a style of being that is the condition for these expressions of a culture. This sequence displays *jogo de cintura* as a spontaneous enjoyment of improvisation, expressed in fluid movements accompanied by samba.

The second sequence is very different in tone.[51] Hélio Oiticica emerges out of the darkness into the dim evening light of an abandoned urban commercial space.[52] He is wearing only a pair of tight green and silver biker trousers, silver shoes, and *Sac Bólide 4* (1967), which is a large plastic sack made of colorless, transparent plastic (Bólide 52, Sac Bólide 4, 1966–7).[53]

[50]Here I am offering a way of thinking of meaning as emergent that I think would be congenial to Oiticica's suggestion that the color white has meaning. See note 39.

[51]It follows the title *"parangol' helium."*

[52]This sequence has been identified as taking place in a street in Leblon in prosperous southern Rio, a world away from the favela of Mangeira in the north of the city.

[53]Written at the opening of the sack are the words: "*Teu amore eu guardo aqui* [I keep your love here]." I am grateful to Ariane Pereira de Figueiredo for identification of this work.

This *Bólide*, I am suggesting, qualifies as a *Parangolé* in the broader sense I have identified.[54] He, like the dancers from the first sequence, manipulates the *Bólide* as he moves. In this case the plastic sack is over his head and shoulders. He distends the sack and at one stage the camera goes up inside it, emphasizing the almost suffocating position in which he puts himself. The mood of this sequence is unsettling and intriguing. Hélio tries out steps or moves, some of them awkward, others slightly more fluid. His movements might be described as a walking that is almost dancing. At times we can glimpse a hint of his enjoying this uneasy experiment and, perhaps also, the viewer's exposure to it. But his enjoyment is quite distinct from that which we were able to observe in the first sequence. If anything, his pleasure seems to be one of intoxicated ecstasy. His improvisation is not an easy-going beginning of a variation on an already established dance, as might appear to be the case in the first sequence. All of this is accompanied by music that borders on noise. We hear painfully high-pitched tones, followed by low rumbling ones and the rhythms are irregular and unsettling.[55] At the end of the sequence, Oiticica disappears into the darkness at the edge of the dimly lit space.

Again here, style is in genesis, but it is more awkwardly self-conscious and more uncomfortable both, it seems, for the participator (Oiticica) and for the viewer. Style is in the foreground and appears alien. This performance presents itself as an "invention" in Oiticica's sense of the term, with the connotation of something that has not yet been said or shown. And just as we can only wait and see where the style will go, we must do likewise for the meanings emerging from this style of movement. I have suggested that emergent meanings are presented by the first sequence insofar as dance steps count as innovative practices within the horizon of a community. In this case, the movements appear to be detached—as is their physical environment—from an existing community. Nevertheless, these dislocated steps are also practices

[54]See Figueirido 2008, 188 for a journal note suggesting that the *Bólides* (1963–7) count as *Parangolés*. See also note 37.

[55]I have not yet obtained a positive identification for this *music*, but it is similar to works by twentieth-century composers such as Ligeti or Stockhausen.

and anticipate a community that is not yet.[56] (After all, Oiticica performs these steps for a camera and for a possible audience.) And while this sequence may appear to operate through style alone, it too points to possibilities of signification. The dialectic between Oiticica's eccentric intervention and its environment, a barren commercial space, evokes questions about the significance of his style. Even when we cannot easily read meanings from his movements, they suggest something more than a way of moving in space. Both style and its meanings are in genesis: they could succeed or fail in being born. The *dance* that is emerging from this experiment is one that has not been danced before: if it succeeds in taking form, a new style (or styles) and new meanings will appear.[57]

Is there any *jogo de cintura* in this second sequence? We may suspect not, for Oiticica's movements are often jerky and might even appear unbalanced. Nevertheless, I would suggest that his bodily movements reveal a deeper significance of what is implied by this verbal expression, through showing the evolution of movement and the risk of its breaking down. He deconstructs *jogo de cintura* as an activity of balancing by highlighting its potential crisis. In doing so, he draws out a deeper possibility within the phrase, highlighting the ongoing project of improvisation that entails both the difficulty and the achievement of kinetic balancing. He thus *shows* something that allows us to go beyond a superficial sense of the verbal expression as implying an immediately harmonious movement. This performance uncovers the potential crisis within apparently harmonious performances such as the first sequence.[58] The evolution of style in the second performance releases emergent meanings and this occurs as a kinetic exploration of improvisation

---

[56]A twist on this suggestion would be that we might think of Oiticica's moves as expressing the culture of the privileged, highly educated, politicized, and artistically motivated *avant-garde* of Leblon and adjacent areas of southern Rio, such as *Jardim Botanico* where the artist lived. The *avant-garde* would then be the representatives of a community only in existence as a possibility.

[57]This would qualify as an instance of what Oiticica calls "unforseen possibilities" (see Figueirido 2008, 180). In referring to Oiticica's movements while wearing the *Sac Bólide* as *dance*, I am using the term in a broad sense for all bodily movements that display "a discovery of the body." See Figueirido (2008, 37) citing a conversation between Oiticica and Ivan Cardoso where he attributes this achievement to samba and rock.

[58]By extension, they do so also for performances that fall somewhere between the harmonious air of the first sequence and the disturbing tone of the second.

that helps us become aware of a deeper nuance within the expression *jogo de cintura*. So the *Sac Bólide* deepens our understanding of the nature and importance of dance for the *Parangolés*, in the narrower sense of the term. A discussion of these visual performances, such as I have only been able to begin here, cannot communicate more than a suggestion of what Oiticica is able to show.

In his performative wearing of the *Sac Bólide*, Oiticica *shows* a crucial point at which style and meaning converge: he presents their relation as an experience within a life. His artistic reflection on that convergence can serve as a beginning of further reflections—both theoretical and artistic—on the necessary connections between stylistics and semantics. His revelation of their dependency also helps retrospectively validate the thesis I introduced at the outset of this chapter and for which I have offered a theoretical sketch. In a nutshell, I have been arguing that no meaning is devoid of style, while style always implies some possible meaning. In the film *H.O.*, Oiticica performs—or dances—the genesis of style at the same time as the birth of possible meaning. Style is in an experimental phase where it may become recognizable or fall apart. Likewise, the significance or meanings facilitated by this style are on the cusp of appearing, but they may also come to nothing. The emergence of new meanings depends on the development of a new style. The performance is one in which style, meaning, and communication are indeterminate, yet they are, problematically, at issue for us. The artwork is saying—or communicating—something to us, but neither we nor Oiticica know yet what. The performance of the emergence of style and meaning is the work of the artwork.

Artworks displaying communicative style are necessarily open-ended and do not *possess* a style: they inhabit a style as an ongoing project. I hope it is clear that this does not mean that any one artwork has to display a plurality of styles, for it may be that a style is unitary but complex and indeterminate. Style is, in such cases, in evolution. It is also the case that not all artworks would fulfill this. I am not saying that communicative style is the only *good* style. I *am* saying that communicative style is able to highlight a reciprocal relation between style and meaning that is often missed. *And further* I am saying that some reciprocity between style and content is the condition of a successful artwork. So a good artwork has as its necessary minimal condition that it operates with some reciprocity between style and content, whether that reciprocity is harmonious or disruptive. Not all good artworks, however, develop this reciprocity in such a way that it becomes visible. Oiticica's *Parangolés*—both in the narrow and, in the case of the *Sac Bólide*, in the broader sense of the term—do just this. One of the ways they stand out is in making the style-meaning relation stand out. The *Parangolés* do so by showing the emergence of meanings within the genesis of style. And this illuminates a condition of the possibility of communication in general.

References

Cardoso, Ivan, dir. 1979. *H.O.* Rio de Janeiro: Collection of Ivan Cardoso. 35mm.

Dezeuze, Anna. 2004. "Tactile Dematerialization, Sensory Politics: Hélio Oiticica's *Parangolés*." *Art Journal* 63(2): 58–71.

Favaretto, Celso. 1992. *A invenção de Hélio Oiticica.* São Paulo: Editora da Universidade de São Paulo.

Figueiredo, Luciano. 2007. "'The world is the museum': Appropriation and Transformation in the Work of Hélio Oicitica." In *Hélio Oiticica: The Body of Colour*, edited by Mari Carmen Ramírez, 105–25. London: Tate Publishing in association with The Museum of Fine Arts, Houston.

—, ed. 2008. *Painting Beyond the Frame.* Translated by Stephen Berg. Rio de Janeiro: Sylvia Roesler Edições de Arte.

Hughes, Fiona. 2007. *Kant's Aesthetic Epistemology: Form and World.* Edinburgh: Edinburgh University Press.

Merleau-Ponty, Maurice. 1945. *Phénoménologie de la perception.* Paris: Gallimard.

—. 1962. *The Phenomenology of Perception.* Translated by C. Smith. London: Routledge.

—. 1964a. "Eye and Mind." In *The Primacy of Perception*, translated by William Cobb, 17–26. Evanston: Northwestern University Press.

—. 1964b. *L'oeil et l'esprit.* Paris: Gallimard.

—. 1964c. *Le visible et l'invisible.* Paris: Gallimard.

—. 1968. *The Visible and the Invisible.* Translated by Alphonso Lingis. Evanston: Northwestern University Press.

Phelan, Wynne H. 2007. "To Bestow a Sense of Light: Hélio Oiticica's Experimental Process." In *Hélio Oiticica: The Body of Colour*, edited by Mari Carmen Ramírez, 75–103. London: Tate Publishing in association with The Museum of Fine Arts, Houston.

Ramírez, Mari Carmen, ed. 2007a. *Hélio Oiticica: The Body of Colour*. London: Tate Publishing in association with The Museum of Fine Arts, Houston.

—. 2007b. "Hélio's Double-Edged Challenge." In *Hélio Oiticica: The Body of Colour*, edited by Mari Carmen Ramírez, 17–26. London: Tate Publishing in association with The Museum of Fine Arts, Houston.

10

St!le-
-in
deconstruction

Laurent Milesi

What we need, perhaps, as Nietzsche said,
is a change of "style."
—JACQUES DERRIDA, "THE ENDS OF MAN"

Introduction

The title of this essay will be economical and to the point: "style-in-deconstruction." But how should one hear or read such a title, the in-different difference in rhythm, tone, or intonation, themselves *mere* elements of style, that articulates the singularly plural hyphens? Unless one means to discuss only whether something called "deconstruction" has anything to say about style or even has style, a style of its own, this title sounds like a flippant reversal of "work in progress" (or "work in construction," as it were): not only would one not arrive at an aesthetically accomplished creation but not even at something called a "style". . . . A most slippery, perilous path down which to travel, one full of stiles and stakes, like crossing the road during what in French is called *l'heure de pointe* (rush hour), where nothing less than *man* might be at stake if one bears in mind the title (and context) of Derrida's essay, "The Ends of Man," from which the quotation in the epigraph, alluding to Nietzsche's *Zarathustra*, was lifted.

Flori-legium: What was style (,) in theory

Like any other time-honored crux, style has enjoyed a vast array of conflicting approaches and definitions,[1] from the now famous adage (astonishingly missing from the first draft) proposed by Buffon in his inaugural discourse at the Académie Française (1753), "le style est l'homme même" (1978, xvii), inspired by one of Pascal's *Pensées*[2] but also consonant with George Puttenham's earlier (1589) dictum in *The Arte of English Poesie* (style as "the image of man" [2007, 233])—and still often (mis)quoted, as in the opening of Lacan's *Écrits* (1966, 9)[3]—to Fredric Jameson's predictable linkage with historical modes of production, for instance in *Marxism and Form*,[4] to Deleuze, in his essay on Melville's "Bartleby," for whom "Style—the foreign language within language—is made up of these two operations [between language and silence]. Or should we instead speak with Proust of a nonstyle, that is, of 'the elements of a style to come which do not yet exist'? Style is the economy of language" (Deleuze 1998, 113, referring to Passerone 1991). Indeed, if, as Paul Valéry famously maintained, style is best envisaged as an *écart* or deviation from the norm—an idea still

---

[1]This "variety of things" that style refers to is echoed for example in the Preface to Brewster (1921, ix).

[2]See fragment 569: "Quand on voit le style naturel, on est tout étonné et ravi, car on s'attendait de voir un auteur et on trouve un homme" ("When one sees natural style, one is quite astonished and enraptured, for one expected to see an author and one finds a man"; Pascal 1995, 1.29. A more ancient origin for the maxim might be Seneca's "Oratio vultus animi est" ("The style is the soul's mirror") (1829, 275).

[3]Often misquoted as "Le style, c'est l'homme," as in Walter Pater's translation in his "Style" (1921, 301), the right formula and its "epigrammatic" contraction are discussed side by side in Ludwig Wittgenstein's *Vermischte Bemerkungen* (1949); see Wittgenstein (1984, 561 / 1980, 78).

[4]"To define style as language which deliberately calls attention to itself, and 'foregrounds' itself as a key element in the work, is to reassert, as over against stylistics, the profoundly historical nature of the phenomenon" (quoted in Lukacher 1986, 178).

endorsed by many a latter-day stylistician[5]—then there should be no harder, more Protean notion, none more resistant to essential pinning down, than style, for which an arch-principle of deviation, if not deviancy, would be constitutive, not unlike the Epicurean *parenklisis* or *clinamen*, that swerve of the atom which "*destine au hasard*" in Derrida's (1984a, 4) "Mes Chances."[6] After all, what we came to understand by style, regardless of its definitional vagaries and of our parochial constituencies, is already a deviation from a more originary meaning, a metonymic slippage from the *stylus* or metal tip used to engrave or *impress* in a wax tablet to the manner of reworking what had been thus incised or *expressed*, as well as a spelling deviancy—*stile* becoming *style*—due to the erroneous association with Greek *stulos*: column, whereas its reconstructed Indo-European root would be **-sti*: to prick, hence sting, stimulus.[7]

"Le style n'est que l'ordre et le mouvement qu'on met dans ses pensées" ("Style is only the order and movement that one puts into one's thoughts"), for Buffon in his *Discours* (1978, 6; see also 1978, 'De l'Art d'écrire', 30; and 1954, 511), who goes on to note that a flowing style is a matter of *construction* and orchestration of ideas, and of rigorous discipline (*sévérité*).[8] Linking words rather than ideas does not lead to style but merely to a gnomonic "shadow"

---

[5]See for example Michael Riffaterre's evolution from a stylistics of such disparities to one recentering on "stylistic context," from (1957) to (1971), as he moves toward a more immanentist, structural stylistics (immanence of the message and structure of the code). With the contribution of the linguistic sciences to the new discipline, now disentangled from criteria of aesthetic evaluation that derived from the old rhetoric, the notion of style as *écart* from a norm becomes no longer viable as prescriptiveness is abandoned (see for instance 1971, 134), although a similar concern for differentiality (versus referentiality) will be reintroduced in Riffaterre's later focus on intertextuality (to the detriment of contextuality, precisely) (see Milesi 1998, especially 15).

[6]All italics in quotations are those of the author quoted unless otherwise indicated.For a development of the structural similarity between Lucretius' theory of the *clinamen* and Derrida's conception of the trace and the *écart*, see Christopher Johnson (1993, 133–6, 138–40, 160–2).

[7]Cf. Buffon, "le style doit graver les pensées" (1978, xiii). "Stimulus" often features in Riffaterre's various linguistic approaches to style in *Essais de stylistique structurale*, (1971, for example 111, 121). See also Pater's "the chief stimulus of good style" (1921, 292).

[8]All translations given are my own unless otherwise indicated.

(*ombre*) of style (Buffon 1978, xiii), and writing as one thinks, that is "naturally," as long as one's thoughts have been logically ordered through the work of reason, is conducive to the *truth* of style: "un beau style n'est tel en effet que par le nombre infini de vérités qu'il présente" ("a beautiful style is such in effect only through the infinite number of truths which it presents" [xvii]).[9] Only in poetry, history, or philosophy could one hope to find and identify sublimity of style (xviii), according to the overconfident essayist whom George Bernard Shaw (1921, vii) had dumbed down as "the celebrated Buffoon." It is worth pointing out that the object here is the style of the man *of letters* or *écrivain* more generally, and that, contrary to what might be assumed, the Age of Reason did not formally distinguish between literature and philosophy to value (good, true) style but mainly put the emphasis on language being at the osmotic service of a natural expression of thought—cf. Boileau's famous "ce qui se conçoit bien s'énonce clairement" in Canto I of his *Art poétique*, Buffon's (1978, 15) "bien écrire, c'est .. . bien penser," Newman's (1858, 9) "style is a thinking out of language," or Rémy de Gourmont's (1902, 154) "le style est la pensée même."

To my knowledge, Edmond Arnould's *Essai d'une théorie du style* (1851) is the first self-styled attempt at laying out a *theory* of style, or rather an impressionistic *material aesthetics*. It predictably glosses Buffon's celebrated aphorism, echoing the view that style is a truly intrinsic property of the individual(ity):

> Le style appartient à l'individu, comme la langue à la nature, comme le langage à l'humanité. C'est en ce sens, mais en ce sens seulement, qu'il faut entendre la fameuse définition de Buffon: le style, c'est l'homme même. Autrement on risquerait de ne pas arriver à la vérité ou de n'arriver qu'à une vérité incomplète. (Arnould 1851, 3)
>
> (Style belongs to the individual, like language to nature, like [verbal] language to humanity. It is in this sense, but in this sense

[9]Note the contrast with Jean-Luc Nancy's "truth demands a laborious science without style" (Nancy 2008, 61). See also, on the same page in Buffon: "Les idées seules forment le fond du style, l'harmonie des paroles n'en est que l'accessoire"; "Le ton n'est que la convenance du style à la nature du sujet." ("Only ideas form the substance of style; the harmony of words is nothing but its accessory.")

only, that Buffon's famous definition, "style is the very man," must be understood. Otherwise one would risk not arriving at truth or else arriving only at an incomplete truth.)

Thus the general, essential qualities of style (clarity, purity, precision, property,[10] naturalness, harmony) are the results of individual qualities, and "Le style est donc le résultat, l'expression et la marque de l'individualité" (1851, 6). Like Buffon, Arnould resorts to the same "neo-classical" typology and metaphorics of elements of styles (coloring, *dessin*, tone; the analogy with the metal to be stamped with one's personal effigy [cf. Buffon 1978, xvi, xviii, xii; and Arnould 1851, 3, 39–58, 115–41]), and does not discriminate between literature and philosophy but merely between poetry and prose (hence the mention of Descartes, Pascal, La Bruyère, Voltaire, Rousseau, Montesquieu, Buffon among prose stylists), a distinction handed down from Aristotle's *Rhetoric*. And like Buffon as well, he recalls the Platonic idea that "le beau est la splendeur du vrai" (Arnould 1851, 145).

Among the natural as much as cultural foundations and determinations of Arnould's typology of style (e.g. the impact of climate, *race*, nationality, and epoch), evolved from the classical generic modes, one should emphasize the insistence on virility: "la pureté, la netteté, la précision et la vigueur des lignes n'apparaissent dans le style qu'avec la civilisation chez les peuples, avec la virilité chez les individus, c'est-à-dire avec le développement logique des idées et l'art qui en règle l'expression" ("Purity, neatness, precision, and the vigour of lines appear in style only with civilisation in populations, with virility in individuals, that is to say, with the logical development of ideas and the art which regulates its expression"). Thus Madame de Staël and "madame Sand" are generously admitted into this predominantly male pantheon because "[elles] sont venues apporter à l'oeuvre commune des qualités d'esprit et une richesse d'imagination vraiment viriles, tempérées par cette délicatesse de sens et cette douceur *pénétrante* qui n'appartiennent qu'à leur sexe" (["they] have brought to the common work truly virile qualities of spirit and wealth of imagination, tempered by this

[10]Cf. Jonathan Swift's "Proper words in proper places, make the true definition of style" in "Letter to a Young Clergyman" (1898, 200–1).

delicacy of meaning and this penetrating softness which belong only to their sex"; 54, emphasis mine]). Later on, Flaubert, who aspired to write a book about nothing, held only by the strength of its style, and of whose *Madame Bovary* Sainte-Beuve would say in a contemporary review that he wielded his pen like a scalpel, will declare, in a letter to Louise Colet of April 24, 1852: "je conçois un style qui entrerait dans l'idée comme un coup de stylet" ("I conceive of a style which would thrust into the idea like a stiletto/stylet.") Style, then, as clinical stiletto.

A similar equation between style and (individual) power or even potency (puissance) opens Ernest Hello's contemporary venture (1861, 7: "Le style est une puissance"), whose most noteworthy contribution is the forceful attempt to take to its logical conclusion the emphasis on the individual "signature" of style as natural, organic, and ultimately truthful,[11] thus rejecting rhetoric's advice to imitate past masters "mechanically" (15–16; cf. Buffon 1978, xv).

Under the joint influence of the nationalistic agenda in earlier, prescriptive treatises on style, derived from classical rhetoric, and the taxonomic inventory of languages and dialects within a predominantly philological culture, *stylistics* first came to designate the *practical* knowledge of the specific traits of a given language, in particular its figures and idiomatic turns (e.g. Berger 1978; cf. also Novalis's formula *Stylistik oder Rhetorik*, hence the emergence of "practical rhetoric"),[12] before taking on a more literary-critical orientation in the wake of the advent of Saussurean linguistics (see Bally 1902 and 1905) .

---

[11]See Hello (1861): "Notre style, c'est la signature de notre personne apposée sur une idée" (16) [Our style is our person's signature affixed to an idea]; "Le style, c'est la parole humaine . . . elle doit être vraie" (11) [Style is human speech . . . it must be true]; "les idées qu'un homme exprime sont la propriété de tous. Mais le style de cet homme est sa propriété particulière" (13) [The ideas which a man expresses are the property of all. But this man's style is his particular property].

[12]As many critics have noted, Novalis may be the first to have used the term to designate this emerging science which was slowly superseding classical but moribund rhetoric, in the formula "*Stylistik oder Rhetorik*," also known then as "practical rhetoric" (Falkmann 1835). In English, *stylistic* (thus spelt), meaning "the art of forming a good style in writing; a treatise on style," was first used as a word in Worcester's *A Universal and Critical Dictionary of the English Language* (1846). See *OED*, vol. XVI, *s. v.* "stylistics."

Running counter to the first timid gropings toward what will become *modern* literary stylistics, which "has privileged reference to the author's individual person, style being in this way identified with an idiolect" (Genette 1993, 128),[13] is the crisis of identity which style has increasingly undergone throughout the nineteenth century, its putative essence being hollowed out by a kind of (self-)consuming pyrography reminiscent of French politician Édouard Herriot's well-known jocular maxim about culture, that it is what remains when one has forgotten everything. Style will thus slowly turn into a minimalist condition, the stripping bare of an author's numerous idiosyncratic variations and flaunted trappings across texts or even within a single text, to a *régime* whose rhythmic invariance could hopefully be recognized *as such*. Whether in literature or theory—supposing one could still pretend to draw a hermetic fault line between the two[14]—style would be something one *naturally* has the moment one forgets to try and acquire it by recognizably artful means, hence "Le meilleur style est celui qui se fait oublier" ("The best style is one that makes itself forgotten"), an aphorism by Stendhal (in his *Journal*) who so admired the Civil Code for its exemplary sobriety that he read a few pages from it every morning (recalled by Genette 1993, 53, 135). Or as Jules Renard concisely put it in his own diary (entry dated April 7, 1891): "Le style, c'est l'oubli de tous les styles" ("Style is the forgetting of all styles")—and here one could think conversely of Joyce's "odyssey of styles" in *Ulysses*, indebted to George Saintsbury's *Specimens of English Prose Style* (1885), in which "style" becomes the compendium, orchestrated into a narrative, of individual or even collective, imitated "period" styles and the differential relation between them. Ultimately, but also paradoxically, to quote French epigrammatist Rivarol (1962):

[13]Genette (1993, 128) further notes: "just as modern criticism has accentuated individual and sometimes sociohistorical aspects of style, classical criticism was much more interested in generic constraints."

[14]Despite the age-old quest, more recently illustrated by Riffaterre, for the essence of literature or literariness—the vexing question, Sartrean or otherwise, "qu'est-ce que la littérature?," going beyond the historicity of the concept recalled by Derrida in "This Strange Institution Called Literature"—there is ultimately no irrefutable proof grounding its difference from something that for instance could be called "theory" (see also Genette 1993, 138, where style is "the place par excellence of conditional literariness").

"Le style n'est rien, mais rien n'est sans le style" ("Style is nothing, but nothing is without style").

In his chapter of *Fiction and Diction* on "Style and Signification," Genette tells a similar story; his initial attempt to find out what style *is* ends in a wild goose chase:

> The classic work by A. J. Greimas and Joseph Courtès, *Semiotics and Language: An Analytical Dictionary*, includes this declaration in the chapter titled "Style": "The term *style* belongs to the realm of literary criticism, and it is difficult, if not impossible, to define it semiotically." Spurred by this challenge, I shall try to sketch out a semiotic definition of style here. But since the semioticians have referred us to literary scholars, I hurry off to find the recent *Vocabulaire de la stylistique* by Jean Mazaleyrat and Georges Molinié, where I read the definition: "*Style*: the object of stylistics." I then rush ahead to find the definition of "Stylistics": there is none. (1993, 85)[15]

Undaunted by this "presumably intentional abstention," Genette then goes on to note that "from Sainte-Beuve to Thibaudet, from Proust to Richard, critics have manifestly considered style too serious a matter to be entrusted, as an autonomous object, to the monopoly of stylisticians" (86–7)—a seemingly offhand dismissal reminiscent of the ambiguous claim that feminism is too important a subject matter to be left only to women, or in Nietzsche's more erudite, because Latinate, injunction recalled by Derrida (1978a, 103): "*taceat mulier de muliere*" ("let woman be silent about woman"). But as Genette (1993, 86) then rightly contends, "The theory of style [note that we are not yet envisaging style of/in theory here] is not stylistics"—especially, I will add, if stylistics is usually conceived as the study of the use of (synchronic, dehistoricized) language in literature (e.g. Toolan 1997)—so that we are faced with a double plight early in Genette's essay: not only do we not know yet what style, nor a theory of style, is, but let alone something ambitiously called, in theory, "style in theory" from

[15]Cf. a similar plight in the Anglo-Saxon world: "Although style is used very frequently in literary criticism and especially stylistics . . ., it is very difficult to define" (Wales [1990] 2001, 370, s. v. "style").

which "style-in-deconstruction" could be demarcated. His essay will therefore unsurprisingly "conclude"—

> As the reader will no doubt have understood, my intention here has not been to establish a new practice of stylistic analysis on the basis of a new definition of style. In a sense, the existing practice, among stylisticians such as Spitzer [in his two-volume *Stilstudien* (1928)], and even more among critics when they apply themselves to the study of style, seems to me more faithful to the reality of style than are the principles of method or the theoretical declarations we have inherited from the discipline. (1993, 140)

—soon before stating in a final, generalizing flourish, taking its cue from one of his earlier, transitory definitions ("Style is the exemplificatory function of discourse, as opposed to its denotative function" [1993, 105]): "The 'phenomenon of style' is discourse itself" (141).[16]

Spurring style: Derrida

Style and truth, style and woman: this is the implicit linkage, one of philosophy's eternal triangles, that Derrida's study of the elusiveness of woman and/as truth famously traces in *Spurs: Nietzsche's Styles*. No matter what forgetting it stages—especially in the section about Nietzsche's enigmatic "I have forgotten my umbrella"—Derrida does not forget to ground his reflection in an appropriately etymological recall (since etymology is the science of truth[17]), yet one suggestive of protruding virility rather than femininity:

---

[16]It would be interesting to contrast this "phenomenality" or *phainesthai* of (true) style with Buffon's shadow (ombre) of style recalled above.

[17]Obviously one should not naively mistake Derrida's frequent recourse to etymology as, literally and indeed etymologically, an appeal to foundational truth in language via historical origins, despite this frequent gesture testifying to the profound historicity of Derrida's deconstructive démarche. Rather, as Culler (1983, 142) observes, "Linkings that stress the etymology or morphology of a word . . . are ways of applying torque to a concept and affecting its force."

> In the question of style there is always the weight or *examen* of some pointed object. At times this object might be only a quill or a stylus. But it could just as easily be a stiletto, or a rapier. . . .
>
> . . . Thus the style would seem to advance in the manner of a *spur* (éperon) of sorts. . . . Or yet again . . . the style might be compared to that rocky point, also called an *éperon*, on which the waves break at the harbor's entrance. . . .
>
> . . . unless it be *already* that gaping chasm which has been deflowered in the unveiling of the difference. (Derrida 1978a, 37, 39, translation modified)

Before *Spurs*, *Glas* had already brought together, via a quotation from Genet (rather than Genette), questions of style, virility, and truth: "Warda [a name which we are told in the previous sentence means 'rose'] cleans her teeth, all day long, with a hatpin she calls her style. She is the one who does not believe in the truth" (Derrida 1986, 58b). (In one of [at least] three "versions" of Nietzsche's "woman," *Spurs* will return to this: "In the guise of the christian, philosophical being she either identifies with truth, or else she continues to play with it at a distance as if it were a fetish, manipulating it, even as she refuses to believe in it, to her own advantage" [1978a, 97].) Derrida's perhaps most formidable text ever is studded with passages about the erectile stem—or style—of a flower, which rises up after the petals part (*s'écartent*). But contrary to Buffon's understanding of style as construction, "The object of the present work, and its style too, is the *morsel*" or bit (cf. also French slang *bitte* ["prick"]), detached "like the grand[est] style" (see Derrida 1986, especially 98b, 127b; cf. also 34b for "the grand style of the flower"). Thus, *Glas* opposes to the virility of an erection (*bande*) of style as (the whole) truth—style as column (French slang *colonne* ["shaft"]), even a *distyle* or double column/style—the *contrebande* of an "érection-tombe" (also in *Glas*, *Spurs*, and *Signéponge/Signsponge* [1984b, 57]), the oblique "antherection of a style *en abyme*" contaminated by (female) castration and associated with Genet's Stilitano (see also Kofman 1984, 144–5).

(S)talking flowers: the marvellous and truly stylish exergue of "White Mythology," which utterly resists translation (but which "style" does not?), had earlier given an inkling of what Derrida's own *florid* style might be like:

> De la philosophie, la rhétorique. D'un volume, à peu près, plus ou moins—faire ici une fleur, l'extraire, la monter, la laisser, plutôt, monter, se faire jour—se détournant comme d'elle-même, révolutée, telle fleur grave—apprenant à cultiver, selon le calcul d'un lapidaire, la patience. (Derrida 1972, 249)
>
> (From philosophy, rhetoric. That is, here, to make from a volume, approximately, more or less, a flower, to extract a flower, to mount it, or rather to have it mount itself, bring to light—and turning away, as if from itself, come round again, such a flower engraves—learning to cultivate, by means of a lapidary's reckoning, patience. [1982b, 209])

What *takes place* here, in Derrida's cultivated writing, which, to echo and slightly alter Anne Dufourmantelle's (2000, 14) words, "gives place to the place otherwise,"[18] is a performatively drawn out, *patient* exfoliation rhythmically spaced out by the work of punctuation, tropically cultivating *patience* (also *dock* in French) as a flower of rhetoric, or turning the flower of rhetoric into the patience-of-style/style-as-patience. A differently "pointed style," therefore, which operates as the linchpin of Derrida's deconstructive syntax and bears some distant, yet uncanny analogy with Hélène Cixous's style, which he had praised in *H.C. for Life, That Is to Say . . .*, as a rhythmic dance. Indeed, let us not forget that *Spurs* tantalizes us with *Distanz*, a distance in which one must also hear a German dance step (*Tanz*) out of step (*dis-*) after the hyphen (cf. 47: "What is the opening step of that *Dis-tanz*?" whose rhythm is already mimed by Nietzsche's writing and his use of the hyphen as a "stylistic effect"):

> Nobody . . . can compete with her when it comes to a genius for, and meticulous calculation of, punctuation—which is, one can never say this enough, the heart and as it were the living breath, the very lungs of the writing. Here punctuation removes itself or gets spirited (away) [*s'enlève elle-même*] by a punctual depunctuation of its very breath, in other words its life, its

[18]See also Derrida (1978a, 120) about style as the non-place of woman, as well as the poematic *hérisson*, soon to be run across, which "takes place, essentially, without one's having to do it or make it" (Derrida 1995a, 297).

> rhythm, its time, and precisely, its speed. The steady slowness with which *I* proceed and which is my *tempo*, the step of my insistence, will only trail [*traîner*], like the train of a dress [*traîne*] or a trail [*traîne*], behind the truly choreographic grace, the aerial evolution, the inspiredness of a writing that dances and sings ceaselessly. By raising all the points of its punctuation. (Derrida 2006, 68)[19]

After this diversion, let us now return to *Spurs* and quote one of its *central* moments or pivots in the unfolding of Derrida's tropic as much as apotropaic *de-monstration*, in a sub-section called "Truths" which segues from a reference to the opening of Nietzsche's *Beyond Good and Evil*:

> At this moment, the truth of woman, the truth of truth, Nietzsche turns it about: [. . .]
>
> Woman (truth) will not be pinned down.
>
> In truth woman, truth will not be pinned down.
>
> That which will not be pinned down by truth is, in truth—*feminine*. This should not, however, be hastily mistaken for a woman's femininity, for female sexuality, or for any other of those essentializing fetishes which might still tantalize the dogmatic philosopher, the impotent artist or the inexperienced seducer who has not yet escaped his foolish hopes of capture.
>
> The divergence [*écart*] within truth elevates itself [*s'enlève d'elle-même*]. It is elevated in quotation marks. . . . Nietzsche's writing is compelled to suspend truth between the tenter-hooks of quotation marks [Derrida (69) will note Nietzsche's tantalizing play on punctuation] . . . Nietzsche's writing is an inscription of the truth. And such an inscription, even if we do not venture so far as to call it the feminine itself, is indeed the feminine *operation*.

---

[19]See also (62): "(nobody knows better how to punctuate, in my opinion, and to punctuate is to write, nobody knows better how to remove or *spirit away* [enlever] punctuation than Hélène Cixous, yes, spirit away—whether it be marked or not, her punctuation is spirited (away) [*enlevée*] . . .)."

> Because woman is (her own) writing [*elle (s')écrit*], style must return to her. In other words, it could be said that if style were a man (much as the penis, according to Freud, is the "normal prototype of fetishes"), then writing would be a woman. (Derrida 1978a, 55, 57)[20]

Nietzsche, the male philosopher who dis-tances woman-as-truth as he dances away in pointed style and stilettos, causes Derrida to wonder, echoing Heidegger's "critical question" (about Nietzsche's Platonism) (1978a, 83), what *genre* (genre or gender) such a (masculine) "pratique stylet" (practiced stiletto) or (feminine) "pratique stylée" (stylish or stylate practice) is, which "cannot be written without the conspired plotting between woman and truth" (83). For Derrida and his antiphallogocentric, miscegenated *écriture du m'ec*,[21]

> the question of style is immediately unloosed as a question of writing. The stylate spur [*éperon stylé*] rips through the veil [*le voile*—of truth-as-unveiling; cf. Greek *aletheia*]. It rents it in such a way that it . . . undoes the sail's [*la voile*] self-opposition, the opposition of veiled/unveiled (sailed/unsailed) [*voilé/dévoilé*] which has folded over on itself. (1978a, 107, translation modified)

Derrida's near-opening gambit had been that

> The title of this lecture was to have been *the question of style.*
>
> However—it is woman who will be my subject.
>
> Still, one might wonder whether that doesn't really amount to the same thing—or is it to the other. (1978a, 35, 37)

This raises the question of phallogocentrism as that which returns to the Father-as-the-same and the proper versus what could be a more feminine "radical alterity" and exappropriation, soon before

---

[20]For the style as fetish, see also *Glas* (1986, passim, especially 209a for its relation to truth). For the staging of generalized fetishism in *Glas*, see Kofman (1984, 132–9, and 145–51 ["De la question du style à celle de Stilitano ou l'écriture du m'ec"]). One would need at this point to insert a discussion of the *fetishization* of style.

[21]See Kofman (1984, 150). Castrating the *mec*, or French slang for "bloke," here also short for *je m'écris*, Kofman's trenchant formula hints at the disarticulation of an erectile style in Derrida's writing.

leaving floating in the air between the masculine and the feminine the necessity to *articulate* the French word *voile* (1978a, 37, 39). After enough patient unfurling, half mimicry half simulacrum, after it has been made "to pass through the gauntlet of Nietzsche's warring styles which inscribe woman in many guises" (Kamuf 1991, 53), the initial assertion will be contradicted into "woman, then, will not have been my subject" (Derrida 1978a, 121),[22] and "for this very reason" (a double-edged phrase omitted in the translation, crucially so if only because it implicitly recalls the *classical* equation between the claims of reason and the claims of style),

> there never has been *the* style, *the* simulacrum, *the* woman. There never has been *the* sexual difference.
>
> If the simulacrum is ever going to occur, its writing must be in the interval [*l'écart*] between several styles. And the insinuation of the woman (of) Nietzsche is that, if there is going to be style, there can only be more than one.[23]
>
> . . . At least two spurs. The anchor [*l'ancre*, an *encre* with a differ*a*nce] is lowered [*lancer*, an anagram of *l'ancre*], risked, lost maybe in the abyss between them. (Derrida 1978a, 139)

Tropes as much as apotropes, "the styles and the spurs of the title both invoke pointed instruments with which to rend the castrating veil of feminized 'truth' or with which to protect oneself from its castrating thrusts" (Kamuf 1991, 354). But by the end of this polytropic journey, what is left of dis-articulated *style*, of the implicit question *what is style*, could be made to echo the end of "*Che cos'è la poesia?*" whose question to the essence of poetry or "ontology of the poetic"[24] took the form of the parable of a hedgehog (*istrice*) hazardously attempting to cross a motorway (*autostrada*):

---

[22]Cf. the well-known "prefatory" opening of "Outwork, Prefacing" in Derrida (1981, 3): "This (therefore) will not have been a book."

[23]This *plus d'un* has to be read alongside Derrida's famous definition of deconstruction as "*plus d'une langue*—more than a language and no more of a language" (Derrida [1989, 15]).

[24]Cf. De Man (1989, 156): "French literary theory has more and more felt the need for an ontology of the poetic as preliminary to a study on such a highly integrated level as that of style," before selecting Blanchot as "the writer who has perhaps gone furthest in the formulation of such an ontology."

> Recall the question: "What is . . . ?" . . . "What is . . . ?" laments the disappearance of the poem—another catastrophe. By announcing that which is just as it is, a question salutes the birth of prose. (Derrida 1995a, 299)

Style, then, might be what chances to remain when one has given up all fetishistic hopes and claims of potency and essential appropriation, so that, through the "atomystics of the letter"—rather than a Genettian "atom*i*st" vision of style "that pulverizes style into a collection of significant *details* (Spitzer) or marked *elements* (Riffaterre)" (Genette 1993, 124)[25]—language would come and, rather than be ordered (Buffon), it would *dictate* to the writer as an *arrivant* and an *event*. The historical allotropics of style, from its manly, ordered constructedness in the "Age of Reason" or Enlightenment to its castration and feminization

in/by deconstruction – from the old aestheticized morality of style keyed to great "men" and minds to a deconstructive "ethics of style" which might usher in the "end of man" – is staged in the rhythmic versatility of (the woman) Nietzsche's style*s* (un)veiled/(un)sailed, thus dis-articulated by Derrida . . .

As early as "Tympanum," Derrida had written that "The logic of the event is examined from the vantage of the structures of expropriation called *timbre* (*tympanum*), *style*, and signature. Timbre, style, and signature are the same obliterating division of the proper" (Derrida 1982b, xix). Thus, as Lukacher writes, "Style is what philosophy can't hear, what defers voice from reference, and what renders the identity of sense into the drift of difference" (Lukacher 1986, 195).[26]

---

[25]Leo Spitzer's monumental two-volume *Stilstudien* (1928) set a landmark in the development of a more literary stylistics and critique of literary styles, grounded on recurrent textual details correlated to an author's ideas, as opposed to the descriptive stylistics inherited from the Bally-Saussure school, which focused on *faits de langue*. Michael Riffaterre's blend of semiotic and stylistic criticism aimed at isolating the determining invariants of literariness (see n. 5 above)

[26]Lukacher 1986, 195.

Style-in-deconstruction

No wonder therefore that, more than 20 years later, in an improvised exchange with Hélène Cixous on style first published in a joint French-Spanish publication, Derrida's initial response will be to emphasize the "difficulty" inherent in this notion, soon adding that "whatever one thinks of the word *style* . . . this question [concerning the 'singular appropriation of language in the act of writing-speaking' for which Mercedes Coli had chosen the word 'style'] surely can't be addressed to both of us jointly, because if there is something we don't have in common, it is style; if something like style exists!" (Segarra 2010, 200).

Derrida's response is twofold, each direction being an extension of the differentiated conception of style staged in *Spurs* as well as earlier in the essay "Qual Quelle: Valéry's Sources," for instance—note, importantly, the resonance with "Tympanum":

> The timbre of my voice, the style of my writing are that which for (a) me never will have been present. I neither hear nor recognize the timbre of my voice. If my style marks itself, it is only on a surface which remains invisible and illegible for me. *Point* of [*point de*] *speculum*: here I am blind to my style, deaf to what is most spontaneous in my voice. (Derrida 1982b, 296)

Point de style, rather than pointed style, or style as blind *punctum*:[27] if style is understood *a minima* as *a singular way of signing* what one writes, speaks, does, etc., whose inimitability can be recognized because of similarities, regularities, returns, recurrences, and implicit norms, then Derrida claims he does not have (a) style in that sense, nor especially *one* he can identify as his:

> For each text, whether small, short or long, there's a new charter and this charter orders me to write differently each time. And when I say differently I mean even in the grammar, the length of sentences, a different style. Of course I don't deny that there may

[27]Cf. Barthes (1993, 26–7): "A Latin word exists to designate this wound, this prick, this mark made by a pointed instrument . . . it also refers to the notion of punctuation . . . these marks, these wounds, are so many points." *Punctum* is also a cast of the dice (26).

> be recognizable things . . . ; but this recurrence, this resemblance, what one thinks one recognizes, is by definition accessible only to the other. What returns as the same or as what looks similar in a very different text of mine, which I sign, can be legible, visible, sensible only for the other and not for me. . . . The idiom, idiomaticity—if there's any—is what can't be reappropriated; *idiom* means in Greek what is proper: *idiotès*. I would set down as an aporia and logical necessity that what is proper can't be appropriated, what is proper to me is what I can't reappropriate. In other words, I would be the last one to be able to see my style, in a way.[28] (Segarra 2010, 200–1)

If, for a faithful deconstructionist critic like Culler (1982, 120), style presupposes recognizable features that produce distinctive effects which can therefore be repeated, such a reappropriation cannot be performed by oneself. Derrida further characterizes that mistrusted insistence of the proper:

> If one now wants to use the word *style* with a slightly sharper edge to it . . . there is something pointed at stake; style is pointed. I wrote a little book on Nietzsche called *Nietzsche's Styles*, in which I insist a lot on the sharp, phallic nature of the point. Style is the pointed tip with which one writes. Therefore the insistence on determining the idiom as style, in the figure of style, is what I would call a phallocentric insistence, which consists in thinking that writing is a gesture of inscription with a decisive, incisive point, and that where this decisive, incisive, cutting, sharp point is lacking, there's no style. . . . Style now is thus an old academic or phallocentric category in which the style is the man [le style, c'est l'homme]—and then I must understand man in the sense of man, not woman. It is the inscription at its most incisive, penetrating, violent . . . but there can be great forms of writing [*écritures*] without style in that sense. Basically I am not sure

---

[28]Cf. one of Genette's attempts at a definition of style, following Roman Jakobson: "Style is nothing else but the aspect—let us call it *perceptible*—that constitutes what Jakobson called a text's 'perceptibility'" (1993, 113). Let us recall that etymologically *theoria* used to denote the putting into speech of something seen, *monstration* as witnessing, which remains implicit in any act of de(-)monstration. See Godzich (1986, especially xiii–xv) and Milesi (2004, especially 51–2).

> whether I'd like to make a claim for style; if I was told "now would you rather be considered as somebody who has style or as somebody who has no style?" I would find it very hard to answer. And I think that if I was obliged to, in the end, I'd say, with some precautions, "I'd rather not have style."
>
> . . . if I replied, "I don't want to have style," or "After all I'd rather not have style," it is because if one really writes with style, if style is the last word, nothing else happens. If I write with the incisive, decisive authority of someone who makes things happen, who does what he says, nothing happens. (Segarra 2010, 200–1)

As the beginning of the quotation indicates, Derrida would at best have "styles," as many styles as the variety of writing opportunities dictates . . . perhaps as many as Roland Barthes had *stylos*, that latter-day avatar of the ancient stylus—in his dismissal of the one model he abhors, the *stylo bic* or biro, Barthes even makes the connection between style and *stylo*. *Stylo in theory* therefore:

> I have an almost obsessive relation to writing instruments. I often switch from one pen to another just for the pleasure of it. I try out new ones. I have far too many *stylos*—I don't know what to do with all of them!
>
> . . . I've also used pen nibs . . . In short, I've tried everything . . . except Bics [*pointe bic*], with which I feel absolutely no affinity. I would even say, a bit nastily, that there is a "Bic style" [*style bic*], which is really just for churning out copy [*pisse copie*], writing that merely transcribes thought.
>
> In the end I always return to fine fountain pens [*stylos à encre*]. The essential thing is that they can produce that soft, smooth writing I absolutely require. (Barthes 1991, 178)

Therefore, for Derrida, one must agree to give up on appropriative authority, relinquish forceful intervention, and surrender to the chance aporetic encounter with language as unexpected *arrivant* for something *else* to happen as an event, for which *style* is perhaps no longer an *appropriate* name. If style as what is traditionally proper to the self cannot be appropriated, made to come into one's own—the etymological parsing of *Ereignis* or event—and if, as is generally admitted, style is a critical choice among language's possibilities in a given situation of expression, then the event—and advent—of style for deconstruction, which is concerned with what comes *before* the critical moment (such as *différance* before the articulation of differences), "style-in-deconstruction" before the critical inscription of rhythm, tone, and intonation, would precede in arche-writing what is more commonly called "style."

Thus, in a reversible formula for which one needs a "double hearing" (Dufourmantelle 2000, 18) in the aural wake of Derrida's famous "tout autre est tout autre," the singularly plural "style-in-deconstruction" ~~IS~~ style in deconstruction and, for the same reason, ~~IS NOT~~ style in deconstruction since its rhythmic spacing, the unappropriatable *différance* that haunts its very medium, "pulls itself back from unveiling" (Dufourmantelle 2000, 2). Just as style was and was not Derrida's subject as he was writing about the elusive tropicity of woman and/as truth in *Spurs*, then my proposed "style-in-deconstruction," even if it does not *articulate* style, will not have been my subject. Hence:

The retrait of style

What Genette referred to as the "atomist" or "punctualist" conception of style runs a twofold risk, according to him,

> of having difficulty determining the marked elements . . ., and, above all, of privileging, even if involuntarily, a mannerist aesthetic for which the most remarkable (in both senses of the word) style will be the one that is the most highly charged with features. (1993, 124)

This risk has eventually to do with the conjunction of what Genette called earlier the *attentional* character of figurativeness, which makes it "a perfect emblem of style" (121), and of what he rightly sees as the reversibility of operations of figurability and "the signifying value of the zero degree" (124) (cf. of course, Barthes's precursor study of that emptying of style he called *écriture blanche* in *Writing Degree Zero* [1968]). And to Daniel Delas's dismissal of the objection, in his preface to Riffaterre's *Essais de stylistique structurale*, that "an excess of style kills style," Genette replies that such an implicit idea of dosage or even absence of style presupposes an inconceivable separability between language and style (125).[29]

In a discussion of the "Will to Style"—a phrase which he borrows from Jameson's analyses about Conrad in *The Political Unconscious*—Ned Lukacher (1986, 179) writes that "The notion of the 'end of style' [which Jameson associates with dehistoricized postmodernism] cannot of course be separated from the notion of the overcoming of metaphysics," a proposition which should be related to Lukacher's idea, still based on an interpretation of Jameson, that the overcoming of style is "something like the end of history itself . . . is an event that has never occurred but whose possibility defines the very nature of style. Style is defined in the continuum between the possibility of an absolutely private language and that of an end of style" (183).

Lukacher then evokes the moment in Hegel's style "when the language of philosophy is called into question by the language of literature that it attempts to appropriate," "when Hegel wants to express his own style, when he wants to impress his own character into the text of philosophy by citing the text of Shakespeare [i.e. when he turns to Hamlet's image of the 'old mole' towards the end of *Lectures on the History of Philosophy*]" (Lukacher 1986, 180), before turning to Heidegger's linkage of the question of style and the question of history in Nietzsche:

> For Heidegger's Nietzsche, philosophy realizes its will to power through the question of style. Philosophy has therefore failed to realize its will to power because it has failed to pose the question of style; that is, it has failed to pose the question of its own language. (1986, 183)

For Nietzsche, according to Heidegger, Hegel "marks the end of the classical style," and with Wagner we reach the "complete dissolution of style" (1979, 135). Nietzsche's solution to the impossibility

---

[29]The relation between language and style has been a hugely vexing source of controversy: Arnould already says that "Ni le langage ni la langue ne sont le style. Le langage impose au style ses lois, les mêmes au fond que celles de la raison" (1851, 2). In *Writing Degree Zero* (1968, 13), Barthes famously wedges *écriture* in between language and style. This incidentally is not what Deleuze negated when he called style "the economy of language" (1997, 113).

of returning to the classical, rigorous style of the eighteenth century, now stripped of its humanizing presuppositions, is "the grand style" (135) glimpsed piecemeal in bits detached from *Glas* before, a new will to power overcome by the "will to style" that "utterly transforms the self by undoing the very opposition (classic/romantic, active/passive) that defines the notion of style," thus changing the very nature of the historical self (Lukacher 1986, 184). It is also in this sense that Derrida understands the question of style in the distant preface to Heidegger's *Nietzsche* that *Spurs* in effect is—and, as we saw, in the dialogue with Hélène Cixous. In Lukacher's words: "to locate the dispossession or expropriation within the event of appropriation" (185). Further, "like Nietzsche's umbrella, style in this sense of dispossession and expropriation is what we tend to forget. Recollection is a figure for learning to read the style of the history of metaphysics" (186)—cf. Stendhal's "the best style is the one that allows itself to be forgotten"—and words like *différance* "are terms through which we attempt to describe man's dispossession of language" (180). So, to return once more, what can "style-in-deconstruction" be, since Derridean deconstruction does not claim it can, nor does it wish to, overcome metaphysics, but just reinscribe it in its effect(s) by redrawing its margins and retracing its lines? What is "style-in-deconstruction," which therefore does not ring the death knell of "style," grand or otherwise, in philosophy, even though it seriously questions its generic delimitation, for instance by prizing open the demarcation between philosophy and poetry or literature?

In "The Supplement of Copula: Philosophy Before Linguistics," also published in *Margins of Philosophy*, Derrida had observed that "the question of metaphor is no more to be asked in the margins of metaphysics than metaphorical style and the use of figures is an accessory embellishment or secondary auxiliary of philosophical discourse" (1982b, 184). As is well known, the following essay in the collection, "White Mythology: Metaphor in the Text of Philosophy," whose opening flourish I quoted earlier, will take up the book's overall theme—how philosophy listens to the sound of its own voice and makes it resound in its inner ear or tympanum by appropriating other discourses—as metaphysics' *usurious* incorporation and neutralization of poetic metaphors. Starting from a reading of Anatole France's *Le Jardin d'Épicure*, which ends on the tropological *figure* of *usure* (wear and tear, and usury), Derrida's study leads to a systematic argument about the role of metaphor in the field of philosophy, both as erasure of the original figure and surplus remaining from this initial forgetting, and therefore also about the indissociable link between the *usure* of metaphor and the metaphor of *usure* in the impossibility to account for the founding *metaphor of metaphor* and totalize the entire structural chain of metaphorics, to capitalize on such a linguistic surplus through any scriptural economy.

But this principle of "tropic supplementarity," the "extra metaphor, remaining outside the field that it allows to circumscribe, [which] extracts or abstracts itself from this field, thus subtracting itself as a metaphor less" (1982b, 220, translation modified), can somehow be seen to haunt deconstructive writing, whose double *ambiguous* syntax orchestrated by *différance* (e.g. *plus d'usure*), which attempts to think form and force at once via a performativity in effect, may eventually allow the Derridean *economy of style*, notwithstanding its choreographic versatility, to be reassigned to an identifiable, *proper* style (for similar remarks on this Derridean economy, see Johnson 1993, 57–64, 32). Thus, and not only given his formidable success, the deconstructive *performateur* would have perversely become, against his own resistance to circuitous models of economic (re-)appropriation as that which returns to the Father-as-the-Same, the *père formateur*—here I am sending back to Derrida his own partly facetious remark on the *perverformative* in "Marx and Sons," where he also recalls that "in all of my texts of at least the past twenty-five years, all my argumentation has been everywhere determined and *overdetermined* by a concern to take into account the performative dimension (not only of language in the narrow sense, but also of what I call the trace and writing)" (1999, 224).[30]

This is in substance what I had tried to argue more tentatively some 20 years ago in an essay on the double bind and "trans-lation" between the *usure* of interpretation and the interpretation of *usure*,[31]

---

[30]To my knowledge, Henri Meschonnic's lengthy study "L'écriture de Derrida" (1975, 401–92) is the first to have emphasized the performativity at work in Derrida's disseminative writing (see for example 472), albeit in a mostly wrong-headed critique of deconstructive textuality and philosophy. See also Steinmetz (1994, 118–19), for the view of Derrida's textual performance as a radicalization of Austinian performativity.

[31]See Milesi (1995, 205–29, especially 225–9).

and which I would like now to prolong in the light of the stunning first two pages of Derrida's sequel to "White Mythology," "Le retrait de la métaphore," following Paul Ricoeur's (1978, 330–48) objections to the earlier essay in *La métaphore vive* (1975).[32]

While providing in the first part a patient refutation of Ricoeur, "Le retrait de la métaphore" elaborates on the "structure of quasimetaphoricity" allegedly more originary than the distinction between metaphor and concept, and analyzes it in terms of the Heideggerian notion of the trait (*Zug*) and its cognate derivatives: *Bezug* (rapport), *Entziehung* (retrait), etc. The essay starts off with a two-page-long performative *dérive* on (not-so-)*metaphorical* means of transport, a vertiginous tour de force pegged on to Derrida's teasing opening manoeuvre about the passing (itself) (away) of metaphor (itself what the Latin language translated into *translatio*), its most pervasive re-mark economically coinciding with its *retrait* or withdrawal, which *translates* into yet another untranslatable *exercice de style* in deconstruction:

> Qu'est-ce qui se passe, aujourd'hui, avec la métaphore?
>
> Et de la métaphore qu'est-ce qui se passe?
>
> . . . s'y représentant comme une énorme bibliothèque dans laquelle nous nous déplacerions sans en percevoir les limites, procédant de stations en stations, y cheminant à pied, pas à pas, ou en autobus (nous circulons déjà, avec l'"autobus" que je viens de nommer, dans la traduction et, selon l'élément de la traduction, entre *Übertragung* et *Übersetzung*, *metaphorikos* désignant encore aujourd'hui, en grec, comme on dit, moderne, ce qui concerne les moyens de transport). *Metaphora* circule dans la cité, elle nous y véhicule comme ses habitants. . . . De ce véhicule nous sommes d'une certaine façon—métaphorique, bien sûr, et sur le mode de l'habitation—le contenu et la teneur: passagers, compris et déplacés par métaphore.
>
> Étrange énoncé pour démarrer—dites-vous. . . . Étrange ensuite parce qu'il n'est pas seulement métaphorique de dire que nous

[32]By far the most thorough discussion of what is at stake in the controversy can be found in the chapter on "De la métaphore restreinte à la métaphore généralisée (Ricoeur)," in Steinmetz (1994, 141–70).

> habitons la métaphore et que nous y circulons comme dans une sorte de véhicule automobile. Ce n'est pas simplement métaphorique. . . . Ni métaphorique, ni a-métaphorique, cette "figure" consiste singulièrement à changer les places et les fonctions: elle constitue le soi-disant sujet des énoncés . . . en *contenu* ou en *teneur*, et encore partielle, et toujours déjà "embarquée," "en voiture," d'un véhicule qui le comprend, l'emporte, le déplace au moment même où ledit sujet croit le désigner, le dire, l'orienter, le conduire, le gouverner "comme un pilote en son navire."

Still adrift on *dérives* and derivations, Derrida carries on:

> Je viens de changer d'élément et de moyen de transport. Nous ne sommes pas dans la métaphore comme un pilote en son navire. Avec cette proposition, je dérive. La figure du vaisseau ou du bateau, qui fut si souvent le véhicule exemplaire de la pédagogie rhétorique . . ., me fait dériver vers une citation de Descartes.
>
> Je devrais donc interrompre décisoirement la dérive ou le dérapage. Je le ferais si c'était possible. Mais qu'est-ce que je fais depuis un moment? Je dérape et je dérive irrésistiblement. J'essaie de parler *de* la métaphore, de dire quelque chose de propre ou de littéral à son sujet . . . mais je suis, par elle, si on peut dire, obligé à parler d'elle *more metaphorico*, à sa manière à elle. . . .
>
> C'est pourquoi depuis tout à l'heure je me déplace d'écart en écart, de véhicule en véhicule, sans pouvoir freiner ou arrêter l'autobus, son automaticité ou son automobilité. . . . Je ne peux plus arrêter le véhicule ou ancrer le navire, maîtriser sans reste la dérive ou le dérapage (j'avais rappelé quelque part que le mot "dérapage," avant son plus grand dérapage métaphorique, avait rapport avec un certain jeu de l'ancre dans le langage de la marine . . .).
>
> Si donc je voulais interrompre le dérapage, j'échouerais. Et cela au moment même où je me retiendrais de le donner à remarquer. (Derrida 1987, 63–5; cf. 2007, 48–50)

After his celebrated aphorism, Buffon (1978, xvii) had stated that "le style ne peut donc ni s'enlever, ni se transporter ni s'altérer"

("Style can therefore not be lifted away, nor be transported, nor be altered"). Indeed, how can one translate, that is to say, transport such a style without altering it "structurally"? If, writes Barthes (1968, 13), "style is never anything but metaphor," and if *metaphora* is always already, in our Western heritage, another name for transport and trans(-)lation, then Derrida's style *is* transport and carries us away (*nous transporte*), leads us astray or *se-duces* us. *Like* a woman fanning herself both tropically and apotropaically with the truth she (un)veils without believing in it. And if style is metaphor and being what withdraws itself from it (see Steinmetz 1994, 168), how can style *be* something and how can one answer the aporetic question: "What is style?"

Like metaphor, Derrida's style *se re(-)tire de lui-même*, remarks itself as it withdraws itself, *se passe de lui-même* (Derrida 1987, 93), and not only to his own blind gaze. It is a *pure* means (of transport) without destination and with only transitory passengers (like Derrida's substitutable chain of self-deconstructing terms), an epochal, generalized rhetoric of *écarts*. As Derrida repeatedly claimed, since deconstruction does not depend so much on individual lexemes for its effect as on the articulation of an at least double syntax,[33] its (aesthetic, political) performativity lies not so much in Austin's *How To Do Things with Words* (1975), even when these designate quasi-originary operations like *différance* or dissemination, as in Iser's "Doing Things in Style" (1974, 179–95).[34] In Derrida's hands, philosophical *demonstration* is displaced into style in and as de-monstration, that is, as we saw, in *theoria*. But insofar as it aims to breach an event, yet inevitably belongs to the generalizable structure of eventhood, which falls under the spell of the deferred re(-)presentation of presence—and let us not

[33]Against the claim and critique, forcefully formulated by Meschonnic, that, even when it puts the emphasis on syntagmatic (i.e. in a sense syntactical) operations, Derrida's etymologizing linguistics is exclusively paradigmatic and privileges lexicalism. See Meschonnic (1975, 477, 481), discussed in Steinmetz (1994, 163ff.).

[34]Recalling Joyce's well-known statement "Don't talk to me about politics. I'm only interested in style" (184), Iser concludes that style "does not capture reality but imposes upon it an historically preconditioned form" (192) and that "Joyce exposes the characteristic quality of style—namely, that it imposes form on an essentially formless reality . . . all styles are relative to the historical conditions that shape them" (193). Joyce's "chronological exhibition of style shows clearly that they are all metaphorical" (194).

forget that style, writes Hegel in the *Aesthetics*, is the "inherently necessary mode of representation" (quoted in Lukacher 1986, 197)—"style-in-deconstruction," like the trait in "The Retrait of Metaphor," or the trace (whose German equivalent, Derrida recalls in *Spurs* [1978a, 41], is *Spur*) in Derrida's own *epigrammatology*, even like the *whole* of deconstruction *itself* in the quip toward the close of "Letter to a Japanese Friend,"[35] ~~is nothing~~ —but cf. above Rivarol's "Le style n'est rien, mais rien n'est sans le style" . . . *nichts*, and therefore not only Nietzsche and his or her styles. Its de-monstrative inscription or incision, like the self-erasing trace or *différance*, "n'arrive qu'à s'effacer" (i.e. manages only to erase itself / arrives only by erasing itself) (Derrida 1987, 89)—or to use a half-baked pun, not the usage of self-raising flour but the *usure* of the self-erasing flower is the main ingredient in style-in-deconstruction, one that, unlike Joyce's (1975, 265) "selfreizing flower" of a girl in *Finnegans Wake*, *se passe d'elle-même* rather than affects and auto-affects itself (German *reizen*: to irritate, stimulate, appeal to, annoy, provoke). Derrida's "style" exceeds the question "What is?" in the same way as the poematic, in the form of the metaphoric and metaphorizing hedgehog, "which in the same stroke exposes itself to earth and protects itself—in a word . . . the retreat [*retrait*] of the *hérisson*" (1995a, 253), finds it perilously hard to (translate itself a)cross the *autoroute* to the other side, and may indeed be left distressed, stranded, or *routed*.

In "Istrice 2: Ick bünn all hier," the sequel to "*Che cos'è la poesia*?" Derrida gives us one more oblique chance to approach what I would finally like to risk calling the poematic nature of his style, which, not unlike Nietzsche's (apo)tropics, "remains profoundly estranged from the work and from the setting-to-work [*mise en oeuvre*] of truth" (1995b, 303; cf. 312), parergonally or exergonally set off against the absolute truth of a Hegel or *Igel* (German for "hedgehog") stranded in the left or "sinister" column of *Glas*. We saw earlier that the style of *Glas* is the *morsel*, detached "like the grand[est] style," and the portent of this remark can now be counterpointed against the fragment on the fragment from Schlegel quoted by Derrida via Nancy and Lacoue-Labarthe's *The Literary Absolute*, followed by their own gloss:

---

[35]Derrida (1987, 32; 1997, 75; 1991, 275). See also Milesi (2007, especially 31–4).

> Like a little work of art, a fragment must be totally detached from the surrounding world and closed on itself like a hedgehog. . . . The fragmentary totality, in conformity with what one should venture to call "the logic of the hedgehog," cannot be situated at one point: it is simultaneously in the whole and in each part. Each fragment is valid for itself and for that from which it is detached. The totality is the fragment itself in its finished individuality. (Derrida, 1995b, 302)

Against the setting-to-work of truth in the Schlegelian "logic of the hedgehog," which style classically was, as was the poem for Heidegger, "the point would thus be to remove what I am calling the *poem* (or the *poiemata*) from the merry-go-round or circus that brings them back in a circular fashion, i.e. economically, to *poiein*, to their poetic source, to the act or to the experience of their setting-to-work in poetry or in poetics" (Derrida 1995b, 304; cf. 1995a, 297). Thus *nothing doing* with *poiesis* for Derrida's humble *hérisson*, but doing this nothing in the *retrait* of a differ*a*ntly economic style which does not bring (back) home the *truth* of style.[36]

—What with all your diversions and hedgings, I feel that I have been taken for a pointless ride, *mené en bateau*, or led astray up a garden path lined with flowers and roots, rather than safely to the other side of the *(auto)route*, which is where I was expecting to be transported, if not carried away, at the end of this protracted journey, during which you have been *travelling in style* indeed. In *Les Styles de Derrida* (1994), Rudy Steinmetz had at least managed to sketch a tripartite evolution, from the "critical" style of an ethics of decision (the "breaching" of deconstruction) to the "explosive" style of an aesthetics of dissemination (the surplus of *différance* in writing), to the "implosive" style of a poetics of invocation (the formalizing rarefaction surrounding the logic of the gift and of the *cendre*, from *est* to *reste*) (1994, especially 175–6n9, 181). But you've given us only a lecture in deconstruction, however you wish to hear this, with historico-theoretical fits and starts, instead of a style of the same.

---

[36]Cf. Derrida's (1978b, 22) necessity "to seek new concepts and new models, an economy escaping th[e] system of metaphysical oppositions." See also Harvey (1986).

—But what if the pointless point of "style-in-deconstruction" was precisely in the drifting, an experience or voyage that attempts to cross a boundary to the other side? Style-in-deconstruction, if something like that exists, "is" to be located interstitially, as in the Mallarméan *entre* deployed in *Dissemination*, among its chance destinerrancies which one will never be able to subject. Style as *écart* not from a prescriptive norm but between differ*a*ntial *traces*, two palindromes which run in contraflow as if to seductively mime the incessant specular play of what in truth amounts to the same—or is it to the other (cf. Derrida 1981, especially 352–3, 363–4).[37]

References

Arnould, M. Edmond. 1851. *Essai d'une théorie du style*. Paris: Hachette.

Austin, J. L. 1975. *How to Do Things with Words*. Oxford: Oxford University Press.

Bally, Charles. 1902. *Traité de stylistique française*. 2 vols. Heidelberg: Winter.

—. 1905. *Précis de stylistique*. Geneva: Eggimann.

Barthes, Ronald. 1968. *Writing Degree Zero*. Translated by Annette Lavers and Colin Smith. New York: Hill and Wang.

—. 1991. "An Almost Obsessive Relation to Writing Instruments." In *The Grain of the Voice: Interviews, 1962–1980*, translated by Linda Coverdale, 177–82. Berkeley: University of California Press.

—. 1993. *Camera Lucida: Reflections on Photography*. Translated by Richard Howard. London: Vintage.

Berger, Ernst. 1878. *Lateinische Stilistik für obere Gymnasialklassen*. Celle: Capaun-Karlowa'sche Buchhandlung.

Brewster, William Tenney, ed. 1921. *Representative Essays on the Theory of Style*. New York: Macmillan.

Buffon, Georges-Louis Leclerc, comte de. 1954. *Oeuvres philosophiques de Buffon*. Edited by Jean Piveteau with the collaboration of Maurice Fréchet and Charles Bruneau. Paris: PUF.

—. 1978. *Discours sur le style: A Facsimile of the 12*[mo] *Edition*. Introduction and notes by Cedric E. Pickford. Hull: Hull French Texts.

[37]On the anagrammatological relationship between *écart* and trace, see Johnson (1993, 111–18).

Culler, Jonathan. 1982. *On Deconstruction*. Ithaca, NY: Cornell University Press.

—. 1983. *On Deconstruction: Theory and Criticism After Structuralism*. London: Routledge.

De Gourmont, Rémy. 1902. *Le Problème du style: Questions d'art, de littérature et de grammaire, avec une préface et un index des noms cités*. Paris: Mercure de France.

Deleuze, Gilles. 1997. "He Stuttered." In *Essays Critical and Clinical*, translated by Daniel W. Smith and Michael A. Greco, 107–14. London: Verso.

De Man, Paul. 1989. "Modern Poetics in France and Germany." In *Critical Writings, 1953–1978*, edited by Lindsay Waters, 153–60. Minneapolis: Minnesota University Press.

Derrida, Jacques. 1972. "La Mythologie blanche. La métaphore dans le texte philosophique." In *Marges de la philosophie*, 247–322. Paris: Minuit.

—. 1978a. *Spurs: Nietzsche's Styles*. Translated by Barbara Harlow. Chicago: University of Chicago Press.

—. 1978b. *Writing and Difference*. Translated by Alan Bass. London: Routledge.

—. 1981. *Dissemination*. Translated by Barbara Johnson. London: Athlone.

—. 1982a. "The Ends of Man." In *Margins of Philosophy*, translated by Alan Bass, 109–37. Brighton: Harvester Press.

—. 1982b. *Margins of Philosophy*. Translated by Alan Bass. Brighton: Harvester Press.

—. 1982c. "White Mythology: Metaphor in the Text of Philosophy." In *Margins of Philosophy*, translated by Alan Bass, 207–72. Brighton: Harvester Press.

—. 1984a. "My Chances/*Mes Chances*: A Rendezvous with Some Epicurean Stereophonies." In *Taking Chances: Derrida, Psychoanalysis, and Literature*, edited by Joseph H. Smith and William Kerrigan, 1–32. Baltimore: Johns Hopkins University Press.

—. 1984b. *Signéponge / Signsponge*. Translated by Richard Rand. New York: Columbia University Press.

—. 1986. *Glas*. Translated by John P. Leavey, Jr and Richard Rand. Lincoln, NE: University of Nebraska Press.

—. 1987. "Le retrait de la métaphore." In *Psyché: Inventions de l'autre*, 63–5. Paris: Galilée.

—. 1989. *Mémoires: For Paul de Man*. rev. ed. Translated by Cecile Lindsay et al. New York: Columbia University Press.

—. 1991. "Letter to a Japanese Friend." Translated by David Wood and Andrew Benjamin. In *A Derrida Reader: Between the Blinds*, edited by Peggy Kamuf, 270–6. New York: Harvester Wheatsheaf.

—. 1992. "This Strange Institution Called Literature." In *Acts of Literature*, edited by Derek Attridge, 33–75. New York: Routledge.

—. 1995a. "*Che cos'è la poesia?*" In *Points . . . Interviews, 1974–1994*, edited by Elisabeth Weber, translated by Peggy Kamuf et al., 288–99. Stanford: Stanford University Press.

—. 1995b. "Istrice 2: Ick bünn all hier." In *Points . . . Interviews, 1974–1994*, edited by Elisabeth Weber, translated by Peggy Kamuf et al., 300–26. Stanford: Stanford University Press.

—. 1997. *Of Grammatology*. Corrected Edition. Translated by Gayatri Chakravorty Spivak. Baltimore: Johns Hopkins University Press.

—. 1999. "Marx and Sons." In *Ghostly Demarcations: A Symposium on Jacques Derrida's* Specters of Marx, edited by Michael Sprinker, 213–69. London: Verso.

—. 2006. *H.C. for Life, That Is to Say. . . .* Translated with additional notes by Laurent Milesi and Stefan Herbrechter. Stanford: Stanford University Press.

—. 2007. "The *Retrait* of Metaphor." Translated by Peggy Kamuf. In *Psyche: Inventions of the Other*, vol. 1, edited by Peggy Kamuf and Elisabeth Rottenberg, 48–80. Stanford: Stanford University Press.

Dufourmantelle, Anne. 2000. "Invitation." In *Of Hospitality: Anne Dufourmantelle Invites Jacques Derrida to Respond*, translated by Rachel Bowlby. Stanford: Stanford University Press.

Falkmann, Christian Friedrich. 1835. *Practische Rhetorik: Praktische Rhetorik fur die obern Klassen der Schulen und zum Selbstunterrichte als zweite, umgearbeitete Ausgabe des Hülfsbuchs der deutschen Stylubüngen*. Hannover: Hahn.

Genette, Gérard. 1993. "Style and Signification." In *Fiction and Diction*, translated by Catherine Porter. Ithaca, NY: Cornell University Press.

Godzich, Wlad. 1986. "Foreword: The Tiger on the Paper Mat." In Paul de Man, *The Resistance to Theory*. Theory and History of Literature 33, ix–xviii. Minneapolis: University of Minnesota Press.

Harvey, Irene E. 1986. *Derrida and the Economy of Difference*. Bloomington: Indiana University Press.

Heidegger, Martin. 1979. *Nietzsche*, vol. 1. Translated by David Farrell Krell. New York: Harper and Row.

Hello, Ernest. 1861. *Le Style: Théorie et histoire*. Paris: Victor Palmé.

Iser, Wolfgang. 1974. "Doing Things in Style: An Interpretation of 'The Oxen of the Sun' in James Joyce's *Ulysses*." In *The Implied Reader: Patterns of Communication in Prose Fiction from Bunyan to Beckett*, 179–95. Baltimore: Johns Hopkins University Press.

Johnson, Christopher. 1993. *System and Writing in the Philosophy of Jacques Derrida*. Cambridge: Cambridge University Press.

Joyce, James. 1975. *Finnegans Wake*. London: Faber and Faber.

Kamuf, Peggy, ed. 1991. *A Derrida Reader: Between the Blinds*. London: Harvester Wheatsheaf.

Kofman, Sarah. 1984. *Lectures de Derrida*. Paris: Galilée.

Lacan, Jacques. 1966. *Écrits*. Paris: Seuil.

Lukacher, Ned. 1986. *Primal Scenes: Literature, Philosophy, Psychoanalysis*. Ithaca, NY: Cornell University Press.

Meschonnic, Henri. 1975. "L'écriture de Derrida." In *Le signe et le poème*, 401–92. Paris: Gallimard.

Milesi, Laurent. 1995. "*Plus d'usure*: Dante, Shakespeare, Pound, Derrida." In *Usure et Rupture: Breaking Points*, Colloque de Tours, Septembre 1993, edited by Claudine Raynaud and Peter Vernon, 205–29. Tours: Publications de l'Université.

—. 1998. "Inter-textualités: enjeux et perspectives (en guise d'avant-propos)." In *Texte(s) et Intertexte(s)*, edited by Éric Le Calvcz and Marie-Claude Canova-Green, 7–34. Amsterdam: Rodopi.

—. 2004. "The Stakes of Theory," in "Whither Theory? / Où va la théorie?," special issue, *Tropismes* 12: 43–62.

—. 2007. "Almost Nothing at the Beginning: The Technicity of the Trace in Deconstruction." In *Language Systems after Prague Structuralism*, edited by Louis Armand with Pavel Černovský, 22–41. Prague: Litteraria Pragensia.

Nancy, Jean-Luc. 2008. *The Discourse of the Syncope: Logodaedalus*. Translated by Saul Anton. Stanford: Stanford University Press.

Newman, John Henry. 1921. "Literature." In *Representative Essays on the Theory of Style*, edited by William Tenney Brewster, 1–26. New York: Macmillan.

Passerone, Giorgio. 1991. *La linea astratta: Pragmattica dello stile*. Milan: Angelo Guerini.

Pater, Walter. 1921. "Style." In *Representative Essays on the Theory of Style*, edited by William Tenney Brewster, 284–310. New York: Macmillan.

Puttenham, George. 2007. *The Art of English Poesy*, edited by Frank Whigham and Wayne A. Rebhorn. New York: Cornell University Press.

Ricoeur, Paul. 1975. *Le métaphore vive*. Paris: Seuil.

—. 1978. "Meta-phor and meta-physics." In *The Rule of Metaphor: The Creation of Meaning in Language*, translated by Robert Czerny with Kathleen McLoughlin and John Costello. 330–48. London: Routledge and Kegan Paul.

Riffaterre, Michael. 1957. *Le Style des Pléiades de Gobineau: Essai d'application d'une méthode stylistique*. Société de Publications Romanes et Françaises LVII. Geneva: Droz; Paris: Minard.

—. 1971. *Essais de stylistique structurale*. Présentation et traductions de Daniel Delas. Paris: Flammarion.

Rivarol, Antoine de. 1962. *Maximes, pensées et paradoxes. Suivis de, De l'universalité de la langue française, Lettres à M Necker, Esprit de Rivarol.* Edited by Pierre-Henri Simon. Paris: Le Livre Club du Libraire.

Saintsbury, George. 1885. *Specimens of English Prose Style.* London: Kegan Paul.

Segarra, Marta, ed. 2010. "On Style (A Question to H. Cixous and J. Derrida)." Translated by Laurent Milesi. In *The Portable Cixous*, 199–206. New York: Columbia University Press.

Seneca, Lucius Annaeus. 1829. "Epistola CXV." In *Pars prima sive Opera Philosophica*, vol. 4, edited by Marie Nicolas Bouillet, 274–83. Paris: Dondey-Dupré.

Shaw, George Bernard. 1921. "Preface: The Infidel Half Century." In *Back to Methuselah: A Metabiological Pentateuch*, vii–ci. New York: Brentano's.

Spitzer, Leo. 1928. *Stilstudien.* 2 vols. Munich: Hueber.

Steinmetz, Rudy. 1994. *Les Styles de Derrida.* Brussels: De Boeck-Wesmael.

Swift, Jonathan. 1898. "A Letter to a Young Clergyman, Lately Entered into Holy Orders." In *The Prose Works of Jonathan Swift, D.D.*, vol. III: *Swift's Writings on Religion and the Church*, vol. I, edited by Temple Scott. 195–217. London: George Bell and Sons.

Toolan, Michael. 1997. *Language in Literature: An Introduction to Stylistics.* London: Arnold.

Wales, Katie. 2001. *A Dictionary of Stylistics.* Harlow: Longman.

Wittgenstein, Ludwig. 1980. *Culture and Value.* Edited by G. H. von Wright and Heikki Nyman. Translated by Peter Winch. Oxford: Blackwell.

—. 1984. *Werkausgabe*, vol. 8. Frankfurt-am-Main: Suhrkamp.

11

"This song to come, this reader to become": The style of paradoxical anachrony in Blanchot's "René Char"

Mario Aquilina

Maurice Blanchot poses inescapable questions for theoretical discussions of style.[1] Operating on and around the margins of literature, philosophy, and literary theory, he is undoubtedly one of the great stylists of the twentieth century. However, style in Blanchot's work is more than just a signature, the flourish of a paraph that identifies his writing; the more fundamental issue it raises concerns what can be called the *conceptual force* of style in the relation between style and thought, both in terms of the role style plays in the unfolding of thought as well as in the effect that style may have on readers. Indeed, these are two closely related aspects of style in Blanchot.

One of the most important but also constitutionally slippery terms associated with Blanchot (1982) is "fascination," which, it can be argued, names the effect of Blanchot's style on the reader.

[1]Without the invaluable comments and mentoring of Ivan Callus, Timothy Clark, James Corby, and Gloria Lauri-Lucente, this chapter would not exist. For this, and more, I thank them.

This notion, which remains unclearly defined, perhaps because it is ultimately indefinable, appears in various passages relating to writing, as in Blanchot's claim that "to write is to surrender to the fascination of time's absence" (30), an atemporal time in which "my relation to [the present] is not one of cognition, but of recognition, and this recognition ruins in me the power of knowing, the right to grasp" (31). For Blanchot, "fascination" involves a relation in which "what is ungraspable" is also "inescapable" and in which one can never "cease reaching" what, paradoxically, cannot be reached (31). The attraction toward something that can never be grasped completely, and that, therefore, keeps one at bay, opens a space or a "moment of fascination" that, as Blanchot puts it, is "bathed in light which is splendid because unrevealed" (33). The object of our fascination—gleaming behind impassable darkness—"robs us of our power to give sense" in that it "no longer reveals itself to us, and yet it affirms itself in a presence foreign to the temporal present and to presence in space" (32). Fascination thus gestures toward a relation that is characterized by an essentially paradoxical dynamic—an encounter marked by separation, an attraction that also holds back.

The effects of fascination described by Blanchot are also felt in the reader's encounter with his work. Indeed, the feeling of being irrevocably captivated by his writing, which seems to demand one's complete surrender, seems to be not at all uncommon. And yet, while being drawn toward Blanchot, there is often the sense that one is somehow held off and repelled, unable to ever completely comprehend or feel in possession of his texts. It is almost as though there is a spell of fascination that draws the reader ever closer to Blanchot while simultaneously leaving him outside, unable to grasp or understand that which draws him closer. It is a spell that, as Jacques Derrida suggests, calls for a "pas d'é-loignement," that is, simultaneously, a "step" ("pas") of distancing and a "stop" ("pas") to this separation (1986, 37). This fascination, at the same time attractive and repellent, is inherently paradoxical. As Blanchot himself writes, "whoever is fascinated doesn't see, properly speaking, what he sees. Rather, it touches him in an immediate proximity; it seizes and ceaselessly draws him close, even though it leaves him absolutely at a distance" (1982, 33). The desire to get closer and yet, in so doing, feeling more and more the withdrawal, the distance from Blanchot's writing, marks the experience of reading Blanchot, in which a paradoxical dynamic of imbrication and rupture—what Timothy Clark calls "a knot of proximity as separation"—is at work (1992, 137). This presents prospective readers of Blanchot with a difficult scenario, poignantly expressed by Roger Laporte: "Devoting oneself to Blanchot's work is hardly a soft option: there is always the fear that, after fifty years of work, one may be no further forward than on the first day, at least if one measures possible progress in terms of clarity" (1996, 33).

The magnetizing and yet distancing effect of the fascination that Blanchot's texts exert is in part the effect of Blanchot's style of writing, a style that is as elusive as it is instantly recognizable. If Blanchot's style can be described as "difficult," it is arguably not so due to any excessive obscurity in his terminology—a critique often leveled at Jacques Lacan, among others. Style in Blanchot is not simply decorative or opaque superficiality laid over ideas in order to dazzle readers. It is also not just mannerism. Nor can it be simply explained as an intentional resistance strategy drawing attention to form in an attempt to shock the alienated reader of late capitalism into thinking, as Fredric Jameson accounts for Theodor Adorno's peculiar style (Jameson 1971, ix–xix). However, while Blanchot's terminology is not as obscure as Lacan's, and his sentences are not as grammatically convoluted as Jameson's or Adorno's, the cumulative effect of Blanchot's style is at least as vertiginous and unsettling.

Forming part of a tradition of writers that also includes Friedrich Nietzsche, Martin Heidegger, and Derrida—a tradition that touches with varying degrees of intensity the indeterminate borders between literature and philosophy—Blanchot writes with and toward a style of fascination that, rather than serving as a dress of thought, has a productive, formative, and conceptual force. My claim is that style in Blanchot is not the form that follows content but actually that which produces the conceptuality while simultaneously being its necessary expression or reflection. As will be shown through a close reading of Blanchot's essay on "René Char," style in Blanchot functions according to a dynamic of what can be called *paradoxical anachrony* through which style impossibly precedes the thoughts which it expresses.

In "René Char"—originally published in a 1946 issue of *Critique* and then included in *La Part du feu* in 1949—style is crucial. The essay was translated into English by Charlotte Mandell in 1995 and it is this translation that will be the focus here. Admittedly, this plan is burdened with several difficulties, not least of which is the fact that Blanchot's style—elusive enough in his native French—is being read and commented on in translation. This may, for some, be a sufficient reason not to attempt such an undertaking. Style, one may argue, is untranslatable and, therefore, any discussion of stylistic features in a text, if it is to avoid being reductive, should engage with the original version. Commenting on Blanchot's style in translation is surely reading at one further remove from the object of study, that is, from a point too distant from the original to say anything significant. This view of translation has contributed to the practice being "regarded as a baneful pretension." The translator, as Blanchot himself has remarked, is often seen with the same suspicion of an "enemy of God" as he tries to profit from reconstructing the Tower of Babel that God decided to destroy (1997, 58).

Significantly, this anxiety seems to be shared by many of Blanchot's translators. A cursory glance at their reflections on the issue reveals that they tend to draw attention to the untranslatability of certain stylistic features in his texts. Mandell, for instance, starts her "Translator's Note" to *The Work of Fire* precisely by pointing out the inadequacy of translating Blanchot's language and style. The title, "La Part du feu," immediately poses formidable difficulties because no English equivalent can be found that captures the polysemy and allusive density of the French phrase. For the translator of "La part du feu," therefore, "The Work of Fire" can only be an approximation to the original (Mandell 1995, ix–x). Similarly, Peter Banki criticizes John Gregg's translation of "L'Attente l'oubli" as "Awaiting Oblivion" because, in translating "l'attente" as "awaiting," Gregg introduces grammatical coherence when this is lacking in the original. Gregg is deemed guilty, not of deducting something from the original, but of changing it or adding to it in a way which leads to its misrepresentation (Banki 2000, 179). Perhaps most revealingly, in the case of *Faux pas*, Mandell retains the French words in the English title but she feels that even they are unsatisfactory (Mandell 2001, xi–xii). Despite the fact that the French expression "faux pas" is also used in English, like Pierre Menard's version of Cervantes's Quixote, the words in the translation or "second" version are both the same and yet different to the original as they do not carry the same connotations in the two languages. The meanings the two titles convey, due to the different contexts, are not the same and, hence, translation is seen as failing to an extent. Ultimately, Blanchot's translators seem to fit Blanchot's own description of the translator as a "nostalgic" and "strange" man who always feels as "lacking in his own language all of what the original work promises in present affirmations" (1997, 60). They are always divided, always feeling that their language is unable to be a worthy vessel of the original while at the same time they cannot be at home in the original itself.

However, while the translators' emphasis on the difficulty of their work is to be expected, so is their ultimate justification of the task that makes them what they are. Thus, Mandell herself reminds us that "inadequacy . . . is part and parcel of any translation" and not only those of Blanchot's texts (1995, x). Admittedly, the problems seem to be somewhat accentuated in the case of Blanchot because his texts are heavily reliant on style, some aspects of which, such as paronomasia and punning, pose particular problems to translators. However, there are other features of his style which may be more translatable, and Mandell, like some others, has managed to provide English-speaking readers with convincing renditions of Blanchot.

Blanchot himself approaches the question of translation from a radically different perspective to that of his own translators. Translations are often judged in terms of whether they capture the essence of the original by transposing into a second language what is "at home" in the "primary" text. Indeed, guilty admissions by translators of the inadequacy of their work presuppose such an understanding of the process of translation. They see themselves as having the task—assigned to them by the original—of reproducing the meaning of the original in another language. However, in discussing Walter Benjamin's "The Task of the Translator," Blanchot writes that there is an element of untranslatability in a text, a foreignness of the language to itself that, paradoxically, *demands* translation. It follows that translation, for Blanchot, is not meant "to make the difference disappear" by producing an equivalent version in a foreign language. It is, on the contrary, "the play of this difference" (1995, 58).

Blanchot revisits Benjamin and his suggestion that translations should try to make a gesture toward a superior language where all the mysteries of different languages would be reconciled. Benjamin writes how "languages are not strangers to one another, but are, a priori . . . interrelated in what they want to express" (Benjamin 1968, 72). This does not mean that translation aims at producing a "likeness to the original" because the original itself inevitably changes, along with its context, through time and the translator can only ever access the "afterlife" of the original (72). The interrelationship among languages is, for Benjamin, a "kinship" of "intention" rather than similarity or likeness in meaning. Indeed, this intention, which is manifested in different modes through different languages, can only be realized through "the totality of [the various languages'] intentions supplementing each other" and thus producing what he calls "pure language." As Benjamin writes, "all individual elements of foreign languages—words, sentences, structure—are mutually exclusive." However, these different languages "supplement one another in their intentions" toward a "pure language" (74). For Benjamin, translation does not so much erase the foreignness of languages as it allows the original to rise toward pure language. The task of the translator is not that of finding an alternative way of conveying the meaning of the original but of discovering in the language of translation the "intention" that can produce an echo of the original. Translation attempts to integrate various tongues into a "true" or "pure" language where all languages harmonize, a language which is impossible to achieve in practice and yet approachable through translation. From this perspective, translation and primary text function as broken "fragments of a greater language, just as fragments are part of a vessel" (78). The fragments of a broken vessel are clearly not "like one another" but they "must match one another in the smallest detail" (78).

Building on but eventually swerving away from Benjamin's understanding of translation being conducted as if there were the possibility of moving toward a "superior language" or a "complementary unity" of different modes of intention, including those of both the original and translation, Blanchot suggests that translation accentuates the difference, the otherness, and the foreignness that exists within the original itself (1997, 58). Through its otherness, the translated text rekindles the difference to itself that makes the original call for translation in the first place, while making visible the otherness of language in the so-called original text through a process not of resemblance but of what Blanchot calls "identity on the basis of an alterity" (59). Translation "translates" or accomplishes the future "becoming," the drift toward the other always already present in the original itself. The effect that this has is that of the same work appearing in what seem to be two versions in two foreign languages rather than in an original and in a foreign language. Consequently, rather than having to be a source of perpetual anxiety due to the impossibility of achieving a "true" copy of the original in another language, translation becomes the "original" art of mastering and accentuating "difference" rather than sameness (58).

Now, the foreignness of language even when it is expected to be at home in itself is precisely what Gilles Deleuze identifies as being the mark of style. For Deleuze, in fact, a great stylist is someone who does not conserve the conventional syntax of a language and has the ability to create a foreign language within his own language through syntax that pushes the language to its limits. The language inhabited by the writer is made to "stutter" and "stammer" by being pushed to "its limit, to its outside, to its silence" (Deleuze 1997, 113). Translation thus becomes that which, rather than inevitably failing to capture untranslatable style, actually reiterates and recreates style's foreignness in another foreign language.[2] Style is not that which is necessarily lost in translation but that which calls for translation, both into a different language and, in the sense used by Derrida in "Des Tours de Babel," into commentary. This, as Derrida shows, reverses the structure of debt implicating the original and the translation. The debt is not simply that owed by the translator to the original but also that owed by the original which, in demanding translation, "begins by indebting itself *as well* with regard to the translator" (Derrida 2002, 118). It is in response to this demand for commentary and translation that I approach Blanchot's style in the English translation of "René Char," in which style is of the essence because not only does

[2]In "The Task of the Translator," Benjamin quotes Rudolf Pannwitz's theory of translation, which includes the idea that a translator should allow his "language to be powerfully affected by the foreign tongue." The translator, for Pannwitz, "must expand and deepen his language by means of the foreign language" (as quoted in Benjamin 1968, 81). What Deleuze adds to Benjamin and Blanchot is, precisely, the focus on style.

Blanchot write about Char's language and style but he does so in an essay where the stakes for style are indeed high.

Style, as a subject of discussion, is arguably not a central thematic concern in Blanchot's oeuvre. Essays where Blanchot discusses the topic directly like, for instance, "The Pursuit of the Zero Point," are rare. In this 1953 essay, Blanchot critiques Roland Barthes's definition of style as physiognomic or biological necessity. While Barthes defines style as a "germinative phenomenon, the transmutation of a Humour" (1977, 11), Blanchot asks whether it is the flesh and blood writer who writes a text or "the wholly other . . . the very demand to write," a demand that employs the name of the writer only to disappropriate him (Blanchot 1995b, 148). "The Pursuit of the Zero Point" is indicative of the angle Blanchot usually takes in relation to the question of style. While style is often understood as a manifestation or outcome of the writer's individuality, Blanchot speaks of the writer as also being dispossessed by the writing rather than simply preceding the text and leaving his stylistic fingerprints on it. Furthermore, the paradoxical anachrony that marks Blanchot's style and that is at the heart of the relation between style and thought in his work is central to the relationship between the writer and writing, which Blanchot sees as defying the linear concept of production; for him, writing is not simply the product of the writer as an individual but, simultaneously, dependant on the writer for its existence and the source of the writer's status as a writer.

Blanchot's essay on "René Char" anticipates several such motifs which would then dominate *The Space of Literature*. Through the economy of the work envisaged by Blanchot, the writer or poet no longer precedes the text in a relationship of chronological anteriority. Instead, a paradoxical structure appears whereby the emergence of the work is contemporaneous to the erasure of the writer. In writing, the writer desires, as it were, that which has already erased him. While the economy of the work is developed at length in *The Space of Literature*, the temporality or, rather, the paradoxical anachrony which characterizes it, is already crucial in Blanchot's essay on Char. Rather than in terms of the notion of poetry as an expression of the human self, a notion that T. S. Eliot famously denounces in "Tradition and the Individual Talent," Blanchot conceives the writer as "second to what he makes" and "subsequent to the world he has brought to life." This results in an oxymoronic understanding of poetry as being both "the writer's work, the truest impulse of his existence," and also that which "causes him to be, what must exist without him and before him" (Blanchot 1995c, 99). The poet is the master of the poem. He is its origin. And yet the poem anticipates the poet, "for it is in the poem that the complete and completely free presence of beings and things is realized," and it is here that "the poet manages to become what he is" (105). According to Blanchot's conception of literature, before the work has been written, there was no one to write it.[3]

In highlighting the "anteriority of poetry" and in declaring that "the poet exists only after the poem," the essay on Char, like *The Space of Literature*, seems to rule out the possibility of understanding style as an expression of the writer's individuality (99). Yet, intriguingly, the notion of the erasure of the poet in poetry is developed in an essay whose style is, in many ways, singularly identifiable as Blanchotian.

The style of Blanchot's critical work evolved during his long career and one cannot presume to offer a monolithic description of his entire oeuvre. His earlier style, while already singularly Blanchotian, is closer to the traditional language of criticism than that of his later fragmentary texts such as *The Writing of the Disaster* and *The Step Not Beyond*. However, there are various features that are tangible across many of his essays, one of which being what can be called the "structure" or "movement" of his essays. Blanchot's critical essays enact a constitutional fragmentation which frustrates readers who expect the conventional statement-exposition-conclusion development. There is no easy way of getting to know Blanchot as his essays tend to be notoriously difficult to paraphrase. They proceed slowly, examining ideas, extending thoughts as far as they can go. They ponder words and often prefer to turn back on themselves repeatedly rather than moving forward toward a resolution, a compromise or the triumph of a conclusion. By the end of a Blanchot essay, the reader is bound to have found more questions than answers. Some may argue that what is called "style" stops short of such overarching structural issues and that style is more identifiable with the

[3]Blanchot's conception of poetry is clearly influenced by Martin Heidegger, whose work often serves as a starting point for Blanchot in *The Space of Literature*. See "The Origin of the Work of Art" (2002).

specific language and words of a text rather than the construction and development of an argument. However, the fragmentation of the structure as well as the elusive nature of its development is a reflection of the vertiginous language of his text at a more basic linguistic level. Indeed, what Kenneth Douglas describes as the fundamental experience of reading Blanchot, that is, a feeling of "vertigo" caused by "fundamental anguish before [an] absence of foundation, [a] nothingness," is created by both the structure of the text and the style of fascination that characterizes Blanchot's writing, and which this essay has been engaging with from the start (Douglas 1949, 85).

When reading Blanchot, our full attention is required at all times but we are seldom rewarded with clear and neatly packaged conclusions. And yet, the reader, a subject of fascination, reads on and reads again without aiming at complete possession or grasping of the text. Following the distinction Blanchot develops in *The Infinite Conversation* and elsewhere, between the reader and the interpreter critic, or between the lightness of reading and the reductiveness of interpretations which seek to determine "what we must read and how we must read it," one can say that reading Blanchot as Blanchot's style demands involves a double movement of listening and letting go, an openness to a process that flows with its own rhythms and tempo and that exercises a powerful fascination on us (1993, 318). In an introduction to Philippe Lacoue-Labarthe's *Typography: Mimesis, Philosophy, Politics*, Derrida invokes the need of being patient and of learning how to "listen to [Lacoue-Labarthe], and to do so at his rhythm" (Derrida 1998, 3). Analogously, it can be argued, Blanchot finds an essentially Blanchotian countersignature in Derrida, who provides a series of readings of Blanchot collected in *Parages* that fully respond to Blanchot's "viens" ("come"). Blanchot's style of fascination demands a paradoxical attentive abandonment, a step toward his texts that, true to the "pas" ("step" and "stop") of fascination, is always already interrupted (Derrida 1986, 11).

This vertiginous fascination brought to bear by Blanchot's writing is traceable, at least in part, to a central incision of Blanchot's style, particularly in his early criticism, that is, its heavy reliance on paradox. As Rodolphe Gasché contends in an important essay on Blanchot, paradox "is the necessary but insufficient condition for the happening, of the chance of literature" (1996, 38). Blanchot's conception of literature is paradoxical; it is built on an interaction of opposites that are somehow not subjected to linear chronology. Indeed, a dominant and recurrent stylistic mark in Blanchot's essays is what I have been calling paradoxical anachrony, which, apart from contributing heavily to what Douglas refers to as the "vertigo" that the reader experiences, has a powerful conceptual and formative force. In this respect, the term *paradoxical anachrony* is meant to capture the twofold operation of style in Blanchot's writing, an operation that problematizes chronological linearity in the relation between style and thought. On the one hand, Blanchot's style seems to be a necessary effect of his paradoxical conception of literature; on the other hand, this paradoxical conception of literature would be almost impossible to formulate without the style of his work. In other words, Blanchot's writing, at one and the same time, *thematizes* and *performs* paradoxical thoughts that defy sequentiality.

Paradoxical anachrony is at work in Blanchot's "René Char," an essay concerned with the seemingly illogical economy of writing in which Blanchot inscribes the relation of the poem to the poet and reader.

> The poet is born by the poem he creates; he is second to what he makes; he is subsequent to the world he has brought to life and concerning which his ties of dependency reproduce all the contradictions expressed in this paradox: the poem is his work, the truest impulse of his existence, but the poem is what causes him to be, what must exist without him and before him, in a superior consciousness wherein are united both the obscurity of the depths of the earth and the clarity of a universal power to establish and justify. (1995c, 99)
>
> (Le poète naît par la poème qu'il crée; il est second au regard de ce qu'il fait; il est postérieur au monde qu'il a suscité et par rapport auquel ses relations de dépendance reproduisent toutes les contradictions exprimées dans ce paradoxe: le poème est son œuvre, le mouvement le plus vrai de son existence, mais le poème est ce qui le fait être, ce qui doit exister sans lui et avant lui, dans une conscience supérieure où s'unissent l'obscur du fond de la terre et la clarté d'un pouvoir universel de fonder et de justifier.) (1949, 104)

This is arguably a signature passage of the early Blanchot, a long sentence that keeps oscillating between the two sides of an opposition without, however, ever achieving a dialectical synthesis or resolution. Paradoxes abound: "the poet," we read, "is born by the poem he creates." Chronological linearity is shattered as the poet is presented as subsequent to that which he precedes, being "second to what he makes." Paradox presents itself in various ways in this sentence and it moves the writing forward in a series of modulations that repeat by rephrasing the previous statement. The passage starts with three paradoxes contained within singular and distinct clauses. The first two clauses, "The poet is born by the poem he creates" and "he is second to what he makes," are short, almost aphoristic in form. The third clause—"he is subsequent to the world he has brought to life and concerning which his ties of dependency reproduce all the contradictions expressed in this paradox"—is longer, syntactically complex, and it also introduces the second part of the sentence where Blanchot formulates the paradox involved in the economy of the work once again. In this second part, starting with "the poem is his work," the opposition is expressed through the use of the coordinating conjunction, "but," rather than being contained within an individual clause as is the case in the three clauses forming the first part of the sentence. Once again, each of the two sides of the irresolvable paradox is laid out through repetition. The first side of the opposition is stated twice with "the poem is his work" and, then, "the truest impulse of his existence." The second side of the opposition is also stated twice: "the poem is what causes him to be" and also "what must exist without him and before him." Moreover, in the final clause, where Blanchot speaks of the superior consciousness within which the poem exists, Blanchot introduces yet another opposition, a paradox within a paradox, as it were, as this consciousness is presented as uniting darkness and light, that is, "both the obscurity of the depths of the earth and the clarity of a universal power to establish and justify."

This passage, with its vertiginous style of paradoxical anachrony, is an account of an irresolvable relation between the poet and the poem. As Gasché (1996) illustrates in a discussion of "Literature and the Right to Death," Blanchot's conception of the relation between the writer and his work does not end in a Hegelian sublation into a higher ring of the dialectic chain but is an infinitely recurring paradox, a suspended irresolvability of oppositions. The sentence from the essay on Char shows Blanchot grappling with similar paradoxes. Through it, one gets the impression that Blanchot is trying to make the impossible leap from the inevitability of sequentiality and linearity in writing to the simultaneous presentation of oppositions. Blanchot's paradoxical style is fundamental, albeit necessarily imperfect, for the formation of Blanchot's paradoxical conception of literature and it is hard to see how Blanchot could have written about literature in a different way.

Blanchot's style, however, is here not only characterized by its peculiarly paradoxical syntax but also by its concentrated interplay of connotations and associations. This paronomastic density can be seen in a passage which, in Blanchot's essay, immediately precedes the one quoted above:

> The relationships between a poem and a reader are always of the most complex kind. It is not true that poetry can do without being read, and that the poem must haughtily ignore the reader; yet previous to any reader, it is exactly the role of the poem to prepare, to put into the world the one who has to read it, to force him to exist starting from this still half-blind, half-composite that is the stammering reader involved in habitual relationships or formed by the reading of other poetic works. It is the same for the reader as for the poet. Both poet and reader of this poem take their existence from it, and are strongly aware of depending, in their existence, on this song to come, this reader to become. This is one of the mysterious demands of poetry's power. (1995c, 98–9)
>
> (Les rapports d'un poème et d'un lecteur sont toujours des plus complexes. Que la poésie puisse se passer d'être lue, et que la poème doive ignorer orgueilleusement le lecteur, cela est faux, mais dans la mesure où, antérieur à lui, c'est justement le rôle du poème de préparer, de mettre au monde celui qui doit le lire, de l'obliger à être à partir de ce composé, encore à demi aveugle, à demi balbutiant, qu'est le lecteur engagé dans les relations habituelles ou formé par la lecture d'autres œuvres poétiques. Il en est du lecteur comme du poète. Tous deux, poète et lecteur de ce *po*ème, reçoivent de lui leur existence, et sont fortement

> conscients de dépendre, dans leur existence, de ce chant à venir, de ce lecteur à devenir. C'est une des mystérieuses exigences du pouvoir poétique.) (1949, 103–4)

In evoking the impossible chronology of the relation between reader and poem, Blanchot weaves an intricate web of what can be termed *birthing* language. Mandell translates Blanchot's "mettre au monde"—used to describe how the poem creates the reader—as "put into the world," but the expression can also be translated as "give birth to." And what the poem, as a mother, creates or gives birth to is a "half-blind, half-composite that is the stammering reader," a dependent infant. Yet, impossibly, the infant reader is already "formed by the reading of other poetic works" and thus, to an extent, he predates the poem which gives him existence.

The birthing language is found again in the parallel description of the poet's relation to the poem. Like the reader, the poet is "born by the poem he creates," echoing the Christian mystery of the Conception whereby Mary becomes her "Maker's maker" (Donne 1994, 244). Both poet and reader are mutually implicated in a relation of "becoming" with poetry. Blanchot conceives the poem as a "song to come" (chant à venir) that is concurrent to the "reader to become" (ce lecteur à devenir).[4] Thus, "to come"—understood as future promise but also, possibly, as sexual fulfillment—and "become"—understood as creation—are inextricable. The sexual and birthing connotations continue as the poet is "subsequent [in time] to the world he has brought to life [created] and concerning which (par rapport auquel) his ties of dependency reproduce (reproduisent) all the contradictions expressed" in a series of paradoxes. The ties of the poet's dependency on the poem "reproduce" a series of contradictions, where the verb "reproduce" (suggesting both "to create an offspring" and "to produce again") embodies the simultaneity of time and birth paradoxes that mark Blanchot's conception of the poet's relation to the poem. The contradictions are "reproduced" through—are an offspring or repeated instances of—the poet's "rapport" (relationship) with the poem. The poem's relations with the poet and the reader are both productive of paradox and determined by a paradoxical economy. As Blanchot puts it,

---

[4]All quotations in this paragraph are taken from (Blanchot 1995c, 98–9) and, in French, from (Blanchot 1949, 103–4). The cited passage is quoted above in text.

what is at stake is an impossible future becoming, "one of the mysterious demands of poetry's power." Blanchot's style of paradoxical anachrony is fundamental in capturing that which Blanchot sees as *poetic* in Char, that is, the openness to the "to come" or to the future ("à venir" and "avenir"). Crucially, however, it is important to note that this style makes Blanchot's writing itself veer toward the poetic, toward that which, like a "song to come," inscribes its own reader. In so doing, style in Blanchot demonstrates a certain resistance to the imposition of rigid borders between philosophy and literature or poetry.

Blanchot's style, while being essentially paradoxical, is also elusive and constitutive through its reliance on paratactic "modulation," that is, the repetitive reformulation of a statement through various subsequent phrases often not connected with conjugations. Intriguingly, and yet again indicative of the inherent hybridity of Blanchot's writing, parataxis is a style feature that Blanchot identifies as a defining characteristic of René Char's poetic language. In *The Infinite Conversation*, Blanchot writes about the force of "juxtaposition and interruption" in Char's fragmentary speech, which he describes as a "new kind of arrangement not entailing harmony, concordance, or reconciliation." Apart from being paratactic, Char's poetic language offers "the torment of contrariety that opposes one term to another, but not in order to arrive at a totality where the *for* and the *against* are reconciled or merge" (1993, 309 emphasis mine). Perhaps, it would be difficult to find a better description of Blanchot's own paradoxical style than his own evaluation of Char's language in this essay.

Indeed, Blanchot's writing and Char's poetic language as discussed by Blanchot himself share important affinities and this is perhaps one of the reasons why Char, like Hölderlin, Kafka, Mallarmé, and very few others, keeps appearing in Blanchot's essays. Char's poetry, in analogous ways to Blanchot's prose, enacts a complex self-turning that makes language itself tangible. These stylistic similarities are not only a form of coincidental parallelism between the two writers but rather invite Blanchot to actually integrate Char's language with his own in his essay on the French poet. In his critical essays, Blanchot often creates what Douglas calls a "new blend of his own personal language and that of the writer he is examining" (Douglas 1949, 88). Blanchot's style often follows, embodies, and extends the language of the writer he is engaging.

In many ways, his reading of Char and others is a performance of his paradoxical conception of reading as an attentive abandonment to the read. This is something which is particularly evident in the essay on Char which abounds in quotations and citations.

> The poem is the truth of the poet, the poet is the possibility of the poem; and yet the poem stays unjustified; even realised, it remains impossible: it is "the mystery that enthrones" (*Alone They Remain*), "the meaning that does not question itself" (*Leaves of Hypnos*). In it are united, in an inexpressible and incomprehensible connection, the obscure depths of being and the transparency of awareness that grounds, the "exquisite, horrible, moving earth" and the "heterogeneous human condition"; for this exalted meeting, in which each "grasps the other and qualifies the other," precedes all qualification, escapes all determination, and signifies only its own impossibility. (1995c, 100)
>
> (La poème est la vérité du poète, le poète est la possibilité du poème; et cependant, le poème reste injustifié; même réalisé, il demeure impossible: c'est "le mystère qui intronise" (*Seuls demeurent*), "la signification que ne s'évalue pas" (*Feuillets d'Hypnos*). En lui s'unissent, dans un rapporte inexprimable et incompréhensible, le fond obscur de l'être et la transparence de la conscience qui fonde, la "terre mouvante, horrible, exquise" et la "condition humaine hétérogène," car cette rencontre exaltée dans laquelle l'un l'autre "se saisissent et se qualifient mutuellement," précède toute qualification, échappe à toute détermination et ne signifie précisément que sa propre impossibilité.) (1949, 109–10)

Here, apart from the paratactic syntax and the various modulations of paradox that characterize the passages analyzed above, one can see Blanchot's blending of Char's poetic language into his critical register through a combination of citation and paraphrase. Blanchot integrates a series of short quotes from Char into his own writing, thus letting Char's language inhabit his essay. Char's poetry, whose peculiar and unusual style and syntax make its language almost different to itself, as if it were a foreign language within language, is that which calls for translation or commentary and inevitably becomes part of Blanchot's text. This, in turn, accentuates the element of foreignness in Blanchot's own language, creating an unhousedness or difference to itself that calls for translation into yet another foreign language. Extending Blanchot's thought about translation,—also discussed above in relation to his reading of Benjamin's "The Task of the Translator"—it may be said that reading Blanchot in English is not necessarily a lamentable loss of a more authentic original.

Style, therefore, is a form of signing but it is also more than that. In "René Char," style is not merely a way of conveying Blanchot's ideas about literature and about the French poet but an enabling of these same thoughts through language. The performative force of his style gives Blanchot's language something of what Mallarmé attributes to poetry, that is, the ability not simply to express meaning but to create it (Blanchot 1995a). Blanchot folds the language of René Char rigorously into the language of his own essay, thus creating a stylistically singular exploration of not only Char's poetry but also of his own paradoxical probing of the question of literature. Blanchot does not use Char instrumentally by trying to mould Char's poetry into some preexisting model of thought that he would like to put forward. What we witness in Blanchot's encounter with Char are rather two writers that respond to the same demand, who inhabit a common space in their relation to literature. As such, Blanchot reads Char more as a writer reading another writer than a critic explaining and understanding a poet. The conception of style that arises is non-teleocratic, a mode of writing that relinquishes power and identity. Style, as it appears through a reading of Blanchot, is an event and not intended as an expression of the individuality of the self, even if, ironically, Blanchot conveys these ideas through a peculiarly recognizable style.

Paradox, modulation, parataxis, and a peculiar mode of merging Char's language with his own are some of the stylistic devices that make Blanchot's style Blanchotian in an essay which questions the writer's ownership and control over his own language. Blanchot's style of paradoxical anachrony, the length of his repeatedly modulated sentences and clauses that oscillate continuously from one edge to another of a thought, and the inhabiting of the foreign language of the other and its own otherness, make Blanchot's texts a source of powerful fascination for readers who are left unsure, uncertain, and never really in complete possession of that which they read. This has important implications for how to read

Blanchot, for how Blanchot should be read. In a sense, readers of Blanchot run the risk of succumbing to a state of passive enthrallment that, as Kevin Hart puts it, "makes us stall" (Hart 2004, 140). It is not insignificant, in this respect, that Blanchot sees childhood as the paradigmatic "moment of fascination" (1982, 33). The implications, however, also extend to the more general question of the role of style in the interface between philosophy and literature. Thus, it could be said that fascination permeates our response to not only Blanchot's writing but also to that of others, who like him, in walking the tightrope between the philosophical and the poetic, step forward *with* style and *through* style. Fascination, after all, is also the "experience of the person in prayer before an icon," the experience of "being drawn endlessly toward the divinity" (Hart 2004, 140). Confronted by that which, like the divine, is fascinating, "one is transfixed, unable to escape," as if from a "ghostly spectacle" (126).

References

Banki, Peter. 2000. "To Translate Blanchot?" *Oxford Literary Review* 22: 178–84.

Barthes, Roland. 1977. "What is Writing?" In *Writing Degree Zero*, translated by Annette Lavers and Colin Smith, 9–18. New York: Hill and Wang.

Benjamin, Walter. 1968. "The Task of the Translator: An Introduction to the Translation of Baudelaire's *Tableaux Parisiens*." In *Illuminations: Essays and Reflections*, edited by Hannah Arendt, translated by Harry Zohn, 69–82. New York: Schocken Books.

Blanchot, Maurice. 1949. "René Char." In *La part du feu*, 103–14. Éditions Gallimard.

—. 1982. "The Essential Solitude." In *The Space of Literature*, translated by Ann Smock, 21–34. Lincoln, NE: University of Nebraska Press.

—. 1993. *The Infinite Conversation*. Translated by Susan Hanson. Minneapolis: University of Minnesota Press.

—. 1995a. "Myth of Mallarmé." In *The Work of Fire*, translated by Charlotte Mandell, 27–42. Stanford, CA: Stanford University Press.

—. 1995b. "The Pursuit of the Zero Point." In *The Blanchot Reader*, edited by Michael Holland, translated by Ian Maclachlan, 143–51. Oxford: Blackwell Publishers.

—. 1995c. "René Char." In *The Work of Fire*, translated by Charlotte Mandell, 98–110. Stanford, CA: Stanford University Press.

—. 1997. "Translating." In *Friendship*, translated by Elizabeth Rottenberg, 57–61. Stanford, CA: Stanford University Press.

Clark, Timothy. 1992. *Derrida, Heidegger, Blanchot: Sources of Derrida's Notion and Practice of Literature*. Cambridge: Cambridge University Press.

Deleuze, Gilles. 1997. "He Stuttered." In *Essays Critical and Clinical*, translated by Daniel W. Smith and Michael A. Greco, 107–14. London: Verso.

Derrida, Jacques. 1986. "Pas." In *Parages*, edited by John Leavey, translated by Tom Conley and James Hulbert, 19–116. Paris: Editions Galilée.

—. 1998. "Introduction: Desistance." In *Typography: Mimesis, Philosophy, Politics*, by Phillipe Lacoue-Labarthe, edited by Christopher Fynsk, 1–42. Stanford, CA: Stanford University Press.

—. 2002. "Des Tours de Babel." Translated by Joseph F. Graham. In *Acts of Religion*, edited by Gil Anidjar, 102–34. New York: Routledge.

Donne, John. 1994. *The Works of John Donne*. Ware: Wordsworth Poetry Library.

Douglas, Kenneth. 1949. "Blanchot and Sartre." *Yale French Studies* 3: 85–95.

Gasché, Rodolphe. 1996. "The Felicities of Paradox: Blanchot on the Null-space of Literature." In *Maurice Blanchot: The Demand of Writing*, edited by Carolyn Bailey Gill, 34–69. London: Routledge.

Hart, Kevin. 2004. *The Dark Gaze: Maurice Blanchot and the Sacred*. Chicago: University of Chicago Press.

Heidegger, Martin. 1971. "The Origin of the Work of Art." In *Poetry, Language, Thought*, edited and translated by Albert Hofstadter, 15–86. Cambridge: Cambridge University Press.

Jameson, Fredric. 1971. *Marxism and Form: Twentieth Century Dialectical Theories of Literature*. Princeton, NJ: Princeton University Press.

Laporte, Roger. 1996. "Maurice Blanchot Today." Translated by Ian Maclachlan. In *Maurice Blanchot: The Demand of Writing*, edited by Carolyn Bailey Gill, 25–33. London: Routledge.

Mandell, Charlotte. 1995. "Translator's Note." In Blanchot, *The Work of Fire*, ix–x. Stanford, CA: Stanford University Press.

—. 2001. "Translator's Note." In Blanchot, *Faux Pas*, translated by Charlotte Mandell, xi–xii. Stanford, CA: Stanford University Press.

12

V for style: Gilles Deleuze on a mobile cusp

Marie-Dominique Garnier

Very small linguistic shifts express upheavals and reversals in the concept.

—GILLES DELEUZE, *DIFFERENCE AND REPETITION*

"Style is not the man, style is essence itself" (Deleuze 2003, 48). Confronted by Gilles Deleuze's affirmation in isolation, readers might be taken aback by what appears to be a contradictory statement which articulates in its first half a critique of Buffon's epigram on style and man, while apparently returning to more essentialist, idealistic terms in its second half. The sentence's post-humanist opening, in other words, is strangely at odds with its tail end (an oddity augmented by the use of the quintessential adverb *itself*, in the very style of Buffon which it sets out to discredit). But in order to be read at all, such a statement must be relocated within a context, a milieu, on a plane, as it were, of stylistic consistencies. Reading Deleuze implies screening and scouting a space of adjacencies, of interconnected, neighborly units of "writing"—in which writing "itself" is at bay, challenged by what pertains to other domains of expression, whether tactile, aural, rhythmic, or respiratory. Deleuze's statement deploys itself in a fluid textual surround, colored both by what follows ("essence is in itself difference" [48]) and by its immediate metamorphic precursor: "*une essence est toujours une naissance*" (1964, 62)—"an essence is always a birth" (2003, 48; a translation which has no other choice but to leave, somehow, the "gist" of it all untranslated).

Deleuze's original French is the locus of a stylistic event in which a small-scale, phonetic interval reforms *essence* into *naissance*—soldering one to the other, operating in the parasitic or contagious mode, against the grain of etymology—as befits a philosophy which prefers the herbescent to trees and roots. In the context of this new, unheard-of homophony, the concept of essence is literally made to swerve from its received humanist acceptation. Something like an acoustic machine emerges from Deleuze's singular assemblage of *essence* to what appears to be only a chance phonetic partner, a stray body-double (*naissance*)—a machine that runs transverse and requires a sense of orality as much as writing. The newly yoked pair of terms responds neither to paronymy, which would involve the sharing of a common root, nor to the "pun" species, a pun being implicitly and etymologically based on a logic of points/puncturing/punctuating, one which is conceptually foreign to Deleuze. *Essence* in the vicinity of *naissance* forms, rather, a differential machine, a system of literal cuts which borrows a spare part (a loose *n*) from the end of the indefinite article *une* and reconnects it to form the following word, thus engineering a new oral/literal product. The quasi-homophony in standard spoken Parisian French of *une naissance* and *une essence*, based on the required phonetic liaison, becomes a case of incremental growth by literal addition (*n+essence*). Occurring in the intervallic space between word boundaries, between a final consonant and the initial vowel of the next word, Deleuze's liaison creates a nearly reversible pattern in which the first term becomes, like the second, a matter of growth and outgrowth—no longer an abstract concept but a rearrangement of displaceable, mobile cut-off points. By extension, style-as-essence forms a transitive alliance with its companion concepts, *naissance* and, in the same paragraph, difference. A subdued becoming-feminine colors Deleuze's birth-related assemblage, a step in the territory or non-territory of birth and birth-giving. But if style-as-essence has anything to do with birth, with coming-into-being and emergence, with being born or giving birth, it does not necessarily follow that style is "woman herself"—to paraphrase and parody Buffon's statement.

Naissance occurs in parasitic fashion, as a non-genealogical, unplanned declension or mutation in writing. Italicized, *naissance* seems to take its own slanted path, to veer off any possible straight or "essential" course, in the *clinamen* mode, rewriting what it veers from into what sounds, but is not, its opposite number (*n-essence*). Essence becomes *naissance*; becomes flux; is secreted out, oozes forth, following the same differential path as one of Deleuze and Guattari's later strokes of style in their joint rewriting "the secret as secretion" (1987, 287).

Deleuze's 1964 conception of style as essence in *Proust and Signs* is intimately linked to his contemporary work on difference and repetition, both terms appearing in the above-mentioned paragraph under consideration—a connection analyzed by Ronald Bogue in an important essay on Deleuze's style, in which he argues that Deleuze's apparent "standard expository prose" is "a ruse, a means of divesting oneself of personality in order to investigate a non-personal individuation," and that, rather than a conventional style, what we have is of the order of a "Deleuze effect" (Bogue 1996, 11). But what this effect materializes remains to some extent elusive—apart from Ronald Bogue's argument in favor of the applicability of the three "styles" of Spinoza (imported from the last text of *Essays Critical and Clinical*) to Deleuze's own (Bogue 1996, 17–18; see also, further, below in this essay).

Difference and Repetition offers almost unexplored ground for forays into Deleuze's style. While belonging to the driest of genres—academic philosophy—the book departs from the unwritten rules of the genre by trying its (differential) hand at discrete, less than perceptible stylistic experiments. What follows is a study *in* rather than *on* style—based on close, parasitic readings which, in tick fashion, fix themselves on the surface of writing, on the scent of what *Difference and Repetition* identifies as "very small linguistic shifts," minor or imperceptible changes out of which "upheavals" and "reversals" can emerge (Deleuze 2004, 300).

When asked by interviewer Claire Parnet whether he thinks he has style—in the "S for style" entry of the *Abécédaire* (Boutang, Deleuze, and Parnet 2004)—Deleuze playfully exclaims: "oh la perfidie!" ("oh the treachery!"), before answering "le style c'est la vie" ("style is life"), adding that he never balks at the thought of having to rewrite a page ten times over, if rewritten it must be. From the reader's perspective, if a block of Deleuze (and Guattari)'s writing often requires to be read more than once, it is amenable, too, to differing forms of reading or "riding," to discontinuous, stochastic modalities of harnessing or bootstrapping. Their "style," which remains to be approached, if not rendered perceptible, involves moments of capture, of tactile or rhythmic adhesion. Beneath the severe guise or disguise of what seems to be the classic style of a philosopher who describes himself as "classic," Deleuze's near-imperceptible traits are even more salient—by their absence—in translation.

Another way of addressing the question of style in Deleuze is to bypass language, meaning, and the "signifier"—against which *A Thousand Plateaus* has engineered a war machine (e.g. in one of Deleuze and Guattari's war cries, "Experiment, don't signify and interpret!" [1987, 12])—in order to capture apparently minor, recurrent surface effects, semi-perceptible cracks or inflexions in writing. The question of Deleuze and language has been analyzed in detail by Jean-Jacques Lecercle in an exemplary study which concludes on the importance of "style" as "a permanent feature" from *Proust and Signs* to Deleuze's last book, *Essays Critical and Clinical*—style being an "apparently *passé* concept" which Deleuze prefers in his last book to "the new-fangled concept of writing," because it "has the requisite ambivalence": "it seems to refer primarily to the art of language . . . and yet it replaces language within a wider range of semiotics" (Lecercle 2002, 256). Lecercle takes up Deleuze's earliest definition of style in *Proust and Signs*, "where it is defined (strangely, for anyone who has read the rest of the *œuvre*) in terms of reaching for essences, interpretation, metaphor and metamorphosis" (256). The "strangeness" of Deleuze's definition can be qualified, however, as soon as one begins to notice what happens to the term *essence* itself at a literal or molecular stylistic level, as soon as one begins to relocate it on the terrain of differential repetition: once *essence* becomes *naissance*. An excrescence, a letter-in-excess brings the closed, essentialist, "passé" system to the point of overload—a status which looks ahead to what *Difference and Repetition* calls, in its last sentence, "the state of excess." The book's final paragraph concludes, and yet continues to gape wide open, on a non-final "*pointe mobile*," perhaps one of Deleuze's closest approximations or mobile definitions of style (2004, 304).

On the "mobile cusp" of style

The foreword to *Difference and Repetition* advises its reader in paradoxical fashion to read the end of the volume first, to operate, as it were, from behind or enter through the back-door: "conclusions should be read at the outset" (Patton 2004, xiv). At the far end of the book's last, restless words, the eye (or any alert sign-receptor ranging from flair to tactile sensitivity) hits upon what the translation renders as a "mobile cusp," a phrase that cannot but call the strongest attention to itself. It occurs at the end of the last subdivision in the conclusion's five-part recapitulation of the volume—in Deleuze's detailed narrative of the "long error [of] the history of representation" and of the necessity to discredit analogy (and by extension metaphors) in favor of univocity (2004, 374).

"*Pointe mobile*" occurs in a carefully wrought textual milieu which bears the mark of several stylistic effects including homonymy (*voix/voies*) and strings of alliterations on the letter *m*. Deleuze's point or, rather, feminine *pointe* materializes the very "tip" of difference itself:

> Le *Tout est égal* et le *Tout revient* ne peuvent se dire que là où l'extrême pointe de la différence est atteinte. Une seule et même *voix* pour tout le multiple aux *mille voies*, un seul et même Océan pour toutes les gouttes, une seule clameur de l'Être pour tous les étants. A condition d'avoir atteint pour chaque étant, pour chaque goutte et dans *chaque voie*, l'état d'excès, c'est-à-dire la différence qui les déplace et les déguise, et les fait revenir, en tournant sur sa pointe mobile. (Deleuze 1968, 388–9, emphasis mine)
>
> (. . . this "Everything is equal" and "Everything returns" can be said only at the point at which the extremity of difference is reached. A single and same *voice* for the whole *thousand-voiced* multiple, a single and same Ocean for all the drops, a single clamour of Being for all beings: on condition that each being, each drop and *each voice* has reached the state of excess—in other words, the difference which displaces and disguises them and, in turning upon its mobile cusp, causes them to return.) (Deleuze 2004, 304, emphasis mine)

At this stage, several remarks must be made about Paul Patton's translation, which in the space of a short paragraph swerves from the original in three instances. In translation something vital is annulled, wiped off, or perhaps simply bypassed in a moment of (understandable) exhaustion: nothing is made of the fact that Deleuze circulates two spellings, two slightly, imperceptibly differing signifiers, not one: (1) *voix* ("*voice*"), (2) *voies* (trails, paths, or ways). Deleuze's stylistic choice of repeated *v*-words (as well as perfect homophones) literally performs and enables aural repetition while maintaining a minor graphic difference (here phonetically annulled). It is the key, albeit minor, factor which graphically yet imperceptibly experiments with difference-and-repetition (to the effect that Paul Patton's otherwise admirable translation fails to render justice to it, leaving it unperceived, unacknowledged, untranslated).

Deleuze's *v*-differential-effect, one might argue, is far from incidental or cosmetic. A few pages earlier, his *defense* of a new kind of affirmative repetition was scaffolded on the possibility of having "two significations for one signifier" (a phrase Deleuze mentions having borrowed from Joachim of Flora), which in the present instance *voies* and *voix* exemplify and experiment with to the letter, by releasing two semantic options for what sounds like one and the same signifier (Deleuze 2004, 297). To the letter, Deleuze's syntagm enacts univocity in its choice of French homophones—admittedly impossible to render in translation. Patton's single use of the same word, *voice*, annuls, however, Deleuze's differential choice. Mistranslation recurs, to a greater degree, when Deleuze's "chaque voie" ("each and every path") becomes, less than comprehensibly, Patton's "each voice."

Two more deviations from the original can be culled from the same page: Deleuze's "extrême pointe de la différence" differs significantly from its rendering in English as "the point at which the extremity of difference," were it only because, once reverse-engineered into French, "the point at which" would unfailingly become "*le* point," in the masculine, thus skirting Deleuze's feminine tropism or "becoming-*pointe*." "*La* pointe" is incomparably more restless than its masculine counterpart, compared to "*le* point" which sticks to its sole signified: a dot, a punctuation mark, a full stop. A *pointe*, in French, liberates a flux of practical, hands-on acceptations: a tip, a top, a spinning top, the ballpoint of a pen, a stylus, the spinning corner of a rolling die, the pointed foot of a ballerina dancing en pointe. Deleuze is interested in a differential "tip" as much as in what makes difference "tip" over or "tilt" differentially, shift gear, reach an apex and spiral on itself (and on its differential selves-to-be) in whirling dervish fashion. Deleuze's *pointe* is, therefore, the exact opposite of a "point" or of a full stop —stopping being entirely irrelevant at this mobile, open-ended "stage," at the precise moment (endowed with much momentum) when such a "starting" term is given prominence.

A third stylistic twist occurs in Patton's rendering of Deleuze's "*pointe mobile*" as "mobile cusp." In contradistinction to a "*pointe mobile*" which conjures up the (invisible) image of a die or the tip of a cone or of a spinning top, the choice of "mobile cusp" runs the risk of placing difference in the confines of post-symbolist aestheticism. No writing, no gambling, no spinning game, no Bergsonian cone can be inferred from the less than mobile image or "analogy" of the cusp. "Cusp" pertains to several fields: astronomy, botany, and geometry, where it designates in turn a pointed end, a fixed apex, the horns of the crescent moon, and (in geometry) the point at which two branches of a curve meet and stop, or "at which the moving point describing the curve has its motion exactly reversed" (*OED*, s.v. "cusp"). A cusp, for short, can hardly be mobile. Here, in the absence of a specific context, the term may be mistaken for a late Symbolist trait, having previously performed as one of the markers of a decadent prose of the kind used, for example, by James Joyce in *A Portrait of the Artist as a Young Man,* where the term appears in Stephen Dedalus' description of Thoth: "the god of writers, writing with a reed upon a tablet and bearing on his narrow ibis head the cusped moon" (1991, 227). The image of the cusp remains, in non-Deleuzian fashion, riveted to the domain of representation and analogy, as well as ill assorted to the "state of excess" called for in the last sentence.

The word *excès*, too, requires to be read in the vicinity of previously disseminated *x*-terms. What is at work in Deleuze's homophonic variations on *voix* and *voies* involves playing a (practical) game with the mark of the plural, with the inscription of a rarer plural suffix in French: *-x*, here repeatedly suffixed to *aux* in "aux mille voies," "aux étants," "aux distributions" (Deleuze 1968, 288). In such a word as *voix*, however, *x* is an invariable fixture, interchangeably singular and plural. Recurrent uses of *x* appear in

Deleuze's earlier analysis of "the power of simulacra," as if that phonetically excessive *x* literally performed as a stand-in (an equivalent, not a metaphor) for simulacra: "the power of simulacra is such that they essentially implicate at once the object = x in the unconscious, the word = x in language, and the action = x in history" (Deleuze 2004, 299). Repeated and displaced in Deleuze's cursory analysis, a mobile *x* recurs, shifting from a singular to a plural use—a transparent, untranslatable mark of univocity as much as an unknown variable. A third *x* occurs in the "state of excess" ("l'état d'excès") which precedes the "pointe mobile." At the outer end or "tip" of the sentence, that active *pointe* performs in excess, endorsing more than one acceptation.

A chain of earlier "points" or *pointes* could be traced across the entire volume, the surface of which they repeatedly pierce like (or as) continental or ocean-formed islands. They hark back, in part, to Hegelian logic, such as "the point of contradiction" (Deleuze 2004, 44). But the restless and arresting, affirmative quality of Deleuze's singular mobile *pointe* isolates it from Hegelian dialectics. One could list, among its implicit precursors, the cone-shaped diagrams of Bergson's *Creative Evolution* and *Matter and Memory* ("a multiplicity formed by the virtual coexistence of all the sections of the 'cone'" [Deleuze 2004, 247]), and the "spinning" mode of Nietzsche's eternal return—part of Deleuze's thesis in *Difference and Repetition* being that the concept of identity be made to "revolve around the Different" (2004, 44).

V for Deleuze: The point of reading

No translation of Deleuze in any language will, it goes without saying, take into account such infinitesimal differentials and micro-variations, although, as we are reminded a few pages earlier in *Difference and Repetition*, what happens at an infinitesimal linguistic level is of paramount importance: "very small linguistic shifts express upheavals and reversals in the concept" (Deleuze 2004, 300). But what exactly does Deleuze mean by "very small linguistic shifts?" What do those "shifts" do? To what extent are they "linguistic"? How shifty or makeshift are they? In this precise occurrence, Patton's translation fits the contours of Deleuze's text with such perfection that nothing is lost in the process: each "v-word" found in the French original, each of these words hired to do what they say to the letter, to spin and revolve repeatedly on the pointed tips of their embedded *v*, finds its way into the English translation—as "upheа*v*als and re*v*ersals" (Deleuze 2004, 373) ("boule*v*ersements, ren*v*ersements" in the original). A *v* occurs and recurs as a shared embedded micro-engine at the core of each "signifier"—which seems to "signify" otherwise, to beckon or emit contagious signals within a common gaseous milieu. Repeatedly, series of *v* are released in the "atmosphere" of Deleuze's writing, made to crystallize into rhythmic aggregates, stepping stones, inorganic wings or corridors of acceleration in the reading pace—performing here the part played elsewhere by the variable *x*.

Without giving in to the temptation of codes, ciphers, and anagrammatic overdetermination, tracing those minor "shifts" is one way of following the concrete, hands-on, life-imbued methodology of a practical philosophy—one in which concepts and "life" interact. No actual code in the semiotic sense rests on such stray uses of *v*, only a (literally) virtual code, which may have the same degree of immateriality as a sign in Proust, or as a "Cipher," a rhythmic force in a war machine (Deleuze and Guattari 1987, 390). Deleuze's uses of *v* emit intermittent, mute variations on a letter that never remains a letter for long. Its variable geometry can accommodate, in turn, a graphic fold, a Roman cipher, a Bergsonian cone-shape, an inflexion, a French circumflex accent in the shape of a dot-sized volcano, a portable island (in other words an "île," to recall the singular object of one of Deleuze's very first published essays, "Causes and Reasons of Desert Islands" [2002, 13]).

The "style" of the concluding page of *Difference and Repetition* emits what could be termed a quasi-code: a leaky, furtive chain of graphic/phonetic/rhythmic signs that stop short of solidifying into stable signifiers or of pointing to a precise referent (cone/dice/pointed shoe/stylus . . .). The earlier uses of *v* found, for example, in the *voie/voix* coupling recur in most of the concepts found on the last page: "re*v*enir," "ren*v*ersement," "indi*v*iduant," "uni*v*ocité" (Deleuze 2002, 388). They grow, like the embedded *v* of *devenir* or (literally) like Henry Miller's grass, mostly in the midst of words, or in the midst of *Difference and Repetition*, if one agrees to see the "pointe mobile" on which it ends as a paradoxical midst and milieu. Whether envisaged as a graphic fold, a *v*-effect, a factor of speed, an exhaling, that "*pointe mobile*" ceases to be metaphorical.

The *v* in the recurring concept of "répétition *v*êtue" ("clothed"); the strangely inverted *v* of Deleuze's myriad circumflexed words; the *v* in "*v*rai coup de dé" and "*v*eritable," the two *v*s of "le *v*éritable uni*v*ersel," the *v* of "ou*v*rir," "déri*v*é," "di*v*ise," and "distributi*v*e," used in the space of two pages (Deleuze 1964, 386–8); the many returns of "in*v*estir" (213) and of the *v*estiary. What is at stake here might be approached, in "anexact but rigorous" terms as Deleuze and Guattari put it when describing Riemanian multiplicities, as a "minor" tongue tunneling through language, a tongue in which vehicle and tenor coalesce (Deleuze and Guattari 1987, 483). Deleuze's multiple "*v*oice" or style breathes, in part, with the help of those "vents" in writing, vestigial pre-signifying *pointes* or graphs found across the philosophical corpus, which contribute to its "readability," to its zones of velocity and coefficient of transitivity. No computer-analysis would serve the purpose of establishing a taxonomy of *v*-effects, or *v*-affects—a non-calibrated concept. In Deleuze's practical philosophic style, one in which philosophy is not differentiated from its object, a letter never ceases to exit its literal frame. A letter can become a propagating path for the power of repetition—each newly stammered *v*-word stumbling onto new bifurcations: some *v*s will endow a word with a micro-cinematic moment or momentum; within a word, behaving as turning tops; others will perform in the guise of cyphers or roman figures (*V* for five), or as diacritical marks (the circumflex accent of two of Deleuze's favorite words, *île* and *vêtir*), or as non-signifying one-letter-word formations exchangeable with the English phoneme [vi:], itself a perfect or imperfect substitute for the French noun *vie* ("life"), in a mindless, subject-free moment of translation-by-contamination or sound propagation. "*V*-e/affects" are, for short, simulacra, "entities with no fixed identity, contradictory or disguised entities in which the dimension of an unlimited and illogical becoming is revealed" (Bogue 1989, 56). In this regime of "universal variation," some *v*s, disguised into *A*s, will stand on their heads, initiate new cracks, breaks, or rhizomes in writing.

Imaging thought

One of the most striking pages in *Difference and Repetition* is devoted to learning (*Apprentissage*) and to the figure of the learner:

Apprendre, *l'Apprenti*—both capitalized, brought up in the last section of "The Image of Thought," in which the question of signs is addressed:

> Problems and their symbolic fields stand in a relationship with signs. . . . An apprentice is someone who constitutes and occupies ("in*v*estit") practical or speculative problems as such. Learning ("*A*pprendre") is the appropriate name ("qui con*v*ient") for the subjective acts carried out when one is confronted with the objectivity of a problem . . . whereas knowledge ("sa*v*oir") designates only the generality of concepts or the calm possession of a rule enabling solutions. . . . The apprentice, on the other hand, raises ("élè*v*e") each faculty to the level of its transcendent exercise. With regard to sensibility, he attempts to give birth ("faire na*î*tre") to that second power which grasps that which can only be sensed . . . from one faculty to the other is communicated a violence which nevertheless always understands ("comprend")[1] the Other ("*A*utre") through the perfection of each . . . we never know in advance how someone will learn ("*v*a apprendre," by means of which loves ("*A*mours") someone becomes good at Latin. . . . The limits of the faculties are encased ("s'embo*î*tent") one in the other in the broken shape of that which bears and transmits difference. There is no more a method for learning than there is a method for finding treasures, but a *v*iolent training, a culture or *paideïa* which affects the entire indi*v*idual. . . . Culture is an in*v*oluntary ad*v*enture ("le mou*v*ement d'apprendre, l'a*v*enture de l'in*v*olontaire"), the movement of learning which links a sensibility, a memory, and then a thought, with all the cruelties and violence necessary. . . ." (Deleuze 2004, 164)

The practical activity of reading this passage involves close proximity between text and reader, between the dense surface of Deleuze's prose and the unexercised Deleuzian "Apprentice" confronted to what in retrospect is as much a cinematic as an acoustic/ graphic textuality. The high frequency of *v*-words here, one might argue, could be attributed to sheer coincidence or to a fixated finder's blinding desire to read a sign into a text.

---

[1] "Understand" here is a case of mistranslation, Deleuze's original verb "comprendre," being used in the Latin sense—the sense it retains in English in "comprehensive"; the proper equivalent here would be "to comprehend," to include, or "to involve."

Alliterating *v*-words, however, saturate Deleuze's style to the point of exhaustion, with such insistence that they pierce the surface of twinned patterns (as in "a*v*enture de l'in*v*olontaire") and key-concepts—of *deVenir* (becoming) and *éVènement* (the E*v*ent); of Vectors, V*ie*—occurring in the title of Deleuze's posthumous essay "*L'Immanence: Une* Vie" ("*A Life*"); of V*itesse* (speed) and Variation; of Venus, in or out of furs. What if *v* was a minimally "broken shape," the "broken shape of that which bears and transmits difference" (Deleuze 2004, 205)?

A principle of multiplicity made letter, *v* gives voice and body to Deleuze's paradoxical way of turning truisms on their heads, of acting as a master of inversions and reversals (of Platonism). Under the "cipher" *V* can be listed (at least) five pseudo-taxonomic headings: (1) a folded, divisive, forking, schizo-letter; (2) an upturned A (for *Apprentice*, *Anti-*, *Autre*, *Aion*, *Alice*, *Albertine*, and many other conspicuous returning figures across the corpus); (3) an inflexion, a circumflex accent (on *être* and *île*, or, to stick to the previous quotation, on *naître* or *s'emboîtent*); (4) a portable introduction to the concept of "flight" or *lettre volante* (a two-winged, flying letter), rather than a *lettre volée* (a purloined letter); (5) an excursus in the (untilled) field of non-semantic, nonsensical phonetic transfers, in which [vi:] becomes *vie (life)*.

Deleuze in V points

Grabbing Deleuze by the forelock of a graphic/acoustic (non)-sign may not only serve to contradict those who tend to believe there is no such thing as writing or style in Deleuze (a statement generally involving, by contradistinction, Derrida)—it may also help to reformulate the question of what *vie* involves, in other words to deflect accusations of vitalism often directed at Deleuze (and Guattari). The last chapter of *Bergsonism,* entitled "Élan Vital *as Movement of Differentiation*," which happens to be chapter V, reflects, above all, on the concept of intensity or "vibrations" (Deleuze 1991, 92) on the possibility of a non-contradiction between dualism and monism, for which is found "a point of unification [which] is itself virtual" (93). *Elan vital* involves differentiation and "ramified series" (95), to the extent that division itself divides. Deleuze writes:

> There are two types of division that must not be confused . . . In the first type, it is a reflexive dualism, which results from the decomposition of an impure composite. . . . In the second type it is a genetic dualism, the result of the differentiation of a Simple or a Pure: it forms the final moment of the method that ultimately rediscovers the starting point on this new plane. (1991, 96)

This second form of dualism—the "genetic" dualism—belongs to the same "plane" as the end of *Difference and Repetition*, where Deleuze's spinning top or mobile tip (or "mobile cusp") is the "point" at which a new plane is made possible. *V*, similarly, forms and reforms a minimal rhizome—a strange "graphoneme" inviting haptic fingers (rather than phenomenological eyes) to follow the divided path of its valley fold.

In Ronald Bogue's essay on style, three stylistic categories (fluctile, aerial, fiery), the same categories that Deleuze had previously developed for Spinoza, are (convincingly) applied to Deleuze himself. Bogue writes:

> if Spinoza's stream of proofs and demonstrations flows with a calm, majestic serenity, Deleuze's river of definitions is more turbulent, full of eddies and whirlpools. . . . If Spinoza's book of fire is isolated in the scholia of the *Ethics,* the Deleuzian counterpart is interspersed throughout his texts. . . . The "aerial" Spinoza emerges in part 5 of the *Ethics* when the geometric method gives way to a "method of invention that proceeds by intervals and leaps, hiatuses and contractions, like a dog searching for something rather than a reasonable man expostulating." (Bogue 1996, 20)

However exemplary the style of Ronald Bogue's own analysis, and the pointedness of the dog image (of the pointer species, perhaps), it is a philosophical and typographical mistake to mention Spinoza's "*part 5* of the *Ethics*" (emphasis mine). Spinoza never wrote a part 5. He wrote a part *V*—which Deleuze inscribes with its Roman figure, unmistakably quoting "*le livre V*" (Deleuze 1993, 184; Deleuze 1997, 149). Taking its cue (or its *v*) from Spinoza's *Ethics*, the composition of *Difference and Repetition* also includes a final chapter *V*, followed by a conclusion, as required by the genre—a conclusion itself carefully and formally divided into V subparts. The last sentence in chapter V, the one which immediately precedes Deleuze's conclusion, ends in an uncouth fashion, on that strangely misplaced, colloquial and un-Deleuzian adverb "e-n-f-i-n," in "cette tendance à l'intériorisation de la différence *enfin*" ("this tendency to interiorize difference at long last/for short") (Deleuze 2004, 335). As is the case for the book's appendage or "*pointe mobile*," there is nothing final or conclusive in this "*enfin*," which does not at all refer to what comes "in the end." "*Enfin*," in this idiomatic, colloquial, spoken use, might best be translated as "if you like" or "for short," or "you know what I mean." It is devoid of any sense of finality, only disguised or made to perform as such. Far from putting a final stop to an academic disquisition, it recodes language as a principle of voluble, uncurbed quintuple arrangements, acting as a portable war-machine: a five-letter word.

Bogue's (1996, 91) conclusion that "one looks in vain for . . . linguistic experimentation in Deleuze," an experimentation of the kind Gherasim Luca and Beckett tried their poetry and prose at, might be qualified as follows: experimentation does occur in Deleuze, one might argue, though not exactly in a "linguistic" format. The *v*-effects or "*v*-affects" this essay attempts to trace do not fall within the precincts of language, and remain on the outer edges of semiotics. They proceed extempore, in a way, as virtual moments actualized (or not) in reading, moments which only reading can turn into mobile lines of flight. Deleuze's folded letter happens, rather, as a let/ter: as an outlet or out-letter, a leaky vessel in the shape of a funnel, a line of dripping, a cone-shaped *infundibulum*.

"Fuite" into "flight": Style-in-translation

Among the foremost concepts coined by Deleuze and Guattari, the *ligne de fuite* emerges, in the French version of *A Thousand Plateaus*, as a composite assemblage involving geometry, escape routes, and plumbing. If the term *fuite* taken in isolation is only minimally related to the "flight" of Brian Massumi's rendering, a "line of flight" operates in a divided way, which somehow relates it to its French counterpart. *Fuite* involves two semantic directions: leaving, leaking—both mentioned by Massumi in his introductory note on the translation: "*Fuite* covers not only the act of fleeing or eluding but also flowing, leaking, and disappearing into the distance (the vanishing point in a painting is a *point de fuite*). It has no relation to flying" (Massumi 1987, xvi).

Yet *flight* provides a vibrant, recognizable equivalent of the sensation of actually reading Deleuze. Flying occurs from the first page of *Spinoza: Practical Philosophy*, which Deleuze prefaces with an excerpt from Malamud's novel *The Fixer*, inviting the figure of a character who describes the experience of reading Spinoza as a moment of fast-track traveling "as if there were a whirlwind at my back," or "as though you were taking a witch's ride" (Deleuze 1988, 1)—a description equally applicable to Deleuze and Guattari, to their *v*-ridden, wind-blown texts. Similar terms are used in Deleuze's account of the process of thought in Foucault, which, Deleuze (1990b, 129) explains, "is like a wind that blows at our back and moves us forwards by gusts and starts"—in the flight, or hedge-hopping mode. Of Foucault's own lines of flight Deleuze writes in *Negotiations* that "we ride such lines whenever we think bewilderingly enough or live forcefully enough" (1995, 110) ("nous chevauchons de telles lignes chaque fois que nous pensons avec assez de vertige ou que nous vivons avec assez de force" [1990b, 149–50]). The original "vertige" or vertigo of thinking connects two planes—flying, and reading—as do the folded "v"-patterns of Deleuze's differential style.

The difficult task of translating Deleuze and Guattari's concepts recently received new exposure in *Deleuze et Guattari à vitesse infinie* (Rosanvallon and Preteseille 2009), a study which isolates the term *auto-survol* from the last pages of *What Is Philosophy? Autosurvol*, or auto-overflight, describes the plane of immanence on which the field of perception becomes unified: "it becomes unified by flying over itself" ("*en se survolant*") (as cited in Deleuze and Guattari 1994, ix–x, my translation). For the translators of *What is Philosophy?*, it is a mistake however to translate *survol* by anything connected to actual flight, since *survol* is imported from Raymond Ruyer's *Néo-finalisme* (1952), in which it is used "to describe the relationship of the 'I-unity' to the subjective sensation of a visual field." Therefore, they explain, they have chosen to render it by *survey*, directing readers in a footnote to the translators' choice in *Logic of Sense*, where *survolant* is also rendered by *surveying* (Hugh Tomlinson and Graham Burchell, in Deleuze and

Guattari 1994, x; see also Deleuze 1990a, in which *survolant* is translated as *surveying*). One of the imperceptible reasons why *survey* has been preferred is perhaps that its syllables harbor the same mobile "point," the same pair of wings as *survol*, the same internal *v*—which literally assumes part of the task of thought, part of its vertigo, while resisting the pressure for metaphors. No alphabet, it goes without saying, contains such a "letter" for long. Deleuze's *v*s grow both initially and internally, in the midst of words, thus impeding watertight classifications. They could only appear in a non-ABC primer of "V-losophy" or "philosoVi:," a tentative discipline requiring a pair of *v*-shaped antennas to feel its way about—the void.

The void? René Schérer, Deleuze's lifelong friend and colleague at the University of Paris 8-Vincennes, begins his book on Deleuze by reminiscing the circumstances of the philosopher's death on November 5, 1995 (more fives). Schérer avoids the difficult, painful task of commenting on his friend's death in philosophical terms, arguing that the event "gardera son mystère" ("will retain its mystery" [Scherer 1998, 10, my translation]); that Deleuze "flew away," chose to evaporate, to become imperceptible. To this end, one might add, the panes of a window had to be opened, into and beyond the angle of a *V*, before a body flew and fell, committed to the void (or the volcano) of Avenue Niel in Paris. A strange Deleuzian line, a line in a "state of excess" remains as an after-effect, a "line" insistently spelt and respelt in the chain of mobile letters that form the name of Avenue N-i-e-l, a name ready to respell a line or a *lien* in stray formation.

In the chapter of *Negotiations* that immediately precedes the fifth and last one (chapter V, devoted to *Politics*), one reads: "we need both wings, as Jaspers would say, just to carry us, philosophers and non-philosophers, towards the same final point" (Deleuze 1990, 166)—in the original French: "Il faut les deux ailes, comme disait Jaspers, ne serait-ce que pour nous emporter, philosophes et non-philosophes, vers une limite commune" (Deleuze 1990b, 225).[2] Deleuze's "limite commune" is not quite the "final point" found

[2]My own attempt at retranslation: "it takes two wings, as Jaspers would say, were it only to be flown, philosophers and non-philosophers alike, towards a common limit." There is no reason to translate "limit" (a line) by "point," when one is in the least familiar with Deleuze's dislike of points (in the masculine) as opposed to pointes or lines.

in the English translation. Nor is this sentence the final one on the page. Deleuze adds, against all odds: "it takes all three wings, nothing less, to form a style, a bird of fire" ("il faut trois ailes au moins pour faire un style, un oiseau de feu")—by which he refers to Spinoza's three tongues, to the three styles that operate beneath the smooth surface of Spinoza's Latin: concepts, affects, and percepts. Three wings? One too many? Not if Deleuze's bird of fire is understood in non-metaphorical fashion—understood as a singular assemblage: two wings to fly, one extra wing (or feather) to write, in the aviary mode.

References

Bogue, Ronald. 1989. *Deleuze and Guattari*. New York: Routledge.
—. 1996. "Deleuze's Style." In *Deleuze's Wake: Tributes and Tributaries*, 9–26. New York: State University of New York Press.
Boutang, Pierre-André, Gilles Deleuze, and Claire Parnet. 2004. *L'Abécédaire de Gilles Deleuze, Avec Claire Parnet*. Paris: Editions Montparnasse. DVD.
Deleuze, Gilles. 1964. *Proust et les Signes*. Paris: Presses Universitaires de France.
—. 1968. *Différence et Répétition*. Paris: Presses Universitaires de France.
—.1973. *Proust and Signs*. Translated by Richard Howard. New York: Allen Lane.
—.1981. *Spinoza Philosophie Pratique*. Paris: Editions de Minuit.
—. 1988. *Spinoza, Practical Philosophy*. Translated by Robert Hurley. San Francisco: City Lights Books.
—. 1990a. *The Logic of Sense*. Translated by Mark Lester. New York: Columbia University Press.
—. 1990b. *Pourparlers 1972–1990*. Paris: Les Editions de Minuit.
—. 1991. *Bergsonism*. New York: Zone Books.
—. 1993. *Critique et Clinique*. Paris: Les Editions de Minuit.
—. 1995. *Negotiations 1972–1990*. Translated by Martin Joughin. New York: Columbia University Press.
—. 1997. *Essays Critical and Clinical*. Translated by Daniel W. Smith and Michael A. Greco. Minneapolis: University of Minnesota Press.
—. 2002. *L'Ile déserte et autres textes: Textes et Entretiens, 1953–1974*. Edited by David Papoujade. Paris: Les Editions de Minuit.
—. 2003. *Proust and Signs: The Complete Text*. Translated by Richard Howard. Minneapolis: University of Minnesota Press.

—. 2004. *Difference and Repetition*. Translated by Paul Patton. New York: Athlone Press.

Deleuze, Gilles and Félix Guattari. 1987. *A Thousand Plateaus*. Translated by Brian Massumi. Minneapolis: University of Minnesota Press.

—. 1994. *What Is Philosophy?* Translated by Hugh Tomlinson and Graham Burchell. New York: Columbia University Press.

Joyce, James. 1991. *The Portrait of the Artist as A Young Man*. New York: Signet Classics.

Lecercle, Jean-Jacques. 2002. *Deleuze and Language*. Basingstoke: Palgrave.

Malamud, Bernard. 1964. *The Fixer*. New York: Farrar Straus and Giroux.

Massumi. 1987. "Notes on the Translation and Ackowledgments." In Gilles Deleuze and Félix Guattari, *A Thousand Plateaus*, translated by Brian Massumi, ix–xv. Minneapolis: University of Minnesota Press.

Patton, Paul. 2004. "Translator's Preface." In Gilles Deleuze, *Difference and Repetition*, vii–x. Athlone Press, Continuum: New York.

Rosanvallon, Jérôme and Benoît Preteseille. 2009. *Deleuze et Guattari à vitesse infinie*. Paris: Editions Paul Ollendorff.

Ruyer, Raymond. 1952. *Le Néo-finalisme*. Paris: Presses Universitaires de France.

Schérer, René. 1998. *Regards sur Deleuze*. Paris: Editions Kimé.

13

Styling theory *à la mode cixousienne*

Janice Sant

The stylus is incisive: its pointed tip punctures the wax tablet upon which it inscribes the signs, one at a time. Cautiously, the hand guides the stylus across the blank slate and carves the text into being. The other end of the stylus, however, is blunt and flat. It can render the surface smooth again, allowing the writer to retouch and correct, if and when necessary. Yet before the stylus styles or restyles, there is, for Hélène Cixous, a more decisive puncture, namely, the stigma. The collection of essays in her 1998 *Stigmata: Escaping Texts*, as she explains in the preface, "share the trace of a wound" (2005a, xi). Like the pointed end of the stylus, the stigma "carves out a place for itself" (xiii). Not only, however, for Cixous makes a fortuitous discovery: in the world of plants, the stigma is part of the pistil, the female life-bearing part of the flower, where the male pollen germinates. The stigma extends outwards from the ovary through the stalk to capture the pollen and start the process of flowering.

Insofar as "what is dead and what will live share the same bed," as she puts it, Cixous does not fear her stigmata: "I do not want the stigmata to disappear. I am attached to my engravings, to the stings in my flesh and my mental parchment" (2005a, xiv). Hence, the stigma and the stylus function in parallel ways. They both take away and give birth, scar and sow life. The stigma wounds the flesh and germinates the pollen; the stylus carves the tablet and gives birth to the text. This conflict between life and death is not alien to Cixous who thinks of the scene of writing as a battlefield in which multiple conflicts come to pass. She does not try to tame the tempest on the page; neither does she shy away from the bloodshed. Rather, in Cixous's hand the stylus turns stabbing instrument as she attempts to enter the interiority of her subject and to delve beyond the skin's wholesome outer layer.

Clearly less politically charged than some of her early manifesto-like texts, the essays gathered in *Stigmata* celebrate lesions and resurrections alike. The sheet of paper becomes the locus for conflict and the stroke of the writer's pen is testimony to the turmoil of the writing experience. Even before the first mark is inscribed, Cixous feels the struggle that presents itself at the very inception of thought when the writer must perforce translate the language of thought into the language of writing. No matter how fast the scribbling hand hastens on, it is ill suited to keep up with the speed of thought. Indeed, the chasm between the two languages grows wider when the writer pauses to look back at the text in order to erase and revise. Such are the gestures that Cixous refuses to perform. In rejecting the idea that *error* is something that the writer must avoid and, failing that, must erase, Cixous may be seen to refuse the blunt end of the Roman stylus. Overcoming the temptation to take a backward glance, she scrawls thought as it hurtles forward without end. The result is a text that is characterized by a rawness of style, which lays bare the spontaneous nature of thought.

In a letter to Martin McQuillan in which she explains why she cannot write the "Post-Word" to a volume of essays on "Post-Theory," Cixous describes poets as those "who, at lightning speed, want to write, write, *before*, in the still-boiling time before the cooled fall-out of the narrative when we feel and it is not yet called such-and-such, this, him or her. Tempest before the immobilisation, the capture, the concept. Where there is already the murmur of words but not yet proper-name-words" (1999, 211).[1] Cixous seems to point at theory's time or the time *for* theory and suggests that the poetic, unlike the theoretical, is true to life precisely because it is concerned with the *before* of the text. If theory, like an appendix or afterword, is what follows the word, the poetic is

---

[1]All italics in quotations in this chapter are those of the author quoted unless otherwise indicated.

what precedes the very birth of the word. More than a foreword or a word before the word, the poetic is to be found *before* the beginning in which the word was. Understood as that which succeeds the literary thing it contemplates, theory is always positioned at the *post*; its time is always, therefore, the time *after* the literary event or happening. As Cixous tells Mireille Calle-Gruber in an interview, she is wary of the term "theory" and its implications:

> What is most true is poetic because it is not stopped-stoppable. All that is stopped, grasped, all that is subjugated, easily transmitted, easily picked up, all that comes under the word concept, which is to say all that is taken, caged, is *less* true. Has lost what is life itself, which is always in the process of seething, of emitting, of transmitting itself. . . . There is a continuity in the living; whereas theory entails a discontinuity, a cut, which is altogether the opposite of life. I am not anathematizing all theory. It is indispensable, at times, to make progress, but alone it is false. (Cixous and Gruber 1997, 4)

Guarding against the fatality of the concept, Cixous is on the side of life (see Derrida 2006b and Stefan Herbrechter's essay in this volume). What interests the self-proclaimed poet is, in fact, the poetic which seems to call for an altogether new *temps* (time/tense). Neither past nor present nor future, the poetic belongs to the time of the *pre*-present which is in a perpetual state of arrival. Rather than seeking to capture the essence of the text as theory tends to do, the Cixousian text sees before the word and gives right of way to the happening of thought in its (pre-)nascent state.

Similarly, Jean-Luc Nancy, writing in "The Birth to Presence," proposes to merely "expose" and "abandon" thought at its inception (1993, 5). He makes a distinction between the "*verb*" that traces the passage of thought and the discourse that "*names*" it conclusively (4). He goes on to argue that thought at its birth very often falls prey to philosophical appropriation and suffers irremediable loss when it is passed over into what he describes as "ornamentation" or "the repetition of philosophy" (5). The obsession of the Western philosophical tradition with representation has had the adverse effect of limiting thought's reach. Nancy underlines the importance of thought's coming into being: "Not form and fundament, but the pace, the passage, the coming in which nothing is distinguished, and everything is unbound. What is born has no form, nor is it the fundament that is born. 'To be born' is rather to transform, transport, and entrance all determinations" (2). Hence, thought in its nascent state is still uninhibited by the conventions of form. Nancy elaborates that the "poverty of thought" is "a matter neither of 'genre' nor of 'style'. It goes much further. It is, quite simply, a question of knowing, in a voice, in a tone, in a writing, whether a thought is being born, or dying: opening sense, ex-posing it, or sealing it off (and wishing to impose it)" (4). Both Cixous and Nancy may be seen to oppose the birth of thought to the death of theoretical and philosophical conceptualization.

For many Anglo-American readers whose first encounter with the work of Hélène Cixous is very likely to come under the misleading category of "French feminist theory," the assertive claim quoted above that theory is an act of "immobilization" and is therefore allied with death may seem counterintuitive. The volume *Stigmata*, first published by Routledge in 1998, is classified as "Literature," "Philosophy," and "Gender Studies," whereas the 2005 edition—published by Routledge Classics—appears as "Literary/Critical Theory," "Feminist Literature and Theory," and "Literature and Gender Studies." The categories are so varied and general that they seem to be of very little help as an introduction to the genre of the book. Indeed, as shall be made clear in what follows, any attempt to classify or pin down a text by Cixous is highly problematic since her work resists such formalization. Nonetheless, in view of the questions posed by this volume, it is worth asking why *Stigmata*, while it is classified as such, is never simply theory understood in a conventional sense. Given that the essays inhabit the very space opened by theory through their devoted reflection on the literary, the rubrics are not entirely erroneous. However, it should be immediately evident to the reader, not least given Cixous's contempt for rigid generic strictures, that such writing does not fall neatly within the genre of *theory*.

This essay seeks to delve into how Cixous does *theory* while simultaneously refusing to do it in *its* (own) style. Her claim that "theory alone is false" and that yet, at the same time, it is "indispensable" is indicative of her choice to style theory alternatively. Paying particular attention to "Writing Blind: Conversation with the Donkey," one of the essays in *Stigmata*, this essay explores Cixous's fascination with the instant of thought's gestation and outlines the ways in which she attempts to transmute thought into a writing that flees that which "threatens to fix, to nail, to *immobilize* [it] in, by, death" (Cixous 2005a, xii). As she is quick to point out, the "first and best ally in the evasion is the poetic use of the languages of language" (xii). Indeed, Cixous's *styling* of theory is clearly poetic. As Derrida writes in his epigrammatic foreword to this volume, the texts in *Stigmata* are, to be sure, "a great poetic treatise" (2005, ix).

In "Writing Blind," Cixous explores the genesis that occurs before writing and the possibilities of tracing this "nudity from before all clothing" (2005b, 187). Itself a performative text that inscribes the writing it describes, this text may be seen to evade the fixity of theory by refusing to conform to the rigor of theoretical discourse. In spite of its essentially theoretical strain—this is a text that explores the *writing* (*l'écriture*) of writing—it indiscriminately blurs the distinctions between the autobiographical, the fictional, the poetic, and the theoretical. In an effort to remain true to the realm of "no more *genre*," as she describes it, Cixous abides by one law alone, that is to say, the lawlessness of blind writing (185). She warns the "policeforce reader" not to expect the accepted: the book "does not fit the description. It does not answer the signals. It does not get a visa" (199). Crossing borders *sans papiers*, Cixous has little patience with the constricting rules of genre and the laws of property and propriety. The distinctive quality that emerges in this essay may be introduced using Cixous's phrase "fugue style" (2005c, 45). Coming from the Latin word *fugere* meaning "to escape," the word "fugue" points at the motif of flight that has a central place in the Cixousian oeuvre. In her seminal "The Laugh of the Medusa" (1975) Cixous incites women to action and calls for a "*new insurgent* writing" that can come into being by means of flight (1976, 880). *Voler*, which in French plays on the two meanings "to steal" and "to fly," is essentially a woman's gesture. Thrilled to turn both burglar and bird, Cixous relates this stealthy flight to an act of defiance against the Law:

> What woman hasn't flown/stolen? Who hasn't felt, dreamt, performed the gesture that jams sociality? Who hasn't crumbled, held up to ridicule, the bar of separation? Who hasn't inscribed with her body the differential, punctured the system of couples and opposition? Who, by some act of transgression, hasn't

> overthrown successiveness, connection, the wall of circumfusion? (1976, 887–8)

In her more recent texts, Cixous also progresses through flight. The text escapes (remember the subtitle of her volume: "*Escaping Texts*") and the writer, fugitively, runs after it. Both the text and the writer, therefore, are on the run. The question, here, is: What are they fleeing?

In a word: *Master-y*

Well known for her notion of *écriture féminine*—a term she coins in "The Laugh of the Medusa"—Hélène Cixous proposes a writing that does not fall under the hegemony of patriarchal rule. In a text from the 1970s, "Castration or Decapitation?," Cixous wages war against the cast-iron hierarchical oppositions embedded in Western culture and attacks the structures of what Derrida has termed "phallogocentric" discourse.[2] She writes: "There's work to be done against *class*, against categorization, against classification—classes. 'Doing classes' in France means doing military service. There's work to be done against military service, against all schools, against the pervasive masculine urge to judge, diagnose, digest, name . . . not so much in the sense of the loving precision of poetic naming as in that of the repressive censorship of philosophical nomination/conceptualization" (1981, 51). Defiantly, Cixous turns her back on the schoolmaster who dictates the purportedly correct male-centered text and inscribes, in its stead, a text that upsets the order of (the) class.

In the opening paragraphs of "Writing Blind," Cixous leaves the broad daylight of apparent certainties and rejoices ecstatically in the act of closing her eyes to the Law. She delights in the fact that the word "*passage*" does not stay in line. To the Francophone ear, it splits into two words: "*Pas sage* (ill-behaved/unwise)" (2005b, 186). She hears an interdiction, warning her against choosing the path of error. Yet she is not deterred; on the contrary, unexplored territories intrigue her. Like Eve in the Garden of Eden,

---

[2]This Derridean neologism combines the notion of "phallocentrism" to that of "logocentrism." It refers to the dominance of the word in certain forms of essentially male-dominated modes of reasoning and conceptualizations of the world.

whom Cixous admires for not having heeded the Word of God the Father, she succumbs to temptation. Deliberately, she strays into the anarchic night which is uninhibited by constricting rules of so-called proper comportment. The experience of letting go is described as follows: "When I close my eyes the passage opens, the dark gorge, I descend. Or rather there is descent: I entrust myself to the primitive space, I do not resist the forces that carry me off. There is no more *genre*. I become a thing with pricked-up ears. Night becomes a verb. I night" (185). Descending into Hades, where Eurydice naively waits for Orpheus to bring her back to the world of the living, Cixous enters the untrodden path of darkness. Recall Maurice Blanchot's description of Orpheus's role: "His *work* is to bring it [the essence of night] back to the light of day and to give it form, shape, and reality in the day" (1982, 171). Notwithstanding their disparate motives, however, both Orpheus and Cixous forgo the possibility of giving orderly shape and form to "night."

In the realm of "no more *genre*," as the French word suggests, both literary and sexual difference are driven, Lethe-wards, into oblivion. To be sure, Hélène Cixous claims that her very being undergoes a metamorphosis into "thing." In the night prior to fixed stereotypical identities even the certainty of the writer's identity is in question. Indeed, the "I" voice in the text slips in and out of the more indefinite "we." The unified person-subject is renounced in favor of an anonymity that Cixous embraces. Not only does she abolish the *author* (or master of the text) from the scene of writing, but she also does away with the writer in order to give pride of place to a more humble profession, namely, that of the scribe who merely listens to and notes down the dictates of the book. For in the fecund time of profusion that precedes the concept, "nothing is proper, nothing is of its own" (Cixous 2005b, 188). Rather, everything exists in a boundlessness that cannot be easily translated into text. Cixous writes that the "book"—a word replete with Mallarméan and Blanchotian overtones—happens in a suddenness that is alien to the linear progression of the written text: "A book is just about round. But since to appear it must adjust itself into a rectangular parallelepiped, at a certain moment you cut the sphere, you flatten it, you square it up. You give the planet the form of a tomb" (194). In an attempt to retain the book's spherical nature, Cixous weaves the text through her preferred modes of progress: "In language I like and I practice the leap and the short-cut, ellipsis, amphibology, speed and slowness, asyndeton" (191). Indeed, sentences and paragraphs progress musically only to be interrupted abruptly by unexpected pauses. Words take their liberties and transgress their dictionary definitions. Turning a blind eye to the law, the word "night" refuses to stay in its category of words. It slips out of the class of nouns and transmutes into verb: "I night," Cixous, now blind, asserts.

It may appear that this primordial darkness in which established rules are turned on their head is anterior to, and hence ignorant of, the conventions of *proper* writing. A devoted guardian of the unconscious, Cixous's blind writing is, in fact, reminiscent of Julia Kristeva's semiotic approach to language that offers a critique of meaning and its underlying laws. In the influential *Revolution in Poetic Language*, Kristeva makes the distinction between the "*phenotext*" and the "*genotext*" (1984, 86–9). Whereas the former refers to univocally determined texts that obey the rules of communication, the latter points at texts that unleash the semiotic drives of the earliest stages of the subject. The poetic impulse of language, as she explains, preserves traces of the pre-symbolic state. For Kristeva, these two textualizations cannot be thought of as self-sufficient autonomous texts. As Dawne McCance (1996, 147) succinctly explains, "signification requires both the semiotic and symbolic modalities: even as the metalanguage of a monological subject, signification cannot completely close off the semiotic, and neither is there any possibility of meaningful signification outside the pro-positioning of a conscious subject." Indeed, Cixous's blind writing functions within similar parameters. It is clear that the desire to write theory while at the same time fleeing its signature rigor compels her to bring together the poetic and the theoretical in the very act of giving birth (in the French sense of *donner le jour*) to the text.

The pervasive presence of the first-person pronoun, as well as the apostrophic "you," in "Writing Blind," underscores the text's pronounced lyrical quality. The personal address first surfaces as Cixous invites the reader to partake in the act of writing: "Let us close our eyes. The night takes me. Where do we go? Into the other world. Just next door. So close yet so difficult to access. But in a dash we are there" (2005b, 186). True to the desire to capture the punctuality of the instant, Cixous describes the writing experience as it happens in the immediate present tense, refusing as she does so to turn the text into a system or prescriptive program. This is a text that refuses to believe in "mechanical fabrication," or "models" (195, 197). Rather it embraces the element of surprise and allows the text to retain its fragmentary and telegraphic quality: "Astounding or stunning sentences come by surprise. Like divine messages: prophecies of the present. If only we heard ourselves! If only we saw ourselves! If only we read ourselves" (195). The urgent tone that emerges in these sentences is present intermittently in this work and can be seen, in certain instances, to give way to a more reflective and personal tone as is evident in the following extract:

> *About the person whose name is You*:
>
> I write you: I write to you and I write *you*. I will never say enough what (I) my writing owes you.
>
> I address myself to you. You are my address.
>
> Each book is in a certain way a letter that wants to be received by you.
>
> But it is not *for* you that I write: it is *by* you, passing through you, because of you ——— And thanks to you each book takes every liberty. Crazy liberty, as you say. The liberty to not resemble, to not obey. But the book itself is not crazy. It has its deep logic. But without you I would be afraid of never being able to return from Mount Crazy. But I can lose myself without anxiety because you keep me. This book is not a narrative, it is not a discourse, it is a poetic animal machine, the grain of its skin is pure poem. Because you keep watch, this book gives itself the freedom to escape from the laws of society. (Cixous 2005b, 199)

Arguably, this could not be more distant from what one may expect a theoretical treatise to read or sound like. Having no qualms about not being taken seriously as a theorist, Cixous does not style theory in what may be traditionally deemed proper to it. The style of the above extract is, in fact, reminiscent of Derrida's *envois* in *The Post Card* where the identity of the addressee in the carefully divulged intimate exchanges remains blanked out. Like Derrida,

Cixous does not disclose the identity of the person "whose name is You." At times, it seems that she too is at a loss for answers regarding the identity of the subject-less pronouns that people this text. This is evident, for instance, in the asyntactical phrasing of the question: "Me is thus the meeting place between my sighted soul and you?" (Cixous 2005b, 187).

The discursive quality of the text is sustained through the intrusions of autobiographical anecdotes that intersperse the text. These brief interludes, which read more like journal entries or notebook jottings, welcome the Air France employee, her sometimes disapproving mother, her prematurely lost father, her brother and her daughter into the fabric of the text in sentences that bring the very life of the writer's everyday world to the fore. There is no rule for what must remain outside the theoretical text and what is granted rightful access into it. In pondering the very issue of what should be barred from and what should be let in the text, she writes: "I do not know where outside happens or if the text is inside, inside outside or if the text is itself outside, or if the outside is in the text. This is what happens when one writes what happens" (Cixous 2005b, 193). The suggestion is that writing "what happens," or more generally, writing *itself*, should not leave anything *outside*. Indeed, if Cixous were to have it her way, the Bible would faithfully report the conversation that she imagines Abraham had with his donkey on his way to Mount Moriah. In a delightfully unexpected dénouement to her argument, she declares: "I would like to give the donkey the floor. One does not say foolish things [bêtises] to a donkey, do you agree? Nor to a cat" (190). Following her own dictates, she allows her cat inside the text, claiming, as she does so, that it brings her "closer to the formation of [her] soul" (202). Judged by her own yardstick, Cixous cannot be found guilty of straying from the path of her subject, that is to say, that of writing blind. For this entails including anything that the writer feels and thinks as she writes. The text, therefore, is not centered around a particular concern or subject, as such. Rather it merely comes into being as the scribe faithfully records the "discontinuous elements" (189) as they present themselves.

The multiplicity of tonalities and voices in this text destabilizes the notion of a single *author*. Indeed, this essay may be described, to use Derrida's words, as "a choreographic text with polysexual signatures"—one that does away with the monological and monosexual voice (1988, 183). Yet by the same stroke, Cixous creates a text that is essentially singular in its style and, one may argue, remarkably Cixousian. Paradoxically, the writing that attempts to free itself from the author's distinguishing *signature* is evidently hard put to attain such anonymity precisely because few writers are willing to give right of way to such flightiness. Evidently, Cixous manifests a relentless resolve to do theory in her own style. Fugitively, she shifts from poetical address to theoretical insight, from assertive declarations to unanswered questions, from the certainty of daylight to the indeterminacy of nighttime. This serpentine labyrinth on the way to writing challenges the reader's conventional modes of reading while slipping in and out of existing genres. Her mode of styling theory, far from abiding by the laws of convention, poses a challenge to classification and the very notion of *genre*. As Derrida writes in *Geneses, Genealogies, Genres and Genius*, Cixous's texts, indeed, "every single letter" of her texts is "incommensurable with any library supposed to house them, classify them, shelve them." Still more provocative, he adds: "Bigger and stronger than the libraries that act as if they have the capacity to hold them [works of great writers like Homer, Shakespeare, Joyce and Cixous] . . . they derange all the archival and indexing spaces by the disproportion of the potentially infinite memory they condense according to the processes of undecidable writing for which as yet no complete formalisation exists" (2006a, 15). Indeed, in "Writing Blind" Cixous may be seen to mix a number of genres: namely, autobiography, the dialogue, the diary, the fragment, the letter, and the lyric. And, to this inventory, one may add the dream and the notebook—two essentially Cixousian modes of writing.[3]

Derrida explores the intricacies of this blending of genres in "The Law of Genre" where he opens with the interdiction: "genres are not to be mixed," only to call into question this seemingly indisputable law (1980, 55). By sleight of hand, he lifts the ban against the mixing of genres, arguing that the very notion of genre is made possible through an a priori counter-law of "contamination" and "impurity" (57). The issues relating to propriety and

---

[3]Cixous (2004; 2006) has published selections from both her notebooks and her dream journals. See also what Derrida (2006b, 75–6) says about Cixous writing "by dream."

belonging that are fundamental to discussions of genre are thus severely challenged. Rather than compromising the strength of the law of genre, however, Derrida argues that the counter movement against the law legitimizes it further.[4] In "Title (To Be Specified)," he maintains that such subversions "would have no force without the instance of the law they seem to defy; they would have no reason for it without drawing reason from it, without provoking it" (1981, 22). It follows, therefore, that genres *are* to be mixed; indeed, it is "impossible not to mix genres" (Derrida 1980, 57). Hence, Derrida's argument would seem to fall in line with Gérard Genette's well-known assertion in *The Architext* that no text can lay claim to being free from genre (1992, 83).

Yet in Derrida's view there is, in fact, a way to avoid getting caught up in the system. In relation to Blanchot's elusive "*La folie du jour*," he argues that a text can free itself from generic determination through "a sort of participation without belonging" (1980, 59). Blanchot's indecisive *récit*, he comments, seems to exist "to make light of all the tranquil categories of genre-theory and history in order to upset their taxonomic certainties, the distribution of their classes, and the presumed stability of their classical nomenclatures" (63). Whereas Derrida maintains that each text bears a "trait" that signals its genre, he asserts that such a trait is, perplexingly, what can never *belong* to any genre or class. Rather, this trait, which is always already "remarkable," "excludes itself from what it includes" (64). This barely perceptible grafting can never fully take root as a result of what Derrida has called the "clause or flood-gate of genre." He explains: "The clause or flood-gate of genre declasses what it allows to be classed. It tolls the knell of genealogy or of genericity, which it however also brings forth to the light of day. Putting to death the very thing that it engenders,

---

[4]Derrida's argument in this essay is exceedingly close to Blanchot's stance in the essay "At Every Extreme" where he writes: "We must rather think that, each time, in these exceptional works in which a limit is reached, it is the exception alone that reveals to us this 'law' from which it also constitutes the unusual and necessary deviation. It seems, then, in novelistic literature, and perhaps in all literature, that we could never recognize the rule except by the exception that abolishes it: the rule, or more precisely this center, of which the certain work is the uncertain affirmation, the already destructive manifestation, the momentary and soon negating presence" (Blanchot 2003b, 109).

it cuts a strange figure; a formless form, it remains nearly invisible, it neither sees the day nor brings itself to light" (65). This "strange figure," it would appear, rests on the penumbral margins of the established Wor(l)d, existing in an in-betweenness that frees it from determination. To return to Nancy's words in "The Birth to Presence," this is the figure of a text—or a thought—that is still "being born."

Likewise, Cixous's formless text holds on fast to the moment of birth and refuses to cut the umbilical cord that binds it to the pre-natal. As Peggy Kamuf writes in her reflection on Derrida's reaction upon first reading Cixous, Cixous brings forth "an absolutely im-possible child, the first-born of a new kind, as yet unbaptized and uncleansed by the world's belief" (2009, 28).[5] Yet this before*ness*, however true to the poetic, paradoxically immobilizes the text (in spite of its volatility) in a perpetual state of becoming. As *sage-femme* (mid-wife) of *écriture féminine*, Cixous stresses that such writing is always in passing: "her writing can only keep going" (1976, 889) and "writing is not arriving" (1993, 65). As such, the Cixousian text hesitates between the *pre*-present (not yet) of birth and the future (to come) of the passage. Thus retaining the promise of a future. In "To Give Place: Semi-Approaches to Hélène Cixous," Kamuf insists that Cixous's style of doing theory calls for an approach that goes beyond the commonly held view (within Anglo-American circles) of French feminist theory. Taking her cue from Toril Moi's reading in "Hélène Cixous: An Imaginary Utopia," she chooses to describe Cixous's theoretical writing as "semi-theoretical" (2005, 118; see Moi 2002, 100–2). She argues that this "contaminating non-category of the 'semi-'" describes Cixous's *theory* more fittingly for it allows for the hesitation in-between genres that is characteristic of her texts (2005, 119). She writes: "A semi-name is not altogether there, it does not name a presence, nothing that *is*; rather, it calls for something to present itself otherwise. If semi-theory responds to, is responsible for, this semi-effacement that carries so little weight in the present, it is because it gives place to that which as yet has no name: a future" (119). Yet, arguably, it is precisely this futurity that betrays the text. In seeking to evade the death of theory, the text does not

[5]For Derrida's reaction upon first reading Cixous, see Derrida 2006b, 7, 147–8.

cease escaping into a(n) (im)possible future. As Blanchot elaborates in "The Book to Come," the time of the work is suspended between the future that "will never abolish" and the "past future perfect" that "will not have taken place" (2003a, 241). Consequently, one waits *without end.*

And whereas the lure of what is yet to come is undoubtedly beguiling, one cannot help but question, on the side of, and with, Cixous: "*Mais quand donc arrivera le futur?*" (Cixous 2010, 26). Published in *Le rire de la Méduse et autres ironies* (2010), Cixous's brief essay entitled "*Un effet d'épine rose*" traces the trajectory of "The Laugh of the Medusa" 35 years after its publication. In a tone that is markedly different from the manifesto that held so much promise for writing, Cixous may be seen to take a backward glance and acknowledge that the laughter of the Medusa has somewhat abated. While challenging the reader's conventional modes of reading, experimental or avant-garde writing also places the onus (and, hence, the responsibility of the future of the book) on the reader. In *H.C. for Life, That Is to Say . . .*, Derrida envisages a time when Cixous *will* be read: "I foresee, therefore, and I foretell, I announce what will take place one day, when one reads her [*quand on la lira*] at last" (2006b, 135). This time may perhaps mark the instant when the present readily coincides with the future and the text, no longer an escapee, proclaims, not the birth *to* presence but, rather, and finally, the birth *of* presence.

References

Blanchot, Maurice. 1982. "Orpheus's Gaze." In *The Space of Literature*, translated by Ann Smock, 171–6. Lincoln: University of Nebraska Press.

—. 2003a. "The Book to Come." In *The Book to Come*, translated by Charlotte Mandell, 224–44. Stanford: Stanford University Press.

—. 2003b. "At Every Extreme." In *The Book to Come*, translated by Charlotte Mandell, 107–10. Stanford: Stanford University Press.

Cixous, Hélène. 1976. "The Laugh of the Medusa." Translated by Keith Cohen and Paula Cohen. *Signs* 1(4): 875–93. www.jstor.org/stable/3173239.

—.1981. "Castration or Decapitation?" Translated by Annette Kuhn. *Signs* 7(1): 41–55. www.jstor.org/stable/3173505.

—. 1993. *Three Steps on the Ladder of Writing*. Translated by Sarah Cornell and Susan Sellers. New York: Columbia University Press.
—. 1999. "Post-Word." Translated by Eric Prenowitz. In *Post-Theory: New Directions in Criticism*, edited by Martin McQuillan, Graeme Macdonald, Robin Purves, and Stephen Thomson, 209–13. Edinburgh: Edinburgh University Press.
—. 2004. *The Writing Notebooks of Hélène Cixous*. Edited and translated by Susan Sellers. New York: Continuum.
—. 2005a. "Preface: On Stigmatexts." Translated by Eric Prenowitz. In *Stigmata: Escaping Texts*, xi–xvi. New York: Routledge.
—. 2005b. "Writing Blind: Conversation with the Donkey." Translated by Eric Prenowitz. In *Stigmata: Escaping Texts*, 184–203. New York: Routledge.
—. 2005c. "In October 1991. . . ." Translated by Keith Cohen. In *Stigmata: Escaping Texts*, 43–62. New York: Routledge.
—. 2006. *Dream I Tell You*. Translated by Beverley Bie Brahic. Edinburgh: Edinburgh University Press.
—. 2010. *Le rire de la Méduse et autres ironies*. Paris: Galilée.
Cixous, Hélène and Mireille Calle-Gruber. 1997. *Rootprints: Memory and Life Writing*. Translated by Eric Prenowitz. New York: Routledge.
Derrida, Jacques. 1980. "The Law of Genre." Translated by Avital Ronell. *Critical Inquiry* 7(1): 55–81. www.jstor.org/stable/1343176.
—. 1981. "Title (To Be Specified)." Translated by Tom Conley. *SubStance* 10(2): 4–22. www.jstor.org/stable/3684327.
—. 1988. "Interview: Choreographies." Translated by Peggy Kamuf. In *The Ear of the Other: Otobiography, Transference, Translation*, edited by Christie McDonald, 163–85. Lincoln, NE: University of Nebraska Press.
—. 2005. Foreword to *Stigmata: Escaping Texts*, by Hélène Cixous, ix–x. Translated by Eric Prenowitz. New York: Routledge.
—. 2006a. *Geneses, Genealogies, Genres and Genius: The Secrets of the Archive*. Translated by Beverley Bie Brahic. Edinburgh: Edinburgh University Press.
—. 2006b. *H. C. for Life, That Is to Say. . . .* Translated by Laurent Milesi and Stefan Herbrechter. Stanford: Stanford University Press.
Genette, Gérard. 1992. *The Architext: An Introduction*. Translated by Jane E. Lewin. Berkeley: University of California Press.
Kamuf, Peggy. 2005. "To Give Place: Semi-Approaches to Hélène Cixous." In *Book of Addresses*, 114–31. Stanford: Stanford University Press.
—. 2009. "Outside in Analysis." *Mosaic* 42(4): 19–34.
Kristeva, Julia. 1984. *Revolution in Poetic Language*. Translated by Margaret Waller. New York: Columbia University Press.

McCance, Dawne. 1996. "*L'écriture limite:* Kristeva's Postmodern Feminist Ethics." *Hypatia* 11(2): 141–60. www.jstor.org/stable/3810268.

Moi, Toril. 2002. "Hélène Cixous: An Imaginary Utopia." In *Sexual/Textual Politics: Feminist Literary Theory*, 100–25. New York: Routledge.

Nancy, Jean-Luc. 1993. "Introduction: The Birth to Presence." In *The Birth to Presence*, 1–6. Translated by Brian Holmes. Stanford: Stanford University Press.

14

Theory . . . for life

Stefan Herbrechter

Je vis comme si j'avais quarante vies . . .
. . .
Je me fuis de vie en vie.
. . .
Moi par moi délogé, remplacé,
Par d'autres plus puissants habitants
Ma vie sans moi par une vie où je serai
Pourra se remplacer.
[I live as if I had forty lives
. . .
I escape from life to life
. . .
Me by myself dislodged, replaced
By other more powerful inhabitants
My life without me by a life where I will be
Can be replaced.

—ARMAND ROBIN, "*Quarante vies [Forty Lives],*"
Ma vie sans moi

Style de vie—life, in theory

There is a rather funny moment in *Derrida*, the film, when Derrida tells an anecdote about his mother reprimanding him for misspelling difference with an "a." This is a moment that might encapsulate in many ways the question about theory and style, style in theory, theory as style, and the theory of style. Is it really necessary for theory to make life so difficult, so counterintuitive? This essay is not intended as some counterattack on apparent everyday-life populism in favor of an intellectualism removed from practical usefulness—as if the non-theoretical was always to be found on the side of *real* and *useful* life, practical life, or living, whereas theory, by implication, would somehow be removed from life, dead, maybe even death itself, at least on the side of death. Instead, this is an attempt to see theory on the side of life, asking whether theory has a life, a life of its own, whether theory actually might *be* life, not just alive but somehow *for life*, at least more than death, and thus it is also an attempt to show that there is life in theory, still and always, that one can dwell in theory, actually live, in theory, that one might somehow, and indeed maybe always and only, live in theory.

In theory, one should have a life. Many people would say, instead, that maybe a theorist should get a life, meaning that he or she should get out more. Presumably, to experience the *real* life, the buzz, the hum, the pleasure of living life to the full, to consume life. Life is time is capital and thus indulgence; life is what you make it: the meaning of life is "x"—to be determined. Interestingly, this rather intimidating phrase, "the meaning of life," has recently been resurfacing with increased regularity. In fact, there seems to be a new urgency in the meaning-of-life-thematic to be seen in the proliferation, or should that now read pro-*life*-ration, of *life* issues. Maybe what is at stake here, in theory, is, and maybe has always been, nothing less than the undefinability of life itself.

Deconstruction, poststructuralism, theory, has a deep affinity with what Derrida calls "*plus d'une langue*" (1988b, 38)—no longer (just) one and *at the same time* more than one language, which, arguably, might be the most accurate description of a plurilingual life, or a life in language(s). *Plus d'une langue*, as maybe the most existential stance of theory, creates a curious remove from any particular language, but not in the form of transcendence—one can never transcend language as such nor can one transcend a language, not even one. It is rather a peculiar, slightly tragic experience, at least momentarily, of some inbetweenness, of being or living in translation, even if this position is always reconstructed, *posthumous*, so to speak, after the effect and affect. Theory is therefore not unrelated to a very specific understanding of *life-writing*, namely of a life in languages, or life-in-languages. It is therefore more than just (a linguistic) style, if style means a particular form or appearance, or character, as an antonym to substance or content. The whole point, or style, of theory, instead, is to show that form and content, appearance and reality, life and death, or style and substance cannot be separated.

Style as a way of life, *style de vie*, is an expression that follows the same *onto-logic* described above in relation to language(s). Just as you can dwell, at least temporarily, between language(s), you can inhabit the space in between ways or styles of life, between life(s). It is not so much a suspension of life but a kind of dehiscence, an interruption, even though time does not stop, unfortunately, at least not biological time, Heideggerian time or being-towards-death.

It is useful to remember that one of the major spin-offs of theory in the Anglo-American academy is almost entirely an investigation into style in the sense of lifestyle, namely cultural studies. Raymond Williams's definition of culture as a way of *life*, or the so-called anthropological, nonnormative, or descriptive definition of culture, quickly led to a pluralization of styles, and lives under investigation. In particular, subcultural analysis flourished following the postmodern aestheticization of *life* as the result of the pluralization of *lifestyles*. Dick Hebdige's influential *Subculture: The Meaning of Style* (1979) uses Jean Genet's subversive style of revolt as an analogy for the meaning of subculture. Style is "intentional communication," he claims: "The communication of a significant *difference*, then (and the parallel communication of a group *identity*), is the 'point' behind the style of all spectacular subcultures" (Hebdige 1979, 100, 102).[1] The *monstrosity* of style—literally and in the etymological sense of "showing," "giving to see" (cf. Latin *de-monstrare*)—lies in its *revoltingness* and the revolt speaks through its style. But, most importantly, style is recognized by Hebdige as a signifying practice—arguably the most central

[1]All italics in quotations in this chapter are those of the author quoted unless otherwise indicated.

phrase of poststructuralism and theory. Signifying practice is precisely that which problematizes the distinction between content and form, style and substance, all the while, quite ironically, foregrounding language. The medium is the message, but precisely for this reason, medium and message cannot be dissociated. Lifestyle is a shared signifying practice which creates its own subjects: "*le style, c'est le sujet pris et torturé par le langage* [style is the subject caught in and tortured by language]," as Michel Arrivé explains in relation to Lacan and his style ("*Lacan sur le style, sur le style de Lacan*," in *Qu'est-ce que le style?* (1994, 76). Rather than simple "ornament" [*parure*] or idiosyncrasy [*tic*], style is inscribed or even prescribed in concrete subject positions, as Michel Riffaterre, in the same volume on style, agrees, citing Buffon's aphorism: "*Le style c'est l'homme même* [style is the man, person or human himself or as such]" (Riffaterre 1994, 283).

The notion of inscription is of course inscribed into the very concept of style with its etymology of stylus, the marking of wax tablets, and with it the entire question of memory, the trace, or the archive. Style is a historical inscription, or a reflection of its time but it is also an attempt to transcend time and to "make a difference," as Edward Said explains in his last, unfinished book *On Late Style*: "Any style involves first of all the artist's connection to his or her own time, or historical period, society, and antecedents; the aesthetic work, for all its irreducible individuality, is nevertheless a part—or, paradoxically, not a part—of the era in which it was produced and appeared. This is not simply a matter of sociological or political synchrony but more interestingly has to do with rhetorical or formal style" (Said 2006, 134).

Theory's lifeblood is language, and language, quite literally, is an issue of life and death, for theory. The literal or rather *letteral* understanding of language in this way is what constitutes theory, even its essence, the truth of its style—which is another aspect of the phrase living in language(s). That is arguably what is most fascinating in theory, namely its awareness of linguistic relativity and linguistic inevitability, *at the same time*, language's finite-infinite play, encapsulated in Derrida's famous aporia: "Yes, I only have one language, yet [French: *or*, yet, therefore] it's not mine" (1998, 2). This has nothing to do with the idea of a "prisonhouse of language," nor with any hermeneutic notion of a "*Haus der Sprache*."

As Paul de Man pointed out in "The Resistance to Theory," an essay he starts by evoking "this autonomous potential of language" which he finds in literature and rhetoric: "The resistance to theory is a resistance to the use of language about language. It is therefore a resistance to language itself or to the possibility that language contains factors or functions that cannot be reduced to intuition" (1986, 12–13). However, one has to add, that theory itself is not immune to this resistance. Theory *is* the resistance in more than one sense, including an *autoimmunitarian* one. Resistance to theory is the resistance to language understood in precisely the way outlined above. One could argue that the resistance to theory is a resistance to an ontological understanding of language. For de Man, as we know, the resistance to theory is itself theoretical and can therefore never be overcome, nor can theory *die* because it always *survives* in the language of *self-resistance*. However, de Man's prophecy might have been too optimistic for theory's flourishing (which, as he said, would be indistinguishable from its fall). Post-theoretical times tell the story of increasing exasperation with theory. It is said that style has killed theory, and worse, that theory's style is killing language, and since style is indissociable from writing, theory might be one giant thanatography.

As John Schad writes at the beginning of his volume *life. after. theory*: "the moment of 'high' theory appears to have passed" (2003a, ix). However, the "After" in his title, he explains, is meant as "in pursuit of": "Could life be in pursuit of theory? Could life ever imitate theory? And, indeed, what is 'life'?" (x). He puts life in inverted commas and claims that "theory has made us wary of the idea of Life, or indeed any other organicist master-word" (172). But however wary of life one might be, its *style*, life's style, constantly inscribes itself into the matter of the universe which, of course, means that life as living present is only ever accessible as trace, or *différance* and in deconstruction, which turns deconstruction, or theory, into a kind of *life-writing*; "it is, however, life implicated in death, or *thanatos*," as Schad explains, "hence Derrida's conceitful talk of his 'auto*biothanato*heterographical opus'" (173). Theory is, in a sense, what *remains* of life, the traces of life's meaning, reconstituted and interpreted in a fashion, or style. "If life is, necessarily, *after*-life; if all living is a form of 'living-*on*' . . . then theory is very much a form of life," Schad concludes (176).

How then to account for the recent resurgence in the theoretical interest in life. Two examples of the resurgence of the phrase, "meaning of life," are Rupert Read's *Philosophy for Life* (2007) and Terry Eagleton's *The Meaning of Life* (2007). Both probably want to be understood as treatises on life-affirmation, but both, inevitably, are inscribed in a *clear and present danger* logic. The threat of imminent death—of humanity, for example—heightens the sense of and brings out the best in life, or so it is hoped. Read, in his "Conclusion: Philosophy for Life" summarizes: "The first decade of the third millennium is a time of vast peril and vast opportunity for humankind" (2007, 135). "Philosophy can be a radical and powerful tool for starting something good," as long as it reminds us of our "embeddedness in the ecosystem" (136) and urges "a certain humility in the face of the wonder and horror of human life" (137). Rather less humility, interestingly, is required in relation to *style*, where Read confidently proposes to "reclaim politics" by reclaiming "the English language" (137), following Wittgenstein and Chomsky, back from its *metaphysical* to its *everyday use*. This no-nonsense commonsensical, pragmatist, and eminently realist approach is designed to make philosophy relevant again to "our actual lives": "Philosophy *for* Life. . . . That is, philosophy *on the side of* life. The fundamental question of the twenty-first century is whether human life as we know it, human civilization, will survive at all" (138). The call to arms for a change in philosophical-*cum*-life style predictably ends in a threatening promise or a promising threat: "We will sink or swim together" (139).

So was theory, then, merely some stylistic aberration, one may ask. Eagleton, who famously turned his back on theory, who, one could say, has gone over to the other side, seems to think so, as his equally blatant *no-frills* approach makes clear: "There is a sense in which those who deny the reality of the human condition also deny global warming. Nothing ought to unite the species as effectively as the possibility of its extinction. In death, at least, we come together" (Eagleton 2007, 140). Eagleton, however, in the end retreats to a form of contemplative cynicism: "No doubt our continuing wrangles over the meaning of life will prove to be fertile and productive. But in a world where we live in overwhelming danger, our failure to find common meanings is as alarming as it is invigorating" (175).

Theory for life, that is to say . . .

Given the general disenchantment with theory, is there life after *theory? "Is there life after deconstruction?"*

—LODGE 1990, blurb

Derrida's last book, *H.C. pour la vie, c'est à dire . . . (2002), H.C. for Life, That Is to Say. . . (2006)*, is all about sides, and in particular about being on the side, especially on the side of life and/or on the side of death. It is also a book about an extraordinary friendship between Hélène Cixous who is, as Derrida claims, always on the side of life, and Derrida himself, who, as he explains, cannot be on her side. Nevertheless, it is a friendship *for life*. Derrida explains the title in an interview with both Cixous and himself in *Magazine littéraire* entitled "*Du mot à la vie* [From (the) Word to Life]": "*C'est pour la vie*—wants to express both loyal and unfailing friendship, forever [*à jamais*], for life but also for life [*pour la vie*] which for her [*chez elle*] is an affirmation, a taking sides for life that I never managed to share. I'm not 'against life' but I'm not 'for life' as she is. This dissonance [*discordance*] is at the heart of the book—and of life" (Derrida and Cixous 2004, 26). But Cixous is quick to add that Derrida is nevertheless "fiercely [*farouchement*] for/on the side of/in favour of [*pour*] life. But otherwise. *In/quiètement*" (26). *In/quiètement*—with a slash between *In* and *quiètement*: worriedly, anxiously, uneasily, but also calmly, both worried and calm, apparently, at the same time. Un/easily for life, or maybe uneasy about life? How is that possible? How to take sides here, between Cixous, who is all for life in the affirmative and unreservedly, and Derrida who is "un/easy" about life and about the very idea of taking sides, but all the more conscious of death, which, however, as Cixous explains, and Derrida endorses, is not a side, not a side to *be* on. Death is not a side because it is the annihilation of life, and therefore one cannot be on its side, because one cannot be on the side of death, where death *is*, precisely, by negotiating being.

Undoubtedly, despite this difference, what brings Cixous and Derrida together is their curious relationship to language, a language shared but through their respective "monolingualism of the other," the almost tragic remove from one's *own* language, in their case French, which for Cixous is the cause of her *algériance* and, for Derrida, his *nostalgérie*, their mutual autobiographies-in-translation or life (in) writing. "*Au commencement, il y a le mot* [At the beginning, there is the word]," "*Du mot à la vie* [From (the) word to life]," as the interview says: "Yes, at the beginning is the word. . . . As if I was thinking nothing before writing: surprised by such a resource of the French language that I didn't invent, and I do something with it that wasn't programmed but which was already made possible by some lexical or syntactical treasure" (Derrida and Cixous 2004, 26). Language invents; in other words, language is alive with words: "*Tout me revient, mais depuis la langue—qui se passe de moi en passant par moi*" (26). Which is, of course, untranslatable because it is already the experience of translation, but translation into and within one's supposedly *own* language—*being*, translated, but also being-translated by and in language. Everything comes back to me but also belongs to me. I'm responsible for it—*tout me revient*, but ([*mais*], but one might even have expected *or* here, as in "*je ne parle qu'une langue, or c'est n'est pas la mienne*") it comes back to me *from* language, *depuis*, from or ever since, language, which always precedes, maybe even *life*, language *before* life. It is this ontological love of language that Cixous admires in Derrida as if it was her own: "I envy his titles. His hypersensitivity as to what these words in French conceal both *folittéralement* and *philosophoniquement*" (26). Untranslatable, again: madness, literally, or the madness that lies in taking language literally, and the idea of doing philosophy through (homo)phony, philosophonics . . . as for example in *H.C. pour la vie* where the C for Cixous is a (near) homophone to *c'est* for "it is"—Hélène is for life, and "that is to say [*c'est à dire*]," which is translation itself: that is to say, in other words, the figure of translation even within (one) language, but also that which has to be said, which always remains to be said—an injunction.

So how to make sense of this "for life" and "that is to say"? And why would Derrida not be on the side of life, at least not as *affirmatively* as Cixous and maybe also many others who recently have helped to shift the discussion, maybe the whole of *theory* toward life, or the issue of life, for life—theory for life? Cixous's power, Derrida says, her might, her *puissance*, lies in her ability to *jump* and to replace, or in her speed and transgression, maybe even the ignoring of boundaries:

> This nullification of the border, this passage of the forbidden between the public and the private, the visible and the hidden, the fictional and the real, the interpretable and the unreadable of an absolute reserve, like the collusion of all genres, I believe, is at work at every moment. It is the very work of her writing, its operation and its opus, which, although literary through and through, also goes beyond literature, just as it goes beyond autobiography. And my hypothesis will be that the excess and surplus of this passage precisely passes through *life*, a word that becomes all the more obscure. (Derrida 2006, 12)

Life—italicized in this passage—becomes more and more obscure, the more the boundaries are *transgressed*. Much of theory has been about the transgression of all sorts of boundaries, so much so that theory is almost synonymous with this transgressing movement, a movement that is most recognizable in a certain combative style, situating itself both before and beyond an identified boundary that is or remains to be transgressed. And, one could argue, the result of it has been an *outbidding* of boundary transgression. Finding—or cynics would say, inventing, one could also say mounting—the boundaries that are to be transgressed, theory raises the stakes with every transgression. Power becomes more powerful, life more mysterious, and life in turn becomes the ultimate boundary that contemporary theory has set itself to transgress, or might already have transgressed.

What is thus at stake in theory is life, theory for life, theory *à jamais* and *pour la vie*. A notion of life *before* death or maybe "out/side" death—life whose other side would precisely no longer be death, as Derrida understands Cixous's affirmation:

> I do not know whether, more than her, sooner than her, better than her, anyone will have ever given me to think what *to live* means. Not that she taught me how to live—that is not the same thing, and it could sometimes resemble its exact opposite, I mean "learning how to die." Not that in giving me to think what to live might mean, she assured me that living meant something, something in relation to which thought and knowledge would go hand in hand and would grant us something, giving us over to something firm and reassuring. No, giving me to think what amounts to living even beyond any will-to-say [*vouloir-dire*],

> beyond any "that is to say," and maybe even beyond any will, beyond a living or a life that would still depend on a will, a will-to-live [*vouloir-vivre*], beyond any knowledge, any power, and any contradiction, for example between living and dying. (Derrida 2006, 16–17)

These are so many "beyonds," so many superlatives and hyperboles to evoke the *miracle* of believing the unbelievable—which, according to Derrida, is the only true *faith*, faith in life, because believing the believable would not require the impossibility that faith demands, the possible-impossible, that is to say life without death—*pas de mort, la vie sans mort.*

Life *itself*, however, resists translation, which would be its arrest or death. Instead, it is language or life, but not as a question of choice, because there is no *other side* from which to choose, for example between life or death. And this has been the case for theory from the very beginning. It is not as if we had just discovered life, as an object of knowledge or science, as the phrase "life sciences" might suggest. *Au commencement la vie la mort*, René Major writes (1999), referring to Derrida and the inseparability and undecidability between life and death, deathlife or lifedeath, which gives rise to *différance*, or spectrality, and turns ontology into hauntology. "Living, by definition, cannot be learned. Not by itself/not by oneself, not by life from life [*de la vie par la vie*]. Only by or from the other and by death," "living just like dying cannot be learned [*ne s'apprend pas*]," as Jean Birnbaum quotes (from *Specters of Marx*) in Derrida's "last interview," *Apprendre à vivre enfin* (Derrida 2005, 15–16). Instead, *lavielamort* is the experience of life as *living-on* as *survivre, survivant, survivance*, even before any notion of "*Dasein*" or ontology in general. As Derrida explains in *The Post Card*, reading Freud's "death drive" and François Jacob's *La logique du vivant*, side by side: "If death is not opposable it is, already, *life death*," and in doing so, he undoes a whole tradition of "life science," from the start, for which "[t]he end of the living, its aim and term, is the return to the inorganic state, The evolution of life is but a detour of the inorganic aiming for itself, a race to the death. It exhausts the couriers, from post to post, as well as the witnesses and the relays" (1986, 355). It is "send[ing] oneself the message of one's own death" or "keep[ing] oneself from death" in a movement of reappropriation (which is "the most driven drive," but also the drive in which "life death are no longer opposed," or on two sides): "Before all else one must auto-affect oneself with one's proper death (and the self does not exist before all else, before this movement of auto-affection), make certain that death is the auto-affection of life or life the auto-affection of death" (355–9). The immanence of death in life causes the auto-immunitarian instinct for which Western metaphysics, if such a thing exists, is so infamous. It is a war-like state that is reproduced in every self, in every subject, but can it really be overcome or maybe *outlived*, which is something completely different from a Derridean sense of *survived*, or haunted living? "I am at war with myself," Derrida says, "it is true, you cannot possibly know to what extent, beyond what you might guess, and I'm saying contradictory things which are, let's say, in real tension constructing me, make me live, make me die. This war I sometimes see it as a terrible and painful war, but at the same time I know that this is life" (2005, 49). Life is at war with itself, or maybe even at war with *its* self. That's life—*c'est la vie*. Or rather, *c'est la survie*, which is the only knowledge of life possible: "living-on is an original concept that constitutes the very structure of what we call existence, the *Dasein*, if you wish. We are structurally survivors, marked by this structure of the trace, or the testament" (54). The mistake that should not be made, however, is to equate Derrida's idea of life as surviving with some form of morbid thanatography (death inscribed within life) or as necropolitics (i.e. politics as the power over life and death, still understood as two sides of a choice) (on necropolitics see Mbembe 2003, 11–40). As if there were two sides, one turned toward death and the past, and the other, turned toward life and the future.

This much Derrida agrees on with Cixous; there is only affirmation: "deconstruction is on the side of the yes [*du côté du oui*; which is the only side possible], of the affirmation of life" (54): an *unconditional* affirmation of life. "*La survivance, c'est la vie au-delà de la vie*. Life beyond and more than life [*La vie plus que la vie*]" (55), "for surviving is not just what remains, it is the most intense life possible" (55). Derrida credits Cixous with occupying that side, the only one possible, of life and still, he regrets not being able to join her, on her side, the side of life, simply because: "If I were on her side, I could not speak of her nor tell her anything whatsoever" (2006, 21). He could not speak of her or about her, or of life nor death, which, of course would be worse than death.

"Indeed, when one is *on the side of*, one is not close; one has to be on the other side, on the other side of the other, in order to be close. When one is on the same side, paradoxically, one is not close, there is no longer any distance or proximity; neither speed nor slowness" (38).

So how indeed does *she* do it? Being on the side of life, unconditionally, while continuing to write—a curious form of life-writing indeed: "life, whence everything derives and detaches itself and toward which everything comes and comes back. Life has no other, it has no other side; and all the sides, all the asides, all the sidesteppings leave their traces on the same side of the same vein" (Derrida 2006, 39). It is the resulting undecidability—being on the same but *only* side which calls for the decision, which, for Derrida, has to pass through the experience of the impossible but can only be affirmative: "Because it is undecidable, one can decide and settle only for life. But life, which is undecidable, is also, in its very finitude, infinite. What has only one side—a single edge without an opposite edge—is in-finite. Finite because it has an edge on one side, but infinite because it has no opposable edge" (48). *For* life, to be *for life*, the whole mystery lies in the *for*. What comes *before* life, from which position to be *for* or *against* life, from which side to argue? That is precisely why it is impossible to be against life, why there is only one side, always already *for* or *before* life. It is the life of the other, for the life of *me*: "before the being-for, and even the being-of-life-for, there would be the life-for-life, the *for-life*, which at once gives and replaces life with life in view" (87–8). Living for the sake of living—that might be the definition of Cixous's writing, for Derrida.

Life-writing

A discourse on life/death must occupy a certain space between logos *and* gramme, *analogy and program, as well as between the differing senses of -program and reproduction. And since life is on the line, the trait that relates the logical to the graphical must also be working between the biological and biographical, the thanatological and thanatographical.*

(DERRIDA 1988a, 4–5)

So why then, as Derrida insists, stay turned toward death? Is it merely a question of style, or lifestyle, as if there were two *styles de vie*, maybe also two *styles de déconstruction*, the one turned toward death, nostalgerian, all the while enjoying life and affirming everything "*parce que c'est passé, fini* [because it is passed, finished]"—the last words of "*Apprendre à vivre enfin*" (Derrida 2005, 55); or the other, on the side of life for life, which certainly does not mean ignoring death, rather *outliving* or *outspeeding* death, overtaking it: "Death counts for her, certainly, on every page, but she herself does not count" (Derrida 2006, 158), "*mais elle, elle-même, elle ne compte pas*" (Derrida 2002, 136). There is an ambiguity in "*elle*": Who does not count, death, in the feminine, *la mort*, or her, *elle*? Death *herself*, death *as such*, or Cixous, *her self*, what or who does not count? And what does *counting* mean in this context?

Cixous's, it appears, would be the missing *logique de la vivante*, not Jacob's logic of the living, but of the living—feminine, like *la vie*, opposed to a masculine, *le vivant* or in the plural universal *les vivants*. And this is precisely what is at stake in theory, today, but arguably, already from the beginning: "*le vivant*," the undecidability between life and death, or the living-on (*survivance*). That which is neither on the side of death, which is no side, nor entirely identical with life, on the other side of life, maybe, where all forms of life and nonlife, organic and anorganic seem to proliferate, machines, cyborgs, viruses, genes, molecules, minerals, plants, and so on. Maybe this is a neo- or even ultravitalism somehow liberated from the very notion of *life*, or from an ontology of life, and entirely turned toward the living presence, whatever in life is *living*, some kind of pure force, the "*élan vital*" without the heroism of life, or "bare life," "*zoē*," as opposed to "*bios*," as Agamben claims (1998, 1–2).

It remains to be seen, however, as Christopher Johnson remarks in "*La vie, le vivant*"—his contribution to *L'animal autobiographique* —"whether this new science (e.g. 'life science,' '*les sciences de la vie*') is not, in the end, finally [*à la fin, enfin*] a science of death, ultimately following the economy *of* death *in* life" (Johnson 1999, 361). It is thus not surprising that there is so much talk of *life* in theory these days, life in all its forms. On the one hand, there is the irreducible plurality of life-forms, while, on the other side, there seems to be life itself, bare life, *zoē*, *bios*, with their associated forms of bio-, necro- or, at worst, thanatopolitics. It is as if the *end of man*, the apparent antihumanism of theory, thematized in the landmark Colloque de Cerisy in 1980 on "*Les fins de l'homme*" (Lacoue-Labarthe and Nancy 1981) had finally, and ironically, given birth to *life*, life after people so to speak, posthumanist if not posthuman, arguably post-theoretical, but at least hopefully post-anthropocentric. The posthumanist (bio-zoo-thanato-) politics of life which is starting to see the day under these new circumstances comes in various forms. Donna Haraway, for example, understands it as "multi-species flourishing" (2009, 131). It becomes clear that the last borderline was always going to be life—from the theory wars to the culture wars to the science wars and, maybe, now *life wars*. And with regard to the danger (the desire for *and* anxiety of), the possibilities of *posthuman* life, theory has been shifting rapidly, maybe all too rapidly, and it has raised the stakes to embrace the war *for* life, which increasingly looks like the war *on* life, and raises the question of life's *precarity*, as Judith Butler puts it in her *Precarious Life* (2004), to address the escalation of biopolitics, and the generalization of the *state of exception*, by attempting to re- or neo- *vitalize* itself. Facing the general posthumanizing drive, it is important to remain mindful of the potentialities but also critical of the speed with which desires are taken for inevitabilities. It is worth recalling life to the letter, so to speak—*du mot à la vie* and back. Affirming life seems to require, literally, saying *yes* to life, first. But even affirming life is not the same as living; it is not the same as living (a) life. Theory, of course, cannot *be* life, even though it may be trying hard these days to theorize what life *is*—theory as *life-writing*.

To give just a few examples and a few names that are key to this revival and pro*life*ration of life in theory today: on the one hand, on the one side, the side of death probably, are the late followers of Aristotle: from Hannah Arendt to Michel Foucault and Giorgio Agamben, who are all in their own way thinkers of *biopolitics* based on the impossible but necessary distinction between *bios* and *zoē*. To complicate matters, according to Agamben, this is a distinction that modernity has blurred and continues to do so, which gives rise to the idea of the *state of exception*, the exposure of *bare life*, which, in turn, becomes the main *material* for and the main *stake* of modern politics.

On the other hand, the other side, maybe the side of life, are the late followers of Spinoza, Bergson, and Darwin. Deleuze and

Guattari and Rosi Braidotti, to name just these as examples, who are proponents of a new *vitalism* based on the idea of *biocentrism* (presumably opposed to metaphysical anthropocentrism). Biocentrism is to be seen as the celebration of all life, of life as life, life in all its forms, including material everyday life and even life in its technological forms (i.e. the life or lives of the future). A life is here understood as *pure immanence*, in the Deleuzian sense, which, in a sense, only makes this proliferation of life—*bios* and/or *zoē*—thinkable, because it coincides with the advent of life technologies that go far beyond any modern *technologies of the self* (see Deleuze 2001). Titles like *Bits of Life* (Smelik and Lykke 2008), *Life as Surplus* (Cooper 2008), *The Politics of Life Itself* (Rose 2007), *Biocapital* (Rajan 2006), *On Creaturely Life* (Santner 2006), *Inventive Life* (Fraser 2006) or *Wetwares: Experiments in Postvital Living* (Doyle 2003) and so many others underscore this. While Agamben's argument in *Homo Sacer*, *Remnants of Auschwitz* and *The Open* has been widely discussed, it might be enough for the present context to focus on one example from the neo-vitalist side. Rosi Braidotti accuses Agamben and arguably the whole *phallogocentric* philosophical tradition, including Derrida, of a fixation on Thanatos or necropolitics. Instead, she, on her side, the side of life, supposedly, argues that the emphasis should fall "on the politics of life itself as a relentlessly generative force. This requires an interrogation of the shifting inter-relations between human and non-human forces. The latter are defined both as in-human and as post-human" (Braidotti 2007). In short, Braidotti claims, "death is overrated," and what in her view constitutes the potentialities of posthuman politics calls for a shift from "bio-power and necro-politics" is "the primacy of life as *zoē*," as "vitalistic, prehuman, generative life" (Braidotti 2008, 177). In order to oppose and escape the traditional humanistic necropolitical tendency she follows Deleuze and Guattari in their attempt to "trespass all metaphysical boundaries" by celebrating a "becoming animal, becoming other, becoming insect, becoming machine," in short, embracing becoming a "posthuman" body: "a living piece of meat activated by electric waves of desire, a script written by the unfolding of genetic encoding, a text composed by the enfolding of external prompts," which is Braidotti's take on *life-writing* (Braidotti 2008, 180). This "becoming corpse" (2006, 40), which she understands as a "Spinozist ontology" (40), is set against the "metaphysics of finitude" (40), which negates life and overrates death, according to her, seen from her side. It is affirmative, or the affirmation of life itself, neomaterialist, feminist, and embodied and above all eco-logical and postanthropocentric. It is worth quoting some passages at length in order to get an impression of Braidotti's style and speed:

> I am developing . . . a sustainable brand of nomadic ethics. The starting point is the relentless generative force of *bios* and *zoē* and the specific brand of transspecies egalitarianism that they establish with the human. The ecological dimension of philosophical nomadism consequently becomes manifest and, with it, its potential ethical impact. It is a matter of forces as well as ethology. (2008, 183)

And, only two paragraphs down, she accelerates:

> The vital politics of life as *zoē*, defined as a generative force, resets the terms of the debate and introduces an ecophilosophy of belonging that includes both species equality and posthumanist ethics. (2008, 183)

And, gathering speed, on the next page:

> I propose a posthumanistic brand of nonanthropomorphic vitalism. To defend this position, I start from the concept of a sustainable self that aims at endurance. (Braidotti 2008, 184)

Over pages and pages of programmatic life force follow and almost reach escape velocity:

> A higher form of self-knowledge, through an understanding of the nature of one's own affectivity, is the key to a Spinozist ethics of empowerment. It includes a more adequate understanding of the interconnections between the self and a multitude of other forces, thus undermining the liberal individual understanding of the subject. . . .
>
> At this point, it is important to stress that sustainability is about decentering anthropocentrism. The ultimate implication is a

> displacement of the human in the new, complex compound of highly generative posthumanities. In my view, the sustainable subject has a nomadic subjectivity because the notion of sustainability brings together ethical, epistemological, and political concerns under cover of a nonunitary vision of the subject. . . . "Life" privileges assemblages of a heterogeneous kind. Animals, insects, machines are as many fields of forces or territories of becoming. The life in me is not only, not even human. (2008, 189–90)

These passages are characteristic of Braidotti's style: relentless, driven, forceful, full of life, obsessed with, *performing* transgression, one could say. Without question, Braidotti would be on the side of Cixous. Theory for life, that is to say . . . for all the promise and necessity of posthumanism, as a *critical* and theoretical step toward embracing the challenges of *our* residual humanism, *our* anthropocentrism, *our* necropolitics, you name it. You *NAME IT*—that is to say. At this juncture, it seems the necessity arises to slow down and ponder the question of the power of naming *it*? For life has the capacity to name itself, as Derrida describes in referring to Cixous's style: ". . . *une puissance d'hétéronomie* . . ." (2003, 59). Cixous's power of heteronomy, the naming of the other, and the speed in which this happens is also a political gesture which is not free of metaphysical necropolitics in speaking *for* the other. As tempting as it might be to agree with Braidotti, who is here seen as an example of a certain post- or neovitalist posthumanism paradigm gathering momentum, questions remain. For example, the question concerning the rather liberal use of the copula "is," proliferating wherever there's a question of life. And it might be worth pausing to see whether theory, while entering the deadly life wars, might have to change its way of speaking *to* life and *about* life. Theory . . . for life, after all, is itself a *style de vie*: theory for life, that is to say . . .

References

Agamben, Giorgio. 1998. *Homo Sacer: Sovereign Power and Bare Life*. Translated by Daniel Heller-Roazen. Stanford: Stanford University Press.

—. 1999. *Remnants of Auschwitz: The Witness and the Archive*. Translated by Daniel Heller-Roazen. New York: Zone Books.
—. 2004. *The Open: Man and Animal*. Translated by Kevin Attell. Stanford: Stanford University Press.
Arrivé, Michel. 1994. "Lacan sur le style, sur le style de Lacan." In *Qu'est-ce que le style?*, edited by Georges Molinié and Pierre Cahné, 45–61. Paris: Presses Universitaires de France.
—. 2006. *Transpositions: On Nomadic Ethics*. Cambridge: Polity.
—. 2007. "Bio-Power and Necro-Politics: Reflections on an Ethics of Sustainability." *Springerin, Hefte für Gegenwartskunst* 2. www.springerin.at/dyn/heft_text.php?textid=1928&lang=en
—. 2008. "The Politics of Life as *Bios/Zoē*." In *Bits of Life: Feminism at the Intersections of Media, Bioscience, and Technology*, edited by Smelik Anneke and Nina Lykke, 177–92. Seattle: University of Washington Press.
Butler, Judith. 2004. *Precarious Life: The Powers of Mourning and Violence*. London: Verso.
Cooper, Melinda. 2008. *Life as Surplus: Biotechnology and Capitalism in the Neoliberal Era*. Seattle: University of Washington Press.
Deleuze, Gilles. 2001. *Pure Immanence: Essays on Life*. Introduction by John Rajchman. Translated by A. Boyman. New York: Zone Books.
De Man, Paul. 1986. *The Resistance to Theory*. Minneapolis: University of Minnesota Press.
Derrida, Jacques. 1986. *The Post Card: From Socrates to Freud and Beyond*. Translated by Alan Bass. Chicago: University of Chicago Press.
—. 1988a. "Otobiographies: The Teaching of Nietzsche and the Politics of the Proper Name." Translated by Avital Ronell. In *The Ear of the Other: Otobiography, Transference, Translation*, edited by Christie McDonald, 1–38. Lincoln, NE: University of Nebraska Press.
—. 1988b. *Mémoires—pour Paul de Man*. Paris: Galilée.
—. 1998. *Monolingualism of the Other; or, The Prosthesis of Origin*. Translated by Patrick Mensah. Stanford: Stanford University Press.
—. 2002. *H.C. pour la vie, c'est à dire. . . .* Paris: Galilée.
—. 2003. *Genèses, genealogies, genres et genie*. Paris: Galilée.
—. 2005. *Apprendre à vivre enfin: Entretien avec Jean Birnbaum*. Paris: Galilée.
—. 2006. *H.C. for Life, That Is to Say. . . .* Translated by Laurent Milesi and Stefan Herbrechter. Stanford: Stanford University Press.
Derrida, Jacques and Hélène Cixous. 2004. "Du mot à la vie: un dialogue entre Jacques Derrida et Hélène Cixous." Edited by Aliette Armel, *Magazine littéraire*, 430: 22–9.
Dick, Kirby and Amy Ziering Kofman, dirs. 2002. *Derrida*. New York: Jane Doe Films Production. DVD.

Doyle, Richard. 2003. *Wetwares: Experiments in Postvital Living*. Minneapolis: University of Minnesota Press.
Eagleton, Terry. 2007. *The Meaning of Life*. Oxford: Oxford University Press.
Fraser, Miriam, et al. eds. 2006. *Inventive Life: Approaches to the New Vitalism*. London: Sage.
Haraway, Donna. 2009. "Becoming-with Companions: Sharing and Response in Experimental Laboratories." In *Animal Encounters*, edited by Tom Tyler and Manuela Rossini, 115–36. Leiden: Brill.
Hebdige, Dick. 1979. *Subculture: The Meaning of Style*. London: Methuen and Co.
Johnson, Christopher. 1999. "La vie, le vivant: Biologie et autobiographie." In *L'Animal autobiographique: Autour de Jacques Derrida*, edited by Marie-Louise Mallet, 353–68. Paris: Galilée.
Lacoue-Labarthe, Philippe and Jean-Luc Nancy, eds. 1981. *Les Fins de l'homme—à partir du travail de Jacques Derrida*. Paris: Galilée.
Lodge, David. 1990. *After Bakhtin*. London: Routledge.
Major, René. 1999. *Au Commencement la vie la mort*. Paris: Galilée.
Mbembe, Achille. 2003. "Necropolitics." Translated by Libby Meintjes. *Public Culture* 15(1): 11–40.
Rajan, Kaushik Sunder. 2006. *Biocapital: The Constitution of Postgenomic Life*. Durham: Duke University Press.
Read, Rupert. 2007. *Philosophy for Life*. Edited by M. A. Lavery. London: Continuum.
Riffaterre, Michel. 1994. "L'inscription du sujet." In *Qu'est-ce que le style?*, edited by Georges Molinié and Pierre Cahné. 283–312. Paris: Presses Universitaires de France.
Robin, Armand. 1970. *Ma vie sans moi*. Paris: Gallimard Poésie.
Rose, Nikolas. 2007. *The Politics of Life Itself: Biomedicine, Power, and Subjectivity in the Twenty-First Century*. Princeton: Princeton University Press.
Said, Edward W. 2006. *On Late Style*. London: Bloomsbury.
Santner, Eric. 2006. *On Creaturely Life: Rilke, Benjamin, Sebald*. Chicago: University of Chicago Press.
Schad, John. 2003a. "Preface: What Are We After?" In *life.after.theory*, edited by John Schad and Michael Payne, ix–xi. London: Continuum.
—. 2003b. "Epilogue: Coming Back to 'Life'." In *life. after. theory*, edited by John Schad and Michael Payne. London: Continuum.
Smelik, Anneke and Nina Lykke, eds. 2008. *Bits of Life: Feminism at the Intersections of Media, Bioscience, and Technology*. Seattle: University of Washington Press.

15

Learning to style finally: Lateness in theory

Ivan Callus

> *Actually, as a matter of fact,* always that:
> as if I were as one dead.
>
> —Roland Barthes

Other essays in this collection have stressed motifs of birth in their exploration of style in theory. For instance, they have drawn attention to themes of parturition and epenthetic accretion and their effect on the modulation of style in literary and theoretical texts (Jean-Michel Rabaté's and Marie-Dominique Garnier's do this in their analyses of Joyce and Deleuze respectively). They have also recalled the birth of the very idea of style and the generation of the language of literature (as in Gloria Lauri-Lucente's or Mario Aquilina's or Janice Sant's, which focus respectively on the impetus thereto of Petrarch and Blanchot and Cixous, or indeed in Chris Müller's, which considers the originarity of language itself and cues reflection on whether being must always go before style). Additionally, they have looked at how style, once born as effect or affect, reproduces its own vitality (examples are Stefan Herbrechter's, which traces the *la vie la mort* theme and its trajectories in French theory, or Laurent Milesi's, which studies deconstruction's conceptual and compositional recasting of style's histories, or those of contributors like Stuart Sillars and Giuseppe Mazzotta and Saul Anton, which survey crucial filiations and compulsions in the thought of style).

Style's many births are therefore extensively reviewed in this volume. Death, however, is a theme that is just as explicitly present. It would not be difficult to trace throughout an interest in the decline of style, and thence in a related waning of the theoretical (as in James Corby's essay, for instance, which is certainly readable in this light in view of its interest in finitude's implications for style *and* man, or Stefan Herbrechter's again, where the co-presence of death in the *style de vie* of theory *is* the theme). My purpose in itemizing all this is not to provide an inventory of the diverse leitmotifs of birth and death in this volume, or of the multiple lives that style ekes out across all the theories it finds itself between in these pages. It is, rather, to foreground the context against which I consider, below, not the end (or death) of style (or theory), but what happens to style and self-styling (assuming one can have the one as an attribute and the other as a deliberated strategy) when one is *sub umbra mortis* (as one always is, though awareness of the diminished scope for gradation in the approach is what changes everything in the sense of an ending). The *style de mort* of theory, in passing, will be considered.

Accordingly, this valedictory essay in the volume focuses on lateness. It considers the style of the experience of being late: of being—discretely and perhaps even simultaneously—tardy; *or* placed where "lambent peaks" (Whitman 1892, 404) loom; *or*, indeed, dead.[1] The testamentary, the experience of (self-)mourning, the counter-identification with the dead, and the autothanatographical will all feature in an attempt to reflect on what happens to style—and to its viabilities and tones—when all moves toward expiration.

*

Unlike that improbable and discomposing utterance at the end of Edgar Allan Poe's short story "The Facts in the Case of M. Valdemar"—"I am dead" (1982, 103)—the statement "I am late" does not put semantics or pragmatics out of countenance. Even

---

[1]Given this chapter's subject matter, it seemed appropriate to cite the 1892 edition of *Leaves of Grass*—the "deathbed edition," as Whitman thought of it.

the anticipation that we shall have been late, where a present is rendered to which presence cannot be delivered, tends not to do so. Like the White Rabbit in the first chapter of *Alice in Wonderland* we have all said, "Oh dear, oh dear, I shall be too late" (Carroll 2009, 10). The future tense in such contexts does not diminish the sense that we are incorrigibly late, but it registers a lateness in process rather than one that is finite. We tell ourselves that we are late, that we are experiencing lateness already, but that we are not yet, in fact, late. "I shall be late" is more defusing than "I am late," but one dreads saying "I shall be *too* late," where the unpunctuality, now irredeemable beyond any forebearing (a transgression admitted by that *too*), inflicts finality on the present missed and on presence denied. We all recognize this because unless we have clear days and iron discipline, self-announced states of lateness are an everyday embarrassment. Lateness: beyond brinkmanship, punctual only for consequences and for others to tell us we'll be late for our own funeral. Daily, we are a little late, just like we die a little every day. Lateness, then, is something we know. We live out life living it down.

So let us consider these two sentences, "I am dead" and "I am late." Their temporalities will exercise us throughout this essay. Both suggest, though very differently, the experience of being out of time. One is unearthly and unthinkable, the other mundane and never far from thought. Yet they could be near-synonymous if the scarcely conceivable rhetoric of autothanatography were to be indulged. Autothanatography—the inconceivable writing that bears witness to and records the perduring experientiality of one's own death or, more thinkably, the process of one's own dying—presents a quite unusual set of challenges to the imagination and to critical interpretation, not to mention to our sense of reality.[2] I shall return to this later. Here, let us recall the obvious: lateness can also mean "recently deceased" (*OED*, s.v. "late"). One can speak, for instance, of the late Edward Said, or the late Jacques

[2]In the space available, the important distinction between death and dying which is developed in the work of Maurice Blanchot, notably in Blanchot/Derrida 2002, cannot be explored and is assumed as assimilated context here. The term *autothanatography* is here used in the awareness of the unfeasibility of longer introduction; on this topic see, for instance, Burt 2009 and Callus 2005—but especially Derrida's comments on the "autobioheterothanatographical" in "Circumfession" (Derrida 1993, 213).

Derrida, or the late Hans-Georg Gadamer. If it is possible to do so it is because their passing away is still vivid to some degree in cultural memory. In this sense one cannot say "the late Dante," "the late Immanuel Kant," or "the late Mozart," as those deaths are not present to our recollection (though the *Requiem* of one of them is). However we do resort, of course, and with a clear sense in our mind of the referent, to the different connotations of, say, "the late Beethoven," or more precisely of "late style in Beethoven" (see Adorno 2002), in consideration of the thought and works that characterize the composer's later period and render them interestingly distinct from earlier writings. What is late, then, has associations that go beyond tardiness. It can also refer to work produced in the time of maturity. It draws attention to periodization: to the discernment of distinctness across early, middle, and more seasoned phases in the writings of authors we might wish to critique. In *The Late Derrida*, for instance, in an essay called "Dead Again," W. J. T. Mitchell delimits the late period of Derrida quite precisely. This refers to the writings, he says, from 1994 to 2004 (2007, 2).[3] The view of Herman Rapaport (2003) of the later Derrida, by contrast, extends from work written after 1987. Clearly, therefore, and just like the forgetting by philosophers of their umbrellas, lateness is a fit subject for criticism and theory.

Of course, there is nothing novel here. The pertinence of lateness is now a commonplace. Adorno provides an important prompt; Edward Said is the other obligatory point of reference. Prompted by Adorno's, Said's reflections on the late style of a number of figures led to a series of monographic lectures delivered at Columbia and elsewhere in the 1980s and 1990s and collected together, in a poignant irony, in his *posthumously* published book *On Late Style* (2006). Christopher Ricks' *Beckett's Dying Words*, Martin Crowley's *Dying Words: The Last Moments of Writers and Philosophers*, Simon Critchley's *The Book of Dead Philosophers* and, as Stuart Sillars points out in his essay here, the work of Russ McDonald and Gordon McMullan on Shakespeare's late style provide further examples of the critical scrutiny directed at what it is that writers, philosophers, and theorists write and say when life and death run close. Indeed, there is an important distinction to

[3]The periodization in question was first mentioned by Mitchell in a letter sent out to potential contributors to *The Late Derrida*.

be made here. It is that between, on the one hand, texts periodized as late, as belonging to maturer years, when perhaps some refocusing or even rejection of earlier work takes place; and on the other texts that can be identified as consciously written in anticipation of death, and in response to the awareness that the writing at hand might well be one's last. In this essay, the lateness that interests me is the latter. I am interested in what happens in writing tasked with "lastness," particularly when the texts are theoretical. Is there a loss of nerve there, possibly to be thought of in the light, for instance, of Wallace Stevens' alleged deathbed conversion to Catholicism, or in terms of the rather different example of the appearance of a more pronounced religious register in the later Derrida, about which more will be said below? But what, in those texts, are the challenges to style? How might theory help us read those challenges? How is theory itself styled when its condition is terminal?

This essay can only broach these large questions. The broaching must start with acknowledgment. The essays by James Corby and Stefan Herbrechter in this volume have already been penetrating about the issues involved. From a rich array, I would want to recall these lines in particular.

> Instead this is an attempt to see theory on the side of life, asking whether theory has a life, a life of its own, whether theory actually might *be* life, not just alive but somehow *for life*, at least more than death, and thus it is also an attempt to show that there is life in theory, still and always, that one can dwell in theory, actually live, in theory, that one might somehow, and indeed maybe always and only, live in theory. (Herbrechter)

> An anticipation of death discloses one's life as a whole and affirms the nonnecessity of one's life on both an existential and existentiell level. Reacquainting us with the thrown-projected temporality of our existence, this intimation of death prompts us to take a stand on our being. We are lifted out of our inauthentic, unthinking absorption in the world and become aware of our potential to style our own existence. As Heidegger puts it: "Being-towards-death is the anticipation of a potentiality-for-Being of that entity whose kind of Being is anticipation itself." Our relation to death, then, is manifested and affirmed specifically in our styling existence *as* styling existence. To forget death is to

> abandon style and become unfree. In choosing one possibility among a number, we style, we choose life, but a life that is, however gradually, ending. Our style is our finitude; finitude is our style. (Corby)

After this, there is a superfluity in almost everything I could bring to bear. The incisiveness in those two discussions is exemplary in running together the sense of finitude and its implications for how one must *dwell, live, die* in theory: existing thereby *in style*, so that one is always styling, style-ish, re-styling, re-styled. *Style in theory* is nothing more than this and *all* of it: life; death; the writing of life and death; the awareness of genesis, trace, end.[4] It can take place in literature, in philosophy, in the writing in between.[5] Here, however, the concern is not that, nor indeed a fuller exploration of the challenges in literature, theory, and philosophy that Herbrechter's and Corby's essays open onto. Rather, in what is admittedly a retreat from those imponderables, I would wish to bring into closer view the rawness of an experience that lies this side of those challenges, where theorization does not dis-intimate mortality. It involves the wrestle with writing when one knows one's terminality all too intimately. It is the immediacy of the experience of secession from life that I would like to bring to view, and what happens to writing and to style when they find themselves wended therein, therefrom, thereto. Inevitably, there is poignancy in that. Perhaps, it has to be said, there is a touch of the elegiac, not to say the sentimental. The tone, therefore, may be a little off. But we are at the end—so be it. The risk must be run.

*

An altogether paradoxical experience of contrary tardiness and anticipation tends to be at play in texts written in the time and space of self-conscious precariousness. They contrive an early chancing upon the reception of the corpus from which they spring and which they possibly seek to subtly re-author as they append

---

[4]There is a strong tradition in deconstruction in support of this idea. See the texts cited in Stefan Herbrechter's essay in this volume, but also—to select invidiously from a vast literature—Smith 1995 and Marrati 2005.

[5]Theory's congruence with a writing *in between* has been prolific (just within Derrida's work see, for instance, Derrida 1986, 1987, 1992, 2006).

themselves to it.[6] What is thereby bequeathed is one last attempt, possibly a corrective one, to bring to notice what it might have been desirable to say had writing not been out of time. If the phrase "I am late" is implied by such texts it is because the sense of the expiration of one's being gains inexorably upon the writing, forestalling it even as the text takes shape in the attempt to resolve itself before it is exceeded. Explicit or everywhere implied, the phrase acknowledges the text's inadequacy in relation to the text's desired effect. It practically announces that one is, in effect, already dead, or might just as well be, and hence attests to what is felt to be most urgent at the last.

In regard to that, the phrase "living on borrowed time" is not less precise about what it denotes simply by being overused. In this experience of lateness, *of being late for one's own death*, the awareness of dying imminently bears the disembodied sense of having survived oneself. One can write from that surviving mind, from that surviving thought. But it is possible, too, to write as if from that surviv*ed* mind, from that surviv*ed* thought. The "desubjectivation" that Gerald L. Bruns speaks about in *On Ceasing to Be Human* (2010) can occur there, and it is possible to recall the experience of saying "I am a process with no subject," in this sentence which gives a book by Philip Beitchman (1988) its title.[7] "[S]urvival," Derrida tells us, "structure[s] every instant in a kind of irreducible torsion," that of "a retrospective anticipation that introduces the untimely moment and the posthumous in the most alive of the present living thing, the rearview mirror of a waiting-for-death [*s'attendre à la mort*]" (1993a, 55). We could look to Blanchot's narrators in his *récits* (e.g. 1987, 1997, 1998, and Derrida 2004b), many of whom live and write that survival. Their experience is the experience of the autothanatographical. The crepuscular settles there—even

---

[6]One of the most remarkable recent examples of this appending is provided by *Maurice Blanchot: Passion politique* (Blanchot 2011, 45–62), which presents in facsimile and transcription a previously unpublished letter by Blanchot to Roger Laporte, rationalizing (but not excusing) political affiliations and positions struck earlier in life.

[7]Bruns develops the idea of desubjectivation in a chapter that takes as its context Foucault's work, rather than Derrida's, which provides the focus here; the scope for contrast and the comparison is rich and instructive. See Bruns (2011, 47–60), and Beitchman (1988), where the authors discussed are Tzara, Beckett, Leiris, Blanchot, Joyce, Sollers, and Des Forêts.

despite the vertigo of the luminousness and fascination which, as Mario Aquilina reminds us in his essay for this volume, such writing produces. As we shall see when encountering Derrida's reflections on this survival, however, there is scope for affirmation too. It is strange, perhaps, that affirmation springs there, where we figure ourselves dead, as the epigraph from Barthes reminds us we can. But if there is one thing that distinguishes theory, as that epigraph indicates, it is the singular readiness of its practitioners—Barthes, Blanchot, Derrida, de Man, etc.—to witness others *or themselves* writing in both the object *and* the subject position of the prosopopoeic stance, precisely to write "as if I were as one dead" (see Barthes 2009, 108). To pick up on the essay by Stuart Sillars in this volume, there is a strange process of ethopoeia at play there, deriving from the wish to empathize with the dead and more peculiarly still with the experience of the consciousness of oneself dead. In that writing between life and death, which there become indistinguishable and interpenetrative, the texts in question come closest to articulating theory as the discourse between literature and philosophy. The style of theory, one starts to suspect, is therefore what it is because theory is where it is *not* incongruous to write like that: "as if it were possible, within such limits," to cite the title of an essay by Derrida which starts, significantly, with this line: "Despite the lateness of what is beginning here, we can be quite sure that it won't be a question of some kind of last word" (2005, 73). Note, in formulations like this title or the epigraph from Barthes, the inescapability of the subjunctive, the recurrent yet suppressed tense of the autothanatographical. If nothing else, then, theory has form in this regard. Indeed, it has *the* form, we could say. Which of course makes it crucial to ask what theory does, how it styles itself, when it itself writes (of) itself as if *it* were a dead discourse. This occurs, it is to be presumed, in the displacement at work in late theory, where late style arrives tenuously or not at all, ever and thereafter. *Theory after theory*, or to put it differently, *style after style* is what we are then concerned with.

We shall come to that in the last section of this essay (I am, incidentally, avoiding the route here of responding to these questions by taking refuge in the theoretical pieties concerning the thinking of *post-* and *ana-* [see Lyotard 1992]). Meanwhile, forewarned (above) by the prospect of the sentimental in all this, we might well ask: can we *not* be stirred by late style? Shakespeare put it well: "the tongues of dying men / Enforce attention like deep harmony" (*Richard* II, 2.1.5–6). Fugitive writing may be more than ordinarily anguished by fear of futility, and that must resonate. The stresses of what Said calls "[t]he relationship between bodily condition and aesthetic style" also obtrude (2006, 3). Indeed, late style may quite possibly be undone by its own infirmity: it may be entirely weak and flat, for all the immensity of its moment. It may fail to measure up to earlier work even as it seeks to be an apotheosis of earlier writing, urgently hoping that it could instigate realignments in various readerly and critical relations to the writer's corpus. This is presumably the work which, written in the face of oblivion, one would most *not* wish to see consigned there. Cruelly, in such writing there is already something spectral, out of the order of time. Yet the problem is that it derives all too much from the corporeal, for it is fixed in the terminal. "This is what I will have written at the end, thought at the end, when I was too late to do more," is what it says. Consequently it has investments in the future anterior even as it reaches the reader, inevitably, as a *billet* from a past that cannot be recovered, but also as a *billet* to the future whose memory it seeks to lay a claim on. For all these reasons it is doubtful if there is any writing which is more nakedly interpellating or individuating. This, after all, is the work in which one signs off an existence.

So what *does* happen to style, *in extremis*? If there are signature effects to style—a possibility that recurs across these essays in this volume—what happens in texts written in awareness of terminality, when signing off on a lifetime's work and thought? What occurs when the stylus is felt to tremble? How are valedictory texts styled, particularly in the work of theorists who may have written at length on style itself, but also on death and mourning—as, indeed, Blanchot and Derrida have? Does style change there? Is it retained, heightened, transformed, toned down, dispensed with, recanted? What are the choices of style, styling, stylishness, or stylelessness toward the end, in the midst of intimations of lateness? At that stage, must a different style add itself to the repertoire?

The choices made then are *performances* of lateness. Humanly, they have to be. Let us recall two of these performances, both *spoken* rather than written. Neither comes from theory. "See in what peace a Christian can die," Joseph Addison, that master of eighteenth-century stylistic decorum, is supposed to have said at the end, in a statement that doubtless resonated more to contemporaries' sensibilities than it does to ours. "So here it is at last, the distinguished thing," we are told that Henry James said toward his end, in what must surely be the most characteristically styled of late performances (see Edel 1968). If these statements, which are priggish or magnificent (depending on one's outlook) sound a little rehearsed, perhaps we should remember that all last testaments are a little like that. They prepare us for the intuition that in written final performances—there where autothanatography comes into its own—the sense of a styled departure can be even more overwhelming. Style can help take the edge off both the momentariness and momentousness of such writing. There, where candor is most expected and important, some degree of dissimulation may be expected.

If this writing *in extremis* is *performed*, the distance between what one would like to say and what one might end up saying may rarely be sharper. That is why tone, as much as or more so than style, becomes significant. It is what we must be alert to. And tone, which, even more than style, is difficult to get right at the most *vital* of times, is surely more difficult still at the end, when vitality ebbs. It will never have been more vital to get it right, when one is aware that one still *is*, after all—when, in other words, one is not yet quite one with stillness. The imminence of stillness in the stilling of writing—a stilling willed just long enough to write that one is about to be late, that one is, indeed, already late—must always induce a little breathlessness, even while it is a writing that affects punctuality. "I am just in time—in time, just—to write this, to bequeath this," it says. This contrivance of being in time, still, when one is all too palpably soon to be out of it, can lead to spurious neatness, deliberation, style—even there where the untidiness, confusion, and randomness of the end can overtake those other qualities. It is not for nothing, after all, that in José Saramago's *Death at Intervals*—a novel about a country where people stop dying but where they eventually start dying again, so that lateness takes on all kinds of unprecedented associations—there is a reference to the "authorised opinion of a grammarian" who notes that death (allegorized as a woman in the narrative) "had simply failed to master even the first rudiments of the art of writing" (Saramago 2008, 102). There is decorum there, of a sort. One does not necessarily expect grammatical or stylistic poise where the poise of life declines. But otherwise it remains a pleasing conceit, this idea that we can pattern, even sign, death and departure. The conceit invites the idea of a punctual matching of terminally inscribing moments to such consistency as can be discerned in the build-up that will have been a life. The writing of lateness, then, attempts *design*, even there where the assertion of an identity which is terminal cannot contemplate what might be called, rather gauchely, *(de)signing*. It seeks to (de)sign the *punctum* of an exhausted *stylus*: ahead of any pointlessness in death and of being (over)taken.

Commenting about that effort in Said, Michael Wood notes that "late evenings, late blossoms, and late autumns are perfectly punctual—there isn't another clock or calendar they are supposed to match" (2006, vi). But this other kind of lateness, the human all too human one, can only affect punctuality and matching as it runs out of both clock and calendar. *Matching*, indeed, is part of the problem here. Matching expectations, matching consistency, matching identity, matching previous styles and tones and dispositions and outlooks in previous writing are what is looked for—*or not*, as the signature in the late work can always, in fact, be appended to an abjuration of what preceded it, not to mention the possibility of disappointment in the face of any evidence of late decline. And it is here that the idea of style as separable category returns. If we are (*concesso non dato*) to countenance the idea that style is an assumed or designed attribute, rather than an integral and nonpartitive element embedded in the very personality of writing, and if we all become, in a manner of speaking, philosophical toward the end, do we thereupon tend to write more in the manner of philosophy: in respect, that is, of some ethic of stylessness that imposes itself at that stage? Is style to be indulged in the end, and does it feel inauthentic if it is? If so, how and why is that impression conveyed? In other words, is style in theory to be allowed to be between literature and philosophy *pour la vie*, but tendentially on the side of the latter toward *l'instant de ma mort*? Is style in theory, then, readable as the oscillation and uncertainty between literature, *pourvu que ça dure*, and philosophy, *à l'heure de notre mort*?

In *Learning to Live Finally: The Last Interview* (which carries the text of an interview originally published in *Le Monde*), Derrida (2004a, 2007b) unsettles those questions in reflections which are all too terminal. They are pronounced in full knowledge that he would be dying soon (he passed away less than two months later). As anticipated, tone must orient us, for we are to expect that awareness of terminality occasions in late, or autothanatographical, texts, something disorienting when they are Derrida's, whose "work of mourning" explored lateness in so many diverse forms. Yet for that reason if there is anyone who could deliver this strange pedagogy aimed at learning to die—or style—finally, then Derrida is surely an apt candidate. As we shall see, however, he disclaims that.

Before getting there, some quick comparative work on terminal self-fashioning is needed. It ought to feature texts that are not theoretical, or literary, or philosophical, for there is a broader poetics of lateness to be remembered. What are the conventions there, and what might the analogues, such as they are, be? While an exhaustive review cannot be provided here, a few examples are considered in the next section.

*

Beyond the apologia, or the self-authored obituary, or the versions of the desire to write one's own epitaph, the rhetoric of lateness—"this is what I was thinking, at the end, about the end (of my work, of my life, of myself, of ending generally . . .)"—might be usefully compared to the act of the writing out of one's will. We could then speak of testamentary autothanatography, as it were. Now the language of wills, we know, is as arid as its effects can be munificent. If we remember the oddity of certain wills it is only because in their overwhelming majority they lack any individuating style, policed as they are by the legal and procedural wording that deters whimsy. Like philosophy, as a certain tradition has it, the law is expected to be above style. In the most serious and earnest of contexts, then—and philosophy and law will claim prerogatives there—style, though not quite absent, is codified. It is made subject to formats and procedures, as academic writing is. (Even a collection on style has to have its style cramped, and the present editors' discussions on appropriate calibration across the volume of that cramping, on the basis of the protocols of academic writing, were extensive.) And indeed, the fact that style guides like *The Chicago Manual of Style* can go into their sixteenth edition is tremendously interesting. If style (or certain styles in certain contexts) can be re-codified by those who lay down its law, it is because it is apt to serially and renewably transgress custom, infiltrating singularity and capriciousness where norms and convention had been instituted.

The difficulty, of course, is whether one expects testamentary autothanatography—this odd genre, written *as if I were dead*, that only literature and theory quite countenance—to be spared of style or, conversely, to fully indulge style (whatever that may mean). Some inevitable degree of pathos in the registering of (self-) loss will feature, but ironization and aporia may predominate even in the autothanatographical. There are too many examples to cite in confirmation *and* contradiction of that, but some examples can be mentioned quickly, without commentary: Petrarch's *Testament*, Chateaubriand's *Memoires d'outre tombe*, Keats's letters, Althusser's *The Future Lasts a Long Time*. Anyone looking for further examples could do worse than refer to Julian Barnes's *Nothing to Be Frightened Of*, a memoir which doubles up as a text probing the nothing that Montaigne desired . . . to be informed of. "If I were a maker of books, I would keep a register, with comments, of various deaths," Montaigne wrote (I, 20; 1958, 62: this prefigures similar ideas in Rilke 2008). To that outlook, learning to die finally is learning how to style final dying, taking further Montaigne's observation that "Cicero says that to philosophize is nothing more than to prepare for death" (I, 20: 56). As learning outcomes go, it is at least more configurable than discovering if late style recedes into nothingness because nothingness obviates style.

I would therefore like to move on to Derrida's *Learning to Live Finally*. The stakes are high because Derrida is among the most personal of theorists, because death always shadowed his work, and because if one is to read about style in theory and about theory's late style one cannot but go to deconstruction, because "theory sooner or later turns out to mean deconstruction. Deconstruction is 'high theory', the theoretical essence of theory" (Redfield 2003, 5). If we are to observe the late style of theory, then, we must witness deconstruction *in extremis* and risk morbid, even distasteful voyeurism as we read *Learning to Live Finally*. So one is moved—to ask: does this late text, turned inward and endward, deconstruct lateness in theory? Does it even deconstruct anything at all? Or is lateness in theory, like justice, famously, not to be deconstructed, not least because it would be insensitive to do so? (see Derrida 1991). For indeed, the question of sensitivity about death runs throughout this chapter. Clearly, there is more than simply a grammar of death and dying, as death establishes a law. This is particularly felt in funeral orations, which must always be beyond reproach, unquestionable. What is said in the context of death, in other words, cannot be challenged—death proscribes it. To do so would be, at the very least, insensitive. Death authenticates and underwrites.[8]

Before addressing that, one last comparison (one must always try to decently defer the end). Derrida's last interview bears comparison with the last and testamentary text of another academic: Randy Pausch. Pausch, who died in 2008, was not a literary or critical theorist. His discipline was human-computer interaction and design. Like Derrida, he would die of pancreatic cancer, in his case at the age of 47. In September 2007 Pausch gave a talk at Carnegie Mellon called "The Last Lecture: Really Achieving Your Childhood Dreams." He did so in keeping with a Carnegie Mellon tradition that invites prominent academics to deliver a talk focused on what they would choose to lecture on if they knew that the occasion would be their last lecture. In the case of Pausch, the wager was all too literal. Living, indeed, on borrowed time, Pausch aimed to offer some suggestions on self-fulfillment in available time. Extraordinarily, he would manage to deliver another lecture in Virginia a month later—on time management (the last lecture is never the last . . .). "The Last Lecture" became, very quickly, a public event and an internet phenomenon. Tens of millions viewed the recording on YouTube, and it subsequently was expanded and published as a book that became a bestseller. In effect, Pausch had written a self-help, live-your-life-better book—months before death. It is, indeed, hard not to be moved. Ezra Pound's words are apt: "There are few things more difficult than to appraise the work of a man suddenly dead in his youth; to disentangle 'promise' from achievement, to save him from that sentimentalizing which confuses the tragedy of the interruption with the merit of the work actually performed" (1970, 118). Notice that testamentary autothanatography, it seems, is beyond critique. But what testamentary autothanatography does call for is notice, and recollection of its legacy. And here, on the last page of Pausch's last text, is the important "head fake," as he calls it, the revelation of what was being

[8]I am grateful to James Corby for discussions on this point, and to Laurent Milesi for conversations on the paragraphs that follow.

held in reserve and what everything was tending to: "The talk wasn't just for those in the room. 'It was for my kids.'" (Pausch and Zaslow 2008, 206).

Testamentary autothanatographies, indeed, move the *lettore modello* (Eco 1985) they choose to position. They are a little pre-scribing in regard to our recall. Derrida's last text, as it happens, is not dissimilar. How, indeed, does he approach it, this theorist who reminded us in *Aporias* that meetings between two friends are shadowed by foreknowledge that one must die before the other, who was alive to the *autobioheterothanatographical* in writing, whose work of mourning was sustained and infelt? The answer may surprise those who suppose deconstruction's texts inattentive to the play of the personal and lacking in emotional inflection. In opposition to that supposing, consider these words. They are reproduced in facsimile and translated form in *The Late Derrida* and—in a pre-scribing of ceremony and memory—written by him to be read by his son at his graveside. They need no framing.

> Jacques wanted no rites and no orations. He knows from experience what an ordeal it is for the friend who takes on this task. He asks me to thank you for coming and to bless you. He beseeches you not to be sad, to think only of the many happy moments you gave him the chance to share with him.
>
> Smile for me, he says, as I will have smiled for you until the end.
>
> Always prefer life and constantly affirm survival . . . I love you and am smiling at you from wherever I am. (Derrida 2007a, 244)

Tone, we said, would orient us, but here it directs us. "Always prefer life," on the side of death . . . but that, perhaps, depends on how we choose to remember. As we shall see below, the (late) style we recall is informed by the style of remembrance. It is as well, therefore, to draw attention to two different styles of reception of Derrida's lateness—and hence of theory's lateness and of the style of theory after theory. (Prior deferral obliges further deferral before the end, to which this will serve as a foil.)

Jean-Luc Nancy reminds us that Derrida deconstructed the concept of generation and that he could no longer bear being referred to as the last of the sixties generation. Nevertheless "[i]t's as if with Derrida, it was not just a great or even a very great philosopher who had passed away but . . . an entire epoch, that is, an entire chance for philosophy" (Nancy 2007, 209). With the passing of theory, then, it is *philosophy* which is bereft. Derrida's is in that case the passing of the chance of an entire style, one might say, of philosophy, or of theory. Nancy is not blinkered about the conflicting responses to that passing. He suggests that "Derrida's is the destiny of a certain greatness that exceeds the ones it inhabits and, in a certain sense, devastates him" (2007, 211). In death, as in life. For every loyal, impeccably styled, and keenly felt tribute to his passing there is a diminishing shabbiness (on this, see Caputo 2006). Perhaps none is as distressing, Nancy tells us—including to himself, Nancy, a friend to both Derrida and Giorgio Agamben—as Agamben's response, in life, to Derrida's work, a response which to Nancy showed itself as "extremely unjust," born from a "refus[al] to read the texts," from a reaction that is "aggressive and unscholarly" (2007, 217). This blatant and unargued hostility, Nancy tells us, pained Derrida. It is enough to induce us to reread the texts, of Derrida, of theory, in as unaggressive and scholarly a way as we can, if we are not to *oublire* theory (see Cixous 1997), to *forgetread* theory. Let me then turn—we are indeed at the end, beyond deferral—to *Learning to Live Finally: The Last Interview.*

*

In the end one must say only as much as one ought. Derrida's last interview, conducted by Jean Birnbaum, runs to only 31 pages in the octavo-sized book that carries the English translation. The obligation is clear. Appropriate proportion in length, style, and tone must be observed in commentary.

Birnbaum is suitably tactful. "You haven't hidden the fact that . . .," he says. Derrida interposes immediately. He admits to being "very seriously ill" but cuts to say that "we are not here to issue a medical report" (2007b, 21–2). We are decorously recalled to the genealogies of late style. Birnbaum notes that the phrase providing the original French title, *apprendre à vivre enfin*, had appeared at the start of *Specters of Marx*, ten years earlier. Derrida himself glosses this in the interview: "to mature, but also to educate: to teach someone else and especially oneself." It can also mean "to teach . . . a lesson," to "teach you how to live" (23). There is "a concern for legacy and death" in *Specters of Marx*, Derrida explains, an interest in how "to *accept* or, better, to *affirm* life" (emphasis in the original). But, he says, he has "never *learned-to-live*" (24). Accommodation to "absolute mortality," related to "the old philosophical injunction since Plato: to philosophize is to learn to die," is something in which he "remain[s] uneducable." Now "the time of the reprieve is rapidly running out," that "temporary reprieve [*en sursis*]" which we, "who are all survivors . . . have been granted." Survival out of reprieve, *la survie* out of *le sursis*, is something he feels keenly and with "melancholic revolt" when cast as "the final representative of a 'generation'" (24–5). And as "life is survival [la vie *est* survie]," positioned between the Benjaminian elaboration of "*überleben* . . . surviving death . . . and *fortleben, living on*," he can retrospectively cast "[a]ll the concepts that have helped me in my work, and notably that of the trace or of the spectral," to "what I call 'originary mourning,' that is, a mourning that does not wait for the so-called 'actual' death" (26).

There is enough here to note that the temporalities of impending and "actual death" are problematized by consciousness, language, and writing when a pre-scribing sense of *fortleben* steals upon such *überleben* as one is afforded or affords oneself. The distinction between "I am late" and "I shall be late," made at the beginning of this essay, is worth recalling here, not least because it can be linked to the discussions in *Speech and Phenomena* of the idea that "[t]he statement 'I am alive' is accompanied by my being dead, and its possibility requires the possibility that I be dead; and conversely" (96–7). This is pointed out by Geoffrey Bennington (2008), who had earlier written about Lyotard's later period and who studies these relations to good effect in *Not Half No End: Militantly Melancholic Essays in Memory of Jacques Derrida*. He comments that it is surely "no accident" that "final (or always only penultimate) thought" leads to "formulations . . . always and everywhere struggling with teleological structures" (2010, 60). Bennington suggests that on the model that this gives rise to, "'Life' . . . would be described as an inhibited tendency towards an *autos* or *ipse* that would however, if achieved, be the end of life" (61). That is why "the 'auto-' in auto-affection, auto-nomie, auto-biography would then be affected by a +R effect, part of the hospitality of the host to the guest or the ghost: *autro-affection, autro-nomy, autro-biography*" (61). Recasting thereby the *la vie la mort* conceit, and having reminded us of the passage in *Of Grammatology* where it is observed that "Auto-affection constitutes the same (*auto*) by dividing it," Bennington concludes, "And that's life, death" (60–1).

But is this not too theoretical—too much in the style of theory? Why theorize still at the end, (im)properly, on the point of (another's) death? A man, associable with theory itself, is about to die; perhaps it is decorous, after all, for him to die in theory, not least because theory itself might or might not be waning here: "We are talking about a sort of *provisionally bygone era*, and not about such and such a person," Derrida himself observes (2007b, 28). Theory, provisionally bygone, reasserts its styles, however. Derrida reaffirms "the strict taste for refinement, paradox, and aporia" (28). Style in theory is suddenly reasserted, leading to and prompted by Birnbaum's remark on Derrida having "invented a form of writing, a writing of survival [*survivance*], which is suited to . . . impatience of fidelity" (30). Here is Derrida's (self-)justification of that writing, *in* that writing:

> To renounce, for example, some difficult formulation, some complication, paradox, or supplementary contradiction, because it is not going to be understood . . . is for me an unacceptable obscenity. (2007b, 30)
>
> If I had invented my writing, I would have done so as a perpetual revolution. For it is necessary in each situation to create an appropriate mode of exposition, to invent the law of the singular event, to take into account the presumed or desired addressee; and at the same time, to make as if this writing will determine the reader, who will learn to read (to "live") something he or she who was not accustomed to receiving from anywhere else. One hopes that he or she will be reborn differently, determined otherwise, as a result: for example, these grafts of poetry onto philosophy, which are anything but confused, or certain ways of using homonyms, the undecidable, or the ruses of language, which many read in confusion because they fail to recognize their properly *logical necessity*. (2007b, 31)

"These grafts of poetry onto philosophy": a reaffirmation that the late style of late theory is ever between literature and philosophy.

Derrida will hint, later, that his kind of *lettore modello* has that in-between quality of 'writer-thinkers, poets' (34). This is consistent with the well-known statement in *Acts of Literature* on his having the "dream of a writing that would be neither philosophy nor literature" but which would have "the memory of literature and philosophy" (1992, 73). There is no abjuration then, not when Derrida is emphasizing the immanence of lateness, whence lateness is dynamic as much as it is periodization:

> At the moment I leave "my" book (to be published) . . . I become, appearing-disappearing, like that uneducable specter who will have never learned how to live. The trace I leave signifies to me at once my death, either to come or already upon me, and the hope that this trace survives me. This is not a striving for immortality; it's something structural. I leave a piece of paper behind, I go away, I die: it is impossible to escape this structure, it is the unchanging form of my life. . . . I live my death in writing. It's the ultimate test: one expropriates oneself without knowing exactly who is being entrusted with what is left behind. Who is going to inherit, and how? Will there even be any heirs? (2007b, 32–3)

This restatement of the dilemma of late style, of late writing, of theory late to correct its own provisionally bygone character, takes on one last twist. Birnbaum provides the cue when he asks, "might not deconstruction be considered an interminable ethics of the survivor?" (2007b, 50). Derrida assents, with a qualification that sets forth the style of theory *in extremis*—the last answer to a last question—in the bequeathal of the thought of life not only *not* placed under erasure (as might once have been the style), but affirmed and, indeed, *blessed*:

> We are structurally survivors, marked by the structure of the trace and of the testament. But, having said that, I would not want to encourage an interpretation that situates surviving on the side of death and the past rather than life and the future. No, deconstruction is always on the side of the *yes*, on the side of the affirmation of life. . . . This surviving is not simply that which remains but the most intense life possible. . . . When I recall my life, I tend to think that I have had the good fortune to

> love even the unhappy moments of my life, and to bless them. (2007b, 51–2)

A head fake? Possibly. It is not the tone we might have expected, but it is the tone to go with. And we must remember that the style of theory is never more infelt than when it is remembering itself to itself. Consequently there are two things to note here. They turn on grace and graciousness.

First, one may be one's own *lettore modello* at the end. One may have written the end—or styled it—for *oneself.* This return to the *auto*, the *ipse*, is cast differently to the envisaging reported in Bennington, above. The legacy to the subjectivity *one would have wanted*—to keep with the past conditional tense that punctuates Barnes's *Nothing to Be Frightened Of*—can be styled in recognition that, as Jean-Luc Marion otherwise notes in "The Final Appeal of the Subject," what is to be sought is grace:

> What succeeds the subject is the very movement of irremediable difference which precedes it, insofar as the subject is given to itself as a *myself*, to which any *I* claiming authenticity only offers a mask, doubly belated and radically secondary, or even originally deceptive. More essential to the *I* than itself, the gesture that interlocutes appears, freely but not without price, in the figure of the claim—as that which gives an I as a *myself* rendered to *itself*. Grace gives me the *myself* to *itself* before the *I* even notices itself. My grace precedes me. (1996, 104)

The grace Marion speaks of is not end-determined, but it is perhaps never more desirable than at the end. One may or may not want to leave with style, but one may settle for the settling of grace and knowing oneself blessed.

The second point is cued by the knowledge that we can allow ourselves graciousness at least, if grace is not forthcoming. We remember that in terminal relation Blanchot and Foucault—very different men with very different casts of thought—were each open to the other's work. We may choose to follow the style of that openness in thinking the other *as I imagine him*, in thinking *the thought from outside* (see Foucault/Blanchot 1990). As theory's "heirs"—to reuse Derrida's term—there is an injunction upon us there. We know that the first ethics of the survivor is memory, and that the generation Derrida survived only for so long and on behalf of whom he expressed "melancholic revolt" (2007b, 25) has bequeathed—theory. There is something to carry forward then, and we are bound to receive the legacy.

So, lest we forget: there is no entry at all for *style* in the Index to a key text about theory's legacy of itself to itself, *Theory after "Theory"* (Elliot and Attridge 2011). Doubtless a mere detail, probably not worth remarking; indeed, certainly not, for indices never point us to style, anyway, even if and because it is immanent. But we may already be in the *oublire* of style in theory. Or perhaps not. There is ample evidence, in texts like Bennington's own *Not Half No End*, J. Hillis Miller's *For Derrida*, Michael Naas' *Derrida From Now On*, or Nicholas Royle's *In Memory of Jacques Derrida*, of the *early* styles of the reception of the late Derrida having been cast, pre-scribing memory and commemoration. We have already seen that the style of theory is in the end, to some minimal but significant extent, the style of our reaction to it, to how we remember its style, to how we receive its wagers on how we would react to its being late (or, quite simply, dead, more than provisionally bygone). The hope is in the *style de (sur)vie* in the *style de mort* of theory. Whereupon theory must be *late* for its own lateness: unpunctual, intent on non-arrival at the very idea of its own passing. Yet we would probably want theory to be neither. Neither dead, that is, nor intractable about arriving after itself, its style unregistered in some of its own contexts. But perhaps we need not worry. Theory's style is to be in between, ever—and nowhere. Neither literature nor philosophy (it is still encountering itself as discourse), neither originary nor dead (it was never very intent on the absolute), it is late because it is like a principle of the undecidable, uncertain about r(e)cognition of its own style. In that lies its style, its blessing, its grace.

References

Adorno, Theodor W. 2002. "Late Style in Beethoven." In *Essays on Music*, edited by Richard Leppert, translated by Susan H. Gillespie, 564–8. Berkeley: University of California Press.

Barnes, Julian. 2008. *Nothing to Be Frightened Of*. London: Jonathan Cape.

Barthes, Roland. 1977. *Roland Barthes*. Translated by Richard Howard. London: Macmillan.

—. 2009. *Mourning Diary: October 26, 1977–September 15, 1979*. Text established and annotated by Nathalie Léger, translated by Richard Howard. New York: Hill and Wang.

Beitchman, Philip. 1988. *I Am a Process with No Subject*. Gainesville: University of Florida Press.

Bennington, Geoffrey. 2008. *Late Lyotard*. n.p.: Create Space.

—. 2010. *Not Half No End: Militantly Melancholic Essays in Memory of Jacques Derrida*. Edinburgh: Edinburgh University Press.

Birnbaum, Jean. 2007. "Introduction. Bearing Loss: Derrida as a Child." In *Learning to Live Finally: The Last Interview*, by Jacques Derrida, translated by Pascale-Anne Brault and Michael Naas, 8–17. London: Palgrave Macmillan.

Blanchot, Maurice. 1987. *The Last Man*. Translated by Lydia Davis. New York: Columbia University Press.

—. 1997. *Awaiting Oblivion*. Translated by John Gregg. Lincoln, NE: University of Nebraska Press.

—. 1998. *Death Sentence*. Translated by Lydia Davis. New York: Barrytown.

—. 2011. "Lettre de Maurice Blanchot à Roger Laporte du 22 décembre 1984." In *Maurice Blanchot: Passion politique*, edited by Jean-Luc Nancy, 45–62. Paris: Galilée.

Blanchot, Maurice / Jacques Derrida. 2002. *The Instant of My Death / Demeure*. Translated by Elizabeth Rottenberg. Stanford: Stanford University Press.

Bruns, Gerald L. 2011. *On Ceasing to Be Human*. Stanford: Stanford University Press.

Burt, E. S. 2009. *Regard for the Other: Autothanatography in Rousseau, De Quincey, Baudelaire, and Wilde*. New York: Fordham University Press.

Callus, Ivan. 2005. "(Auto)thanatography or (Auto)thanatology?: Mark C. Taylor, Simon Critchley, and the Writing of the Dead." *Forum for Modern Language Studies* 41: 427–38.

Caputo, John D. 2005–6. "Jacques Derrida, 1930–2004," *Cross Currents* 55(4). www.crosscurrents.org/caputo200506.htm.

Carroll, Lewis. 2009. *Alice's Adventures in Wonderland and Through the Looking Glass*. London: Penguin.

Chateaubriand, François René de. 1957. *Mémoires d'outre tombe*. Paris: Gallimard.

Cixous, Hélène. 1997. *Or: les lettres de mon père*. Paris: Des femmes.

Critchley, Simon. 2008. *The Book of Dead Philosophers*. London: Granta.

Crowley, Martin, ed. 2000. *Dying Words: The Last Moments of Writers and Philosophers*. Amsterdam: Rodopi.

De Man, Paul. 1984. *The Rhetoric of Romanticism*. New York: Columbia University Press.

Derrida, Jacques. 1973. *Speech and Phenomena and Other Essays on Husserl's Theory of Signs*. Translated by David B. Allison. Evanston, IL: Northwestern University Press.

—. 1986. *Glas*. Translated by John P. Leavey, Jr and Richard Rand. Lincoln, NE: University of Nebraska Press.

—. 1987. "Envois." In *The Post Card: From Socrates to Freud and Beyond*, translated by Alan Bass, 1–256. Chicago: University of Chicago Press.

—. 1991. "Letter to a Japanese Friend." In *The Derrida Reader: Between the Blinds*, edited by Peggy Kamuf, 269–78. New York: Columbia University Press.

—. 1992. "This Strange Institution Called Literature: An Interview with Jacques Derrida." In *Acts of Literature*, edited by Derek Attridge, 33–75. London: Routledge.

—. 1993a. *Aporias*. Translated by Thomas Dutoit. Stanford: Stanford University Press.

—. 1993b. "Circumfession." In *Jacques Derrida*, edited by Geoffrey Bennington, 3–315. Chicago: University of Chicago Press.

—. 1994. *Specters of Marx: The State of the Debt, the Work of Mourning and the New International*. Translated by Peggy Kamuf. New York: Routledge.

—. 2004a. "Je suis en guerre contre moi-meme." *Le Monde*. August 19.

—. 2004b. "Living On." Translated by James Hulbert. In *Deconstruction and Criticism*, by Harold Bloom, Paul de Man, Jacques Derrida, Geoffrey Hartman, and J. Hillis Miller, 62–142. London: Continuum.

—. 2005. "As If It Were Possible, 'Within Such Limits.'" In *Paper Machine*, translated by Rachel Bowlby. 73–99. Stanford: Stanford University Press.

—. 2006. *H.C. for Life, That Is to Say. . . .* Translated by Laurent Milesi and Stefan Herbrechter. Stanford: Stanford University Press.

—. 2007a. "Final Words." Translated by Gilda Walker. In *The Late Derrida*, edited by W. J. T. Mitchell and Arnold I. Davidson, 244. Chicago: University of Chicago Press.

—. 2007b. "Learning to Live Finally." Interview by Jean Birnbaum. In *Learning to Live Finally: The Last Interview*, translated by Pascale-Anne Brault and Michael Naas, 19–52. London: Palgrave Macmillan.

—. 2007c. *Learning to Live Finally: The Last Interview*, by Jacques Derrida. Translated by Pascale-Anne Brault and Michael Naas. London: Palgrave Macmillan.

Eco, Umberto. 1985. *Lector in fabula*. Milan: Bompiani.
Edel, Leon. 1968. "The Deathbed Notes of Henry James." *The Atlantic Monthly* 221(6): 103–5.
Elliott, Jane and Derek Attridge. 2011. *Theory after "Theory."* New York: Routledge.
Foucault, Michel / Maurice Blanchot. 1990. *Maurice Blanchot: The Thought from Outside / Michel Foucault as I Imagine Him*. Translated by Brian Massumi and Jeffrey Mehlman. New York: Zone Books.
Keats, John. 1952. *The Letters of John Keats*. Edited by Maurice Buxton Forman. Oxford: Oxford University Press.
Lyotard, Jean-François. 1992. "Note on the meaning of 'post-'." In *The Postmodern Explained to Children: Correspondence 1982–1985*, translated by Don Barry, Bernadette Maher, Julian Pefanis, Virginia Spate, and Morgan Thomas, 87–94. London: Turnaround.
Marion, Jean-Luc. 1996. "The Final Appeal of the Subject." In *Deconstructive Subjectivities*, edited by Simon Critchley and Peter Dews, 85–104. New York: State University of New York Press.
Marrati, Paola. 2005. *Genesis and Trace: Derrida Reading Husserl and Heidegger*. Stanford: Stanford University Press.
McDonald, Russ. 2006. *Shakespeare's Late Style*. Cambridge: Cambridge University Press.
McMullan, Gordon. 2007. *Shakespeare and the Idea of Late Writing: Authorship in the Proximity of Death*. Cambridge: Cambridge University Press.
Miller, J. Hillis. 2009. *For Derrida*. New York: Fordham University Press.
Mitchell, W. J. T. 2007. "Dead Again." In *The Late Derrida*, edited by W. J. T. Mitchell and Arnold I. Davidson, 1–10. Chicago: University of Chicago Press.
Montaigne, Michel de. 1958. *The Complete Essays of Montaigne*. Translated by Donald Frame. Stanford: Stanford University Press.
Naas, Michael. 2008. *Derrida From Now On*. New York: Fordham University Press.
Nancy, Jean-Luc. 2007. "Philosophy of Chance." Interview by Lorenzo Fabbri. In *The Late Derrida*, edited by W. J. T. Mitchell and Arnold I. Davidson, 209–22. Chicago: University of Chicago Press.
Pausch, Randy and Jeffrey Zaslow. 2008. *The Last Lecture*. London: Hodder and Stoughton.
Petrarch [F.]. 1957. *Petrarch's Testament*. Edited and translated by Theodor E. Mommsen. Ithaca, NY: Cornell University Press.
Poe, Edgar Allan. 1982. *The Complete Tales and Poems of Edgar Allan Poe*. London: Penguin.
Pound, Ezra. 1970. *A Memoir of Gaudier-Brzeska*. New York: New Directions.

Rapaport, Herman. 2003. *The Later Derrida: Reading the Recent Work*. New York: Routledge.
Redfield, Marc. 2005. *Politics of Aesthetics: Nationalism, Gender, Romanticism*. Stanford: Stanford University Press.
Ricks, Christopher. 1995. *Beckett's Dying Words*. Oxford: Oxford University Press.
Rilke, Rainer Maria. 2008. *The Notebooks of Matte Laurids Brigge*. Translated by Burton Pike. Champaign, IL: Dalkey Archive Press.
Royle, Nicholas. 2009. *In Memory of Jacques Derrida*. Edinburgh: Edinburgh University Press.
Said, Edward. 2006. *On Late Style*. London: Bloomsbury.
Saramago, José. 2008. *Death at Intervals*. Translated by Margaret Jull Costa. London: Vintage.
Smith, Robert. 1995. *Derrida and Autobiography*. Cambridge: Cambridge University Press.
Whitman, Walt. 1982. "Old Age's Lambent Peaks." In *Leaves of Grass*, 404. Philadelphia: David McKay.
Wood, Michael. 2006. "Introduction." In Said, *On Late Style*, vi–xix. London: Bloomsbury.

NOTES ON CONTRIBUTORS

Saul Anton is the author of the critical fiction entitled *Warhol's Dream* (Les Presses du réel, 2007), and the translator of Jean-Luc Nancy's *The Discourse of the Syncope: Logodaedalus* (Stanford University Press, 2008). Having received his PhD in 2010 (Princeton University), he is currently writing two books, *The Vestige of Art: Painting and History in Diderot*, and *Lee Friedlander's* Little Screens*: The Image Between Photography and Television*, which is forthcoming in 2013 from Afterall Books. He currently teaches at The New School and the Pratt Institute.

Mario Aquilina is a Visiting Lecturer within the Department of English and the Faculty of Media and Knowledge Sciences at the University of Malta, where he teaches courses in applied theory, English Literature, and reflective writing. He is currently completing a PhD in English Studies at the University of Durham under the supervision of Timothy Clark. He has presented and published papers on Shakespeare, Borges, Derrida, Blanchot, Jameson, and on style. His current research is on the notion of style in the work of Gadamer, Blanchot, Derrida, and Celan, as well as on the remediation of literature in digital media.

Douglas Burnham holds a personal professorial chair in Philosophy at Staffordshire University in the United Kingdom. He is the author of a number of books and papers on Kant, Nietzsche, and philosophy's relation to the arts, including *Kant's Philosophies of Judgement* (Edinburgh University Press, 2004) and *Nietzsche's* Thus Spoke Zarathustra (Edinburgh University Press/Indiana University Press, 2010). He has written *Wine and Aesthetics* (Blackwell, 2012) with Ole Martin Skilleås, and is compiling the *Nietzsche Dictionary* for Continuum.

Ivan Callus is Associate Professor and Head of the Department of English in Malta. He is the author of papers on contemporary fiction, poststructuralism, and posthumanism. With Stefan Herbrechter, he is editor of the series *Critical Posthumanisms* (Rodopi) and of *Discipline and Practice: The (Ir)resistibility of Theory* (Bucknell University Press, 2004), *Post-Theory/Culture/Criticism* (Rodopi, 2004), *Cy-Borges: Memories of Posthumanism in the Work of Jorge Luis Borges* (Bucknell University Press, 2009), and *Posthumanist Shakespeares* (Palgrave Macmillan, 2012). His current research is on reclusiveness in contemporary literature and culture.

James Corby is a Lecturer in the Department of English at the University of Malta. He teaches courses in literature and philosophy, modern and contemporary poetry, literary theory, cultural criticism, and drama. His principal research interest is in literary and philosophical conceptions of post-romanticism, and he has published articles on Friedrich Schlegel, Fernando Pessoa, Tony Kushner, Philip Larkin, and Cormac McCarthy (forthcoming). With Ivan Callus, he is the general editor of the journal *CounterText* (forthcoming).

Marie-Dominique Garnier is Professor of English Literature and Gender Studies at the University of Paris 8-Vincennes, France, where she teaches Shakespeare, modernism, philosophy, and gender. She has recently coedited a volume on Hélène Cixous, *Cixous sous X* (Paris, Presses de Vincennes, 2010). Her main field of research is the intersection of philosophy, literature, and gender. Recent publications include articles on Derrida and the animal, on Cixous's haecceities/hexeities, and on the poetry of James Joyce (forthcoming). She is also working as a translator, having recently completed the translation of Madeline Gins' *Helen Keller or Arakawa* (1994).

Stefan Herbrechter is Reader in Cultural Theory at Coventry University, United Kingdom. He is the editor (with Ivan Callus) of Rodopi's monograph series *Critical Posthumanisms*. He has published numerous volumes and articles on English and comparative literature, critical and cultural theory, and cultural studies. He is a translator of Stiegler, Derrida, and Hélène Cixous; together with Laurent Milesi, he is the translator of Jacques Derrida, *H.C. for*

Life, That Is to Say . . . (Stanford University Press, 2006). His current research projects involve the relation between multilingualism, autobiography, and deconstruction; notions of alterity and strangeness in literature, theory and culture; posthumanism in literature, film, and mediacultures; and notions of life, politics, and constructions of the future.

Fiona Hughes is a Senior Lecturer in Philosophy at the University of Essex. Her work is principally on Kant's epistemology, Kant's aesthetics and Merleau-Ponty. She is the author of *Kant's Aesthetic Epistemology: Form and World* (Edinburgh University Press, 2007) and *Reader's Guide to Kant's Critique of Aesthetic Judgement* (Continuum, 2009), in addition to a range of articles on Kant, Nietzsche, Merleau-Ponty and the arts.

Gloria Lauri-Lucente is Associate Professor and Head of the Department of Italian at the University of Malta, where she teaches courses in Italian Literature, Comparative Literature, and Film Studies. She is also Director of the Institute of Anglo-Italian Studies. She is the author of numerous papers and book chapters on the lyric tradition, Anglo-Italian Studies, and Film. Her most recent publication is *Jane Austen's* Emma*: Revisitations and Critical Contexts* (Aracne, 2012), which she coedited with Francesco Marroni. She is currently writing *"Mutatas Formas": Posthumanism and Transembodiment in Ovid, Dante, and Petrarch* which is forthcoming from Rodopi. She is also completing a book on literary and cinematic representations of organized crime in Italy and the United States.

Giuseppe F. Mazzotta is the Sterling Professor in the Humanities for Italian at Yale University. His scholarly interests focus primarily on medieval, Renaissance, and Baroque literature and philosophy. He is the author of more than 100 major articles and reviews and has written the following books: *Dante, Poet of the Desert: History and Allegory in the Divine Comedy* (Princeton University Press, 1979); *The World at Play: A Study of Boccaccio's Decameron* (Princeton University Press, 1986); *Dante's Vision and the Circle of Knowledge* (Princeton University Press, 1993); *The Worlds of Petrarch* (Duke University Pres, 1993; rpt. 2000); *The New Map of the World: The Poetic Philosophy of Giambattista Vico* (Princeton University Press, 1999); and *Cosmopoiesis: A*

Renaissance Experiment (University of Toronto Press, 2003). He has also edited numerous volumes.

Laurent Milesi is a Reader in twentieth-century English/American Literature and Critical Theory at Cardiff University, and is a member of the ITEM-CNRS Research Group on James Joyce's manuscripts. He has written numerous essays on Joyce and related aspects of modernism, nineteenth- and twentieth-century (American) poetry, postmodernism, and poststructuralism. He is the editor of *James Joyce and the Difference of Language* (Cambridge University Press, 2003), and together with Stefan Herbrechter translated Jacques Derrida's *H. C. For Life, That Is to Say . . .* (Stanford University Press, 2006). His annotated translations of Cixous's study of Beckett, *Le Voisin de zéro*, as well as of *Philippines*, have both been published by Polity Press (2010, 2011). His recently completed translation of her novel *Tombe* is forthcoming from Seagull Press. He is also preparing a collection of Cixous's shorter essays on Derrida and completing a monograph on "(non-) place" in Derrida's works.

Chris Müller read for a Bachelor of Arts and a Masters degree at Cardiff University and has also spent a year studying at the University of Berne. His main research interests are the phenomenology of emotions and bodily affects, and the intersection of poststructuralist theory, ethics, and technics. He is currently working on his doctoral thesis at Cardiff University. His research draws together the thought of Max Scheler, Martin Heidegger, and Jacques Derrida, under the heading of "shame." He has presented papers on space and memory, deconstruction, Heidegger, shame and technicity, and the relation of philosophy and literature.

Jean-Michel Rabaté, Vartan Gregorian Professor in the Humanities at the University of Pennsylvania, is a curator of the Slought Foundation, an editor of the *Journal of Modern Literature*, and a Fellow of the American Academy of Arts and Sciences. He has authored or edited 30 books on modernism, psychoanalysis, philosophy, and on writers like Beckett, Pound, and Joyce. Recent books include *1913: The Cradle of Modernism* (Blackwell, 2007), *The Ethics of the Lie* (New York: Other Press, 2008), and *Etant donnés: 1° l'art, 2° le crime* (Les presses du réel, 2010). He is currently editing a collection of essays on modernism and literary theory.

Janice Sant read for a Bachelor of Arts (Hons) and a Masters degree at the University of Malta. Her research interests include modern and contemporary poetry as well as critical and cultural theory. She has concentrated particularly on the poetry of Wallace Stevens. She is currently working on her doctoral thesis on the poetics of Maurice Blanchot, Hélène Cixous, and Paul Celan at Cardiff University.

Stuart Sillars is Professor of English at the Universities of Bergen and Agder. Among his books are *Shakespeare, Time and the Victorians: A Pictorial Exploration* (2011), *The Illustrated Shakespeare, 1709–1875* (2008) and *Painting Shakespeare* (2006), all from Cambridge University Press.

INDEX